OFFICIAL LIES

OFFICIAL LIES

How Washington Misleads Us

JAMES T. BENNETT

THOMAS J. DILORENZO

GROOM BOOKS : *Alexandria, VA*

Library of Congress Catalog Card Number 92-072083
ISBN 0-9632701-0-9

Published in the United States by Groom Books,
1800 Diagonal Road, Alexandria, VA 22314

Distributed to the trade by National Book Network,
4720-A Boston Way, Lanham, MD 20706

Printed on acid-free paper
Manufactured in the United States of America
1   3   5   7   9   10   8   6   4   2

Contents

Tables

Authors' Preface and Acknowledgments

PROPAGANDA IS always used to set the stage for public-policy initiatives which inevitably increase the power of government. In his nineteenth-century classic, *Democracy in America,* Alexis de Tocqueville, the renowned French statesman, author, and political philosopher, made frequent references to a "new servitude," a phrase he used to describe the ultimate effect of increasing governmental encroachments into the lives of citizens:

> [A]fter having successfully taken each member of the community in its powerful grasp, and fashioned him at will, the supreme power then extends its arm over the whole community. It covers the surface of society with a network of small complicated rules, minute and uniform, through which the most original minds and most energetic characters cannot penetrate to rise above the crowd. The will of man is not shattered but softened, bent, and guided; men are seldom forced by it to act, but they are constantly restrained from acting. Such a power does not destroy, but it prevents existence; it does not tyrannize, but it compresses, enervates, extinguishes, and stupefies a people, till each nation is reduced to be nothing better than a flock of timid and industrial animals, of which government is the shepherd (Part II, Book IV, chap. vi).

In *The Road to Serfdom,* Nobel laureate F. A. Hayek expanded on de Tocqueville's theme by explaining that the "new servitude" involves the adoption by citizens of the values implicit in public policy which are imposed by governmental regulation and regimentation: "The most important change which extensive government control produces is a psychological change, an alteration in the character of the people. This is necessarily a slow affair, a process which extends not over a few years but perhaps over one or two generations. . . ."

Thus, over time, government propaganda and the public-policy initiatives which ensue alter not only the economic, social, and political environment, but also the psychology and value systems of the citizens. In the long run, propaganda shapes the character of a nation. For this reason, it is crucial for citizens to understand how propaganda is used to enhance the self-interests of those in government at the expense of individual liberty. This book is a first step in that process.

We are indebted to many individuals who assisted our efforts over the past several years. Dan Craig, Josh David, John Furey, and David Spage at George Mason University and Don Ratcliff at the University of Tennessee at Chattanooga provided excellent research assistance; Jane Cashatt provided clerical assistance; and Marianne Keddington edited the manuscript.

Financial support for our research was generously provided by the John M. Olin Foundation, the J. M. Foundation, the Earhart Foundation, the Sunmark Foundation, the Romill Foundation, and the Shelby Cullom Davis Foundation. We also thank The Athens Institute, and John Blundell of the Charles Koch Foundation.

Finally, we offer our sincere gratitude and special thanks to Bill Kauffman, who succeeded so admirably in a most challenging task: translating our economic jargon so that the ideas in this book are accessible to a wider audience. Mr. Kauffman also contributed original writing and research, as well as his considerable editorial skills. We, of course, accept full responsibility for any errors of omission or commission.

OFFICIAL LIES

1

Welcome to the Jungle

---

*In the Great Society it is no longer possible to fuse the waywardness
of individuals in the furnace of the war dance; a new and subtler instrument must weld thousands and even millions of human beings into
one amalgamated mass of hate and will and hope. A new flame must
burn out the canker of dissent and temper the steel of bellicose enthusiasm. The name of this new hammer and anvil of social solidarity is
propaganda.*

   —HAROLD LASSWELL

WHEN MOST OF US hear the word "propaganda," we think of the crude lies
and distortions practiced by the erstwhile Soviet Union and so trenchantly
satirized in George Orwell's *1984*. In its most malignant form, propaganda
divests words of their meanings: "War is Peace," "Slavery is Freedom." A
less direct but no less pernicious tool of the propagandist is euphemism. As
Orwell wrote in his classic essay "Politics and the English Language":

> In our time, political speech and writing are largely the defence of
> the indefensible. Things like the continuance of British rule in
> India, the Russian purges and deportations, the dropping of the
> atom bombs on Japan, can indeed be defended, but only by argu-
> ments which are too brutal for most people to face, and which
> do not square with the professed aim of political parties. Thus

political language has to consist largely of euphemism, question-begging, and sheer cloudy vagueness.[1]

The lie is a third form of propaganda. It was used by Hitler to demonize the Jews and by Stalin to justify the murder or imprisonment of millions of Russian citizens. As Nazi Minister of Information Joseph Goebbels raged: "To arouse outbursts of fury; to get masses of men on the march; to organize hatred and suspicion—all with ice-cold calculation—that is the task of the propagandist."[2] The atrocities committed by these masters of propaganda conceal the widespread practice of propaganda in the United States and other democracies. Propaganda need not entail mass murder. Harold Lasswell, propaganda's foremost American theorist, defined it as "the technique of influencing human action by the manipulation of representations."[3] In plainer language, it is "the making of deliberately one-sided statements to a mass audience."[4]

Professor-cum-politician Eugene McCarthy offered a definition tailored for American politics: "Any kind of information or news—either true or false—used by a government to influence other governments and persons. . . . Generally the word is used as indicating immoral or undignified methods, although within recent years it has become somewhat more respectable."[5]

Indeed, propaganda can be used to further a worthy cause. It originally described efforts by the Catholic church to propagate the faith; Popes Gregory XV and Urban VIII established a College of Propaganda to train missionaries.

Does propaganda have a place in American democracy? Theoretically, in a democracy power is vested in the people. Citizens exercise their power directly by voting on issues or indirectly through their elected representatives. Public policy is thus presumed to reflect, however imperfectly, the will of the people. Government exists to serve that will. As Thomas Jefferson phrased it in the Declaration of Independence, "Governments are instituted among Men, deriving their just powers from the consent of the governed." The subservient nature of democratic government is suggested by the common terms "public servant" and "civil servant." Servants are passive agents who carry out the bidding of their masters.

The relationship between the democratic state and its citizens differs markedly in practice from the theory. In *Capitalism, Socialism, and Democracy*, economist Joseph Schumpeter observed that "human nature in politics being what it is, [politicians and bureaucrats] are able to fashion and, within very wide limits, even to create the will of the people. What we are confronted with in the analysis of political processes is largely not a genuine but a manufactured will."[6] Walter Lippmann called this process "the manufacture of consent," and it is nothing more than the successful implementation of Lasswell's "technique of influencing human action by the manipulation of representations." Government, especially at the federal level, has become increasingly involved in shaping and influencing public opinion and the will of the people.

Propagandists don't have to be monstrous totalitarians or street-corner cranks hectoring passersby. In a far more insidious way, government molds public opinion by providing financial support to political advocacy groups that are supposedly independent of the state. Our earlier book, *Destroying Democracy: How Government Funds Partisan Politics*,[7] documents how hundreds of millions of taxpayers' dollars are funneled each year to advocacy organizations through grants and contracts. The ostensibly private recipients use this pelf to finance lobbying, campaigning, and grass-roots organizing on various public-policy issues. Virtually all of these subsidized groups advocate the expansion of existing government programs and the initiation of new ones. (The bureaucracy rarely funds its critics.)

Of course, the government itself seeks to manipulate public opinion by generating reams and reams of its own propaganda. James Beck, a former solicitor general of the United States, railed against "bureaucracy and its propaganda" in his 1933 book, *Our Wonderland of Bureaucracy*:

> Publicity has become a potent factor in the growth of bureaucracy . . . which loudly vaunts its usefulness from the housetops by newspaper articles, reports, radio broadcasting and bulletins. . . . To accomplish their ends they seize every opportunity, not only to promote the interests of their services but incidentally to suppress or explain away any news, which might reflect unfavorably on their bureau.[8]

> The bureaucracy, at the expense of the tax payers, is ever at work to increase the importance and prestige of their several bureaus and . . . to secure greater recognition. . . . If Congress at times weakly yields to these powerful propaganda organizations, it is because they are organized and are an appreciable force at the polls, while the tax payers and consumers are unorganized and inarticulate.[9]

Despite the overabundance of state-produced and -directed propaganda, "the cause-and-effect relationship between government efforts to influence public opinion and the spread of pernicious notions has been neglected or ignored."[10] This dearth of research is largely due to the difficulty in obtaining data. In 1913 Congress made lobbying by the executive branch illegal:

> No part of the money appropriated by any enactment of Congress shall, in the absence of express authorization by Congress, be used directly or indirectly . . . to influence in any manner a Member of Congress, to favor or oppose, by vote or otherwise, any legislation or appropriation by Congress whether before or after the introduction of any bill or resolution proposing such legislation or appropriation. . . . [18 United States Code 1913]

This law also forbids "using appropriated funds for paying 'publicity experts,' " a laudable stricture that is easily evaded. There is not a single "publicity expert" in all of officialdom; there are, however, "in a bureaucratic wink at a bothersome law," tens of thousands of " 'information officers,' 'public-affairs officers,' 'communications officers,' and 'press secretaries.' "[11] In a gold-medal act of cynical circumvention, the federal government has used propaganda to conceal from the public the fact that it engages in propaganda.

The congressional prohibition on propaganda and lobbying by the executive branch has all the teeth of an Indianapolis Colts goal-line stand. Back in 1933, Representative Louis Ludlow declared: "Bureaucracy thrives by tooting its own horn. No sooner is a bureau established than it goes in for publicity, the object being to glorify itself and make itself strong and secure by publicizing its glorious mission in the world and broadcasting its beneficent works."[12]

In a more academic vein, Peter Woll explains in *American Bureaucracy*:

> The ability of administrative agencies to marshal support in favor of particular programs is often severely tested, and as a result the agencies have frequently created public relations departments on a permanent basis to engineer consent for their legislative proposals. . . . [I]t is obvious that agencies are expending huge amounts of funds, time, and effort on indirect and direct lobbying

activities. Administrative personnel engaged in public relations are not so open about their activities as their counterparts in private advertising and public relations firms, for the myth that the bureaucracy is "neutral" must be maintained if possible. However, through what might be called undercover devices, the bureaucracy engages in extensive lobbying and propaganda activities.[13]

George Orwell would've appreciated the deftness with which the bureaucracy has appropriated the euphemism "public affairs," under which banner it sedulously promotes the programs and policies within its purview.

Dissecting the Belly of the Propaganda Beast

The U.S. General Accounting Office (GAO) distinguishes between the "public affairs" activities of federal agencies and their "congressional affairs." As the GAO puts it:[14]

Public affairs involves efforts to develop and disseminate information to the public to explain the activities of and the issues facing an organization. Following are some of the activities that we consider public affairs:

- issuing press releases on activities;
- responding to press inquiries;
- conducting press conferences and briefings;
- producing leaflets, fact sheets, articles, and periodicals for the general public;
- producing photographic and graphic materials for publications; and
- producing material for radio and television broadcasts.

And on and on and on. The list also includes sending speakers into schools, giving tours and seminars, advertising, and "providing information that is intended to be useful to the public," which is as blanket a clause as "national security" was to the Reagan White House. The GAO then offers this similarly broad definition:

Congressional affairs involves efforts to manage day-to-day contact with the Congress. Following are some of the activities that we consider congressional affairs:

- participating in the selection and briefing of an organization's witnesses for congressional hearings;
- preparing testimony, hearing reports, and follow-up;
- arranging congressional committee briefings on key issues (in conjunction with program personnel);
- providing technical assistance on legislation; and
- furnishing general information and publications in response to congressional requests.

Thus, according to the GAO—as mild a watchdog as ever whimpered—virtually all of the "external" activities of government agencies can be viewed as either "public" or "congressional" affairs. Thither goest 18 United States Code 1913, into irrelevancy.

Since 1973, the General Accounting Office has produced seven reports on public-affairs spending by the executive branch. In its most recent study, issued February 1986, the GAO reckoned the cost of public- and congressional-affairs obligations and the number of full-time equivalent employees engaged in those duties for all thirteen cabinet departments and eighteen independent agencies of the federal government. (See appendices 1, 2, and 3 on pages 269–274.) The GAO report concluded:

> The responding agencies expected to obligate about $337 million for public affairs activities during fiscal year 1985 with almost 5,600 full-time equivalent employees assigned to public-affairs duties. In addition, about $100 million was expected to be obligated in fiscal year 1985 for congressional affairs activities with almost 2,000 full-time equivalent employees assigned.[15]

These figures significantly *understate* the size and scope of the executive branch propaganda industry. As appendix 3 indicates, the Department of Defense is far and away the biggest employer of propagandists, with about 1,300 full-time equivalent employees engaged in public and congressional affairs in fiscal year 1985. Yet Senator J. W. Fulbright, respected then-chairman of the Foreign Relations Committee, stated in his book *The Pentagon Propaganda Machine* that the Department of Defense told the Senate Appropriations Committee in 1969 that there were 4,430 people in the Pentagon "working to shape public opinion."[16] Moreover, more than forty years ago, "the Budget Bureau [predecessor to the Office of Management and Budget] was able to count 42,000 federal publicists, and U.S. information activity has increased enormously over the years even as titles of those who do the work become more shadowy,"[17] according to *U.S. News & World Report*. If 42,000 publicists blared trumpets in a federal work force of 1.96 million, how many government horn blowers must there be in the current federal work force of 3.1 million?

Costs, too, are likely far higher than the GAO's conservative estimates:

Public-affairs and information efforts of the bureaucracy cost taxpayers at least 2.5 billion dollars annually [in 1979], and hidden activities probably send the total far higher.

Washington's propaganda machine is so vast that nobody knows how many civil servants are engaged in trumpeting the works of government. Though official estimates put their number near 20,000, every audit to find the true extent of federal public relations has fizzled because the publicity network is so widespread and the identities and activities of many of those involved are disguised by vague titles.[18]

No one knows the true number of federal employees engaged in public and congressional affairs or the sums spent on these activities. It is doubtful that an accurate tally will ever be obtained. Nor can we reliably measure the extent of government "advertising." For example, although it might be possible to ascertain the total spent on glorifying the U.S. Army ("Be All That You Can Be") and U.S. Postal Service ("We Deliver For You"—as though we have a choice), thousands of public-service ads produced by government agencies are broadcast over television and radio at no cost. Despite its concealment and deception, the U.S. government ranked 39th in *Advertising Age*'s 1991 list of the Leading National 100 Advertisers. Uncle Sam's reported expenditures were $304 million, ranking him ahead of such corporate giants as General Electric, Paramount Communications, IBM, and ITT. (First place went to Procter and Gamble, which spent $2.2 billion on advertising.)[19]

The federal propaganda machine does not operate in a vacuum. Eagerly abetting it are the swarms of interest groups that batten on government programs. For example, the labors of the flacks in the Pentagon to influence public and congressional opinion on weapons systems, e.g., the B-1 bomber, are aided immeasurably by powerful groups, such as the prime contractor, myriad subcontractors, and labor unions. Such coalitions are always well financed, vocal, and they usually get what they want—a reserved porking space at the federal trough. By any standard of comparison, the federal bureaucracy and its special-interest allies are the largest and richest lobby in the world.

Publish and Never Perish

Unbeknownst to most Americans, Washington—and not New York or Los Angeles—is the publishing and filmmaking capital of the United States. Archibald MacLeish, the poet who served as Librarian of Congress and FDR's speechwriter, explained: "The government of a democracy, by virtue of its existence as a democratic government, has a very different function in relation to the making of opinion. It is the government's function to see to it that the people have the facts before them—the facts on which opinions can be formed."[20]

The "facts" that the federal government publishes go far beyond the congressional hearings, executive branch memoranda, IRS tax forms, and paperwork and documents "essential" to the functioning of government. In his zeal to educate the hoi polloi on a wide range of issues, Uncle Sam has built a federal printing establishment without equal in the world. The Government Printing Office (GPO) is the largest federal publishing facility. Boasts its director: "We have . . . 33 acres under our roof, 6,200 employees, of which over 5,000 . . . are in the main plants and well over 100 presses. . . . We are probably the largest . . . printer in the United States." There are also "more than 300 printing plants located in many government agencies."[21]

The GPO's monthly catalog of publications reveals a federal government that can only be called omniscient. Among the bewildering array of topics on which it offers authoritative advice are home and automobile repair and maintenance, personal and business financial management, health and fitness, child care, gardening, and cooking.[22] The GPO offers more than eighteen thousand publications to citizens by mail and through a network of government-run bookstores; *Infant Care: Your Child from 1 to 6*, *Septic Tank Care*, and *Adult Physical Fitness*, while not exactly bodice-rippers, have sold in excess of a million copies each.[23]

The federal government also distributes countless "free" publications as a public-relations strategy. For example, many federal agencies cooperate with the Consumer Information Center (CIC) in Pueblo, Colorado, which runs those cutesy ads on television. The CIC, one of Richard Nixon's numerous illegitimate bureaucratic offspring, publishes the quarterly *Consumer Information Catalogue*, which describes more than two hundred brochures, pamphlets, and periodicals, many of them free for the asking. Consumers can receive up to twenty free tracts per request; topics include "Money Management," "Travel and Hobbies," "Automobiles," and "Gardening." At any one time, the CIC has as many as fourteen million copies of publications in its warehouses.[24]

The astonishing variety of federal publications and the energy with which the government promotes them illustrate two critical points. First, every aspect—every nook and cranny and crevice—of an American citizen's life is viewed by the federal government as a legitimate area of concern. Your septic tank, your kite-flying, your rutabagas: they're Washington's business, too. Second, the federal government is anxious to establish its credentials as an expert source of information on every conceivable subject. When to change your oil? How to potty-train your tyke? What to pack for the trip to Scotland? Washington knows best.

Hollywood on the Potomac

The master propagandists immediately grasped the potential of the cinema. Hitler wrote of Sergey Eisenstein's *Potemkin*: "It is a marvelously well-made film, and one which reveals incomparable cinematic artistry. Its uniquely distinctive quality is the line it takes. This is a film which could turn anyone into a Bolshevik. Which means that a work of art can very well accommodate a political alignment, and that even the most obnoxious attitude can be communicated if it is expressed through the medium of an outstanding work of art."[25]

If Washington hasn't yet nurtured an Eisenstein, it's not for lack of trying. Although southern California is commonly believed to be the world center of filmmaking, the output of the major Hollywood studios pales in comparison with the audiovisual activities of the federal government. Over the years, the bureaucracy has produced—and unwitting taxpayers have financed—more than 100,000 films. (By contrast, Leonard Maltin's comprehensive 1991 *TV Movies and Video Guide* lists 19,000 films.) At one time, the Department of Defense alone had 2,033 facilities for making motion pictures with titles like *Oral Hygiene—Swab Your Choppers*, a how-to flick about brushing your teeth. As *TV Guide* has commented, "Government filmmaking, to put it simply, is a colossus."[26] The size of this colossus is difficult to gauge, but annual federal spending on audiovisual production and distribution runs into the hundreds of millions of dollars:

> According to a little-noticed report issued by the White House Office of Telecommunications in February, 1974, the [federal] government spent at least $375 million in 1972 to produce and distribute films, photographs, and an assortment of recorded programs and audio services. These programs covered a wide range of subjects and were produced by government employees working out of at least 653 federal facilities scattered throughout the government.[27]

No one knows how many films the federal government makes or sponsors each year. Witness the following exchange between Mike Wallace and Maurice McDonald, chief of the audiovisual department of the U.S. Department of Health, Education and Welfare, from a "60 Minutes" segment entitled "Hollywood on the Potomac":

WALLACE: Do you know how many films you make?

McDONALD: No, I can't give you an exact answer.

WALLACE: Do you know how many films you have made in the last two years?

McDONALD: I haven't done a count on them.

WALLACE: Do you know where I would go to get that list? Is there a list?

McDONALD: There is no list.[28]

One estimate has placed the number of "educational" films offered by the federal government at more than fifty thousand.[29] Since 1969, the distribution of federal films has been centralized in the National Audio-visual Center (NAC), located in Capitol Heights, Maryland. The NAC issues an annual *Media Resource Catalog* listing thousands of films on such diverse subjects as history and anthropology, earth science and space science, safety and health at home and on the job, and even medicine and dentistry. Alphabetically, the listings range from agriculture to wounds; their target audiences include everyone from children to the elderly. Their only common trait is that each and every film was produced by federal agencies or by contractors under federal grants.

Some of NAC's film offerings pique one's curiosity; others sound less inviting than two hours of *Ishtar*. On the soporific side of the ledger, *Dental Auxiliary Trigger Situations—Interpersonal Relations* reportedly "discusses interpersonal problems in a dental practice [and] encourages serious thinking about better understanding others, a personal commitment to react more sensitively to others, and self-assessment in relation to the role of the auxiliary as a member of a dental team." We haven't the high threshold for boredom necessary to confirm or deny this précis. Rather more popular are *Female External Genitalia* and *Female Genital Examination—A Humanistic Approach*.[30] Some enterprising minion of the NAC might make a fortune booking showings of that pair.

The thematic concerns of federal film productions are apparently bound-less: "Government films are made on almost any subject imaginable—choking, exercising cattle, terror, racial discrimination. Titles include *Fuel Pump Disassembly*; *Hacksaws, Part III*; *Hospital Housekeeping: Mopping, Two Bucket Method*; *Handling and Storing Apples in Pallet Boxes*; and *Climbing and Working on Poles*."[31]

Hacksaws, Part III is no *Potemkin*. Heck, it's not even *Hudson Hawk*. But it is effective at a different level: it and kindred celluloid waste suggest an omniscient, omnipotent government. Many of the books, pamphlets, films, news releases, studies, and pronouncements that emerge from Washington are seemingly benign; others, as we shall see in later chapters, are not. Some are unobjectionable, if dull; others are chock-a-block with lies. All, however, promote an "official" view of everything from mopping floors to the health hazards posed by a marijuana cigarette. And that is one of the chief dangers of government propaganda: other voices, from other rooms, are made inaudible by the great din of Washington. Dissent is muted, or silenced, or simply cannot find an outlet because government-sanctioned views become, by constant repetition, the accepted wisdom.

Once the central government starts promoting one scientific—or religious or ethical—position over another, the potential for mischief is enormous. Recall Stanley Milgram's controversial experiments at Yale in the early 1960s, in which an authority figure instructed subjects to administer shocks of up to 450 volts to unseen "learners" (really actors), who howled in pain and agony. Milgram's conclusion was distressing: "It is the extreme willingness of adults to go to almost any lengths on the command of an authority [which] constitutes the chief finding of this study."[32]

Despite our heritage of stubborn individualism, many Americans display a disturbing deference to government "experts." Yuri Maltsev, former adviser to Mikhail Gorbachev and now professor at Carthage College in Wisconsin, said that the thing that surprised him most when he moved to this country in 1989 was that so much of the American public actually believed what the government told them.

No earthly authority exceeds that of government; its approval lends even a harebrained idea the air of legitimacy. Its disapproval can be damning; woe befalls the independent man who challenges the official view. As Aldous Huxley wrote of the propagandist: "He must never admit that he might be wrong or that people with a different point of view might be right or that people with different points of view might even be partially right. Opponents should not be argued with; they should be attacked, shouted down, or, if they become too much of a nuisance, liquidated."[33]

The "consent" that government manufactures is not always consonant with the truth—and that is why every American should worry about the propaganda machine that churns away beneath the corridors of power.

2

The Political Economy of Propaganda, or Joe Isuzu Meets Nelson Rockefeller

Capitalism is the best. It's free enterprise. Barter. Gimbels, if I get really rank with the clerk, "Well I don't like this," how can I resolve it? If it really gets ridiculous, I go, "Frig it, man, I walk." What can this guy do at Gimbels, even if he was the president of Gimbels? He can always eject me from that store, but I can always go to Macy's. He can't really hurt me. Communism is like one big phone company. Government control, man. And if I get too rank with that phone company, where can I go? I'll end up like a schmuck with a dixie cup on a thread.

—LENNY BRUCE

WHAT'S SO BAD about government advertising anyway? Isn't it the same, for all intents and purposes, as the Energizer bunny and washed-up jocks hawking Lite beer?

Not really. Economist Joseph Schumpeter elucidated the difference in his classic 1942 book *Capitalism, Socialism, and Democracy*:

The picture of the prettiest girl that ever lived will in the long run prove powerless to maintain the sales of a bad cigarette. There is

15

no equally effective safeguard in the case of political decisions.
Many decisions of fateful importance are of a nature that makes it
impossible for the public to experiment with them at its leisure and
at moderate cost. Even if that is possible, however, judgment is as a
rule not so easy to arrive at as it is in the case of the cigarette,
because effects are less easy to interpret. [1]

In the private sector, irrelevant or misleading advertising can work only
in the short run, for nearly all businesses depend on repeat sales. Customers are unlikely to be seduced—twice—by the "prettiest girl that ever
lived" if the cigarette whose advertisements she adorns tastes like
smoked offal. Despite ballyhoo and big budgets, numerous dumb
products—microwave sundaes, aspirin cream, and of course the Ford
Motor Company's Edsel—have failed to find an audience. Consumers can
experiment with most private goods and services and decide whether or
not they like them. Advertisers may be able to fool some of the people
some of the time, but not forever. In the long run, comparison shopping,
which is facilitated by advertising, will penalize—perhaps by forcing out
of business—those businesses that oversell. Fulsome praise and extrava-
gant claims can't save a dog: just ask Norman Mailer, whose *Harlot's
Ghost* haunts the nation's remainder bins, or Michael Jackson, who discovered with his disappointing album *Dangerous* that sometimes even
multimillion-dollar ad campaigns and public crotch-grabbing can't stimulate sales.

The public sector is another story. Once a government program is
established, it quickly develops a core of supporters among the program's
administrators and beneficiaries, who combine to demand ever-higher
funding levels, whether or not the program is a "success." Consequently,
fundamental changes in public policy are rare, and those that do take place
occur slowly and incrementally. Comparison shopping and consumer
choice have no real analogues in the public sector. Political elections are
held only periodically. Restrictive laws often keep alternative parties off
the ballot: burdensome petition requirements helped keep the two biggest
insurgent parties, the Citizens and the Libertarians, off numerous state
ballots throughout the 1980s. Incumbents have so bolstered their already
strong positions that it is not unusual for members of Congress and state
legislatures to have lifetime tenure. Congressional incumbents enjoy a 96
percent reelection rate. Incredibly, over the last thirty years, there was less

turnover in the United States Congress than in the now-defunct Supreme Soviet. (See chapter 3.)

Our Norman Rockwell ideal of a community of concerned citizens who are given a meaningful choice in competitive elections is deader than Rockwell himself. We can't "throw the rascals out": the rascals have taken over the house, bolted the door, fortified the citadel, and manned the parapets, the artillery of incumbency in hand, ready to mow down the barbarians (i.e., the voters) milling outside the gates.

In the private sector, unlike the public, advertising provides information that facilitates comparison shopping. Think about it: what would happen if we banned newspaper, television, and radio advertising? No Martin Sheen peddling Toyotas, no demure lasses shot through gauzy lenses while extolling feminine-hygiene products, no Michael Jordan dishing out the bull. If you're a TV addict, such a ban might make life on the couch marginally more pleasurable, but venturing outside would become a more expensive proposition. Prices would zoom—and that's not all.

Scholarly studies have found that the legislative and regulatory restrictions that already exist on advertising have generally boosted prices, decreased the quality of goods and services, or both. For example, Lee Benham found that the price of eyeglasses was higher in those states that prohibited advertising by optometrists.[2] Amahai Glazer reported that grocery prices in New York City were significantly higher during a newspaper strike—when newspaper advertising was absent—than before and after the strike.[3] John Cady concluded that restrictions on the ability of pharmacists to advertise prices of prescription drugs drove up the price of drugs. Pharmacists benefitted from these curbs; consumers lost.[4] Restrictions on private advertising also tend to help older, more established businesses— the brand names, if you like. They're already well known; they need not advertise as heavily as newer competitors, who must make consumers aware of their product, their prices, even their existence.

Take the hotel industry. Large chains such as Holiday Inn are the beneficiaries of the restrictions on billboard advertising that exist in various regions of the nation. Billboards—large and small, simple and gaudy, reading "Spend a Night, Not a Fortune" and "You Are Now Two Miles from the World-Famous Stumblin' Inn: Rooms $19.95"—are a primary advertising vehicle for newer hotels that may charge less than the giants for beds that are just as comfortable. (Or just as flea-bitten. Whatever.) Without billboard advertising, the weary traveler is much less likely to find bargains at the Stumblin' Inn along the great American highway. "Spend a Night, Not a Fortune," the billboards beckon to consumers. You'd probably spend both were it not for the much-maligned—and increasingly regulated—industry of advertising.

Playing Monopoly with Government

Comparison shopping is virtually nonexistent in the public sector. Government is usually a monopolist in its provision of goods or services. You say you don't like the Social Security tax? Or the Stealth bomber? Or the U.S. Postal Service? Tough. Unlike, say, cigarettes—where you can smoke Camels or Virginia Slims or roll your own or pound huge No Smoking signs into your front yard—government offers you no choices. You pay your taxes to support its programs or you go to jail. It's that simple.

Think of the many everyday activities that are controlled by choice-denying government monopolies. If you want to mail a first-class letter to a friend, you must use the U.S. Postal Service—or else. Alternatives to the postal monopoly, at least for first-class mail, are prohibited by law. Taxpayers must support the public-school monopoly with their taxes even if their children attend St. Mary's Roman Catholic School down the street—or, indeed, even if they are childless. The same is true for hundreds of other services provided by federal, state, and local governments: pacifists are forced to contribute to the military defense of Europe; vaqueros along the Rio Grande must pay for New York City subway cars; guys who like to recline in Barcaloungers and watch the Bears play the Packers are the compulsory patrons of the National Endowment for the Arts' favored abstract expressionists. There are also countless services that government provides that compete with private firms. In 1981 the U.S. Senate Committee on Small Business determined that federal employees were "operating over 11,000 commercial or industrial activities that the private sector also performs."[5] At the local level, such activities include garbage collection, schools, solid-waste disposal, parking lots, bus systems, airport operation, and public utilities.

Even if government doesn't completely outlaw competition—the old "if you can't beat 'em, enjoin 'em" routine—it still maintains an unfair advantage over private-sector competitors. The capital and operating costs of government enterprises are subsidized by the taxpayers and are exempt from federal, state, and local income, sales, and property taxes; they are immune from minimum wage, securities, bankruptcy, antitrust, and myriad other regulations; and they can exercise powers of eminent domain and borrow at interest rates that are considerably below those paid by their taxpaying competitors.[6] Yes, competition still exists—in the same way that a ball game between the Oakland A's and the Minnesota Twins would be "competitive," even though the Twins had to wear blindfolds and the A's could arbitrarily order Twins' runners off their bases for breaching ever-changing rules written by the A's manager.

Special legislative privileges allow government enterprises to crowd private businesses out of the market, paving the way for monopolies. Economist Richard E. Wagner has concluded: "Whereas the natural state of the private sector appears to be competitive, the natural state of the public sector in a democratic society appears to be monopolistic . . . government is the monopolist par excellence."[7]

If government is a "monopolist par excellence," then why does it advertise? Certainly not as a means of encouraging comparison shopping, as is the case with the private sector. Rather, as Wagner observed, the function of public advertising "would seem to be to promote acquiescence in and to provide assurance about the prevailing public policies. The purpose of public advertising would be to reassure citizens that the fact that their public goods are composed of 60 percent baloney indicates good performance."[8]

We might quarrel with Wagner's disparagement of a fine sausage, but his analysis of the whys and wherefores of public advertising is right on. When governments do provide public (as opposed to private) goods, there is no sound economic rationale for advertising at all. (A brief definition: a public good is one for which there is a known demand; but because of the free-rider problem, private markets supposedly won't provide adequate quantities of it. The problem is not that consumers aren't aware of the product or service, but that "free-riders"—people who can enjoy the product without paying for it—preclude an adequate funding mechanism. If there is already an abundant demand for public goods, as the theory of public goods asserts, it would be redundant for government to advertise to stimulate a demand that already exists.)

Government advertising is not a competitive activity; it is, pure and simple, a propaganda tool used to coax the public into accepting prevailing policies and the political status quo—no matter how misguided, counter-productive, or bollixed up they may be.

Food, Shelter, Sex, and John Kenneth Galbraith

John Kenneth Galbraith is perhaps the best-known popular critic of private-sector advertising. The heart of the Galbraithian critique is the "dependence effect."[9] According to Galbraith's 1958 best-seller, *The Affluent Society*, the only valuable "needs" are ones that are innate to the human mind and are experienced spontaneously. Our "wants," on the other hand, are not spontaneous but are created by the process by which they are satisfied—that is, by the production (and advertising) process. Such wants, Galbraith contends, cannot be urgent or important. Because human wants are factitious, we end up with a social imbalance whereby consumers spend too much of their income on consumer goods and too little on public goods. We have "private affluence amidst public squalor." The average Joe, Galbraith charges, is far too wealthy, wastes too much of his money on consumer goods, and is grossly undertaxed. Following the serpentine curves of Galbraithian logic, the sexy vamp giving us come-hither winks in the beer commercial ultimately leads to a starving baby with rickets in an Appalachian hollow.

Galbraith's is among the most sophisticated, and certainly the best-known, critiques of private advertising. It is also an at least implicit defense of public advertising. Yet his argument, which seemed fresh in 1958, is by now stale and discredited. It has aged about as well as his bête noire, the hula hoop.

Describing the federal government—or most state and local governments—as emaciated and living in "squalor" is ridiculous. Government spending at all levels today accounts for nearly 40 percent of Gross National Product in the United States, yet Galbraith's thesis retains a measure of popularity, especially among political scientists, sociologists, and critics of capitalism.

But we ought to discard Galbraith's theory (perhaps in a refuse heap of New Coke and Billy Beer cans?) and here's why. First, he completely ignores the informational value of advertising, which, as discussed earlier, cuts costs and expands choices for consumers. By ignoring this competitive aspect, Galbraith has vastly understated the social benefits of private advertising. Second, the theory is a *non sequitur*, as Nobel laureate economist Friedrich Hayek demonstrated in a devastating critique of Galbraith's "dependence effect."[10] Hayek wrote: "The innate wants are probably confined to food, shelter and sex," so that "all the rest we learn to desire because we see others enjoying various things. To say that a desire is not important because it is not innate is to say that the whole cultural achievement of man is not important."[11] After all, very few "needs" are independent of the social environment or the example of others. "In this sense," Hayek concluded, "probably all our esthetic feelings [are] acquired tastes."[12]

The absurdity of the Galbraithian argument is shown by applying the argument to the arts. If people do not feel the "need" for something unless it is innate in their own minds, then all of literature—Tolstoy, Shakespeare, Twain, even *The Affluent Society*—would be worthless. Galbraith's theory also suggests that formal education is worthless, for math, science, literature, and history are not innate to students but are revealed to them through the process of education.

Galbraith has his "social imbalance" thesis exactly backwards. Private-sector advertising does not lead to a private sector that is "too large" and a public sector that is "too small," but government advertising acts as so much helium to the ballooning public sector. Or to borrow Wagner's imagery, government labels steak "baloney" and then prohibits private butchers from selling the real thing. Galbraith was right about one thing: advertising *does* contribute to a social imbalance. Alas, he confused the direction of the imbalance.

Government advertising enjoys an additional advantage: it is much more difficult to judge the quality of governmental services than the quality of private goods and services. An inefficient private messenger company goes out of business; an inefficient U.S. Postal Service hikes its monopolistic rates and floods the television with lavish, loving (taxpayer-financed) paeans comparing postal workers with Olympic athletes. As John Kennedy once sagely quipped, "Life is not fair." Furthermore, in the absence of user fees, it is virtually impossible for citizens to know what the real cost to them is of particular governmental goods and services. Ample opportunities for fraudulent advertising exist in the public sector, as we shall see in later chapters. With apologies to John Kenneth Galbraith, we're moving apace to a condition of public affluence amidst private squalor.

The "Credence" Revival

Most government services constitute what economists call "credence services."[13] That is, their quality is difficult to judge, even after they have been consumed. There are also many such services produced by the private sector, such as automobile repair and certain types of medical care. It is difficult for a layperson to judge, for example, whether what's really needed is that new radiator, as Mr. Goodwrench suggests, or whether his daughter ought to get that tonsillectomy her physician recommends.

Private-sector advertising fraud is much more likely to occur with credence services. There are unscrupulous mechanics and avaricious doctors who fleece unsuspecting consumers. But at least in the private sector there are restraints on fraud: deceitful business practices are punishable by law; phony or mendacious ads are subject to regulation; bad advice or quack remedies ("Eat Oat Bran; Pick Up Chicks!") are jumped on by competitors; and consumers do have the option of shopping around for second or third (or fortieth) opinions. In a competitive marketplace, false advertising will be punished, sooner or later, by lower profits or bankruptcy.

Not so in the public sector. Since there is often no competition, there are no competitors to point out false claims. Academics and gadflies, sad to say, don't constitute a countervailing force. So we rely on the fox to guard the henhouse: government is in charge of policing itself. As we've seen year in and year out with the ethics committees, Congress cannot be trusted to keep its own house in order. Oh sure, if pressured by public outcry it'll throw the dying or infirm—Senators Alan Cranston (D-Calif.) and Harrison Williams (D-N.J.)—to the wolves, but true clubmen—four of the Keating Five, Congressman Harold Ford (D-Tenn.), Senator David Durenberger (R-Minn.)—are more likely to be whitewashed than hung out to dry. The ethics committees forgive wrongdoers with a charity, a liberality, a generosity—yea, an astonishing blindness—that goes far beyond the usual bounds of Christian forgiveness. Anyone who believes that Congress can effectively regulate its members' advertising probably bought a case of those microwave sundaes a few years back.

Another advantage that Uncle Sam has over Sam the crooked auto repairman is the fact that government services are often much more difficult to evaluate than even private-sector credence services. Gauging the economic effect of the latest textile import-quota bill or Medicare or the

Strategic Defense Initiative is a lot tougher than deciding whether to purchase a new radiator or repair the old one.

And even if citizens were able to accurately judge the quality of government services or policies, how does one even begin to put an accurate price tag on a particular program? An example: let's say the sloganeers find a new cause—"If government can put a man on the moon, then why can't it take the ping out of my engine?" With bold promises—"By the year 2000, no American will suffer the indignity of a loud muffler"—and unwanted haste, Congress and the president nationalize the automobile-repair business. The new Car Maintenance as a Birthright program is financed by general tax revenues. Gus's Body Shop is now a subsidiary of the federal government. Even if Gus the GS-12 is completely honest in recommending a new radiator that costs, say, $100, we cannot know the true "cost" of the radiator because its purchase is financed out of general tax revenues. The direct "cost" assessed by Gus is $100, but the indirect tax costs of the Car Maintenance as a Birthright program may be much higher.

A good example of this phenomenon is the financing of higher education. Studies have shown that the per-student costs at state universities are from four to six times higher than the tuition charged. Thus, the explicit price paid by the students and their parents is, on average, only one fifth the total price of higher education; taxpayers subsidize the remaining four fifths. Without knowing the true costs and benefits of nationalized auto repair or state colleges, citizens cannot make intelligent judgments about the desirability of those programs.

Government advertising overstates the benefits, while general-fund (and many other forms of governmental) financing reduces the perceived cost to taxpayers. Thus deceived, we get a bloated public sector and a shrunken private sector: Galbraithism turned on its head and set loose on the citizenry.

Are Prices Right?

There is a public-sector version of price competition, although it is severely limited. Local governments within a metropolitan area can compete with one another for population and industry. (In the depersonalizing parlance of bureaucracy, people and shops and factories are reduced to the mere fundaments of a "tax base.") To an extent, citizens are able to "vote with their feet" by moving to lower-tax jurisdictions or jurisdictions with an equivalent tax burden but better services: for example, superior schools. Sunbelt states that have lower tax burdens than Frostbelt states trumpet their comparative advantage in their attempts to attract population and industry.

This is fine as far as it goes, which isn't far. In the private sector, new competitors can enter the market if existing firms are making above-normal economic profits. In the public sector, by contrast, competition generally takes place at the local level between existing governmental jurisdictions; the formation of new governments is rare. Monroe County may tax property at extortionate rates, but it is nigh-impossible for the county's western half to declare itself an autonomous entity and drastically reduce property levies. Furthermore, local government annexations and consolidations have rendered many metropolitan areas monopolistic, leaving only one or a few large jurisdictions responsible for providing all public services. The boa has swallowed the rabbits; where once there were many, now there is often one.

And what of our "monopolist par excellence" in Washington? Who are his competitors? To whom does the pacifist turn? What are the options for the rugged individualist who disdains Social Security? "Voting with your feet," that is, moving to a different country, is the unpalatable answer. And rare is the man whose ties to a particular place—especially his homeland—are so attenuated that he'll willingly expatriate himself for a lower marginal tax rate. Brazil can slash taxes with machetes, but Joe Smith shan't pack up the family and possessions and light out for Rio. (Joe's employer may be a different story.)

When intergovernmental competition is weak, as it almost invariably is, it's up to business to call Washington's bluff; to challenge the claims that the regulators and their publicists make. Alas, many businessmen, especially those heading large concerns dependent on government subvention, have been cowed (or bought) into silence. Representatives of certain industries fear, with some justification, regulatory retribution. A real-estate developer who publicly protests against the zoning process will soon find it impossible to get the necessary approvals for his project. But haven't these titans (and midgets) of industry the same free-speech rights that other Americans have? Well, yes, in the same way that a tenant farmer has the right to confront his landlord in a town meeting. He can speak his mind, if he likes, but once he opens his mouth he'd best hunker down because retribution is coming, sure as sunrise.

Even if we had an informed citizenry, a vocal business community, and a vigilant press, the politicians would still be able to manipulate the flow and content of information. Debt finance, for example, is a politician's dream: it's a scam by which popular programs—and their concomitants, votes and campaign lucre—are financed by saddling future generations with the costs. When the federal government finances a program by issuing thirty-year debt, it is taxing kids who aren't yet old enough to vote; indeed, it's taxing the unborn children of unborn children. If these glimmers in their mothers' eyes could speak, they might adapt the old Revolutionary slogan to their predicament and cry, in unison: "No taxation without gestation!"

Thomas Foley and Robert Michel will have long since departed this vale of tears before the full impact of their handiwork is felt. As Richard E. Wagner concluded:

> Budgetary policy can be used to influence the electoral prospects of incumbent politicians. . . . In general, expenditure programs are vehicles to secure political support, while the taxes necessary to finance those programs will by themselves diminish political support. If the government operates within a balanced-budget constraint, any proposal for expenditure must also entail a proposal for taxation to finance the program. The ability to engage in deficit finance severs this link between spending and taxing. . . . The incumbent party can pursue the vote-increasing ability of expenditure programs without having to bear the vote-decreasing burden of taxation. . . . Political success will be promoted by deficit finance because . . . it appears to politicians and citizens as a less costly way of providing expenditure programs.[14]

A second scam that politicians pull to hide the true cost of their deviltry is to place billions of dollars of spending off-budget or off the books.[15] Like debt finance, this Houdini-esque legerdemain causes a "fiscal illusion" that obscures the true cost of government from the eyes of the hapless taxpaying audience.

This was the m.o. of the spendthrift New York governor Nelson A. Rockefeller, the backslapping heir who liked to joke that he was "too rich to steal." Rocky loved to create off-budget enterprises (OBEs), which financed their operations by issuing revenue bonds. (This can usually—but not always, to Rocky's consternation—be done without voter approval in a referendum.) Theoretically, the bonds finance projects that are paid for by revenues earned by the projects; for example, State University of New York dormitories were supposed to be financed by student room fees. Then again, theoretically, you could be elected president of the United States in 1992—or 1996 or the year 2000—by a write-in campaign. Realistically, it isn't going to happen. And in practice, the fees for OBEs are rarely sufficient to make the projects self-financing: taxpayer subsidies or bailouts are all but inevitable.

Let's take a lesson from the master. (A free lesson, if you live outside New York.) When the Empire State's taxpayers repeatedly refused to approve his own mini-Great Society schemes during his long reign as governor, Rockefeller resorted to the OBE:

> [W]hen voters rejected a $100 million housing bond issue for the third time, Governor Rockefeller created the Housing Finance Authority, which issued massive amounts of [off-budget] debt, at one point in excess of the entire [on-budget] debt of New York State. In 1961, voters rejected a $500 million higher-education bond issue for the fourth time; the Governor created the off-budget State University Construction Fund. In 1965, the voters rejected, for the fifth time, a housing bond issue; the Governor created the Urban Development Corporation. . . . By the time he resigned from office in 1972, 14 months before the state faced default and bankruptcy, OBE debt . . . was approximately four times the amount of guaranteed, voter-approved borrowing.[16]

Every state and most local governments have established a number of off-budget enterprises; OBE spending rivals on-budget expenditures. It happens in Washington, too. The Federal Financing Bank was specifically created as a vehicle for placing spending off the books. Federal credit programs—government sponsored enterprises, loan guarantees, subsidized loans—are a prime means by which government doles out dollars to favored constituencies while deferring or disguising the costs.

In politics, as the Sunday morning pundits remind us with numbing regularity, perceptions are often more important than reality. If the perceived cost of government is lower than the actual cost, then taxpayers may consent to programs that they'd emphatically reject if they carried accurate price tags. Few voters are doltish enough to fall for the promise of a free lunch, but cheap eats, purchased on the OBE discount, are sometimes hard to pass up.

Falling for the Free-Lunch Fallacy

In the private sector, no one expects to get something for nothing. "What's the catch?" you'd probably ask if Gus promised you a free radiator. Businesses exist to make profits, and everyone understands that. Indeed, something-for-nothing promises are a hoary staple of entertainment. Recall the wildly popular television advertisements during the 1980s featuring Joe Isuzu, a compulsive and unctuous liar, slippery as a greased pig, grinning earnestly, absurdly offering to sell the viewer an Isuzu car or truck at a ridiculously low price. The commercials were brilliant at playing to the deep skepticism that most of us feel toward car salesmen; Isuzu's audacious use of a transparent snake-oil peddler like Joe made for a smashing success. (In a fortuitous example of justice through juxtaposition, in 1988 *Newsweek* ran a full-page color photo of Lyin' Joe Isuzu directly opposite a photo of presidential candidate Michael Dukakis, to whom Joe bore a resemblance. The magazine apologized to Governor Dukakis, who lost to a man who pledged not to raise taxes and did.)

Politics is full of smiling Joe Isuzus who promise something for nothing. Alas, they lack Joe's oily sense of humor; the joke is always on us. Although the public holds members of Congress in only slightly higher esteem than paroled murderers, people are extraordinarily gullible when it comes to swallowing the outlandish advertising claims made by government authorities. This phenomenon was observed by Schumpeter nearly half a century ago: "The typical citizen drops down to a lower level of mental performance as soon as he enters the political field. He argues and analyzes in a way which he would readily recognize as infantile within the sphere of his real interests. He becomes a primitive again."[17]

Most citizens are "rationally ignorant" when it comes to most political or public-policy issues. They spend considerable time on personal affairs—paying the bills, going to their children's plays and baseball games—because these are the things that are most important to them, as they should be. They have no real incentives to inspect the government's bills with anywhere near the same vigor or intensity. They care more about filling Kate's cavities than auditing Cape Kennedy. Most people who are busy raising families and looking out for neighbors (or, admittedly, watching "Roseanne") don't see the profit in spending their time guarding the public till.

Again, Schumpeter explains: "When we move still farther away from the private concerns of the family and the business office into those regions of national and international affairs that lack a direct and unmistakable link with those private concerns . . . the sense of reality is so completely lost."[18] He continues: "The great political questions take their place in the psychic economy of the typical citizen with those leisure-hour interests that have not attained the rank of hobbies."[19] The average citizen "expends less disciplined effort on mastering a political problem than he expends on a game of bridge."[20]

There's nothing wrong with this "wise and masterly inactivity," as the curmudgeonly Old Virginia statesman John Randolph phrased it. But public inattentiveness—or rational ignorance—has opened the door to the exchequer to every mendicant and conniving special-interest thief in the land, from agribusiness giant Archer Daniels Midland to General Dynamics to the Museum of Modern Art. These suckers on the public teat then use the propaganda machinery of government to shape public opinion. As 1960s Yippie Jerry Rubin liked to say, power belongs to he who frames the terms of debate. Or as the decidedly un-Yippieish Schumpeter noted:

> [Politicians] are able to fashion and, within very wide limits, even to create the will of the people. What we are confronted with in the analysis of political processes is largely not a genuine but a manufactured will. . . . So far as this is so, the will of the people is the product and not the motive power of the political process. The ways in which issues and the popular will on any issue are being manufactured is exactly analogous to the ways of commercial advertising. We find the same attempts to contact the subconscious. We find the same technique of creating favorable and unfavorable associations which are the more effective the less rational they are. We find the same evasions and . . . the same trick of producing opinion by reiterated assertion that is successful precisely to the extent to which it avoids rational argument and the danger of awakening the critical faculties of the people.[21]

Schumpeter went on to warn readers that political propaganda was far more insidious than its private-sector counterpart because while "the prettiest girl that ever lived will in the long run prove powerless to maintain the sales of a bad cigarette, there is no equally effective safeguard in the case of political decisions."

Can Government Create Jobs?

A hardy perennial that politicians of both parties wear in their lapels is the "government creates jobs" corsage. Since the 1930s, when President Franklin D. Roosevelt sired the Works Progress Administration and the Civilian Conservation Corps, public spending has been viewed as an engine of job creation. Listen to the debate—or should we say the harmonious chorus—the next time Congress takes up the reauthorization of the Highway Trust Fund. Democrats and Republicans alike will wax rhapsodic over the hundreds—no, thousands—no, hundreds of thousands—of jobs they are "creating" by taxing gasoline and the trucking industry.

What you will not hear mentioned is the economic law of opportunity cost. Government jobs are financed by withdrawing resources from the private sector to pay for them, thus diverting resources—and jobs—from the private to the public sector. We destroy a refinery worker's job to create one for the road-crew signaler. The taxes on which this insidious shuffle depends depress the private-sector economy, increasing unemployment. If the government borrows to finance the programs, then private-sector borrowing is reduced, and the economy lags. If the government resorts to money creation, then the resulting inflation reduces the value of private wealth; again, the private-sector economy suffers. The politicians will point with pride to the visible jobs they've created, but who mourns the countless jobs that are lost? The composition of employment may be altered, but no government has yet invented the magic wand that creates jobs out of thin air.

This is no secret. Every economist knows it. The unemployment rate in 1939—after seven years of New Deal "jobs" programs—was higher than in 1932; the alphabet soup of the WPA and CCC evidently lacked potency. The relief effort had employed more than ten million Americans, to no apparent avail.

There is a marvelous line at the end of John Ford's eulogistic western *The Man Who Shot Liberty Valance*: "When the legend becomes fact, print the legend." That is precisely what has happened with government jobs programs. Hell, if public spending created jobs, unemployment would be as dead as the dodo. After all, government spending at all levels now accounts for approximately 40 percent of GNP.

That the legend of government job creation is lustrous still is tribute to the conjunctive power of rational ignoramuses, wily politicos, and aggressive feeders at the Washington trough. Say what you will about construction companies, unions, materials suppliers, and pork-barrel pols, but don't dare call them ignorant.

Can Government Mandate Happiness?

Can government make people happy? Short of conscripting doctors to pay bedside visits to the sick (and Madonna to do likewise for the healthy), how can it boost our "wellness index," as current psycho-medical argot has it? Will we really be better off if we enact the recent spate of proposals requiring employers to provide health insurance, parental leave, day care, and numerous other employee benefits?

If we believe the fustian spun in the august halls of Congress, these goodies can be given to employees at no cost. Because the benefits are paid by employers (and consumers through higher prices), there is no direct increase in the tax burden. And because employers are forced to provide the benefits, they cost employees nothing.

This is straight out of the wish-is-father-to-the-thought school of statecraft. Fiat can no more ensure medicine for the ailing then it can dictate the phases of the moon. If matters were that malleable, poverty would have ended decades ago with the imposition of a high enough minimum wage.

Politicians aren't so unlike the rest of us. They like their jobs and want to keep them; to do this, they must convince their constituents that the benefits they receive from government programs outweigh the costs. Government spending programs win votes and campaign contributions and make politicians more popular, while taxes are unpopular and are a political "cost" to the politician as well as an economic cost to taxpayers.

Regardless of a politician's motives—whether he or she is a self-interested empire builder or an altruistic public servant (or a combination of the two)—staying in office is a prerequisite for achieving his or her objectives. And the government's vast public-relations machinery is utilized to convince the voters that the bounty of government programs—which incumbents readily take credit for—greatly outweighs the costs, which they do their level best to disguise.

Every executive-branch agency of the federal government and their administrative counterparts in state and local government also engage in public-relations activities. Notes political scientist James L. Payne:

"Administrators and others who benefit from funding are hopelessly biased sources of information and opinion about spending programs."[22] Not that these are fundamentally dishonest men; there are honorable and gimlet-eyed bureaucrats, but even they seldom voice their valid complaints about waste or inefficiencies in the programs they administer. Laments one employee of the U.S. Department of Agriculture:

> You have to remember that if you're going to work here, you have to play the game. It's not like the agency will stop you from publishing [an unflattering finding], but they'll tell you that it won't be beneficial for the agency if you do it. And you certainly don't want to get anybody put under the thumb, because that's just hard on everybody.[23]

Bureaucracies are skilled at cover-ups; they're also adept at flacking. As scholar Peter Woll has written, government bureaucrats "engaged in public relations are not so open about their activities as their counterparts in private advertising . . . for the myth that the bureaucracy is 'neutral' must be maintained if possible. However, through what might be called undercover devices, the bureaucracy engages in extensive lobbying and propaganda activities."[24] Operating on Al Smith's maxim that nothing un-American can stand exposure to sunlight, we'll discuss many of those "undercover devices" in later chapters.

If agencies are less than forthright, their privileged clients are often downright mendacious. Economist Gordon Tullock explains, "Special interest groups normally have an interest in diminishing the information of the average voter. If they can sell him some false tale which supports their particular effort to rob the treasury, it pays. They have resources and normally make efforts to produce this kind of misinformation."[25]

Many of the purportedly "private" nonprofit interest groups that lobby for expanded governmental programs are in reality appendages of government. The battery of consultants who feast on government contracts are another ostensibly "private" gang who are literally bought and paid for by their government sponsors. Known as "Beltway Bandits" for their proximity to the highway that girdles the metropolitan Washington area, these firms are supposed to provide objective analyses of governmental programs. Although the mainstream press treats these hired guns as Olympians of impartiality, they are in fact "profoundly biased in favor of the programs they evaluate,"[26] Payne has discovered. As one Beltway Bandit candidly admits, the guiding rule is that "you don't want to antagonize the agency that's funding you."[27] Consequently, "Washington is flooded with hundreds of defective and biased policy evaluations supporting spending programs."[28]

Let us now enter the wonderland of government *mis-* and *dis*information.

3

How Propaganda Builds a Permanent Congress

It's a big pie down in Washington. Each member's sent there to bring a piece of that pie back home. And if you go down there and you don't . . . you come back without milkin' it after a few terms . . . you don't go . . . back.

— Representative MICHAEL "OZZIE" MYERS to FBI agents posing as aides to an Arab sheik

OUR CONGRESS WAS never intended to be a rascal warren of self-advertising career politicians. George Mason hailed it as "the grand repository of the democratic principle of government."[1] Competition in the political marketplace would ensure that elected officials acted in the interest of the citizens. Congress, Mason commented, "ought to know and sympathize with every part of the community."[2] The House of Representatives was to be "the most sensitive barometer of changes in political mood," as David Broder notes, because its members serve terms of only two years.[3]

In his classic *Democracy in America* Alexis de Tocqueville observed that "Americans determined that the members of the legislature should be elected by the people *directly*, and for a *very brief term* in order to subject them, not only to the general convictions, but even to the daily passions, of their constituents."[4] The longer terms of senators and the president make them less responsive to the prevailing public will, but anyone who has ever

33

watched Masters of the Art of Pandering and Poll-watching—Senators Al
D'Amato (R-N.Y.) and Arlen Specter (R-Penn.) come to mind—cannot
suppose that these men are epitomes of dispassion in their Senate ivory
tower.

"Coolly analytical" is hardly a phrase that comes to mind when the
subject is the modern Congress. Our body politic has grown arthritic. We
need change—drastic change. While term limits are no panacea, they hold
some promise of invigorating our elections. When we limit terms of the
legislature (as the Articles of Confederation did) and the chief of the
executive branch (as the Twenty-second Amendment did), the citizen-
politician envisioned by the Founders may reappear.

Who Controls Whom?

The notion that the citizens of a democracy exercise control over their
government through elected representatives is based on the eighteenth-
century writings of Jeremy Bentham, John Stuart Mill, James Madison,
and Alexander Hamilton, and summarized in the dictum, "Officeholders
want to be reelected, and hence will do what the voters want; elections
make it to their interest to further the voters' interest."[5] Or as a scholar put
it, "For most people, no doubt, elections are seen as the primary mechanism through which common citizens control their government. Elections
are, supposedly, the means by which leaders gone astray are replaced by
ones more attuned to popular desires."[6]

The belief in citizen control permeates most of the textbooks on government. For instance, in *Forge of Democracy* Neil MacNeil writes that a U.S.
representative "could violate the sensibilities and the views of his constituents only at the imminent peril of being forced into political retirement."[7]
Roger Davidson and Walter Oleszek opine that "Representatives' actions
are constrained . . . by the threat of defeat. Occasionally members voice
policies or views at odds with those of their district voters; often (but not
always) incumbents subsequently shift their stands to retain their seats."[8]
The literature teems with Pollyannaish paeans to the mom-and-apple-pie
myth that congressmen serve at the mercy of their constituents—ordinary
Joes and Joans who ain't got much money but by golly they've got the vote,
and that's more powerful'n a million bucks! (Tell it to savings-and-loan
bandit Charles Keating and the out-of-state senators who took his money

and joylessly but efficiently did his bidding, in best competent whore fashion.)

Political scientist Robert Burnstein avers that "the myth of constituency control goes largely unchallenged by supporters of democracy because democrats desperately want the myth to be true. If constituencies do not control their representatives . . . what then is the argument for having a democracy?"[9] If the elected agents of the people are able to largely ignore the desires of those same people, then what are we: a democracy or an oligarchy? This is an uncomfortable, nettling question that many feel but few articulate.

The proposition that constituents "control" their congressmen has been subjected to only a few rigorous tests; the evidence in its favor has been described as "weak and ambiguous."[10] After an extensive study of "the myth of constituency control," Burnstein concluded:

> The myth exaggerates and distorts the influence that constituencies have in determining government policy. It exaggerates the influence that constituencies have over their representatives' policy. . . . Constituencies do not control the policies adopted by their representatives. . . . Constituency influence does not flow primarily from electoral threats against those in office, but rather from the initial selection of representatives.
>
> The myth of constituency control is not a harmless folk tale to be passed on to future generations of students. It fundamentally misstates the relationship between the constituency and the representative. It is time for writers and researchers to refrain from perpetuating an essentially incorrect view of how representative government functions in the United States.[11]

If anything approximating control is to exist, according to Burnstein's analysis, there must be frequent turnover among members of Congress because constituent influence occurs primarily in the *initial selection* of elected representatives. The longer one serves, the more formidable his electoral redoubt becomes, and the deafer he grows to the cries from back home.

Taxpayer-financed propaganda is one of the most useful tools by which scared, vulnerable rookie congressmen become calloused, invulnerable veterans. Incumbents have built up an impressive arsenal of self-promoting weapons: the congressional frank, travel and telephone expenses, district and state offices, TV and radio studios, and large staffs that serve—no matter what they tell you—as full-time, round-the-calendar campaign organizations.

The advantages of incumbency are overwhelming; potential challengers, unless they are fabulously rich, gallantly quixotic, or hopelessly mono-maniacal, are usually frightened off. Special-interest groups, operating through political action committees (PACs), contribute almost exclusively to the campaigns of incumbents. These favors may go unremarked, but they do not go unrepaid. Rare is the congressman who issues a press release boasting that the Widget Industry PAC has just forked over $5,000; rarer still is the pol who'll take that gift and vote against the Widget Industry Protection Act.

The Permanent Congress

The Founding Fathers had in mind a citizen legislature, a body composed of men such as Cincinnatus, who left his plow when the public weal demanded, then returned to it when his work was done. Of course this idealized state was never realized; politics has always attracted grifters and crooks with an eye for the main chance. But the early days of the republic saw a high turnover rate: the first congressional election in George Washington's term saw 40 percent of the incumbents lose. In those days of yore, Americans, believe it or not, voted in competitive elections in which the incumbent stood a fair chance of losing. Today, by sad contrast, Congress "has surrounded itself with a moat that challengers find difficult to ford,"[12] as Representative Guy Vander Jagt (R-Mich.) has written. (Vander Jagt, by the way, has served in the House since 1967 and is not noted for his reluctance to employ the powers of his office.)

Election to Congress almost guarantees reelection. In 1988 when 98 percent of House incumbents seeking reelection won, turnover was at an all-time low:

> Over the past decade, only 88 incumbents were defeated. This compares to 97 incumbents defeated in the 1970s, 142 in the '60s and 133 in the '50s. If, over the course of 10 years, only 88 of the 2,175 seats change hands because voters toss an incumbent out and replace him with a challenger, there is something wrong with the system. . . . Mortality rates and age had more to do with

turnover of House seats than competitive elections in competitive districts.[13]

In the 1990 elections, 406 incumbents sought reelection; 391 won, or 96 percent of those who ran; 79 incumbents faced no opponent. And this in a year when "Throw the Bums Out" was a kind of national anthem!

The ordeal, the travail, the horrible tribulations of the poor beleaguered congressman are common themes in the establishment press. These sob stories are belied by the fact that "when a seat does open up, chances are a leading candidate for it will be a former Member of Congress, desperate to get back inside the Beltway."[14] (Twelve former members competed for seats in the 1990 congressional elections.[15]) The reelection rate in the House of Representatives has been 80 percent or higher for the past four decades; since the Watergate elections of 1974, the rate has not fallen below 90 percent; and since 1986, the rate has been 96 percent or higher. A similar pattern is evident in the elections to the Senate. In the Reagan landslide election of 1980, when the Republicans wrested control of the Senate from the Democrats and put out to pasture a stable of liberal warhorses (Birch Bayh, Frank Church, George McGovern, Gaylord Nelson), the reelection rate in the Senate fell to 55 percent. The rate rebounded to 93 percent and 90 percent in the next two elections, and in 1986, when the Democrats regained majority control of the Senate by ousting the most jaundiced Reagan babies (James Abdnor, Paula Hawkins), the reelection rate was still 75 percent.[16] In the 1990 Senate races, 31 of 32 incumbents—97 percent—were reelected.[17]

The advantages of incumbency are so powerful that even the taint of scandal or documented moral turpitude may not be sufficient to oust an entrenched and determined member of Congress. Retirement, disability, and the greatest leveler—death—are the only sure avenues of exit. In recent years, members have survived the scandals of cohabiting with a prostitute of the same sex (Rep. Barney Frank, D-Mass.), seducing a page (Rep. Gerry Studds, D-Mass.), profiting from a suspicious book deal (Sen. David Durenberger, R-Minn.), and steering HUD contracts to friends (Sen. Al D'Amato, R-N.Y.), among other peccadilloes.

Members of Congress are also winning reelection by bigger margins, or they are running without opposition. In the 1988 House elections,

about 70 incumbents [were] unopposed, and most of the rest [were] not threatened. A survey by *Congressional Quarterly*, an authoritative magazine, reported that "fewer than 10 House members" entered the final days of the campaign without a "perceptible advantage over their challengers."

Thus the trend of the last several decades in House elections seems likely to continue. . . . In more than seven-eighths of all House races in 1984 and 1986, the winner received more than 55 percent of the vote, the normal dividing line between what politicians consider competitive and one-sided elections.[18]

According to Common Cause, 94 percent of House incumbents who sought reelection in 1990—382 of 405—ran "financially unopposed."[19] Close elections are a dying breed; many congressmen no longer fear the discipline of Election Day. (Political scientists call this phenomenon "the case of the vanishing marginals.")

Something is very wrong here. Members of Congress, insulated from the bracing winds of competition, are able to ignore their hapless constituents. Voters in most districts are toothless, impotent, pathetic. And a large part of the reason is the propaganda machinery at Congress's disposal. As the American Century draws to a close, we have a dispirited electorate, a weak political opposition, and a permanent, seemingly immovable class of professional politicians. To borrow from David Byrne of the Talking Heads, "How did we get here?"

The Arsenal Against Democracy: The Congressional Frank

Thomas Jefferson asserted that communication between citizens and their elected representatives should be "free, full, and unawed by any" so that it would "give the will of the people the influence that it ought to have."[20] During the nation's infancy, the only means of direct communication other than face-to-face meetings was the mail, so elected federal officials were given the congressional frank, a free-mailing privilege for official mail, to respond to correspondence from constituents. The postage is paid from the annual appropriation for the legislative branch, which is allocated to an account called the Joint Items–Official Mail Costs. The annual Legislative Branch Appropriations Act traditionally makes funds available immediately; funds appropriated for any fiscal year remain available for an additional two years. Neither rain nor snow nor sleet nor a $350 billion deficit can stop congressmen from unleashing their blizzard of missives.

The congressional appropriations for postage for official mailings contains *no* spending limits. As the *Washington Post* notes, "Under current law, the Postal Service is required to handle any amount of mail Congress sends, and make up the difference in cost of delivery by using its own funds if the congressional appropriation is not enough."[21]

It's difficult to object to the theory behind the frank. Citizen-legislator dialogue is essential to a working democracy, and only a Senator Rockefeller could afford to pay postage costs out of pocket. (We are leaving aside the artificial nature of much of this mail; letters to non-contributors are usually written by staffers and signed by "autopens," which are impressive forgery machines.) But take a look at tables 3.1 and 3.2, which are based on reports by the Congressional Research Service of the Library of Congress.[22]

TABLE 3.1

U.S. HOUSE OF REPRESENTATIVES, NUMBER OF PIECES OF INCOMING AND OUTGOING MAIL AND ACTUAL MAIL COSTS, FY 1972–88

Fiscal Year	Incoming Mail	Outgoing Mail	Cost ($ Million)
1972	14,600,000	230,282,524	18.422
1973	40,600,000	207,001,419	18.709
1974	41,905,750	223,617,840	21.781
1975	47,718,903	212,890,050	24.509
1976	51,560,000	294,869,543	38.341
TQ*	N/A	129,721,529	14.925
1977	52,700,000	223,754,223	27.860
1978	100,000,000	334,065,000	35.109
1979	113,000,000	239,734,399	27.729
1980	120,000,000	400,129,816	43.422
1981	161,000,000	262,281,213	29.686
1982	145,000,000	508,156,638	59.894
1983	153,000,000	335,650,314	40.306
1984	200,000,000	586,203,143	67.348
1985	225,000,000	354,291,751	45.308
1986	180,000,000	461,091,864	60.401
1987	157,000,000	338,540,364	44.201
1988	156,000,000	548,465,538	77.852

*Transition Quarter (July 1, 1976, to September 30, 1976) reflects the shift in the beginning of the federal government fiscal year from July 1 to October 1.

SOURCE: John Pontius, "U.S. Congress Official Mail Costs, Fiscal Year 1972 to Present," (Washington, D.C.: Congressional Research Service, June 13, 1989), Table 3.

TABLE 3.2

U.S. SENATE, NUMBER OF PIECES OF INCOMING AND OUTGOING
MAIL AND ACTUAL MAIL COSTS, FY 1972–88

Fiscal Year	Incoming Mail	Outgoing Mail	Cost ($ Million)
1972	N/A	59,796,687	$ 4.784
1973	N/A	86,187,506	7.576
1974	N/A	97,357,698	9.521
1975	N/A	99,492,733	11.467
1976	N/A	106,558,729	14.633
TQ*	N/A	30,194,561	4.250
1977	32,500,000	86,346,092	13.559
1978	37,500,000	96,097,000	13.817
1979	34,200,000	86,526,101	15.214
1980	36,700,000	111,172,349	18.484
1981	35,800,000	133,300,675	24.176
1982	42,700,000	263,608,855	40.143
1983	41,500,000	221,190,032	32.126
1984	42,500,000	338,399,231	43.609
1985	46,200,000	321,982,710	39.852
1986	38,100,000	297,649,018	35.538
1987	50,000,000	156,193,086	19.424
1988	53,800,000	256,532,131	35.508

*Transition Quarter (July 1, 1976, to September 30, 1976) reflects the shift in the beginning of the federal government fiscal year from July 1 to October 1.

SOURCE: John Pontius, "U.S. Congress Official Mail Costs, Fiscal Year 1972 to Present," (Washington, D.C.: Congressional Research Service, June 13, 1989), Table 4.

In the seventeen fiscal years between 1972 and 1988, the Congress spent $1.04 billion in postage to send out 8.74 billion pieces of official mail. Between fiscal years 1972 and 1988, outgoing mail from the House of Representatives increased by 138 percent and the cost of postage rose by 322 percent; for the Senate, the volume of mail sent out rose by 329 percent and the cost escalated by 642 percent—almost two and one-half times the rate of inflation during that period. By comparison, the number of pieces of outgoing mail from the House and Senate combined was less than 50 million in 1954 and did not exceed 100 million until 1960.[23]

The gap—the gulf—the abyss—between incoming and outgoing mail is astounding. One estimate is that "less than 5 percent of franked mail goes out in response to constituent inquiries."[24] The idyllic image of the frank—a hardy yeoman writing by firelight to his citizen-legislator, who sits at Daniel Webster's rolltop desk and thoughtfully pens his response—is a lie. The frank is now a government license to bury voters under mounds of propaganda designed to ensure reelection. Note that the volume of mail and the associated cost of postage is far greater in even years than in odd years, a reflection of the election cycle. This pattern is somewhat more pronounced for the House of Representatives because all 435 members run for reelection every two years, while only about a third of the senators are engaged in campaigns each election cycle.

Stated simply, the congressional frank is now a taxpayer-financed means of distributing political propaganda for congressional incumbents. Representative Morris Udall (D-Ariz.), one of those uncommon men of integrity who somehow stumbled into the House, once complained: "As chairman of the Commission on Congressional Mailing Standards, I have often been appalled by the way some Members have perverted the frank. There can be no doubt that by the use of slick, highly targeted mailings many Members have greatly enhanced their chances for reelection"; and in a similar vein, Senator David Boren (D-Okla.) referred to the frank as a means of sending "campaign propaganda paid for by the taxpayer."[25]

The political nature of unsolicited congressional mail is blatant, often brazen. The aforementioned Senator D'Amato, after receiving only a mild rebuke in 1991 for favor peddling by the limp Senate Ethics Committee, sent out a letter to every household in New York trumpeting his dubious exoneration. Not coincidentally, this disgraceful waste of money occurred just as D'Amato was gearing up for a tough reelection campaign. Or take the case of ex-Senator James A. McClure (R-Idaho), whose conduct is typical—which makes it all the more outrageous. As the *Washington Post* reported:

> Sen. James A. McClure (R-Idaho), who is up for reelection next year [1990], sent out more taxpayer-financed mailings during the first three months of this year than he did in all of 1988, according to records published by the Secretary of the Senate.
>
> The step-up continued during subsequent months with statewide mailings in May and August to all 422,000 postal patrons in Idaho and other mass mailings to specific lists of more than 500 teachers, livestock producers, mining interests, abortion foes, and people interested in gun-control legislation, according to material the senator filed with the clerk's office under Senate rules governing mass mailings.

The $90,300 paid out of the official congressional mail budget to cover the 608,170 pieces mailed by McClure's office between Jan. 1 and March 31 of this year was $27,000 more than what he spent from that same congressional fund in all of 1988. It was far above the roughly $1,300 McClure's campaign committee reported it spent on postage in the first six months of this year, when its overall expenditures totaled $69,000, according to reports filed with the Federal Election Commission.[26]

McClure, after sedulously flushing ninety thousand taxpayer dollars in three fevered months, decided *not* to run again in 1990. He made no restitution to the Treasury. Senator John D. "Jay" Rockefeller IV (D-W. Va.), nephew of the OBE-obsessed Nelson, had mailings that cost $156,300 in 1988 and $32,700 in the first three months of 1989. "By comparison, Rockefeller's campaign committee spent $4,000 on postage in the first six months of [1989]."[27] The family tradition of private parsimony and public profligacy is in good hands.

The liberal reformist group Common Cause, which has labored valiantly on this issue, confirms what we already suspected:

> The cost to taxpayers of franked mass mailings by 100 U.S. Senators during 1987–88 totaled $52,760,528. . . . The 27 incumbent Senators who sought reelection in 1988 spent $20,127,003 of the overall total. These 27 Senators who ran for reelection in 1988 had average 1987–88 franking expenses of 48 cents per household—55 percent more than both those Senators whose terms expire in 1990 and than those whose terms expire in 1992, and 220 percent more than the six Senators who chose to retire in 1988.[28]

Senators who are retiring or who have two or more years before their next campaign typically spend far less than those who face an imminent campaign, as table 3.3 demonstrates. Let us assume that the six senators who retired in 1988 used their franking privilege as it was originally intended—to respond to constituents—rather than as a license to peddle self-glorifying propaganda. We find that the mailing cost per household for the average senator would be approximately fifteen cents. Note that the twenty-seven senators waging reelection campaigns in 1988 spent forty-eight cents per household, or more than three times that amount. The thirty-three senators at the midpoint of their terms spent thirty-one cents per household, more than twice as much as was necessary to respond to constituent mail. The tens of millions of dollars we're talking about are dismissed as "peanuts" by Capitol Hill apologists, but as Senate Minority Leader Everett Dirksen liked to say back in the 1950s, "a million here and a million there and pretty soon we're talking about real money."

TABLE 3.3

FRANKED MAIL EXPENDITURES FOR 1987–88 FOR U.S. SENATORS,
BY REELECTION YEAR

Reelection Year	Mail Cost	Average/Household
27 Senators-1988	$ 20,127,003	$ .48
33 Senators-1990	12,519,655	.31*
34 Senators-1992	17,890,606	.31
6 Retiring-1988	2,223,264	.15

*The states with senate elections in 1990 have almost 20 million fewer households than the states with Senate elections in 1992.

SOURCE: "Franks a Lot: Senators Spend $53 Million in Franked Mass Mailings in 1987–88," *Common Cause News*, June 16, 1989.

The postage budget for each senator is determined by his state's population, but there is a reserve fund for "emergency use." Unused funds can be transferred among members, and the "emergency" designation all too often seems to mean that an incumbent faces a tough reelection campaign.

For example, Senator David K. Karnes (R-Neb.) was appointed to fill the seat of the deceased maverick (and lonely anti-frank crusader) Ed Zorinsky. Karnes blanketed the Cornhusker State with more than a million pieces of mass mail in 1988, including "eight targeted newsletters . . . on topics from taxes to Alzheimer's disease."[29] Republican senators who were not involved in reelection contests transferred $73,000 to Karnes's account; the senator, who ran as a fiscal conservative, withdrew $130,000 from the reserve fund. He lost anyway. Senator Chic Hecht (R-Nev.), another endangered nonentity, also dipped into the reserve fund for $150,000 in a losing effort.[30]

No one uses the frank like a freshman. In our dreams of the world as it ought to be, we picture new congressmen studying classic works of history, philosophy, and economy as they take their places in our hallowed Capitol halls. In reality, those thick books in their briefcases are the House rules, which they will milk for every last buck. The *Washington Post* describes it well:

> Freshman legislators traditionally have been considered to be among the heaviest users of "franked" mail since it provides a way to keep their names before voters, especially in election years. An informal review of mass-mailed newsletters and meeting notices filed by 11 freshman Republican and Democratic members over the last two years seems to support that perception.
>
> The filings at the House Commission on Congressional Mailing Standards showed that in the 19 months since the 11 members took office, the majority sent four or more newsletters and six town meeting notices, though a few sent eight or more meeting notices.
>
> . . . [T]he newsletters for the most part were primarily promotion pieces for the members and a means to encourage constituents to use their services in dealing with the federal government. Some members have even turned the town meeting announcements into artful advertisements for themselves.[31]

The timing gives the game away. Note in tables 3.1 and 3.2 (pages 39–40) that the volume of mail sent in the transition quarter of fiscal year 1976—between July 1 and September 30, 1976—is disproportionately greater than for the remainder of the year. Incumbents would love to stuff every mailbox in the land throughout October and early November, but pesky old regulations prohibit the use of the frank for mass mailings for a period of sixty days prior to a primary or general election.[32] As the deadline nears, House and Senate mail facilities take on the frenetic character of the Oklahoma land rush. Pin-striped Sooners throw everything but the kitchen sink (and their booze cabinets) into franked envelopes. The *Washington Post* reports:

> In one of the biennial rites of incumbency, members of the House and Senate raced to write home to their constituents one last time before their free mailing privilege ended, 60 days before the election.
>
> When the avalanche of outgoing mail bags was counted, the House mailing room held a record backlog of 58 million pieces of mail—enough to send a postal patron mailing to 236 congressional districts. The cost: more than $5 million for the "free" postage.

[The] . . . 67 extra employees hired . . . to help process the last-minute rush might have to be kept on through Oct. 15. Total cost for this year's extra help: nearly $500,000.

Meanwhile, the Senate's mailing department ran three shifts at its printing operation starting in June to keep up with members' work orders because Senate rules won't permit a backlog. All the franked mass mailings were in the mail by the midnight Sept. 9 deadline.[33]

Further darkening this gloomy picture, the conditions under which congressional mail employees work is far from ideal. The *Wall Street Journal* reported "200 employees in the House folding room were working 70-hour weeks without overtime to get out mailings that will help incumbents in the primaries. Sweatshop conditions in the bowels of the Longworth Building?"[34] Oh, well. Some things are more important than the dignity of workers: for instance, the reelection of those workers' tribunes.

Ask an ordinary taxpayer what to do to reduce franking abuses and she'll probably recommend—demand, really—that unsolicited mailings be stopped. Over the years a few doughty souls have advanced this heresy, and have been roundly ignored. The current Congress, to no one's surprise, is moving in the opposite direction. It is considering the construction of a new congressional mailing complex on twenty-five acres of federal land near Bolling Air Force Base. There, "larger, more updated, sophisticated operations" would be constructed to handle the "extremely high volume levels [that] can be expected"[35] to pour from Capitol offices. "About $3 million worth of new printing equipment is to be purchased, including six web-fed presses and 11 sheet-fed presses,"[36] according to one report. Perhaps the edifice will even carry the honored name of a champion franker: the "Al D'Amato Memorial Center for Creampuffery and Propaganda" sounds about right.

Goaded to action by public outrage over Watergate as well as congressional malfeasance, the Congress in the early 1970s created the House Commission on Congressional Mailing Standards (Public Law 93-191) to "issue regulations governing the proper use of the franking privilege."[37] This watchdog had all the pep of a seventeen-year-old basset hound on Quaaludes. For instance, the commission declared, "Members are cautioned on the excessive use of personally phrased references (Member's name, 'I,' 'me,' 'the Congressman,' 'the representative') in newsletters or other mass mailings. Personally phrased references contained in a mass mailing, for the most part, should not appear on the average more than eight times per page." As if that flabby stricture wasn't lax enough, the commission bored a loophole wide enough for Refrigerator Perry to plow through: "The use of personally phrased references in excess of these guidelines, when viewed as a whole and in the proper context, may not be in violation of the spirit and intent of the franking statutes and regulations thereunder."[38]

In other words, Rule B is to ignore Rule A. The commission bowed to public opinion by emphasizing that "it is the policy of the Congress that the privilege of sending mail . . . [is established] to assist and expedite the official business, activities, and duties of the Congress of the United States."[39] Yet it permitted openly propagandistic, self-advertising features such as:

- Tabulation of Member's voting record
- Report detailing the positions a Member took on various legislative proposals
- Notice that a Member will visit various sites in his district to conduct official business with the public
- Comments critical of administration or congressional policies, provided the comments are not presented in a partisan manner
- Invitations to meet and participate with a Member in a public discussion or report on Congress when the meetings are not held under political auspices
- Statements of financial disclosure when contained in a press release or newsletter
- Editorial or issue-oriented cartoons which depict public issues (e.g., energy, inflation, defense) on a nonpolitical basis.[40]

Voter registration and election information or assistance may also be franked as long as it is "prepared and mailed in a nonpartisan manner."[41]

The commission defined a "mass mailing" as "newsletters and similar mailings of more than five hundred pieces in which the content of the matter mailed is substantially identical"; "mass mailings, therefore, are determined by *quantity*."[42] In 1977 Congress limited mass mailings by a byzantine formula: "The total number of pieces of franked [mass] mail during any calendar year may not exceed an amount equal to six multiplied by the number of addresses to which such mail may be delivered in the area from which such member is elected."[43] Again, it sounds good and means nothing. For one thing, notices of members' appearances in their congressional districts do not count against the limitation. Moreover, computer technology and sophisticated mailing techniques have rendered this limitation almost useless, for "targeted" mail is far more effective than crude mass mailings. Tom Kenworthy in the *Washington Post*, newspaper of record when it comes to Congress, explains:

> In political terms . . . nothing is more valuable to a member of Congress than the lists of constituent letters. . . . Think of it this way: Members of Congress normally receive between 250 and 500 letters each week. If the information from those letters is properly coded, a congressional office can develop a near-perfect list for targeted follow-ups. . . . To be able to push the constituents' "hot button" over and over again on an issue he or she cares about . . . is a powerful tool.
>
> The search for the "hot button" has led to creation of an informal network of congressional aides who advise the staffs of new lawmakers on how to establish an effective mail program.
>
> The political benefit of targeted mail is "real simple," said Earl Bender, a direct-mail consultant who has advised Democratic lawmakers on setting up congressional mail programs. "It demonstrates effectiveness and it demonstrates [that the lawmaker] is paying attention to the same issues I'm interested in. . . . It demonstrates more than anything else that this officeholder is interested in communicating with me, that he thinks I am important enough to have a dialogue with."[44]

Consultant Bender's inanities are revealing. Have we really sunk so low that receiving a computer-generated sheet of junk mail constitutes "dialogue"?

We've all gotten questionnaires in the mail from our representatives. Many of us dutifully fill them out, naively supposing that our opinions carry weight. In fact, these questionnaires enable members of Congress to identify members of key interest groups, such as senior citizens, public employees, environmentalists, veterans and military retirees, and pro- or anti-abortion advocates. Gloria Borger of *U.S. News & World Report* explains: "When members send constituents questionnaires that flatter by their very appearance, they use the answers from returns to build their own specialized rosters. A district becomes a conglomeration of lists, categorized by age, ethnic origin, race, opinions or special interest."[45] Out of this mass of information, this dross of demographics, the consultants and computer whizzes alchemize their golden lists. For example, "ethnic directories . . . allow lawmakers to cull the names of almost all Jewish constituents from a computer tape of registered voters."[46] Lists can be cross-classified, sorted, and merged to target specific audiences (e.g., pro-choice Jewish senior citizens who are concerned about the environment and are also military retirees in certain zip codes) with highly personalized messages. High-speed laser printers and automatic signature machines produce documents that few people—this side of a Sotheby's handwriting expert—can distinguish from an old-fashioned letter signed and dictated by a real live congressman.

Personalized computer letters are, for politicians, the greatest invention since the ten-second sound bite. They're far more effective than newsletters, which most Americans in this jaded junk-mail age toss in the trash. Remember that mailings of fewer than five hundred escape the mass-mailing rules; they are sent first class. By sending out small numbers of strategically targeted letters, a member of Congress can carefully cultivate a politically active constituency—at taxpayer expense. Postage, printing, and preparation are all paid from appropriated funds. House regulations stick the taxpayer with the bill for "stationery supplies, design and layout, consultation services, printing services, and mailing list compilation."[47] Even the mailing lists can be legally purchased from consultants and direct-mail factories with taxpayers' dollars.[48]

Since 1985, senators, unlike House members, have been required to disclose publicly the annual costs of their mailings. There are nominal cost limits, based on state population, but once again, the loopholes are wider than Senator Howell Heflin (D-Ala.). Excess campaign funds can be diverted to office expense accounts; postal allocations can be carried over from one year to the next and transferred from one senator to another.[49] Senators who exceed their franking limits simply deduct the overdraft from their office expense account; taxpayer monies ostensibly used to pay staffers can legally pay instead for postage. The franking rules are lax almost beyond belief; by contrast, the house rules at Plato's Retreat are positively draconian. But the more our legislators squander, the more ardently they avow their own undying fiscal responsibility:

> According to projections, House members are about to exhaust the
> $41 million they appropriated for their mail this year [fiscal year

1990], and are headed for a record total of $79 million by the end of the fiscal year.

Recently, the House voted to delete $25 million added to a "dire emergency" spending bill for the rest of the fiscal year to cover some of the extra mail costs. [The] lawmakers who supported the cut could thus claim to have voted to hold down mail costs, although the deletion did not mean less spending. By law, the Postal Service must continue to deliver franked mail even after the appropriation expires.[50]

A deliciously rank example of hypocrisy involves Representative Craig T. James (R-Fla.), who in April 1990 sent a letter to 312,000 households in his district denouncing the "runaway federal deficit [and bragging of] . . . his effort to persuade members of Congress to return to the Treasury their most recent pay increase as a way of setting 'an example of fiscal commitment and responsibility.' By refusing what he called the 'congressional money grab' and returning his pay raise, James saved the taxpayers $7,100 this year. Informing his constituents of this decision cost taxpayers $78,000."[51]

The Honorable James, at least, exhibited a (no doubt unconscious) sense of irony; a far more prosaic money-waster was a member of Congress from New York who "sent a mailing to 180,000 constituents to announce a new bench at a bus stop."[52]

Over in the world's greatest deliberative body, senators engage in the same vapidities. For example, the February 28, 1990, *Washington Post* reported that Senator Rudy Boschwitz (R-Minn.)

> takes the prize for marketing expertise. His letters are targeted to specific audiences. His tone is charming. Last summer he sent a newsletter across Minnesota inviting people to visit "Rudy's Super Duper Milk House"—a booth at the Minnesota State Fair. He said folks could "try some root beer milk, or one of the other flavors we have, or just let me know what's on your mind. I'd love to chat."

He who lives by the targeted mailing can die by it too. Boschwitz won the dubious honor of being the only incumbent senator to lose his bid for reelection in 1990 when he mailed Jewish voters an amazingly tactless letter implying that his Jewish opponent, college professor Paul Wellstone, had proven himself an unreliable defender of Israel's interests by marrying a non-Jew. Ironically, Boschwitz is himself Jewish.

Meanwhile, Senator Dan Coats (R-Ind.), the man who succeeded Dan Quayle,

> sends letters to tell constituents when he doesn't do something. After the Senate debate on the savings and loan bailout bill, Coats wrote, "I felt that the proposed legislation was solid as it stood, and therefore, I did not offer any amendments that would hinder speedy passage." Last year, Coats introduced a bill to cut wasteful congressional spending. Then he sent a mass mailing to announce the bill.[53]

His predecessor, one imagines, would've exhausted his mailing allowance had he informed Indianans every time he didn't have an idea.

In 1989, when a flurry of scandals that reached all the way up to Speaker of the House Jim Wright (D-Tex.) brought that chamber into nigh-unprecedented disrepute, reform was in the air. Proposals to curb self-congratulatory mass mailings by members of Congress were floated; leaders of both parties vowed "ethics and campaign reforms."[54] The Senate Appropriations Committee considered a host of significant strictures: reducing the amount available for postage by more than half; requiring congressmen to disclose the cost of their annual mailings; forbidding the Postal Service to deliver franked mail from a member whose annual appropriation had been spent; limiting each member of Congress to two newsletters a year; and stamping, plain as daylight, the words "mailed at taxpayers' expense"[55] on each franked newsletter. The committee unanimously approved these reforms.

Then the theatrics started—appropriately begun by the junior senator from California. Senator Pete Wilson proposed that *all* franked mass mailings be eliminated and that the $45 million in savings be spent on crack-addicted mothers and babies.[56] The ploy was ingenious and perhaps disingenuous. As the September 28, 1989, *Los Angeles Times* reported:

> Wilson's proposal to ban all congressional mass mailings—including newsletters and town meeting notices—was added as an amendment to the Senate version of the fiscal 1990 legislative appropriations bill. It was seen as a shrewd political maneuver to put lawmakers on the spot by essentially forcing them to choose between tightening a prized perquisite and fighting drugs.

Who dared take the side of dark in this Manichean struggle? The Senate endorsed the measure by a vote of 83 to 8; the House approved by 245 to 137.[57] But a

> funny thing happened on the way to passage. At the start of the conference committee meeting, the leader of the House delegation announced that a "compromise" had been reached with the Senate. Mass mailings would continue; individual member secrecy would prevail; no disclosure required that the junk-mailer's cost came out of the voter's pocket. That was it: no reform.[58]

One modest change was eventually adopted. Under Public Law 101-163, House members may send three district-wide mass mailings per year, half the previous limit of six. Big deal: according to the House Commission on Congressional Mailing Standards, some members routinely send out ten such mailings a year, secure in the knowledge that the old boys' club will wink at the transgression. Those members who shy from open disobedience still find ways to circumvent the new restriction: members of the House have *tripled* their spending on first-class, individually addressed mail.

Consider the record of Representative Steny H. Hoyer (D-Md.), who sent only two newsletters in the past year:

> Hoyer is also targeting senior citizens with a mailing due out this week to about 30,000 households in his Prince Georges County district, and sent an earlier mailing to 10,000 homes of federal employees. His district's 6,500 newly registered voters each got a letter, and each of the district's approximately 210,000 households got newsletters twice. Combined with 262,000 public meeting notices, Hoyer has sent more than 700,000 pieces of mail this year at public expense.[59]

What Hoyer does is perfectly legal, well within the rules—and, to those who stubbornly cling to the old republican ideals of the citizen-legislator, sickening.

Others make no effort to respect the letter of the law. Representative John Porter (R-Ill.), in a summer 1989 newsletter bewailing "the Defense Department's proposed closing of Fort Sheridan in his district," used the "word 'I' 16 different times on one page."[60] This contravened the formal limit of eight self-references per page (which one would think would be enough for all but the most inflated egomaniac), but no matter: Porter went unpunished.

Franking reform has failed, ignominiously so, because some of its alleged champions are pharisees of the first water. The late Representative Silvio Conte (R-Mass.), one of the more colorful characters to sit in the House in recent years, took to the floor to condemn the abuse of the franking privilege as a "Frankenstein monster"; jumbling metaphors, he then asserted that it was time to "cut its head off cold turkey." Nevertheless, Conte, without fail, "regularly mailed the then-limit of six newsletters to his constituents in 1989 and earlier."[61] It was humorous but ineffective, like a drunkard sounding the call for temperance.

If sentiment ever existed in the Senate for franking reform, it had a very short life span.[62] Less than a year after the Senate voted overwhelmingly to eliminate all mass-mailing privileges,

> the Senate Rules Committee . . . consider[ed] a resolution . . . that could result in an increase of nearly 50 percent next year in taxpayer-financed franked mailings by senators.
>
> The new proposal . . . could lead to cancellation of cuts made in Senate mailing privileges made last year. The Senate has been torn between the desire to continue making mass-mailings to constituents at taxpayer expense, and concern that the growing cost of such mailings is politically embarrassing.[63]

Two weeks before the 1990 elections, as "Throw the Bums Out!" had reached a fever pitch, the House hastily passed new rules governing the use of the frank. Henceforth—or at least until the House can quietly reverse itself in the wee hours of a December night—each representative will have an annual postal budget of $178,000; each member's mailing expenses will be published quarterly; the postmaster will monitor each member's allowance and halt mass mailings when the allowance is exhausted; members cannot share allowances or carry them over to the next year; and all mass mailings of over five hundred similar pieces must be reviewed by the House Franking Commission.[64] The House rules are now in basic conformity with the Senate rules.[65] For the time being.

Still, the reforms are largely cosmetic. Mass mailings—propaganda thinly disguised as public service—continue, more or less unabated. As

Charles Babcock ruefully observed in the *Washington Post*, "Both parties teach new members that there are three rules for getting reelected: 'Use the frank. Use the frank. Use the frank.' It would be funny if it wasn't taxpayers' money and degrading to the whole institution."[66]

The frank is only one part, albeit a large and noxious part, of Congress's taxpayer-financed incumbent propaganda machine. For example, both the Senate and the House have television studios that telegenic members use to tape messages for distribution to the folks back home. A satellite service, paid for by the taxpayers, distributes softball "interviews" with House members to television stations in their districts. These interrogations, often conducted by the member's press flack, are about as hard-hitting as a Cuban reporter's fawning interview with Fidel Castro. As one seasoned Hill correspondent notes:

> The satellite service is just one out of an array of electronic media outlets—some paid for by the taxpayers—available to incumbent House members that provides them with almost instantaneous communication links with their districts. It also gives incumbent lawmakers a powerful campaign tool that is seldom matched by their opponents.
>   . . . [P]olitical professionals agree that under the right conditions a House member can improve his standing with the voters if he can be seen and heard regularly on local television and radio.[67]

Each senator has a facsimile machine, which is "the perfect tool to distribute news releases to media in a member's state."[68] The Senate sergeant-at-arms is pushing "an 800 telephone number so that members could conduct from the Senate studio a television call-in show with constituents who would be able to ask questions at no cost." (These "constituents" are often staffers and friends who lob nice juicy home-run pitches.) Also on the drawing board is "interactive teleconferencing," which permits both the senator and his interlocutor to be televised.[69]

The advantages that accrue to politicians who get free (and extensive) mailing and television privileges are enormous. As political scientist David Mayhew writes, the goal of every congressional candidate is "to disseminate one's name among constituents in such a fashion as to create a favorable image but in messages having little or no issue content."[70] During the 1986 elections, $97.3 million, or 24.3 percent of total campaign expenditures of $400.4 million, was used to purchase advertising on radio and television stations; production and consultation costs accounted for an additional $17.6 million.[71] When incumbents, who in almost every race already enjoy a huge edge over their challengers in name recognition, get what amounts to free advertising, is it any wonder they're damn near unbeatable?

Congressional Staff

Senator Daniel Patrick Moynihan (D-N.Y.), whose iconoclastic streak flares redder than his boozer's snout every so often, has made himself mighty unpopular in his workplace with his call for sharp reductions in the size of the congressional staff. (Nebraska's Senator Bob Kerrey, who tried unsuccessfully to grab the brass ring of the Democratic presidential nomination in 1992, has seconded Moynihan's proposal.)

The notion that members of Congress are entitled to taxpayer-provided full-time assistance is only about a century old: senators were not provided with full-time clerks until 1885, and House members got them eight years later.[72] As late as 1861, the legislative branch of government functioned with only 393 employees.[73] At the turn of the century, total employment in the legislative branch was 5,690; this figure remained below 10,000 until 1928.[74] As of April 1990, that number had risen to 38,149—100 times larger than in 1861. (During the same thirteen decades, the nation's population has increased eightfold, from 31.5 million to 248.7 million.)

The real growth has been in personal (as opposed to institutional) aides. Before World War II, "House members got along with only a secretary and a clerk, and senators had an average of four aides each."[75] The numbers have expanded exponentially. Today there are more than twenty-eight staff and committee employees for each member of the House and more than seventy-five for each senator. Compare these hypertrophied staffs with the modest crews of British parliamentarians. The 650 members of the British House of Commons have a *total* of about 1,000 employees to assist them. Members of Parliament "labor with almost no assistance from staff. . . . Most MPs have a part-time secretary to assist them, . . . but almost three quarters of the secretaries do no more than handle the clerical work . . . such as typing letters and answering phone calls. Even so, a few MPs proudly claimed to answer many letters in longhand,"[76] as three American political scientists discovered as recently as 1987.

Between 1946 and 1986, "legislative branch appropriations increased

2,859 percent: six times the inflation rate. The cost of running the legislative branch rose from $198 million in 1966 to $947.2 million in 1976 and
$1.8 billion in 1986, a ninefold increase in 20 years."[77] (The legislative
branch consists of Congress proper as well as a number of federal agencies
under congressional control, such as the General Accounting Office, the
Government Printing Office, and the Library of Congress.)

It costs more than $1.1 billion to run Congress, a 93 percent increase
since 1980. The average senator costs the taxpayer $3.85 million; the
average representative costs $1.31 million. And that's before a single vote
is cast.

Representatives receive a staff budget of approximately $500,000,
which may be distributed among a total of twenty-two employees.[78] The
staff allowance for senators depends upon the population of their states, but
the average is over a million dollars a year.[79] A senator from New York or
California may have as many as seventy or eighty staff members.[80]

Congressional staffers aren't civil servants, cosseted by a web of protec-
tive laws. They can be fired at any time, for any reason, by their boss or
their boss's boss—the voters. The fear that haunts all run-of-the-mill
politicians—defeat—shadows staffers, too. Although many turn cynical,
many other congressional aides develop fanatical loyalty to their boss—
usually referred to as "my member."

To no one's surprise, "congressional staff members are primarily loyal to
their appointing authority—that is, to the individual senator or representative responsible for having put them in their present jobs."[81] This fealty is
manifested, first and foremost, by a relentless push toward reelection. As a
former legislative aide to a respected senator told the authors: "The most
important part of our jobs was thinking up bills or grandstand plays to get
the senator free and positive air time. Good public policy was secondary—
very secondary."

Larger staffs were supposed to permit congressmen to grapple with
complex issues. Political scientist Morris Fiorina describes what really
happened:

> There is an ironic twist to the story of the congressional staff
> expansions. Of all the possible changes ("reforms") that various
> observers have urged upon Congress during the postwar period,
> staff increases are perhaps the least controversial. Congressional
> actions to augment staff numbers and quality are almost univer-
> sally encouraged and applauded. The reason is a naive assumption

about the purposes to which congressmen put their staffs. . . . To reformers, a large professional staff is just the thing to assure better public policies and a more even balance between Congress and the executive branch.

But in reality what are the uses to which congressmen put their staffs? Improved public policy is a goal that most congressmen favor. But reelection is certainly a more important goal. And when given sixteen or eighteen employees to allocate as they see fit, congressmen quite naturally put the lion's share to work on the most important thing, reelection, while perhaps reserving a few for secondary matters such as formulating our country's laws and programs.[82]

A savvy staffer is an invaluable campaign tool. Indeed, "some are hired expressly for their political skills that can be used to help the member gain reelection."[83] As a result, one critic calls Congress a "staff-driven public-relations machine" whose members "mount the national stage by means of press releases, endless bills and amendments, ghostwritten letters and threatening phone calls"[84]—all paid for by a complaisant public.

Consider the distribution of staff members between the members' offices in Washington—which deal, if reluctantly, with the great policy issues of the day—and their offices back home in the district or the state. In 1960 only 4 percent of the Congress operated district offices, and most were open only on an intermittent basis, usually when the congressperson visited the district. District staffers accounted for just 14 percent of the total congressional personal staff.[85] In three decades, these numbers have rocketed upward faster than the national debt. *Every* member of Congress now has a district or state office—sometimes as many as eight.[86] By 1987, 41 percent of House personal staff and 34 percent of Senate personal staff were employed in state or district offices.[87] That's thirteen hundred House and Senate offices across the fruited plains, or more offices than Sears, Roebuck & Co. has retail stores. These thirteen hundred branch offices are peopled by four thousand or so retainers, busily solving constituent problems and burnishing the boss's image.[88]

"Constituent service" has become a raison d'être for many congress-people; it has a much better ring than "thoughtful consideration of the public weal," and the payoff—reelection—is sweeter than any Vegas jackpot. Speaker of the House Thomas Foley and House Minority Leader Robert Michel observe that we have witnessed a major transformation in the demands on the federal government and, correspondingly, in the demands on congressional offices.

Federal government programs increasingly affect the lives of constituents, who quickly learned that they needed help navigating the vast federal bureaucracy. We in Congress responded to the need. We placed more staff in our home offices and made them directly responsible for providing constituent assistance. The home office is our front line and we take great pride in their service. Our constituent services not only solve individual problems, they can improve the quality of life for entire communities.

These activities take good management and a strong work force. Coordinating the disparate activities of several offices hundreds of miles apart is a formidable management challenge—but it is essential to our overall effectiveness as Members of Congress.[89]

It all sounds so pure and innocent. Foley and Michel can warm the cockles of any mugwump heart. What they don't say is that "constituent service" is a highly effective and, happily, noncontroversial way to get your ticket punched every two years. As the *Washington Post* reports:

Members of Congress are finding that the road to political success lies in what they do for the folks back home. . . . The study, conducted by the Congressional Management Foundation, asked the top managers and political aides of members of Congress to rank the "most important factors in solidifying your member's political base." The result? Congressional offices overwhelmingly rank constituent services as most important for political success.[90]

Freshmen learn this lesson quickly and well. They want to be your friend; some *insist* on being your friend. New representative Tom Campbell (R-Calif.) sent out a newsletter with a "clip and save" list that included "locate late or missing Social Security checks; cutting red tape in immigration; problems regarding veteran's hospitals; unraveling regulations involving small businesses; problems with IRS; and fighting job or housing discrimination."[91] ("Babysit for your kids" barely missed the list.) Representative Ben Jones (D-Ga.), memorable for his performance as Cooter on TV's moronic "The Dukes of Hazzard," fair begged the folks back home to call his four full-time case workers "if an application for passports was two months late or if a constituent wanted calendars, agricultural yearbooks, a tour package to help plan a visit to Washington, or 'for a fee,' a flag that had been flown over the Capitol."[92]

These two examples are hardly egregious; they're typical. But they suggest the ways in which Congress has metamorphosed from a deliberative legislature into a pack of smiling ombudsmen who are happy to sic a flunky on Mrs. Smith's lost Social Security check but terrified to debate, or discuss, or even think about, reforming the Social Security system.

Students—and practitioners—of politics know this. In *The Congressman*, Charles Clapp observes:

> Denied a favorable ruling by the bureaucracy on a matter of direct concern to him, puzzled or irked by delays in obtaining a decision, confused by the administrative maze through which he is directed to proceed, or ignorant of whom to write, a constituent may turn to his congressman for help. These letters offer great potential for political benefit to the congressman since they affect the constituent personally. If the legislator can be of assistance, he may gain a firm ally; if he is indifferent, he may even lose votes.[93]

Casework has become the most important activity of congressional offices. Congressional scholar Kenneth Olson ventures that "the chances are good that an analysis of the total time expended by members and their staffs on all congressional work would find casework the leading activity."[94] Does this mean that we have a kinder, gentler Congress that, animated by love and tender concern, has put aside dispute and contention in order to soothe, to succor, to mend the broken hearts of 250 million Americans? Hardly. The perceptive Morris Fiorina notes, "The picture that emerges is that, other things being equal, representatives who are 'running scared' are the most energetic providers of constituency service."[95]

When in doubt, a political proverb ought to go, opt for the innocuous. Plenty of politicians have been damaged by taking stands on war, taxes, gun control, and free speech, but no one—not even a grown man who's made a nice living by answering to the name of Cooter—ever lost an election because he sent out a free calendar. Statesmanship has its rewards, but they are frequently posthumous; it's much easier to expedite, to facilitate, to intervene—to be nothing more than an exalted messenger boy whom the other messenger boys call "my distinguished colleague."

Stripped of the whitewash and the embellishments, what we have is a nationwide network—an octopus, to use novelist Frank Norris's imagery—of tax-funded flunkies whose primary job is to subvert the electoral process—that is, to give incumbents unfair advantages over their already underfinanced challengers. These are thinly disguised campaign organizations run by shrewd operators. Ofttimes no effort is made to mask the fact: in 1988 more than 40 percent of congressmen running for reelection installed a personal aide in a top campaign post.[96] They're bamboozling us, and we're paying for the privilege.

PAC[k]ing Congress

Then there is money, which may not be the root of all evil but certainly is the lifeblood of politics. A citizen of modest means cannot run a serious race for Congress unless he has hocked his soul to the PAC-men. (Admittedly, a rare conjunction of circumstances can produce a maverick unbeholden: Vermont's socialist congressman Bernard Sanders, for instance, or the late Iowa curmudgeon and skinflint H. R. Gross.) A Senate seat, which retails for about $8 million these days, is out of the middle-class citizen-politician's reach, except perhaps in a Vermont or a New Hampshire.

Political action committees (PACs) have been cast as the villain in this long-running morality play, and with good reason. Congressmen, on average, get about half their campaign booty from PACs,[97] which are generally offshoots of labor, business, trade, or ideological associations. PACs can be traced back to the 1896 presidential campaign of William McKinley (brilliantly engineered by the Cleveland shipping magnate Marcus Alonzo Hanna), but detailed information about them and their practices has been available only since 1972, when disclosure of campaign receipts and expenditures was required under the Federal Election Campaign Act of 1971.[98]

There are thousands of PACs, dispensing dollars on behalf of every interest from doctors to truckers. The CIO-PAC, created by the Congress of Industrial Organizations in July 1943, was the first modern PAC, and until 1980 the contributions of labor-union PACs dwarfed those of business. The worm has since turned; corporate PACs are now the biggest player in federal-election campaigns. In the 1988 election cycle, 40,258 corporate contributions totalling $32.4 million were made to House candidates; labor organizations made 12,124 such contributions totalling $27.2 million.[99]

From 1972 through the end of July 1989, senators holding office as of July 1990 had received a total of $158.2 million in PAC contributions. Six senators had received more than three million dollars each; twenty-two received more than two million dollars; and seventy-eight more than one million. Only two senators accepted no PAC money [Herbert H. Kohl (D-Wisc.) and David L. Boren (D-Okla.)].[100] Senators tend to rely less than representatives on PAC money, but even this may be changing. The *Washington Post* reports that "between 1978 and 1988, PAC giving to Senate candidates jumped from $9.7 million, 11.3 percent of total receipts, to $45.7 million, or 23 percent of total receipts."[101] From relatively modest beginnings in the 1972 election, when total PAC contributions were $8.5 million to both incumbents and challengers, these organizations were doling out $106.4 million by 1988.[102]

To adapt a maxim: Better the devil in your hip pocket than the devil outside it. The gadfly ex-California governor Jerry Brown argues that we are governed by only one party: The Incumbent Party. And PAC money is a cornerstone of this one-party system. In 1972 fifty-two cents of each PAC dollar went to incumbents, twenty-five cents went to challengers, and the remainder was donated to candidates running for open seats. By 1982, incumbents received sixty-eight cents of each PAC dollar, challengers received eighteen cents, and only fourteen cents went into open-seat elections.[103]

TABLE 3.4

DISTRIBUTION OF PAC CONTRIBUTIONS BETWEEN INCUMBENTS AND
CHALLENGERS IN THE 1988 HOUSE ELECTIONS CYCLE
($ THOUSANDS)

| *Incumbents Who Received* | INCUMBENTS | | CHALLENGERS | | |
	No.	*Amount*	*No.*	*Amount*	*Ratio*
$500,000 or more	9	$ 4,949.8	9	$ 827.8	5.98
$400,000 to $499,999	24	10,720.5	24	1,153.5	9.29
$300,000 to 399,999	44	15,314.2	39	2,608.2	5.87
$200,000 to $299,999	110	27,651.5	102	5,634.1	4.91
$100,000 to 199,999	184	27,298.5	162	4,387.2	6.22
$ 50,000 to $ 99,999	46	3,637.8	34	1,322.5	2.75
Less than $50,000	23	337.7	21	543.7	.62
Total		$ 89,910.1		$ 16,477.0	5.46

SOURCE: "PAC Support Scorecard: The House," *Washington Post*, May 11, 1989.

Table 3.4 tells another dreary PAC story. The nine incumbents who received more than a half million dollars from PACs were given a total of $4.9 million; their challengers got only $827,837. Any incumbent who has to spend that much is in trouble; these were, for the most part, hotly contested races, yet the incumbents received $5.98 from PACs for each $1 given to the challengers.

The ratios are similar in other categories. The "Less than $50,000" numbers were thrown way out of whack because Representative Craig T. James (R-Fla.) obtained only $2,750 in PAC contributions, while his opponent garnered $444,684. If we disregard that highly aberrant race, incumbents in this category lead their opponents in PAC receipts by a ratio of 3.38:1. In the 1988 House elections, 84.4 cents of the average PAC dollar went to incumbents, 8.6 cents to their challengers, and 7 cents to open-seat candidates.[104] The 105 challengers who received nothing from PACs faced incumbents who collected a total of $18.9 million. The rich are getting richer—much richer.

And what do we make of the bizarre fact that the forty-nine incumbents who faced *no* opposition in 1988 collected more than $7.8 million from PACs? Since Nevada is the only state that offers disgruntled voters a "None of the Above" option, we must conclude that the PACs were buying influence, or, to put it less euphemistically, votes.

PACs make great whipping boys; "goo-goos," as cynics call good-government reformers, can flail away, secure in their own righteousness. But let's flip this coin and look at it from the obverse: of the 408 House members running for reelection in 1988, only seven lost; in 1990, only fifteen incumbents lost. Only the brave (or foolhardy) back a challenger. The deck is so stacked in favor of incumbents that influence-seeking PACs must assume that every member will be reelected and act accordingly. If the Widget Industry PAC backs too many losing challengers, the next omnibus tariff bill is likely to lower duties on widget imports. No favor is ever forgotten in Washington; no bad turn ever goes unpunished.

The findings of the swelling literature on PACs are summarized by liberal sociologist Amatai Etzioni, who notes:

> When lawmakers are elected, and appointed to a committee or subcommittee, they often bring with them a set of unspoken obligations to the PACs who helped get them there. However, those who got it without acquiring sufficient or the "right" kinds of obligations are not immune to the influence of PACs, either; nor

are they inaccessible to new PACs. Congress is kept very attentive to PAC needs, according them exactly the kind of careful husbanding that the public interest deserves, and citizens at large are entitled to, between one election campaign and another. [105]

Scholarly studies of the relationship between voting and PAC contributions have produced mixed results. Links between voting behavior and PAC contributions have been found in the dairy, [106] trucking, [107] maritime, and automobile [108] industries as well as with corporate and union interests. [109] The opposite conclusion—that PAC contributions have little influence on voting behavior—has also been reported in research. [110] No one disputes, however, that PAC contributions buy access and open doors.

Increasingly (and subversively), campaign coffers are being filled by out-of-state—sometimes even out-of-country—PAC money. In the 1988 election cycle, one quarter of all Senate donations were from out-of-state interests. Two years later, half the Senate "received a majority of their large individual donations from out of state." [111]

This isn't always the much-maligned PAC money. Consider Representative Edward J. Markey (D-Mass.), who is chairman of the House Telecommunications and Finance Subcommittee. Markey boasts of his refusal to take soiled PAC dollars, yet over a three-year period he "collected $333,675 in contributions of $200 or larger from donors living outside Massachusetts; about 75 percent of those out-of-state dollars came from people with ties to the telecommunications and financial industries. By contrast, he raised $146,950 from the folks at home." [112] Sanctimony, like love, is easy to feign but hard to disguise.

The rapidly growing foreign influence on domestic politics is even more troublesome. In the 1980s foreign companies began buying up U.S. firms on a large scale. Many companies that operate domestically are wholly or partly owned by foreigners, and these companies make substantial PAC contributions. As the weekly magazine *Insight*—itself a property of South Korean religious leader Sun Myung Moon's empire—revealed:

> Many of these PACs contributed more than $100,000 to campaigns. Brown & Williamson Tobacco Corp., for example, 100 percent owned by Britain's B.A.T. Industries plc, contributed $104,150 to 177 candidates. Joseph E. Seagram & Sons Inc., 100 percent owned by Canada's Seagram Co. Ltd., contributed $174,150 to 153 candidates. Marine Midland Bank Inc., 100

percent owned by Hong Kong's Hong Kong and Shanghai Banking Corp., contributed $104,425 to 88 candidates.[113]

Most members of Congress now have dual constituencies: the folks back home, who've got votes but not much money, and the financial contributors, who may write their checks in offices two thousand miles away. What happens when the interests of those two constituencies collide? Whom, or what, does the congressperson represent? If he sides with what the old Jacksonians religiously called "the people," the money may dry up. If he takes the money and runs, he may sprint himself right out of a job. But the latter fate is improbable. The taxpayer-provided perquisites of power are a nearly impenetrable armor; even if constituents are offended by a vote, to whom can they turn? An unknown, penniless opponent?

The communitarian Etzioni is on the right track when he suggests that plutocracy—the rule of the power of wealth—is replacing democracy, or the power of the people. (The power of unorganized individuals is even more meager.) Ironically, it is the other special-interest groups—rather than "the people"—who check the power of the mightiest interests. Etzioni explains:

> Plutocracy does *not* assume one ruling class, or one power elite. . . . America's power wielders include a variety of groups—corporations and labor unions, big business and associations of small businesses, oil companies and farm associations and banks. They do not all pull in the same directions and they are not in cahoots with one another, like one well-organized tidy bunch. On the contrary, each interest group seeks to tilt the system its own way, so that the riches on the table will roll into its own pockets. Cumulatively, however, they do prevent the government from discharging its appointed duties, from serving the public first and foremost.[114]

Etzioni fails to mention powerful organized groups such as environmentalists and crusaders for the disabled, who are responsible for the passage of laws such as the Clean Air Act and the Americans with Disabilities Act.

Further complicating matters and fragmenting loyalties are the "leadership PACs" that spawned like poison mushrooms in the late 1970s. Through them, congressional money-magnets dish out their excess funds to other candidates, usually incumbents or probable winners of open seats. They do so in order to build up a pile of IOUs that can be cashed in at a propitious time. Congress-watcher Ross Baker writes: "Funding provided by leadership PACs seems to have been decisive in races for such posts as House majority whip (the number three leadership slot), Budget Committee chair, and chair of the House Democratic Caucus (leadership of the entire Democratic membership of the House)."[115]

The king of the leadership PAC was Representative Tony Coelho (D-Calif.), fund-raising whiz and mastermind of the Democratic Congressional Campaign Committee. He put the squeeze on PACs for millions of dollars, which he then distributed through his personal leadership PAC, the Valley Education Fund. This largesse smoothed Coelho's way into the House Democratic hierarchy; he fell, though, and fell hard, resigning in disgrace after an ethics scandal.[116]

The least scrupulous members of Congress—which is like denominating the least humorous members of North Korea's Kim Il Sung family—use PAC money as pocket money. Senators are allowed to use their excess campaign funds to cover office expenses; until 1993, House members may transfer surplus campaign cash to their personal accounts if a) they retire; and b) they were in office before January 1980. Representative Gene Taylor (R-Mo.), no fool, gave up his seat in 1989 and "spent some of his war chest to pay for auto insurance, income taxes and a party for his staff. . . . After donating $52,000 to charity, Taylor wrote himself checks totalling $345,000."[117] Those members who are not eligible to pocket their excess campaign funds can use them "for future campaigns—even for different offices."[118] While the Gene Taylors pocket the pelf, other grafters can take a lesson from convicted crook Mario Biaggi, the former Bronx congressman who

> used $386,064 . . . to pay legal expenses associated with fighting racketeering and other criminal charges for which he was convicted last year [1988] in the Wedtech public corruption scandal. . . . The late Rep. John Duncan (R-Tenn.) willed $604,521 in campaign funds to his family upon his death last year.[119]

Like vampires, politicians heave and foam and lust for the lifeblood of politics. Senator Phil Gramm (R-Tex.) was still raising PAC money in September 1990 for November's race, even though he had already raised $6.2 million to his opponent's $20,000, a ratio of 310:1. Gramm's greedy and voluble House counterpart, Representative Stephen J. Solarz (D-N.Y.), had $1.6 million in the bank when he fleeced PACs at a September 27, 1990, "birthday party" fund-raiser: his challenger had not yet raised the $5,000 minimum that required a filing with the FEC.[120] And the permanent Congress rolls on, and on, and on—flattening the republic underneath.

As *Newsweek* reports, incumbents use

> huge campaign war chests as pre-emptive weapons to effectively blow away opponents before they reach the starting line. Thanks to favorable financing and spending laws—voted in by incumbents to protect themselves—the campaign sums need not be liquidated when an election is over, but rather can accumulate indefinitely. Challenges grow increasingly difficult, elections amount to little more than formalities, debate is squelched and voters end up with with few, if any, choices.[121]

Too Many Congressional Cooks Stir the Public-Policy Pot

Congress used to be a deliberative body that determined broad national policy objectives, enacted legislation to fund the programs that are carried out by the executive branch, and then exercised oversight and review to ensure that the congressional mandates were met. No more. Fund-raising has pervaded and perverted the Congress; its members have lost sight of the forest in their obsessive shaking of the money tree. Many have become involved in the administration of federal programs; they exert pressure on the bureaucracy to grant favors to contributors. Charles Keating and his five Senate errand boys—Alan Cranston (D-Calif.), John McCain (R-Ariz.), Donald Riegle, Jr. (D-Mich.), John Glenn (D-Ohio), and Dennis DeConcini (D-Ariz.)—are walking testaments to our system of government-by-payback.

The oversight function of Congress, ostensibly designed to protect the taxpayer against bureaucratic abuses and failures, has been contorted into a means by which smooth operators repay political debts. For an increasing number of members of Congress, managing programs has become a more rewarding—not to mention more lucrative—activity than setting policy.

The influence-buyers who run PACs understand that the most important work of Congress is done in its committees. A defense contractor is better off buying the tepid support of a member of the Armed Services Committee than the fervent advocacy of a backbencher on the Post Office and Civil Service Committee. A canny new member, therefore, will seek placement on a powerful committee. (Of course members also want to be on committees that have large constituencies back home: an Iowan, for example, will often—but not always—ask to be assigned to the Agriculture Committee.)

The result of all this jockeying is predictable: the last two decades have seen a rapid growth in the number of committees and subcommittees and in their average size. Between 1974 and 1985, "the number of congressional committees increased 14 percent, subcommittees 23 percent and [their combined staffs increased] more than 124 percent."[122] The House and Senate have created more than 250 subcommittees.

Inevitably, jurisdictions overlap; turf wars become confoundingly complex. Consider drug-abuse policy. In 1988 the Congressional Research Service tried to untangle the coils and masses of American narcotics law. Who has jurisdiction over what? Its findings were mind-boggling.[123] Excluding select, special, joint, and ad hoc committees and subcommittees, as well as the House and Senate Appropriations and Budget Committees—and issuing the caveat that "because House and Senate committees and subcommittees are so numerous, it is nearly impossible to identify all panels that could conceivably be involved with drug-abuse policy"—CRS found an incredible total of seventy-five House and Senate committees and subcommittees that are responsible for some aspect of the federal War on Drugs.[124]

One measure of the waste and duplication among these seventy-five committees and subcommittees can be obtained by counting the number of times key words appear in the statements of their activities (see table 3.5). In the House, for example, two committees and six subcommittees examine the issue of drug testing, as do three committees and one subcommittee in the Senate. Seven bodies deal with drug smuggling, while four oversee the interdiction of illegal drugs. Treatment for drug abuse is near the top of the agenda for a whopping thirteen congressional committees or subcommittees.

Leaving aside, until chapter 9, the wisdom of the federal government's War on Drugs, we can see that wasteful duplication is one of its by-products. Congress displays the same curious blend of superfluity and fecklessness when it comes to monitoring other departments and agencies of the federal government. According to the *Wall Street Journal*, Secretary of Defense Richard Cheney complained to the president that

107 congressional committees and subcommittees oversee his department. But that's not all. Every working day, the Defense

TABLE 3.5

FREQUENCY OF OCCURRENCE OF KEY WORDS OR PHRASES IN
THE FY 1988 ACTIVITY STATEMENTS OF HOUSE AND SENATE
COMMITTEES AND SUBCOMMITTEES DEALING WITH DRUG ABUSE

	HOUSE OF REPRESENTATIVES		SENATE	
Key Word or Phrase	*Committee*	*Subcommittee*	*Committee*	*Subcommittee*
Narco-terrorists	1	1	1	1
Rehabilitation	0	3	2	1
Treatment	0	7	4	2
Drug Testing	2	6	3	1
Drug Use/Users	2	9	4	5
Interdiction	1	1	1	1
Smuggling	1	3	1	2
Loans	1	1	0	1

SOURCE: Carol Hardy, "House and Senate Standing Committees and Subcommittees with Jurisdiction over National Drug Abuse Policy," Report #88-634 GOV (Washington, D.C.: Congressional Research Service of the Library of Congress, September 27, 1988), pp. 5–12.

Department receives an estimated 450 written inquiries and more than 2,500 telephone inquiries from Capitol Hill. Each day, according to the report, the department is required to submit to Congress nearly three separate written reports—each averaging more than 1,000 man-hours and costing about $50,000 to prepare. Senior Defense Department officials, meanwhile, spend 40 hours preparing for the average 14 hours of congressional testimony they provide each day that Congress is in session. None of this "oversight," however, prevented such wasteful spending as the massive Defense Department fraud uncovered in 1988 by the FBI.

In the wake of the mismanagement of millions of dollars at the Department of Housing and Urban Development, many members of Congress are calling for increased oversight of HUD. Yet Congress is and has been exercising considerable jurisdiction over the department. During the HUD scandal years, 84 congressional committees and subcommittees had jurisdiction over HUD. Obviously, the oversight was ineffective.[125]

This shouldn't surprise us. Members of Congress themselves complain that they're spread much too thin. No one can become expert in the minutiae of the two or three committees and multiple subcommittees that our representatives serve on. A day has but twenty-four hours, and if eight are allotted to sleep and eight more to begging rich men and PACs for donations, there's not much time left for mastering details. The wonder isn't that scandals occur, it's that they're ever discovered. For when everyone is responsible for oversight, then no one is. A single person or committee with a strong incentive to exercise oversight authority is far more effective than seventy-five congressional cooks stirring the public-policy pot.

Behold the energy-policy maze:

> The House Agriculture Committee's Subcommittee on Forests, Family Farms, and Energy has 13 members; the Appropriation Committee's Subcommittee on Energy and Water Development has nine members; the Energy and Commerce Committee has 42 members; the Government Operations Committee has a nine-member Subcommittee on Environment, Energy, and Natural Resources; the Interior and Insular Affairs Committee has a 17-member Subcommittee on Energy and the Environment and a 22-member Subcommittee on Water, Power, and Offshore Energy Resources; the Science, Space, and Technology Committee has a 14-member Subcommittee on Energy Research and Development; and even the Small Business Committee has an eight-person Subcommittee on Regulation, Business Opportunities, and Energy.
>
> With about 40 of our 100 senators also involved in various aspects of energy policy, the question becomes: Who's responsible for what?[126]

The answer, alas, is nobody.

Oversight Oversights

Studies of congressional oversight have emphasized its absence: "Not much 'oversight' of administration, in a systematic and continuous enough manner to make it mean very much, is practiced."[127] Recurring scandals give ample testimony to the sporadic and ineffective nature of congressional oversight, yet scholars have failed to come up with convincing reasons why Congress makes such a bad monitor.[128] Some blame an alleged lack of "resources"—DCspeak for bigger staffs and higher budgets.[129] Others, a bit more plausibly, cite time constraints. A more nebulous explanation is that "members of the House and Senate have a variety of interests, and the motivation to engage in detailed, continuous oversight is often missing or weak at best."[130] We take a different view. Congress prefers not to exercise oversight because members of Congress are directly responsible for the pork-barrel politics that cause much of the waste, abuse, and corruption in the executive branch.[131]

Every member of Congress—excepting once-in-a-generation skinflints like H. R. Gross—dips his scoop into the pork barrel. Bringing home the bacon (which other people paid for) is a boon to incumbents; indeed, so ingrained is the notion of Washington as a "Great Barbecue" that voters expect their congressmen to ride herd on the pencil-pushers and paper-shufflers and squeeze a veterans' hospital or science grant or at least a lousy bridge out of the bureaucracy. This runs athwart the congressional oversight role: members are supposed to identify waste and prevent its reoccurrence. Ha! Ha! These guys don't want to shut down the boondoggle factory—they want to place new orders! As the *Wall Street Journal* notes:

> What is missing from the congressional hearings on the HUD scandal . . . are details about the role congressmen played as lobbyists encouraging the mismanagement of funds. How often did congressmen call or write HUD officials pressing them to grant housing contracts to their own friends and supporters? As the *Washington Post*, the *New York Times*, and others have reported, several congressmen—even some who have expressed outrage over the scandal—worked hand-in-hand with professional influence peddlers to direct HUD contracts to campaign contributors and influential constituents. Yet, there is no official record of this congressional lobbying.[132]

Nor are we likely to get one.

Micromanagement

Committees and subcommittees are less interested in ferreting out evidence of that hoary old trinity of waste, fraud, and abuse than in "micromanaging" agencies and bureaus to extract pork and favors for monied friends. Congressional directives are becoming more explicit: for example, "in the FY 1986 Labor-HHS-Education Appropriations Bill, the number of new and competing renewal research grants to be supported by NIH [National Institutes of Health] (6,100) was specified for the first time. The Act [P.L. 99-178] . . . provided that $4.5 million . . . be transferred to the departmental management account for the construction of the Mary Babb Randolph Cancer Center in West Virginia."[133]

Medical degrees are notable by their absence on congressional résumés, yet these sages somehow determined that 6,100 was the "optimal" number of research grants. Why not 6,101? Or 5,999? Or 2,337? Affixing the name Randolph to a cancer-research center in West Virginia is understandable; Senator Jennings Randolph was a fine man and a top-flight pork-barreler. But is West Virginia the ideal location for a cancer-research facility? Is it fair to take $4.5 million from taxpayers in South Dakota and Texas to subsidize employment for carpenters and masons in West Virginia—just because a powerful man lives there? Congress is supposed to set broad public policy at the national level, which is then implemented by the executive branch. This poses a problem to favor-giving, money-getting congressmen: what if the bureaucracy is obdurate, wrong-headed, or insensitive to a hack's political obligations? Perish the thought—and the integrity of the oversight process. Gone is the watchdog function, replaced by an effort to micromanage the bureaucracy by steering pork to deserving plates.

A crucial consideration in military matters is not so much whether a weapons system or vehicle works properly or is needed, but whose congressional district or state is enriched by the procurement. Mackubin Thomas Owens explains:

> According to the February 1984 issue of the *Armed Forces Journal*, the Senate Appropriations Committee changed 63 percent of the 1,129 line items of the Fiscal Year 1984 defense budget, and the House Appropriations Committee changed 68 percent. The Armed Services Committee meddled only slightly less, altering 62 percent in the Senate and 58 percent in the House.[134]

> What kind of amendments are typically offered?. . . [A]bout one-fourth of the total qualified as "pure pork"—for example, a sense-of-the-Congress amendment asking the DOD to spend a fair share of its procurement dollars in rural counties, even though few major systems are built in such areas.[135]

Riders to appropriations bills are an excellent way to repay—and incur—political debts:

> Commerce Secretary Robert Mosbacher . . . recently complained that Congress was forcing him to spend money on pork-barrel projects ineligible for funding under established federal guidelines. Five public-works projects proposed for the Economic Development Administration totalling $11.4 million were rejected this year by Mr. Mosbacher as being legally ineligible under EDA guidelines. Mr. Mosbacher was overridden, however, by congressmen seeking the projects for their home states. The secretary was directed in the department's appropriations bill to earmark funding for the five projects, as well as six others that the inspector general of the department determined were "inordinate," "inappropriate," and "flawed with respect to long-existing EDA policies."[136]

Examples of micromanagement are legion.[137] Not even foreign policy is exempt: "In 1989, various laws required 288 separate reports on foreign aid. These laws earmarked the specifics of how 92 percent of military aid would be spent, 98 percent of economic aid, and 49 percent of development aid."[138]

Even after the savings-and-loan disaster (which, in large part, can be traced to the machinations of members of Congress) spilled onto the front pages, dogged congressmen kept writing and calling and hectoring the agencies responsible for bailing out the nation's thrift industry. The *Wall Street Journal* reported that "many of the contacts were routine inquiries, but other interventions were attempts to obtain a desired result from officials."[139] Yet when circumstances cry out for such punctiliousness, members of Congress are nowhere to be found. As the *Washington Post* reports:

> Constituent service also played a role in last year's [1989] Department of Housing and Urban Development scandal, yet Congress took pains to avoid any such conclusion. Instead the House hearings chaired by Rep. Tom Lantos focused on the executive branch and private lobbyists, refusing to examine in depth any role that congressmen themselves may have played in the scandal.
>
> Yet constituent service promotes the political favoritism that is at the heart of the HUD scandal. As Charles L. Dempsey, inspector

general at HUD from 1977–85, put it: "Congress was more interested in getting favors from HUD than in overseeing its operation."

Congress routinely ignored reports of long-standing abuses at
HUD. . . . [T]aken together, the department's inspector general
reports to Congress add up to a year-by-year chronicle of abuses
beginning before the Reagan administration took office. But according to Dempsey, "Through all these investigations, I never
heard from Congress. From 1981 until I retired in 1985, I cannot
recall one telephone call from our House oversight committee."
This, even though HUD itself received thousands of calls from
Capitol Hill. Obviously, the calls were more about "constituent
service"—however loosely defined—than about oversight.[140]

Meaningful oversight of executive agencies and departments would,
perforce, expose congressional connivance in the HUD and S&L scandals.
It is instructive that the Resolution Trust Corporation (RTC), the savings-
and-loan bailout agency, has

proposed logging inquiries [from members of Congress] because it
was ordered by Congress in the bailout law that created the RTC to
avoid "political favoritism and undue influence" when it disposes
of billions of dollars of thrifts and their assets. Members of Congress are sure to be asked by constituents not to sell particular
properties that are important to local communities, or to encourage their sale to certain buyers.

It is just those sorts of inquiries about Lincoln Savings & Loan
Association, whose failure is expected to cost taxpayers about
$2.5 billion, that have cast five U.S. senators in an unfavorable
light.[141]

Nice try, RTC, but it'll never happen. Congressmen who carry water for
powerful interests aren't about to leave a paper trail. The fiscal year 1990
Department of Interior appropriations bill included this restriction: "None
of the funds available under this [bill] may be used to prepare reports on
contacts between employees of the Department of the Interior and Members and Committees of Congress and their staff."[142] The micromanagers
have directed that no records of their micromanagement be kept. The
bullying, the cajoling, the thievery, the waste: they continue unimpeded,
even protected, by our permanent Congress.

Lights, Camera, Propaganda!

Dull, stolid men reciting dry statistics make poor propagandists. They've got no flair, no panache: even C-SPAN junkies want a little spice in their gruel. Movie stars, on the other hand, are a cause-pusher's dream: comely, chiseled, and liposuctioned, they exude superiority. It's hard to take your eyes off them.

Hollywood is ridiculed as a frivolous town, and some of its denizens are stung by the criticism. There's nothing worse than the gnawing feeling that others don't take you seriously; what better way to prove your sobriety and seriousness of purpose than by testifying before Congress on—well, whatever. If you've got a big enough name—say, Paul Newman—or occupy a prominent place in the national couch potato consciousness—say, as the curvaceous slut on an imbecilic sitcom—your appearance will be a full-fledged media event. Consider Meryl Streep, the actress of a thousand voices, who on June 6, 1989, testified at a Senate Labor and Human Resources Subcommittee hearing on pesticide residues in fruits and vegetables that had been prompted by the use of Alar on apples. Ms. Streep admitted

> I think the reason we have all been invited here, as I look around the room and I see so many experts, is we have been invited for what we do not know, which probably will fill the room. But actually, I do not mind representing the constituency of the great mass of uninformed, because I think what we do not know about this issue is the most alarming, and that is coming up over and over in what I have been hearing. What we don't know is a frightening chasm.

What refreshing candor! Who else would be invited to address an assemblage of senators as the tribune "of the great mass of uninformed"? The totality of Streep's expertise, as revealed in her answer to a question asked by Senator Joseph Lieberman (D-Conn.), consisted of "having been involved in this issue for four months."[143] Perhaps four months of (very sporadic) study qualifies one to play opposite Roseanne Barr in *She-Devil*, but it's not long enough to master the scientific question of Alar's effect.

Ed Asner, who seems to have forsaken acting for politics, had a similar experience. A member of Africa Today, an organization concerned about malnutrition, Asner testified before both the House Committee on Interior and Insular Affairs and the House Committee on Science, Space, and Technology. "In February of this year, I was drafted for the cause," he conceded, belying any claim to authoritativeness. Asner freely admitted that his command of the subject matter was less than impressive: "If someone had taken me aside in the '50s when I was doing college plays in Chicago, and told me that 35 years later, I would be testifying for Congress on aquaculture in Africa, I would never have believed it. To be truthful, I *still* don't believe it, for I'm certainly no expert on the subject."[144]

Then why, pray tell, was he called upon to address *two* committees of the U.S. House of Representatives? To ensure the presence of TV cameras and reporters, that's why. The number of stars (and faded stars—white dwarfs, you might say) and public personalities who've enlightened Congress on various and sundry issues include

- Members of the folk-rock group The Grateful Dead—appeared before the Congressional Human Rights Caucus in July 1989 to provide information on rain forests in Malaysia
- Richard Gere—discussed Tibet before a congressional panel in 1988
- Buster Douglas, heavyweight boxing champ for a day or two— testified on low-income energy assistance programs
- Mary Tyler Moore—read a poem about animal trapping to a subcommittee of the House Merchant Marine and Fisheries Committee
- John Denver—regaled the House Committee on Interior and Insular Affairs with the song "Ode to Alaskan Forests"
- Morgan Fairchild—appeared before the Senate Committee on Energy and Natural Resources hearing on the California Desert Protection Act of 1987
- John Ritter—testified before a House subcommittee considering problems of hunger and malnutrition
- Valerie Harper, a member of Love Is Feeding Everyone—appeared before a Senate committee hearing on homelessness in America.

Other Hollywood notables and has-beens who have testified before Congress include Jon Voight (homelessness), Dennis Weaver (hunger relief), Richard Thomas (the arts in America), Lorne Greene (funding for the Department of the Interior), E. G. Marshall (funding for the arts), Richard Dreyfuss (funding for Departments of Labor, HHS, Education, and related agencies), and Robert Redford (nuclear waste disposal). And who can ever forget Jane Fonda, Jessica Lange, and Sally Field tearing up as they briefed senators on the parlous state of the family farm? (The trio was later seen dining at one of Washington's most expensive restaurants.)

Some of these celebrity cameos are justified: James Stewart talking about the colorization of classic black-and-white movies, for instance, or Robert J. "Captain Kangaroo" Keeshan discussing children's television. Actors are citizens, too, and laypeople certainly should be permitted—indeed, encouraged—to give witness before congressional committees. But something is amiss when Meryl Streep, self-described as "uninformed," makes the evening news emoting about Alar while scientists who specialize in the field are ignored because they have charisma deficiencies. It makes fine theater but bad policy.

Staff Infection

No member of Congress wants to be seen as a slug. Even the laziest, stupidest, most torpid representative wants the folks back home to see him as a leader, a doer, and a mover and shaker rather than the passive participant in congressional proceedings that he really is. The best way to be regarded as a "doer" is to *do*—to work hard and think well. But there's an easier way: introduce legislation. No matter if it's shoddy and poorly thought out. All the voters need to know is that Representative Schmoe has tossed "The Drug Abuse, Wife-Beating, and Rainy Weather Prevention Act of 1992" into the hopper, thereby "doing something" about these problems. Tawdry legislation like this is going nowhere, but it sure helps at reelection time.

Congress is awash in a flood of bills. In the 100th Congress (1987–88), 664 of the 8,700 bills introduced were passed. Most of the other 8,036 were designed solely for self-advertisement. Nevertheless, to deal with the deluge (on average, more than sixteen pieces of legislation for each member of Congress), "the House met on 298 days and the Senate on 307. Congressional committees and subcommittees held 7,563 hearings, briefings and other meetings, such as legislative conferences and 'mark up' sessions."[145]

Unfortunately, members probably know more about their showboat bills than the prosaic measures that are actually considered. Virtually all legislation is written by personal or committee staffs, and there is a cost. Comments the *Christian Science Monitor*, "As staffers acquire expertise and Capitol Hill street smarts, they become indispensable to their bosses, often more knowledgeable than members on technical matters. The congressman becomes a dependent."[146] These "indispensable" staff members are an "invisible"—and unelected—government, wielding considerable power.[147] They have "the real power to make or break legislation,"[148] as one observer writes.

In 1989, *Roll Call*, which is sort of the community gazette of Capitol Hill, published *The Almanac of the Unelected*, a book that profiled approximately six hundred of the most influential congressional staff members. As the *Wall Street Journal* reported, one remarkable finding from the profiles was that "many of the people who write the laws have had little or no experience at all working in the private sector, which may explain why so many of the laws they create don't work very well in the real world either."[149] The more onerous a law is, the greater the demand for those who can effectively lobby for its modification or even repeal. It is not unusual for staffers to move from Capitol Hill to corporate lobbies, where they work to circumvent or undo legislation that they once crafted.[150]

Staffers are like anyone else: they like to be flattered and pampered and treated as persons of importance. Committee staffers, especially, accept trips from the same special interests that members of Congress shake down for contributions. For instance, "industries with large stakes in clean air legislation . . . [fly] staff members of influential congressional committees around the country on what the industries call education tours. In some cases, the staff members have spent a night or two at Walt Disney World or in New Orleans' French Quarter." Surprisingly, these expense-paid junkets are legal as long as their ostensible purpose is to make the junketeers "better informed regarding subject matter closely related to their official duties."[151]

In the popular mind, congressional aides are either trusted right-hand men from the district or cynics with hearts of gold, à la Jean Arthur in Frank Capra's classic *Mr. Smith Goes to Washington.* To be sure, Jean Arthurs are still found here and there, but for the most part, senior staffers constitute a cadre of savvy pros who know more about legislation than most members. (Michael Malbin's *Unelected Representatives* describes the institutional arrangements that have made congressional staff a dominant force in the legislative process.[152])

Only in the wake of the Clarence Thomas–Anita Hill flap did most Americans learn that Congress routinely exempts itself from legislation that it imposes on all other Americans. These exemptions include the Civil

Rights Act of 1964, the Equal Employment Opportunity Act, the Civil Service Reform Act, the Fair Labor Standards Act, the Equal Pay Act, the Age Discrimination in Employment Act, the Occupational Safety and Health Act, the Minimum Wage Act, and the Civil Rights Restoration Act.[153] With this double standard, Congress cedes any claim to the high ground of moral leadership; it has, for all intents and purposes, declared itself above the law—a self-righteous and sanctimonious stance that bodes ill for democracy. Is it any wonder that arrogant men who violate the law of the land with impunity pass laws that are somewhat less than Solomonic in their wisdom?

The relatively few pieces of legislation that emerge from congressional gridlock are often breathtakingly fatuous. Journalist John Dutton discovered

> of the 240 public laws passed during the first session of the present Congress, more than one-third (88) had nothing to do with problem solving. They were commemorative bills celebrating such things as National Tap Dance Day, National Job Skills Week, Federal Employees Recognition Week, and National Digestive Disease Awareness Month (May, if you are wondering). The 95th Congress, during the Carter era, passed just 34 such laws. The 100th Congress passed 258 of them.[154]

Congress is good at acknowledging National Asparagus Month and commemorating National Fire Safety at Home—Change Your Battery Day, but rather more substantive matters (like, say, adopting a federal budget) are in the realm of the impossible.[155] As of 1990, Congress had failed to pass a budget in nine of the past ten years, forcing the federal government to operate by the expedient of continuing resolutions and "emergency" appropriation bills.

Congressmen fear substance as a savage fears science, to paraphrase James Russell Lowell. (In fact, the Boston Brahmin poet might have contributed the epigraph to this chapter: "For office means a kind of patent drill / To force an entrance to the nation's till.") Substantive changes in public policy inevitably disturb the status quo—some groups in society win, others lose. Some voters win, some lose. Some are pleased, some are peeved. So we get paralysis, against which the good gray *New York Times* editorialized in December 1987

The first session of the 100th Congress raises the real possibility that one of these years, the national legislature may not simply adjourn for Christmas but actually grind to a halt. Consider the lawmakers' performance in the last few days. They had to pass a law to keep the Government functioning while they battled one more day. The next day they had to do it again.

. . . when it came to legislating, the legislators seemed paralyzed. Even of the most critical task of the year, cutting the Federal budget deficit, the best they could do was to keep it from growing still bigger. Other priorities just collapsed.[156]

This kind of sluggishness is hardly the face Congress wants to show the nation, so when a tricky subject demands action, our fearless leaders hand the ball off to a national commission, a carefully selected group of prominent individuals appointed to "study" a particular issue and make recommendations. President George Washington formed the first national commission to negotiate with the tax rebels in the Whiskey Rebellion of 1794, so there is a long if not entirely honorable tradition of using such commissions to handle politically sensitive issues.[157] A national commission has two major advantages. First, its deliberations take time, and the hot potato may have cooled sufficiently by the time its report appears so that no action is required and no one gets hurt. Second, the commission's findings and recommendations are foreordained. If the prejudices and preferences and angles of commission members are known in advance, then the outcome can be predicted with reasonable certainty. Thus, politicians are assured of the end product they desire, and the Eminent (unelected) Men of the commission will take the flak. Nobel laureate George J. Stigler regarded the national commission as an instrument of political propaganda:

Why . . . form commissions? The most important answer, I am convinced, is that the commission is deemed an efficient instrument of propaganda. The many semi-unanimous voices will somehow sound louder in chorus than the sum of their individual efforts.

The whole art of commissionship is to select honorable and disinterested members who will mostly agree with the position that the creators of the commission desire. This is not so difficult as it may sound, because most honorable and disinterested men of distinction (1) have no very definite ideas on most specific questions (in this they are no different from the rest of us), but (2) have definite, known sentiments and inclinations; and hence are predictable.[158]

That's classic Stigler: caustic, perceptive, dead-solid perfect on target. The Minimum Wage Study Commission, created by Congress in 1977, is typical of its genre. Empowered to "help resolve the many controversial issues that have surrounded the federal minimum wage and overtime requirements since their origin in the Fair Labor Standards Act of 1938,"[159] the commission found that the preponderance of the empirical research suggests that the minimum-wage laws are counterproductive. That politically incorrect finding was conveniently ignored by a commission whose real job was to ratify the status quo. It did so, according to one observer, "by the simple expedient of ignoring its own research. . . . It is so clear that the Commission's recommendations were so predetermined by its composition that it is a source of wonder that it put itself at risk by asking that economic research be done."[160]

Congress has used commissions to reduce the political backlash on a wide variety of issues, including pay raises for its members (which most ordinary people oppose, and most Establishmentarians heartily support[161]), Social Security tax increases, foreign policy in Central America (the commission slavishly followed the Reaganite line), the federal deficit, national productivity and competitiveness, and the MX missile. Congress was unable even to muster the collective courage to shut down obsolete military bases, some of them dating back to the Civil War. President Carter, as part of his intermittent war on government waste, proposed a series of base closings in 1979 that Congress rejected amid great bombast. The closure of the redundant forts, it was said, would "leave the United States almost completely helpless before an air attack by manned bombers or ballistic missiles."[162]

Yet everyone—even the densest hacks—realized what a drain on the Treasury these bases were. So Congress cut another profile in cowardice: a commission was appointed to recommend the elimination of unneeded facilities, and its recommendations were to take effect unless rejected as a whole by majorities of both the House and the Senate. Gutless it was, but it worked. By passing the buck to an unelected body, Congress accomplished what it had been unable to do for years.

The commission addiction grows more severe by the year. In 1989, 122 bills to create 125 federal commissions and boards were considered; one bill proposed the establishment of the Advisory Commission on National Commemorative Events and another recommended the Advisory Commission on National Observances.[163] Apparently, National Digestive Disease Month has become too controversial to handle through the usual legislative process: it demands consideration by a Commission on Frivolity, Frippery, and Foolishness.

The federal bureaucracy also uses panels of "independent experts" or federal advisory committees to ratify its preferences. At the end of fiscal year 1989, 978 advisory committees were operating in the executive branch of government, an increase of 22 over the previous year. Of these, 37 percent were directed by law; 26 percent were authorized by law; 35 percent were established by agency authority; and 2 percent were authorized by presidential authority. A total of 22,960 individuals served as members, 3,474 meetings were held, and 1,079 reports were issued. They cost, in sum, $98.4 million; about half of that represents indirect expenditures for 1,103 man-years of federal staff support. Although the Federal Advisory Committee Act of 1972 requires (with a few exceptions) that each committee meeting be open to the public and that the Freedom of Information Act apply to all papers, records, and minutes, only 53 percent of the meetings were completely open to the public; 23 percent were totally closed, and the remainder were partially closed.[164]

The advisory committee serves the same purpose for the bureaucrats in the executive branch as its counterpart, the national commission, does for members of Congress in the legislative branch: responsibility for actions and blame for errors can be dispersed or, even better, shifted to outsiders.[165] Both Congress and the federal bureaucracy are more likely to bite a marshmallow than the bullet when the time comes to make difficult choices.

What Can We Do?

What can we do to set things aright?

Calls for campaign reform have typically centered on the way elections are financed. Because PACs give a substantial advantage to incumbents, a popular solution is the elimination of PAC contributions. That's a good first step, but banishing PACs is no panacea, for the panoply of taxpayer-financed incumbent benefits would still remain. Restricting use of the frank to responses to constituent letters is a worthy, if hopelessly utopian, goal. One thing is certain: radical reform *must* come from the outside. We should be deeply suspicious of any schemes that incumbents propose: they may sound good, but in practice they're likely to further freeze sitting members in the congressional aspic. Public financing of campaigns, for instance, has long been a cornerstone of Common Cause's reform agenda. Setting aside the justness of taxing citizens to pay politicians' advertising bills, this proposal will achieve precisely the opposite of its intent. Because the taxpayer financing is always linked to spending ceilings, incumbents will be safer than ever. Political scientists agree that a challenger's chances depend largely on his expenditures. This isn't necessarily true for sitting members. Strange as it sounds, incumbents who spend the most are the most likely to lose. Capping spending will cripple challengers—which is probably why House Democrats have enthusiastically supported public financing over the last two decades.

There is but one infallible way to reduce the stranglehold that incumbents have on their congressional seats: limit the term of office. This proposal, hotter than Georgia asphalt in August, is by no means new; twenty-eight states limit the number of terms a governor can serve, and the Twenty-second Amendment holds a U.S. president to two full terms.

The firebell in the night for this issue rang in 1990. Oklahoma voters overwhelmingly passed an initiative limiting the terms of state legislators to twelve years. Voters in California likewise restricted the length of service of elected officials. Colorado voters passed a state constitutional amendment imposing a twelve-year limit on those serving in the U.S. House of Representatives and the Senate; Colorado state officials would be limited to eight consecutive years. Politicians appealed to the courts—how dare mere *voters* meddle in matters of state? To the surprise of cynics, the pols in California lost their suit and shall, in the course of a few years, have to seek productive employment. Dozens of states will follow the lead of these western states in 1992 and beyond.

At the federal level, a constitutional amendment may be necessary to limit congressional terms. Tactically, this may be the way to go as well. Voters in Washington state rejected, by 54–46 percent, a 1991 initiative that would've imposed unilateral limits on the number of terms Washington's congressional delegation could serve. Opinion polls had predicted passage, but the pols turned the tide by making an ingenious argument: if we throw out our experienced, seniority-dripping members (including Speaker of the House Thomas Foley), then other states, especially the hated California, will take advantage of us. The fact that ex-California governor Jerry Brown stumped Washington on behalf of the initiative didn't help matters.

What if we did limit senators to one or two six-year terms and members of the House to three or six two-year terms? Opponents, such as Republican Congressman Henry Hyde (R-Ill.), argue, "A mandatory revolving door for elected officials would only strengthen the grip of the 'permanent bureaucracy' because lack of experience would make the legislators even more dependent on staff."[166]

Hyde is partly right: experienced legislators would be lost, but a great deal of experience in government isn't essential for making policy.[167] Experience may be useful in implementing and managing government programs, but members of Congress should not be engaged in such activities anyway. With term limitation, committee chairmanships would be awarded more on the basis of talent and ability and less on seniority (and its accompaniment, senility). There is no reason to believe that more rapid turnover of federal elected officials would necessarily give more power to staff members and lobbyists. The current system already allocates far too much authority to the unelected. We'd see the frequent reorganization of congressional offices, greatly lessening the incentives for staff members and lobbyists to develop long-term relationships with members of Congress.

In the end, though, it comes down to the virtues of what the New Left called "participatory democracy." We need citizen-legislators, not the careerists of our current self-perpetuating Congress. Democracy is not a spectator sport, as the bumper sticker goes: it depends on the active, informed involvement of people from all walks of life. Frequent injections of new blood into our tired Congress would be a start toward reviving our debilitated body politic.

4

Gimme Shelter, Gimme Food, Gimme . . .

I see one third of a nation ill-housed, ill-clad, ill-nourished.

—President Franklin D. Roosevelt
Second Inaugural Address

EVER SINCE President Roosevelt scribbled that grim (and unfounded) vision into an otherwise ghostwritten second inaugural address, the alleviation of poverty has been an ostensible goal of the federal government. Poverty is a strong word, laden with emotion; it evokes the image of destitute, penniless, and struggling people who survive on the margins of society. In the United States, the richest nation on earth, poverty is an embarrassment. We wonder how so many can live in squalor in the midst of plenty. "If we can put a man on the moon," street-corner philosophers are wont to say, "why can't we cure [fill in your favorite social pathology]?" If government statistics can be believed, poverty is not only prevalent in our wealthy land, it is even increasing—despite the expenditure of hundreds of billions of dollars over more than three decades.

The persistence of poverty can be ascribed to a lack of national will and a feebleness of collective commitment, if such news features as ABC's "American Agenda" are right. The evidence of this national disgrace, given the imprimatur of the federal government, is distressing enough to produce powerful pangs of guilt in the "haves" of our society.

83

No one—liberal, conservative, libertarian, socialist, or other—doubts that there are indigent people in this country who deserve our compassion. But is the government-inspired propaganda on poverty consistent with reality? Are America's "poor" as destitute as the bureaucracy contends?

Poverty Is What We Say It Is

Poverty was officially defined in 1964 by a sprightly woman named Mollie Orshansky of the Social Security Administration. Orshansky's "poverty threshold" was based on a 1955 U.S. Department of Agriculture survey that revealed that families of three or more persons spent roughly one third of their incomes on food.[1] Therefore, the poverty-threshold level of income is set at three times the estimated cost of the USDA's "economy" food plan. (The Bureau of the Census adjusts the threshold annually to factor in the effects of inflation.)

Every household whose income falls below the threshold is labeled "poor." In 1990 the threshold income for a family of four was $12,700,[2] which consigned almost one of every seven Americans to the ranks of the impoverished.

Applying Orshansky's formula to pre-1964 America, we find that in 1947, 32.7 percent of the population was poor; by 1954, the percentage had dropped to 27.9, and in 1959 it had declined to 22.4. The population was booming, however, so the total number of poor remained relatively static. By 1959, a whopping 39.5 million Americans lived below the poverty line. Since the welfare state was largely unformed, the percentage decline in the number of poor during the placid '50s can be attributed to economic growth.

Then came Camelot. President Kennedy sent a message to Congress in 1962 that, as part of his New Frontier, proposed to end the dole and help those in need to help themselves. Poverty would be reduced, he predicted, by giving the poor a "hand" rather than a "handout." As the *New York Times* editorialized:

> President Kennedy's welfare message to Congress yesterday stems from a recognition that no lasting solution to the problem can be bought with a welfare check. The initial cost will actually be higher than the mere continuation of handouts. The dividends will

come in the restoration of individual dignity and in the long-term reduction of the need for government help.[3]

The slain president's initiative was incorporated into President Lyndon B. Johnson's Great Society as a major offensive in LBJ's War on Poverty. Federal government spending on welfare programs (adjusted for inflation) zoomed from $52 billion in 1960—President Eisenhower's final year in office—to about $140 billion in 1969, when the curtain closed on the Johnson tragedy. (That increase was more than two-and-a-half times the rate of inflation during the decade.) Yet despite the Great Society's massive outlays, progress in eliminating poverty was actually slower in the 1960s than it was in the previous decade.

By 1973, the poverty rate had dropped to an all-time low of 11.1 percent. Thereafter it rose, reaching 15 percent at the end of the 1981–82 recession and declining slightly, to 13.5 percent, by 1990. Like the War on Drugs, the government's own statistics suggest at best a stalemate in the vaunted War on Poverty.

If the war's successes are blared from every government rooftop, its costs are less well known. Former Secretary of the Treasury William E. Simon notes:

> From 1965 to 1976 the amount of government money spent for "social welfare" functions broadly defined exploded from $77 billion a year to more than $331 billion—an increase of better than $250 billion in the amount of money being spent each year allegedly to help the needy. Interestingly, the number of poor people in America hardly changed at all during this period—continuing to hover at about the 25 million mark, according to the official figures. . . .
>
> A little arithmetic is sufficient to show that if we had taken this $250 billion increase in social welfare spending and simply given it to those 25 million poor people, we could have given each and every one of them an annual grant of $10,000—which is an income, for a family of four, of $40,000 a year. We could have made all those poor people relatively rich. But we didn't.[4]

(The dollar figures that Simon uses are not adjusted for inflation. They include Social Security benefits but not the additional billions in charitable giving by private individuals and institutions.)

The popular impression—abetted by articles in the middlebrow press bearing titles like "Why There's No Welfare Fat Left to Trim"—is that eight years of Reaganism gutted a wide array of social programs. Not true; in fact, federal expenditures on poverty programs rose throughout the decade of the 1980s, even after adjusting for inflation.[5] In constant 1988 dollars, welfare spending by local, state, and federal governments rose from $156.6 billion in 1980 to $184.2 billion in 1988—an 18 percent increase.[6] By 1988, government at all levels spent enough on poverty programs alone (excluding Social Security; see table 4.1) to give $5,790 to each man, woman, and child below the poverty threshold. That adds up to $23,160 for every family of four—or nearly *twice* the poverty threshold level of income.

TABLE 4.1

GOVERNMENTAL EXPENDITURES ON WELFARE, 1988, BY TYPE, BY
INSTITUTIONAL STATUS, AND BY EFFECT ON INCOME
($ BILLIONS)

Expenditure Type	Total Spending	Noninstitutional Expenditures	Effect on Income
Means-Tested Cash Assistance	$ 47.6	$ 42.4	$26.9
Means-Tested Noncash Food Assistance	21.5	21.5	0
Means-Tested Noncash Housing Assistance	14.7	14.7	0
Medicaid & Other Means-Tested Medical Benefits	66.4	43.2	0
Medicare	11.2	11.2	0
Other Means-Tested Noncash Programs	22.6	22.6	0
Total	$184.2	$155.6	$26.9

SOURCE: Robert Rector, Kate Walsh O'Beirne, and Michael McLaughlin, "How 'Poor' Are America's Poor?" *Backgrounder* no. 791 (Washington, D.C.: The Heritage Foundation, September 21, 1990), pp. 4–6.

One would think that $184 billion would vanquish all gradations of material poverty, from abject to mild. Yet the Census Bureau, arbiter of such matters, estimates that the entirety of welfare benefits reduces the number of "poor" Americans from 33.3 million to 31.9 million—a measly decrease of just 1.4 million.[7] Astoundingly, each person who was lifted out of official poverty cost American taxpayers a staggering $131,570. These statistics confound both logic and common sense.

There are four reasons for this anomaly. First, and most important, the Census Bureau vastly understates the financial resources of the poor by excluding *virtually all welfare spending* in determining their incomes. Only *cash* income is counted, even though most major federal assistance programs offer "in-kind" benefits such as food stamps, public housing, and Medicaid. (Note that the "institutional spending" alluded to in table 4.1 means, literally, spending on individuals in nursing homes and other institutions. In fiscal year 1988, this spending came to $28.6 billion. These individuals are not included in the population surveyed by the census in compiling income and poverty data.)

Despite the Census Bureau's refusal to acknowledge it, noncash assistance is a tremendous boon to the incomes of the poor, especially because many of the programs overlap. (Its effect on their spirit is a matter for debate elsewhere.) Consider food stamps. Children who are assumed to eat three food-stamp-provided meals a day at home also eat taxpayer-subsidized school breakfasts and lunches. Food-stamp recipients are also eligible for Women, Infants, and Children (WIC) assistance, Aid for Dependent Children (AFDC), and commodity-distribution ("free cheese") programs. Federal food programs are intended to do much more than prevent hunger or malnutrition; according to the Congressional Budget Office: "Today, the food stamp program goes beyond providing recipients the wherewithal to increase food consumption and, on the average, for every one dollar of bonus food stamps transferred, approximately forty-three cents is freed for nonfood purchases."[8] The food-stamp program doesn't buy just milk and bread for the needy; it also permits recipients to spend money on other items.

Second, the Census Bureau—intentionally—grossly understates the financial resources of the poor. Assets and wealth are not taken into account in any way; thus, a member of the landed gentry (or indigentry?) whose annual income is low is lumped in with an impecunious junkie. In 1983, for example, the average net worth of "poor families" was $30,000—approximately three times the poverty threshold and five times the average income of the poor.[9] The Census Bureau also fails to count a great deal of income; its own data reveal that the people it deems "poor" spend $1.94 for every $1.00 in reported income. This discrepancy has increased steadily, vitiating the integrity of census statistics.[10] As two researchers note: "Individuals with reported incomes under $1,000 were spending $224 for every $100 of reported income. Add to this consideration the fact that among low-income individuals there would be writers, artists, and actors—people whose earning ability is actually quite high."[11] If Kevin Costner decides to take a year off and lay about the pool, does he really join the tattered legion of the bereft?

A third factor in distorting poverty statistics is the Consumer Price Index, which is used to adjust the poverty threshold each year. A major component of the CPI is the cost of housing. During the inflationary 1970s and early 1980s, the inflation rate was overestimated because the CPI assumed that all homeowners were burdened with high mortgage interest rates. This error was corrected in 1983, when a rental equivalence method of computing housing costs was introduced. Had this approach been used in earlier years, the CPI would have been about 10 percent lower, as would the poverty threshold.[12]

The fourth and final problem is that much of the welfare aid purportedly appropriated for the poor never reaches the poor. Middlemen who bewail the "plight of the poor"—sometimes cynically, sometimes with genuine concern—allocate billions of tax dollars to propaganda rather than relief.[13]

A fleet of organizations, often subsidized by taxpayers as well as the guilt-ridden legatees of huge fortunes (such as the Rockefeller Foundation), employs droves of researchers to study the needs of the poor, evaluate the effects of existing programs, and try to reconcile the two. Despite the usual blather about "objectivity," these analysts inevitably call for additional government spending and greater intrusiveness by Uncle Sam. Past failures—for instance, the widely derided CETA (Comprehensive Employment and Training Act) jobs program, which paid the collegiate sons of political hacks to stand around on shovels—are seldom criticized. To be blunt, the researchers are bought off; their conclusions are foreordained. After all, if the mammoth Department of Health and Human Services gives you a grant to evaluate its work, and you find it to be subpar and say so on paper, you'll not be getting any more HHS dough. The bureaucracy suffers fools gladly, but not critics.

These quasi-governmental private organizations cooperate with the Census Bureau and other departments of government to produce poverty propaganda that magnifies the extent of social ills and makes them appear intractable—indeed, insoluble, at least without massive cash infusions to dispassionate researchers. This chorus, sung in one part by government bureaucrats and in the other by the institutes they subsidize with study grants, ensures that the nation's poverty industry thrives. As one (apparently unsubsidized) analyst puts it:

> The welfare system sustains a nationwide welfare industry of more than 5 million public and private workers. . . . The industry has demonstrated that its goal is not to eliminate poverty, but to expand welfare through increased spending, more benefits and programs, centralization of control in the federal government, and expanded employment in welfare-related services. [14]

Take the nebulous concept of the "poverty gap," or the Census Bureau–calculated amount of governmental assistance that would be required to raise the incomes of all the poor to exceed the poverty threshold. In 1986, for example, the poverty gap was estimated at $64.9 billion. *After* welfare benefits were taken into account, the gap had declined to $48.8 billion. [15] Yet a total of $126.2 billion had been spent on poverty programs for the noninstitutional poor. How could the gap close by only $16.1 billion? Must we spend $7.84 in taxpayers' money for every dollar reduction in the poverty gap? If so, eliminating the 1990 poverty gap of approximately $70 billion would cost us more than a half trillion dollars—or almost half of the federal budget.

Something is amiss. Bureaucratic overhead is a culprit, but even more serious is a government misdefinition of poverty that bears little resemblance to the dictionary definition of a "serious lack of the means for proper existence." [16] We can illustrate this by using the government's own data.

Are the "Poor" Truly Poor?

To F. Scott Fitzgerald's observation that "the rich are different from us," Ernest Hemingway responded drolly, "Yes, they have more money." The poor are different, too: they have less money. But *how* different are the *living standards* of the poor relative to other Americans? The income standard employed by the Census Bureau is arbitrary and deeply flawed; by excluding assets, it greatly overstates the prevalence of poverty in the United States. Using other measures, we can see that the poor, though lacking income, are not so different from the rest of us—and are far better off than others in the industrialized world. If we go looking for a "serious lack of the means for proper existence," that is, lack of shelter and food, we find little evidence of grinding poverty, even in the other America.

We Are Housed

Since the days of Jacob Riis, the stereotypical housing unit of a poor family has been the tenement slum, where entire families are crowded in a single room, without even the most basic sanitary amenities, such as running water and toilet facilities. Rats run the floors, nipping at the toes of malnourished starvelings. Disease, deprivation, and early death are common. This squalor was fact in the early twentieth century, as waves of immigrants washed ashore in the crowded cities of the Northeast. But that was four generations ago. The tenements, so movingly depicted in the muckraking journalism and committed fiction of the Progressive Era, have ceased to exist.

In 1910 the typical American household had an average of 1.13 person(s) per room. By 1987, that figure had declined by more than half, to .48 (see table 4.2). The typical "poor" family household—using the government's own figures—had an average of .56 persons per room in 1987. This is less dense than the *average* American household was in 1970.

TABLE 4.2

AVERAGE NUMBER OF PERSONS PER ROOM IN AMERICAN HOUSING,
ALL HOUSEHOLDS, SELECTED YEARS, 1910–1987

1910	1940	1950	1960	1970	1980	1987
1.13	.74	.68	.60	.62	.50	.48

SOURCE: Stanley Lebergott, *The American Economy: Income, Wealth, and Want* (Princeton, N.J.: Princeton University Press, 1976), p. 258; U.S. Department of Commerce, Bureau of the Census, and U.S. Department of Housing and Urban Development, Office of Policy Development and Research, *American Housing Survey for the United States in 1987* (Washington, D.C.: Government Printing Office, 1989), pp. 38, 40, 88, 90, 146, 148.

By definition of the lexicographers of the federal government, "moderate crowding" occurs when there is more than one person per room in a household; "crowding" implies that there are more than 1.5 persons per room; and "severe crowding" occurs when a household averages more than two persons per room. Table 4.3 reveals that severe crowding has virtually disappeared in the United States; indeed, it had all but vanished by the 1930s. By 1987, only 1.6 percent of the poor experienced crowding; by contrast, 3.6 percent of *all* U.S. households in 1960 were "crowded." Moderate crowding, the condition of 2.7 percent of all households in 1987, described 7.5 percent of all poor households in that same year.

TABLE 4.3

PERCENTAGES OF ALL U.S. HOUSEHOLDS WITH MODERATE CROWDING, CROWDING, AND SEVERE CROWDING, AND WITH BASIC AMENITIES IN SELECTED YEARS, 1900–1987

Type of Crowding	1900	1930	1940	1950	1960	1987	Poor, 1987
Moderate	52	—	20	16	11	2.7	7.5
Crowding	—	—	9	6.2	3.6	0.5	1.6
Severe	8.9	0	0	0	0	0	0
Amenity							
Running Water	2	—	70	83	93	99.6	98.4
Flush Toilet	15	51	60	71	87	99.5	98.2
Electricity	3	68	79	94	99	99.97	99.9

SOURCE: Stanley Lebergott, *The American Economy: Income, Wealth, and Want* (Princeton, N.J.: Princeton University Press, 1976), p. 258; U.S. Department of Commerce, Bureau of the Census, and U.S. Department of Housing and Urban Development, Office of Policy Development and Research, *American Housing Survey for the United States in 1987* (Washington, D.C.: Government Printing Office, 1989), pp. 38, 40, 88, 90, 146, 148.

The physical housing arrangements of the poor are remarkably similar to those of the average U.S. household and much better than the conditions under which the average citizens of other nations live. In Japan, for example, an average household has 0.8 persons per room, far higher than the .56 average for "poor" Americans. Mexicans average 2.5 persons per room; Indians average 2.8.[17] Even in Western Europe, which our social democrats often hold up as the standard against which our polity must be judged, the average household was more crowded (using 1980 figures) than was the typical poor American residence.[18]

Additionally, the living space that a poor American occupies seems even larger by world standards, if measured in terms of square footage, rather than rooms. In former Communist Poland and East Germany, an informal survey conducted in 1991 revealed an average living space of between 125–150 square feet per occupant. This is unbelievably cramped, even by the standards of depressed American inner-city neighborhoods. In America, an efficiency of five hundred square feet, occupied by a single person, would be considered quite small. The average Japanese also occupies incredibly small dwellings, which would make the living area of a "poor" American seem quite spacious. Subsidized townhouses recently built outside Washington, D.C., for "low-income" families are approximately two thousand square feet, and house small families of several people. An affluent Japanese family in Tokyo would almost certainly occupy a smaller living area than these American "low-income" families, whose subsidized units are gargantuan by Eastern European standards. Hence, whether measured by rooms per occupant, or the size of those rooms, "poor" Americans occupy homes that would be considered large by international standards.

Basic amenities—running water, flush toilets, and electricity—are nigh universal in the United States. Almost none of the poor lack these comforts; those who do are likely Thoreauvian free spirits who shun the gadgets of industrial society. As table 4.4 shows, the situation in Western Europe is rather different. The typical Norwegian family is about ten times more likely to lack these facilities than are poor American families. In Japan—widely heralded as a dynamo of wealth and technology that is leaving the sluggish United States in the dust—more than half the population still uses arrangements that many Americans would consider primitive. According to the Organization for Economic Cooperation and Development, a poor family in America is about thirty times more likely to have an indoor flush toilet than the average Japanese family.

Conventional wisdom holds that the houses in which the poor live are dilapidated, decrepit, and badly in need of something more than a paint job. Conventional wisdom is wrong. The 1987 Housing Survey conducted by the Census Bureau indicates that 38 percent of those designated "poor" own their own homes, with a median value of $39,305. Almost half of *all* homes in which the poor live are air-conditioned; their median age is only seven years more than the median age of all U.S. housing units. Only 2.4 percent of these units had significant structural defects, such as foundation or roofing problems. Nine percent of the poor households surveyed com-

TABLE 4.4

PERCENTAGE OF HOUSEHOLDS IN SELECTED COUNTRIES
LACKING INDOOR FLUSH TOILETS OR SHOWER OR BATH

Country	Percentage Without Flush Toilet	Percentage Without Shower or Bath
United Kingdom	6	4
West Germany	7	11
Italy	11	11
Spain	12	39
France	17	17
Norway	17	18
Belgium	19	24
Ireland	22	26
Greece	29	—
Portugal	43	—
Japan	54	17

SOURCE: Organization for Economic Cooperation and Development, *LivingConditions in OECD Countries* (Paris: OECD, 1986), p. 139.

plained that their homes had been uncomfortably cold during the winter because of inadequate insulation, heating capacity, or equipment failure; about half as many of the nonpoor made the same complaints.[19]

And what of possessions? Table 4.5 gives us the provocative picture. Although many of the poor live in central cities where public transportation is available and where even the wealthy shun the auto, more than 62 percent possess one or more motor vehicles; 13.6 percent own two or more motor vehicles. (Among all American households, 89 percent own a motor vehicle.) Almost all the poor have a refrigerator; most have telephones. Significant percentages of poor households also have nonessentials (ascetics might say fripperies) that include air-conditioning, microwave ovens, dishwashers, and garbage disposals. Predictably, poor households that are owner occupied tend to be better equipped than those that are occupied by renters (with the curious exception of garbage disposals). At the extreme, more than 22,000 "poor" households have a heated swimming pool or a Jacuzzi.[20] (This is the kind of choice McNugget that Ronald Reagan loved to chew on during his years on the rubber-chicken circuit.)

TABLE 4.5

PERCENTAGE OF "POOR" HOUSEHOLDS WITH VARIOUS DURABLE GOODS AND
APPLIANCES IN 1987: ALL HOUSEHOLDS AND BY TYPE OF OCCUPANCY

Durable or Appliance	All Poor Households	Owner Occupied	Renter Occupied
One or More Autos*	62.2	77.9	52.4
Two or More Autos*	13.6	21.0	9.0
Air-conditioning	49.0	55.8	44.7
Microwave Oven	30.7	—	—
Washing Machine	56.0	84.6	38.1
Dishwasher	17.0	23.2	13.2
Garbage Disposal	18.9	15.1	21.3
Refrigerator	99.1	99.5	98.9
Telephone	81.3	91.4	75.0

*"Autos" include vans and trucks.

SOURCE: U.S. Bureau of the Census, *American Housing Survey for the United States in 1987* (Washington, D.C.: Government Printing Office, 1989), pp. 40, 46, 90, 96, 108, 154. U.S. Department of Energy, Energy Information Administration, *Housing Characteristics 1987* (Washington, D.C.: Government Printing Office, 1989), p. 87.

By the end of the 1980s, "poor" households were far more likely to own consumer durables, such as televisions and refrigerators, than the typical American family was in the 1950s. There are 344 automobiles for every 1,000 poor persons in the United States, a rate of ownership that is roughly equal to that for the entire population in the United Kingdom and 40 percent higher than the rate for the typical Japanese family.

Food and the Poor

If there is a villain keeping essential vitamins and minerals out of poor bodies, it is the federal Department of Agriculture, which for six decades has systematically raised food prices by a variety of outrageous means. American farmers have been paid to not produce, depressing supplies and boosting prices. Acreage allotments have taken farmland out of production; monopoly pricing schemes have been executed through "marketing orders"; the government has bought and stored and let rot commodities in order to keep prices from falling. Without these byzantine interventions, oranges and sugar and milk would cost the single mother a heck of a lot less in her weekly trip through the Safeway aisles.

Tons of food are destroyed each year just to maintain high prices for farmers. Government warehouses become virtual mountains of dairy and other agricultural products in this insane subsidy to the nation's farmers. At the same time that many of us were distressed about the deficiency of vitamin C in the diets of the poor, federal policies were raising the prices of citrus fruits. Furthermore, by government order, about 40 percent of oranges and 75 percent of lemons grown in California are wasted or destroyed. In 1983, for example, "more lemons were dumped . . . than sold fresh to American consumers."[21] In addition, imports of sugar and other foods and staples are restricted or heavily taxed to protect domestic prices. No doubt some farmers are enriched by such policies, but is it any wonder that some Americans of limited means find it difficult to balance their grocery budget?

In spite of this madness, the poor do not differ significantly in their consumption of food than those in the upper half of income distribution. Consider table 4.6, which compares the food consumption patterns of low-income families with those of high-income families. Overall, poor families consume 95 percent as much meat as wealthier families. (The "poor" eat more poultry and fish than steak, of course.) They eat nearly as many fresh vegetables (92 percent) but considerably less fresh fruits (71 percent). To rectify this deficiency, advocates for the poor ought to demand the abolition of citrus marketing orders and the like; recent efforts at forging an urban poor/free marketeer alliance have been unsuccessful but not unpromising.

Low-income households spend eighty cents on food for each dollar spent by median-income households. Of each dollar spent on food by poor families, thirty-two cents was spent in restaurants.[22] So yes, the official

TABLE 4.6

FOOD CONSUMPTION OF HOUSEHOLDS IN THE LOWEST-INCOME QUINTILE
AS A PERCENTAGE OF THE CONSUMPTION OF HOUSEHOLDS IN THE
UPPER HALF OF THE INCOME DISTRIBUTION
(CONSUMPTION IN POUNDS PER WEEK)

All Meats	Steak	Poultry	Fish	Fresh Vegetables	Fresh Fruits
95	70	109	114	92	71

SOURCE: U.S. Department of Agriculture, Human Nutrition Service, *Food Consumption: Households in the United States, Spring 1977* (Washington, D.C.: Government Printing Office, 1982).

poor do purchase somewhat lower-quality and less-expensive foods than upper-income families, but there is little evidence of malnutrition or serious dietary deficiencies.

Table 4.7 shows the average daily intake of twelve nutrients for three groups: persons eligible for food stamps (but not receiving them); persons in the lowest fifth of the income distribution; and persons in the upper half of the income distribution. The daily nutrient intake is remarkably consistent across incomes. The poor don't get enough calcium, iron, magnesium, and vitamin B_6, but neither do the comparatively rich. The problem, it would seem, is more eating habits than anything else.

Again, Americans do well when we drag in our subcontinental and transatlantic friends. Meat is one of the most expensive items in family diets the world over, and the American "poor" consume far more of it than the average citizen of many other countries (see table 4.8).

TABLE 4.7

AVERAGE NUTRIENTS CONSUMED AS A PERCENTAGE OF 1980 RECOMMENDED DIETARY STANDARDS BY PERSONS IN VARIOUS INCOME GROUPS

| | PERSONS WHO ARE | | |
Nutrient	Eligible for Food Stamps	Low Income	Upper Income
Protein	169	156	168
Calcium	89	79	89
Iron	99	100	101
Magnesium	87	78	86
Phosphorus	131	126	139
Vitamin A	124	144	129
Thiamin	119	113	111
Riboflavin	135	130	133
Niacin	118	120	125
Vitamin B_6	75	71	77
Vitamin B_{12}	142	178	171
Vitamin C	137	134	156

SOURCE: U.S. Department of Agriculture, Human Nutrition Information Service, *Nutrient Intakes in 48 States, Year 1977-78* (Washington, D.C.: Government Printing Office, 1979). U.S. Department of Agriculture, Human Nutrition Information Service, *Food and Nutrient Intakes in One Day, Low-Income Households, November 1979-March 1980* (Washington, D.C.: Government Printing Office, 1980), p. 126.

TABLE 4.8

CONSUMPTION OF MEAT BY AVERAGE CITIZENS IN VARIOUS COUNTRIES
AS A PERCENTAGE OF THE CONSUMPTION OF MEAT BY AMERICANS
IN THE LOWEST FIFTH OF THE INCOME DISTRIBUTION

Germany	France	Italy	U.K.	USSR	Romania	Mexico	Japan	Venezuela	Brazil
75	70	62	57	56	40	39	39	31	27

SOURCE: U.S. Department of Agriculture, Foreign Agriculture, *World Livestock Situation*, March 1990. U.S. Department of Agriculture, Human Nutrition Information Service, *Food and Nutrient Intakes in One Day, Low-Income Households, November 1979–March 1980* (Washington, D.C.: Government Printing Office, 1980).

Low-income Americans eat one third more meat than the *average* West German, nearly twice as much as the British, two-and-a-half times as much as Romanians, almost three times as much as Japanese, and about four times as much as Brazilians. If a "hunger crisis" exists, as some contend, it exists far beyond our shores.

Child Nutrition

Understandably, our children are a focus of nutrition studies. In the midst of American plenty, it really would be unconscionable to permit the off-spring of the poor to go malnourished. Happily, they do not. The evidence comes from a comprehensive 1985 survey by the Human Nutrition Information Service of the U.S. Department of Agriculture. The HNIS discovered that children in families with incomes at 75 percent of the poverty level consumed 54.4 grams of proteins daily—more than the 53.6 grams of protein consumed by children in families with incomes *three times* the poverty level.[23] The figure for black pre-school children was 56.9 grams, compared to 52.4 grams for white children. Both protein and calorie consumption were slightly higher in central cities than in the suburbs.[24]

Regardless of income, American children do very well when we measure their intake of nutrients. Children in families with incomes at 75 percent of the poverty level received more than twice the daily standard recommended by USDA; the same is true of most essential vitamins and minerals (save iron and zinc), where the daily intake of "poor" kids exceeded USDA standards by as much as 50 to 100 percent.[25]

Poverty and Malnutrition

Yet the myth of American malnutrition persists. Even a supposed debunker such as Sylvia Mason of *Fortune* declared in that magazine's May 26, 1986, issue that "the widespread malnutrition of the early 1960s no longer exists." *What* "widespread malnutrition"? Where is the evidence? As early as 1980, the Congressional Budget Office questioned whether the United States was ever afflicted with this problem:

> What are the nutritional problems that are to be addressed by government intervention? Hunger and severe malnutrition are *not serious public health problems* in the United States today although some subgroups of the population may be affected. Despite some limited cases of severe malnutrition found by the Senate Subcommittee on Employment, Manpower and Poverty in the Mississippi Delta in 1967, statements that severe malnutrition exists on a national scale have never been documented, even during the early years of the "War on Poverty" programs.[26]

Moreover, the problems in the Mississippi Delta, where cotton is the principal crop, can be traced *directly* to federal-government policies. The Delta economy was fractured when minimum-wage coverage was extended to agricultural labor in 1966 and cotton set-aside payments, which result in less cotton being planted, were increased. To save on labor costs, planters turned to mechanical cottonpickers, throwing tens of thousands of farm laborers out of work, according to the Department of Agriculture's own admission. Because cotton acreage was reduced at the same time, the demand for labor was lowered even further. Unemployment was severe; without income, buying food became difficult,[27] and the Delta, so rich in cultural heritage, became desperately poor. Never were the region's blues sung with such conviction.[28]

An In-Kind, Gentler Nation?

In 1980 economist Morton Paglin analyzed poverty programs and included the effects of in-kind transfers on the incomes of the poor. He concluded:

Acknowledging the major impact of in-kind transfers in reducing poverty need not make us insensitive to their faults. The in-kind programs are beset with inconsistent eligibility criteria and have failed to coordinate program benefits; they have produced inequities, disincentives, and wasteful administration. But this should not obscure the salient fact that the transfers have been on a sufficiently massive scale to effect a major reduction in the poverty population. It would have been surprising if they had not done so. What is disquieting is the failure to recognize this accomplishment. Social scientists generally have accepted and have given wide currency to the official poverty estimates. It is time for the statistical veil to be lifted so that the poverty problem can be seen in its true dimensions.[29]

By including in-kind transfers, Paglin drew a picture of poverty in the United States that was far more subtle, and accurate, than that painted by federal bureaucrats. In 1975, for example, the Census Bureau's official statistics reported a poverty gap of $16.1 billion, 25.9 million persons in poverty, and a poverty rate of 12.3 percent. Paglin, by contrast, found that in-kind transfers had reduced the poverty gap to $4.1 billion, the number of persons living in poverty to only 7.8 million, and the poverty rate to just 3.6 percent.[30]

Paglin's conclusions jibe with those of an increasing number of economists who have come to view government poverty statistics as at best incomplete and at worst meaningless. "In a meaningful sense," writes Edgar K. Browning, "poverty had become virtually nonexistent by 1973." He is seconded by Roger A. Freeman, who notes that many of those who "have a money income below the poverty level may not be poor in any meaningful sense." The renowned social scientist Edward C. Banfield adds that "most of those who report income below the poverty line are not undergoing hardship."[31]

How have the disseminators of inflated poverty statistics responded to these challenges? Typical is this bizarre disquisition by Leonard Beeghley:

The assertion that the effect of in-kind transfers is to lower the rate of poverty in the United States is very beguiling, mainly because it stems from a simple, but misleading, assumption: that in-kind benefits make those who receive them less poor. Thus, the argument goes, the value of such benefits should be included when calculating the rate of poverty. By implication, the result would be a more scientifically accurate measure. This argument implies that public aid programs are designed to eliminate poverty, a point of view which misrepresents their nature and purpose.[32]

Say *what*? Is Beeghley admitting that the grant eaters and the government employees who design and fight the War on Poverty have goals other than "eliminating poverty"? Well, not quite. Beeghley lamely avers: "Public assistance programs are not designed to eliminate poverty; they are, rather, intended to alleviate some of the problems associated with destitution."[33] This is disingenuous; it is a sophistic exercise in semantics. The point is that after receiving the in-kind transfers, the "destitution" has been alleviated, but government statistics resolutely ignore this. And if the trillions of dollars expended to combat poverty over the last thirty years have been money down a rathole, as the official statistics suggest and as Beeghley claims, then the anti-poverty programs can only be deemed a monumental failure.

Beeghley's logic grows stranger by the paragraph. He goes on to claim:

The poverty reduction literature counts income twice, once on an in-kind basis and once as cash. This is because when measures of poverty reduction are estimated, in-kind income is imputed to the poor . . . without any recognition that the money actually goes to vendors who provide services. Thus, income is attributed both to those who receive benefits and to those who provide them.[34]

What is being alleviated here is the burden of sense. Consider a person earning $3,000 per month after taxes who spends all of it on housing, medical care, food, clothing, and other goods and services. The $3,000 income is attributed to the worker and it also, as it is spent, becomes income for the landlord, dentist, physician, grocer, and clothier. What else is new? The fact that the goods and services are provided "in-kind" rather than paid for in cash makes no difference, for goods and services are not altered by the method of payment. Muddled statistics lead to muddled analysis.

Beeghley's *coup de grâce* in his bludgeoning of logic is

Although it would be nice to think that there are very few poor people in the United States and that the war on poverty has been won because "welfare" eliminates want, such claims are based on methodological sophistry. In the real world where people must obtain food, shelter, and all the other necessities of life, the only way to eliminate poverty is for people to become economically independent.[35]

The last clause is true. But what debased form of "independence" is it when one is tied to the end of a federal-government tether? The system is supposed to give hand-ups rather than handouts; welfare aid was designed to be temporary and to provide opportunity, not a permanent check signed by Uncle Sam.

The standard catalogue of the welfare state's failures is well known and need not be repeated here. Suffice to say that it encourages the breakup of families, the bearing of illegitimate children, and discourages work.[36] Readers looking for a thorough, elegant, and provocative exposition of these failures are advised to consult Charles Murray's *Losing Ground: American Social Policy, 1950–1980* and *In Pursuit: Of Happiness and Good Government.*[37]

The American experience in helping the destitute during the late nineteenth century, nicely described by University of Texas professor Marvin Olasky, stands in stark contrast to the modern welfare state, with its engorged bureaucracy and counterproductive programs.[38] The millions of poor, ragged, huddled immigrants who passed through Ellis Island at the turn of the century came with little more than the clothes on their back and, at best, a smattering of English. No Department of Health and Human Services was there to greet them, so a system of private charity evolved that relieved their immediate needs and helped them achieve, with amazing alacrity, the dreamt-of economic independence. The crowded tenements are mostly gone from our cities today, but newer, more durable pestilences have sprung up. The shame of our cities shall not be extirpated by fatter welfare checks.

The Hidden Agenda of the Poverty Industry

To what end has this blizzard of misleading poverty statistics been unleashed? Herman Miller, in a monograph written for the Bureau of the Census, gives us a hint:

Few statistics reveal as much about the operation of an economy as do those on income distribution. Although the levels of living that are possible in any society are prescribed by the size of the national product, a given output can be distributed in many different ways. It can provide palaces for live kings and pyramids for dead ones, but hovels and hunger for the mass of mankind; or it can be widely distributed and provide reasonably uniform levels for all.[39]

Pamela Roby, in *The Poverty Establishment*, is more explicit: "If American incomes were distributed equally or nearly equally, America would have neither poverty nor a poverty establishment. Our unequal distribution of resources rather than a lack of resources has maintained poverty."[40] Now we see why the bureaucracy has so stubbornly resisted counting in-kind transfers as income: its real motive is the redistribution of wealth, preferably along the lines of Western European or Scandinavian welfare-state democracy. We are to become Sweden, and while that country has its attractions, a dynamic economy and vital culture are not among them.

Large-scale redistribution is supported by most American economists. Edgar Browning stated in 1989 in his presidential address to the Southern Economic Association:

Economists tend to be quite egalitarian in their evaluation of social issues. According to one survey, 71 percent of American economists believe the distribution of income in the United States should be more equal, and 81 percent feel that redistribution of income is a legitimate role for government. Support for these positions is even stronger among economists with academic affiliations, and stronger still among economists with elite academic affiliations.[41]

But is the assumption that underlies the redistributionist argument valid? Is there a "degree of inequality that is quite large"[42] in American life, as the National Conference of Catholic Bishops states in a recent Pastoral Letter?

Not really. The federal government has repeatedly issued reports that wildly overstate the inequality in household incomes. And the more inequality, the greater the need for the federal government to play the good cop. In 1986, for example, the Census Bureau reported that the top 20 percent of households ranked by income received 43.7 percent of total income, while the bottom 20 percent received only 4.6 percent.[43] The top quintile made nine and a half times as much as the bottom quintile. This strikes most of us as unfair. As Americans, we are raised on the small-*d* democratic truth that all men are created equal; the working man is every bit the equal of the executive (and superior to the quick-buck artist). Some disparity in income is fine, but the chasm indicated by the Census Bureau offends some very venerable senses.

The problem is: the Census numbers are bunk. For one thing, they are based on before-tax incomes; under our progressive system of taxation, upper-income families pay a disproportionate share of the nation's taxes while the poorest pay very little. Of course the bureau refuses to include income received in-kind or in the form of government-provided services such as day care, job training, education, and legal representation. No adjustments are made for family size or for the number of workers under one roof. No effort is made to take into account the variation of incomes over the course of a lifetime; for example, college students often have minuscule incomes and are counted among the poor, although a twenty-year-old premed scholar receiving straight As at Yale is not exactly a candidate for a homeless shelter. If all of these factors were taken into account, the distribution of income would be far more equal. Robert Rector and Kate O'Beirne of the Heritage Foundation have tried to do just that (see table 4.9).

To make the comparison consistent, only households with at least one full-time worker were included in the analysis. At the household level, the average after-tax income of families in the lowest quintile was $12,766, or one sixth the average income of families in the highest fifth. There is still

TABLE 4.9

AFTER-TAX DISTRIBUTION OF HOUSEHOLDS WITH AT LEAST ONE FULL-TIME WORKER, PER CAPITA, AND PER WORKER INCOME IN 1986, BY QUINTILES

| | QUINTILE | | | | |
	Lowest	*Second*	*Third*	*Fourth*	*Highest*
Household	$12,766	$22,199	$30,042	$39,792	$76,591
Per Capita	5,479	7,708	9,598	12,858	22,330
Per Worker	5,069	6,500	7,332	8,308	14,499

SOURCE: Robert Rector and Kate Walsh O'Beirne, "Dispelling the Myth of Income Inequality," *Backgrounder* no. 710 (Washington, D.C.: Heritage Foundation, June 6, 1989), p. 12, chart 4.

considerable inequality. This is no egalitarian paradise (or totalitarian nightmare). But the average household in the top fifth contains nearly 50 percent more members than the lowest quintile. We find many single individuals in the lowest fifth; they may be young workers new to the labor force, without children to feed. Most of the families in the top quintile, by contrast, are large. They contain more workers. That they earn more is no big surprise. So if we look at per capita income, the inequality is greatly reduced: members of the lowest-income quintile averaged $5,479 per capita, while individuals in the top quintile received an average income of $22,330. Merely adjusting for family size drastically reduces the income gap between the haves and the have-nots to a factor of four.

Among households in the bottom fifth of the income distribution, only 8 percent have two full-time workers; 54 percent of the households in the top fifth have two or more full-time workers. Common sense dictates that the more full-time workers a household has, the greater its income. Rector and O'Beirne conclude:

> Comparing the post-tax income distribution of working families after fully adjusting for family size and number of workers per family, the most affluent fifth of households have a post-tax per capita income of $14,499 for each full-time worker. The least affluent fifth of households has an average post-tax per capita income of $5,069 for each full-time worker. The remaining gap between the top and the bottom is primarily the result of differences in the productivity levels of the workers in each family. Workers in the more affluent families generally are highly skilled professionals or managers. Workers in the lower-income households tend to be younger and predominantly low-skilled blue-collar and white-collar workers.
>
> On close examination, in fact, the remarkable thing about U.S. society is not the alleged gap between the rich and the poor but the astonishing overall level of equality.[44]

Had Rector and O'Beirne examined the incomes of families over time, rather than for a single year, the degree of inequality would have been reduced even further, for as Edgar K. Browning has found, "lifetime incomes are substantially more equally distributed than annual incomes."[45] Yet the redistributionist drumbeat rolls on.

Too many poverty analysts ignore the myriad lessons that the bearish corpse of the USSR teaches. For seventy years the Soviet Union pledged fealty to the myth of socialist equality. Alas, the New Soviet Man they created was slothful, improvident, and a wastrel in the workplace. With no incentive to work or save, economic output shrinks, and there is less income to distribute. You end up with queues, food shortages, shoddy goods, crowded housing, and a dolorous, dispirited people. You don't even achieve your original goal of income equality. As economist Andrei Kuteinkov wrote of his ancestral land:

> At the top, wealthy families comprise 2.3% of the population. Only one-third of those families have legal sources for their wealth. Below them, a middle class of 11.2% of the Soviet Union. Just half of that category have legal sources for their wealth. Everybody else—86.5%—is poor. In the U.S., high-consumption families account for 20% of the population, middle-class families for 60% and low-income families for 20%.[46]

The income distribution in the former Soviet Union was far more unequal than that in the United States. The Soviet welfare state did little to redress the imbalance, as Kuteinkov noted

> Nor does the once celebrated Soviet welfare state compensate for these inequalities. Social welfare expenditures account for 20% of Soviet GNP, compared to 28.5% in the U.S., but Soviet social welfare disproportionately benefits the Soviet elite. It is the Soviet elite who consume the best of the free health care, use the best of the subsidized recreation facilities and educate their children in the best of the free schools and colleges.[47]

In effect, the Soviet welfare state *increased* income inequality so that "below the crust of Soviet society an enormous, and radicalized, mass of poor people seethe[d] with discontent."[48] The "solution" to inequality can become a horrific problem in its own right.

Burning Down the House

Home ownership is a keystone of the American Dream. For years, a bipartisan coalition of Republicans and Democrats has encouraged housing construction and financing through a variety of federal programs and by permitting tax deductions for mortgage interest. In fiscal year 1991, these various expenditures exceeded $50 billion.

Yet, as with the bewildering array of agricultural programs, the federal government has exacerbated housing problems by adopting rent-control laws, building and land-use codes and regulations, an unwise tax policy, and zoning restrictions. Every one of these measures decreases the supply of housing and increases its cost.

Researcher Cassandra Moore, who studied the severe housing problems in New York City, concluded:

> Despite having spent billions of dollars on housing, New York City has more homeless people, more tenants in subsidized quarters, and more dilapidated and abandoned housing than any other city in the country. It spends 10 times more on housing than the total spent by the next largest cities in America, yet its housing problems put it in a league with many cities in the Third World.
>
> . . . many people fail to realize that the "crisis" is mainly self-inflicted. New York, with its welter of building codes, rent regulations, and taxation policies, has put major roadblocks in the way of maintaining or building low-cost housing.
>
> . . . the media have ignored government's role in creating the problem. Instead, with much hand wringing, a parade of advocates for the homeless has claimed that low-cost housing would put an end to the misery.[49]

Whenever supply is artificially reduced and prices are artificially raised by government actions, those at the bottom of the economic ladder suffer the most. The poor and disadvantaged, the ostensible beneficiaries of our housing programs, are in fact the victims. More and more of them are pushed into the projects, which Supreme Court Justice Clarence Thomas has likened to "concentration camps."[50]

Rent control, long a sacred cow of urban activists, is in fact a bane in hundreds of cities across the country. Socialist Assar Lindbeck, chairman of the Nobel Prize economics committee, points out:

> The effects of rent control have in fact been exactly what can be predicted from the simplest type of supply-and-demand analysis— "housing shortages," black markets, privileges for those who

happen to have a contract for a rent-controlled apartment, nepo-tism in the distribution of the available apartments, difficulties in getting apartments for families with children, and, in many places, deterioration of the housing stock. In fact, next to bombing rent control seems in many cases to be the most efficient technique so far known for destroying cities, as the housing situation in New York City demonstrates.[51]

Fortunately, most cities are not experiencing housing shortages.[52] The urban-affairs specialist Carl Horowitz writes: "The supply and condition of America's housing stock is adequate; demand over the next decade for new housing will lessen; and the current national housing market is not 'tight' with respect either to availability or cost."[53] In fact, the last two decades have seen an unprecedented expansion in the number of housing units, from 68.7 million dwellings in 1970 to 102.7 million in 1987—an increase of almost 50 percent. One third of the nation's current housing stock was built during this period, amid warnings of a critical housing shortage. The growth of housing units between 1970 and 1987 far exceeded the number of new households and the growth in population. Horowitz notes: "For each net additional household, America produced 1.3 dwell-ings, and for each net additional person, America produced almost 0.9 dwellings—and these figures already allow for demolitions and other revenue losses."[54] Over the next two decades the rate of household forma-tion will slacken; baby boomers have, for the most part, already established their households. Consequently, the demand for housing will drop.

Although there is little evidence of overcrowding, and vacancy rates are high, activists are still pressing for more federal spending for construction, leading Horowitz to comment:

Advocates for the homeless who press for expanded federally-subsidized new construction ignore the fact that there are almost 9 million vacant housing units for rent or sale year-round. This is about fifteen dwellings for each homeless person, based on last year's Urban Institute estimate of close to 600,000 homeless per-sons nationwide. These vacant units are not "tenements" or "slums." They contain a median of 4.3 rooms; 95 percent have at least one complete bathroom; and close to half are single-family homes.[55]

Prices have gone up. In constant 1988 dollars, the median cost of a new home increased by 56.7 percent between 1970 and 1988—from $71,783 to $112,500. But this is due largely to improvements in quality. Between 1970 and 1988, the median square footage of new one-family homes rose by 30.7 percent (from 1,385 square feet to 1,810 square feet); the percentage of new homes with central air-conditioning increased from 34 to 75; the percentage with one or more fireplaces went from 35 to 65; and the percentage with 2.5 or more bathrooms increased from 16 to 42.[56] Homes are more spacious and loaded with amenities—of course they cost more. (Building codes and regulations are also responsible for the inflated costs.)

Yet housing remains eminently affordable. Horowitz claims:

> On balance, the evidence from a number of sources indicates that with the exception of a few metropolitan markets on the East and West coasts, a home was one of the economic bargains of the past decade. The 1987 American Housing Survey reveals that the median monthly housing cost for homes with a mortgage was $621; the monthly cost for homes owned free and clear was $203. The respective inflation-adjusted figures for 1980 were $504 and $176.[57]

Actually, higher-priced and higher-quality housing became *more* affordable during the 1980s. The ratio of monthly cost of home ownership to gross income decreased from 32.4 percent in 1980 to 31.8 percent in 1989.[58] In addition, the proportion of home buyers who were purchasing for the first time rose from 32.9 percent in 1980 to 40.2 percent in 1989; one third of the increase occurred between 1988 and 1989.[59]

There are any number of social and political illnesses that afflict this country as the twentieth century draws to a close. Although housing is becoming less affordable for a variety of reasons, a real shortage is not even on the horizon. Now if only the propagandists of Washington, D.C., would realize—or admit—this pleasant fact.

5

Getting Down on the Farm

Most of us dairy farmers are like entrepreneurs everywhere, in that we find there are times when we have to squeeze hard to milk a net profit out of our investments. And, like anyone else, once we started depending on government subsidies to do it, instead of on our own resources, we developed a dependency hard to kick.

—HANNAH B. LAPP
Cassadaga, New York

NO AMERICAN COW is more sacred than the farmer. Year in and year out, nature's noblemen slop at the subsidy trough; in 1991 their hearty meal cost taxpayers over $11 billion in direct subsidies alone, not to mention billions more at the supermarket cash register as a result of "price supports." This voracious appetite for public monies goes unchecked by politicians intimidated by the clout of the farm lobby.

Humorist P. J. O'Rourke, in his gonzo investigations into the arcana of Washington, was overjoyed to find so clear cut a case of right and wrong:

> Everything I've investigated—election campaigns, drug abuse, savings and loan regulation, social security, housing, foreign policy, the environment—has turned out to be a lot more complicated than I expected. . . . Until now. Until I got to the 1990 Farm Bill. Here at last is a simple problem with a simple solution. Drag the thing behind the barn and kill it with an ax.[1]

It won't be that easy. Government farm programs are close to untouchable; they have been made so partly by the singularly successful propaganda campaign waged by the U.S. Department of Agriculture and its beneficiaries. Who, after all, can be opposed to programs that claim to help farms and people taken right out of Currier & Ives prints and Norman Rockwell paintings? (Could it be that the presumed color of farm subsidy recipients—white—has something to do with the lack of public outrage over this form of welfare?)

For decades, Americans have been told that farmers are poorer than city dwellers; that the goal of agricultural policy is protecting small family farms; that fair is fair, and farmers are entitled to earn as much as nonfarmers; that farm subsidies stimulate economic growth; and that farm bankruptcies rend the fabric of society. *None* of these statements is accurate. Nevertheless, they are widely believed. The USDA, ably assisted by agribusiness and agriculture-school researchers, has convinced a large part of the American public that 1) farm businesses deserve special assistance from the government; 2) farm subsidies are in the public interest; and 3) existing farm programs effectively provide such assistance. Consequently, the farm bill sails through at every reauthorization, despite O'Rourke's homicidal fantasies. And the USDA budget rockets upward, from $8.4 billion in 1970 to $48.2 billion twenty years later.

The Ingredients

Although bewilderingly complex, the basic elements of farm policy have not changed significantly since the 1930s, when the Roosevelt administration sought to boost food prices by manipulating the supply of numerous products. The New Deal succeeded in making food more expensive, which admittedly did aid some farmers but harmed consumers—especially the poor, who spend a greater portion of their income on food than do the nonpoor. This regressive tax has contributed to whatever malnutrition exists in America. (Even fawning Roosevelt biographer James MacGregor Burns has conceded that "the 'big boys'—the large commercial farmers, farming corporations, banks and insurance companies—seemed to be getting more than their share of the take" of the New Deal farm programs. Over six decades, at least this hasn't changed.[2])

Price Supports. The federal government began setting price floors under agricultural commodities in 1933; more than 100 commodity groups are now underlain by floors.[3] Farmers are not forced to participate in such programs, but almost all do. Participants pledge their harvest to the federal Commodity Credit Corporation (CCC) in exchange for a year-long "non-recourse loan" that is equal to the support price multiplied by the number of bushels harvested. The farmers are not personally liable for these nonrecourse loans. If prices rise, the farmer repays the loan and sells his goods in private markets. If prices fall, the farmer defaults and the CCC keeps the commodities.[4] The taxpayers subsidize farm losses but do not share in the profits; the game is rigged surer than the 1919 World Series.

Milk. The federal government offers to buy unlimited quantities of milk and milk products from farmers at an above-market price, thus removing billions of dollars worth of dairy products from the market each year. The restricted supply drives up prices, forcing taxpayers to pay twice: first in the form of the subsidy, then at the grocery store. With great pomp and circumstance, the USDA throws a few hunks of cheese to the poor. The irony is that this agency, which makes cheese more expensive, is publicly seen as a benefactor for its occasional giveaways. But of course the cheese is not free, even to the poor. Minimum-wage earners pay taxes, too—in this case, to support a program that pads their dairy bills.

Sugar. Government price supports have set the price of sugar at as high as *500 percent* of the world price for most of this century. During the 1980s, this program cost taxpayers approximately $2 million for every subsidized sugar grower,[5] not to mention the higher prices at the check-out counter. In 1985, for example, the world sugar price was 4.5 cents per pound, while sugar being sold stateside was artificially inflated to 21 cents per pound.[6] All told, the sugar price-support program costs consumers approximately $3 billion per year.[7]

As if price supports weren't enough, domestic sugar interests have slapped strict foreign-import quotas on producers. Thanks to this sugar cartel, less sugar was imported in 1985 than in 1910.[8] Americans suffer—especially the poor. But so do the sugar-exporting countries of the Third World: the Dominican Republic, Guatemala, Brazil, Colombia, Peru, the Philippines, and Panama. By depriving them of a potentially huge export market, we cripple their economies. Preferring handouts to mutually beneficial trade, Washington then appeases these countries with foreign aid, creating client states. (Much as welfare is a sop to lower-income Americans who are the victims of American farm policy.)

Take a Reagan administration brainchild, the "Quota Offset Program," which gives free food to countries that are harmed by America's sugar protectionism. It sounds nice, but the free food has the effect of depressing the price of the same foods in the recipient countries, making it even harder for Third World farmers to earn a living. With the U.S. sugar market closed to them, and domestic markets glutted with Reagan's free food, many of these farmers turned to marijuana and coca-plant production. It is far easier to evade Uncle Sam's zero-import cocaine quota than his sugar interdiction.

Through it all, the USDA defends its sugar program with saccharine propaganda. The 1985 farm bill, for example, sets import quotas on sugar with the stated intention of subsidizing farmers "at no cost to the government." The enormous cost to consumers goes oddly unmentioned.

Protectionism often backfires, and the sugar industry hasn't escaped harm. Due to the dramatic reductions in sugar imports, dozens of sugar refineries have shut down and thousands of workers have been laid off.[9] Artifically high sugar prices have stimulated the development of sugar substitutes such as lower-priced corn syrup. Coca-Cola and Pepsi-Cola no longer use sugar in their soft-drink formulas; corn syrup now has a bigger share of the sweetener market than sugar does. There has also been a sharp increase in the importation of sugar substitutes that are not covered by import restrictions, such as dextrose, high-fructose corn syrup, maple syrup, honey, and molasses.[10]

The response from the industry has been about what you'd expect from a coddled, spoiled-rotten child. More subsidies! Greater production (and protection)! The USDA won't mind, but taxpayers should. Our sugar programs already cost consumers $10 for every $1 in benefits to affluent sugar producers.[11]

Wool. Taxpayers are really fleeced by the "target prices" set for domestically produced wool. In 1987, for instance, the target price was $1.81 per pound, more than two-and-a-half times the market price of sixty-seven cents. So the USDA paid wool growers the difference of $1.14 per pound. In recent years wool subsidies have exceeded $150 million, far greater than the value of wool produced.

Since wool subsidies (or "incentive payments," in government-speak) are based on quantity, the incentives they create are to provide lower-quality wool. Even the USDA concedes that American wool is inferior to foreign wool because of the program's perverse incentive effects.[12] Many textile firms refuse to use the inferior American wool, so 80 percent of the wool purchased by American consumers is imported.

Wool growers look far and wide to find justifications for their privileged status. For example, the 1954 National Wool Act declared that wool was an "essential strategic commodity" for national-defense purposes because it was used in military dress uniforms.[13] When skeptics pointed out that soldiers do not wear dress uniforms in combat, the wool interests smoothly segued into the always effective blather about the necessity of maintaining a positive balance of trade. In truth, wool subsidies *worsen* the balance of trade by creating a lower quality domestic product, which decreases the demand for American wool while increasing the demand for foreign wool.

Then there is the misty-eyed, sentimental argument that without government handouts to sheepherders who sell their sheep unshorn, the salt-of-the-earth folk who earn their living ripping the hair off sheepskins will be out of work and a valuable occupation will be jeopardized—an epoch of human civilization will end.[14] This is a subjective matter, and to each his own opinion, but we're highly dubious that the federal government should be subsidizing the careers of sheepshearers as the U.S. work force prepares for the twenty-first century.

The House Agriculture Committee has even gone so far as to sanction the Orwellian claim that the wool program, particularly its high-tariff component, is in the *consumers'* best interests. Without tariffs, the argument goes, the government would lose revenue, and somehow a leaner Treasury would harm consumers. Of course, lowering tariffs would cut the prices of wool products and greatly *benefit* consumers, but this obvious fact goes unmentioned.

When all else fails, the National Wool Growers Association and its allies argue that more than fifty years of subsidies are only just recompense for the price controls imposed on wool (along with hundreds of other commodities) during World War II. Like most—but not all—demands for reparations, this is preposterously weak, but then ludicrous reasoning and importunate demands are the stock in trade of the Baa Baa Black Sheep crowd.[15]

Cotton. Cotton farmers, too, are guaranteed a specified price for their product that is usually several times higher than the market price. Euphemistically called "marketing loans," these outright gifts amounted to more than $7 billion during the 1986–89 period—approximately $1 million per cotton farmer.[16] In addition, wealthy cotton agribusinesses are eligible for eighteen-month interest-free loans that enable them to speculate on cotton prices. If prices fall, the taxpayers incur the loss; if prices rise, the farmers claim the profits. Pretty good work if you can get it.

Other Price Support Fiascoes. Similarly larcenous price-support programs exist for wheat, rice, corn, tobacco, soybeans, and many other crops. In 1990 the ratios of support price to market price for these commodities were: wheat (1.96/1); rice (3.13/1); corn (2.09/1); cotton (1.57/1); tobacco (.94/1); and soybeans (1.02/1). Yet none dare call them ripoffs. Senator Larry Pressler (R-S.D.), arguably the dumbest Rhodes Scholar ever, declared in 1984 that the government's annual $100 million honey subsidies to beekeepers must be maintained because "without the honey bee to pollinate crops, the diet of American consumers would be limited to nuts, cereal grains, and meat."[17] With drones like Pressler buzzing about Congress, several queen beekeepers have received over $1 million per year in subsidies.

Money for Nothing

Agricultural price-support programs encourage increased production, which leads to surpluses, which in turn depress prices, leading to demands for higher price supports, which cause even greater surpluses. The cycle then repeats itself. This eats up a large bundle of money in a very short period of time. When President Reagan took office, agricultural subsidies amounted to about $4 billion; by the end of his first term they were over $35 billion. Even given the Reagan administration's profligate ways, that's an extraordinary increase.

The USDA is not unaware of the price-support cycle, which it tries to short-circuit by "acreage reduction"—in plain English, paying farmers for *not* growing crops. The New Deal farm programs, the model on which contemporary policies are based, began in 1933 when farmers were paid to plow up more than ten million acres of cotton and to slaughter more than six million pigs. As historian Julius Duscha described it:

> The slaughter was suggested by corn and hog producers at a meeting in Chicago because there was such a surplus of hogs that they had been selling for less than three cents a pound. . . . So the Emergency Hog-Marketing Program was put into effect. . . .

Farmers turned over their pigs to Agriculture Department representatives at eighty processing and meat packing plants throughout the country. The farmers were paid and the pigs were killed.[18]

"Kill every third pig and plow every third row under,"[19] was the popular description of this program; public outrage was widespread. "The government wouldn't let us plant, so we had to go on relief,"[20] was a plaint heard across the heartland. Even the Secretary of Agriculture, Iowan Henry Wallace, admitted to an ambivalence: "To destroy a standing crop goes against the soundest instincts of human nature."[21]

The New Deal's farm cornerstone, the Agricultural Adjustment Act, was planned and administered largely by economists from government land-grant colleges. (We'll return to this marriage of college and state in chapter 8.) As FDR-ophile Arthur Schlesinger, Jr., concedes, "The Agricultural Adjustment bill was essentially a leadership measure devised by farm economists, sold by them to farm organization leaders, sold again by economists and farm leaders in combination to the President, but lacking any basis in public understanding."[22] Everyone, it seems, was for the AAA—except the farmers themselves.

The public protest over the pig killing and plowing-under of land was on both humanitarian and pocketbook grounds. People knew full well that the effect of the policy was to reduce the supply and raise the price of pigs and cotton. In a letter to Secretary Wallace, one woman wrote, "It just makes me sick all over when I think how the government has killed millions and millions of little pigs, and how that has raised pork prices until today we poor people cannot even look at a piece of bacon."[23] The infuriated letter-writer had a sound understanding of the basic principles of supply and demand. How many people today, after decades of relentless government propaganda, have the same clear view of the farm mess?

The pig slaughter, especially, was a public-relations disaster. The New Deal planners learned a valuable political lesson: It's better to pay farmers not to produce than to destroy what they have already produced. Instead of plowing up crops in the field, the USDA started paying farmers to idle some of their land. Typical of such "acreage reduction" schemes was the Payment-In-Kind (PIK) program initiated by the Reagan administration in 1983.

Large subsidies to wealthy corporate farmers had become a political embarrassment, so Congress reluctantly placed limits on the amount of cash subsidies individual farmers could receive. The PIK program was a way of getting around these limitations while at the same time taking credit for supposedly shooing rich farmers from the trough. PIK was limited to farmers who participated in existing acreage-reduction schemes. Under PIK, farmers were allowed to idle an additional 10 to 20 percent of their land and receive certificates redeemable in government-stored grain or cotton. In this way the government returned commodities to farmers that it had already purchased from them at steeply inflated prices and then allowed them to sell those commodities again in private markets.

So many farmers signed up for the PIK gravy train that the USDA had to *buy* more grain to meet the subsidy-seeking farmers' demand, since its stockpiles of surplus corn, sorghum, and wheat were exhausted in the mid-1980s.[24] American families were taxed so that the USDA could purchase agricultural commodities that it *gave* to farmers to bribe them *not* to farm, thereby driving up food prices for families whose pockets had already been picked of tax dollars to pay for the scheme. The PIK program also caused massive unemployment as thousands of fertilizer, farm equipment, and seed dealers were put out of work because of the acreage reductions. One study estimated that sixty thousand agriculture-related jobs were lost in California alone in a single year.[25]

Small family farmers received little from the PIK program, while large corporate farms did very well:

> P. J. Ritchie Farms Corporation received over $5 million worth of government-owned cotton in return for leaving its farmland idle. . . . National Farms Corporation received over $3 million worth of corn from the government as a reward for not planting its own crops. A [U.S. General Accounting Office] survey found that large farmers received an average of $175,000 apiece worth of government crops . . . to compensate them for planting less than in previous years.[26]

The PIK program was just one example of the government's sixty-year policy of paying farmers not to produce food. The USDA hasn't even been able to achieve this perverse goal. According to agricultural economist Clifton B. Luttrell,

> from the beginning, the acreage withdrawal and other supply-control provisions put forward by the [government] were leaky. Farmers soon discovered a variety of methods to maximize their

economic position while adhering to the letter of the law's requirements. When paid to withdraw land from tillage, they retired only their least fertile plots. They practiced more intensive cultivation on the land they kept in circulation. They switched from controlled crops such as corn to noncontrolled crops such as soybeans. For all these reasons, total farm output remained high despite all of the [government's] expensive efforts to reduce the supply of farm commodities.[27]

Price support and acreage-reduction policies are contradictory, but then so is the rest of American agricultural policy. Congress pays farmers to produce less and turns around and subsidizes agricultural research, soil improvement, and chemical fertilization, all of which encourage bountiful production. No wonder farmers complain about mercurial prices and incomes.

The "farm problem" is largely the fault of Uncle Sam, who passes himself off as the savior of American husbandry. Intervention begets intervention begets more intervention, and the taxpayers are herded quietly, with little more than an anemic "oink," to the slaughterhouse. As butchers like to say, every part of the pig is ground and eaten except the squeal.

Smothering Foreign Trade

American farmers produce far more food than is consumed in the United States. One would therefore assume that food exports are voluminous, as befits a land that once aspired to be the "breadbasket of the world." But one would be wrong. American farmers are discouraged from exporting food by USDA "target prices" that are set high above world market prices. It is more lucrative for American farmers to sell their commodities to the government, which will store it (or let it rot), than to sell it to another country.

The USDA, as usual, has a "remedy" for this problem that costs money and fattens government: subsidizing food exports. Under the Agricultural Trade Development and Assistance Act of 1954, which the propagandists christened the Food for Peace Act, the U.S. government agreed to sell to the governments of less-developed countries agricultural commodities in return for the largely inconvertible currency of these poor nations.

Proceeds from the food sales are plowed back into the less-developed countries for "development projects." The act's stated purpose is to "encourage the export of price-supported commodities . . . and to aid agricultural improvement in the developing nations";[28] translated into an honest language, it permits the USDA to dump its agricultural surpluses in foreign countries and pay off their rulers to ensure compliance with U.S. foreign policy.

Dumping agricultural products in Third World countries depresses the price of the homegrown commodities in those countries, thus undercutting indigenous farmers. And the development aid, as economist P. T. Bauer has demonstrated, is typically of the government-to-government variety. Seldom does it reach the bushman or peasant woman; rather, it goes to build monuments to vanity and environmental destruction. Foreign aid bails out foreign politicians, especially the Westernized urban elite in many African and Latin American nations that exploit rural people by imposing price controls on food. These controls create food shortages and drive many farmers out of business and into the cities, intensifying the shortages. The appropriate policy response would be to deregulate food prices, but American agricultural subsidies permit these oppressive governments to forgo (or at least to delay) the common sense option.[29]

USDA bureaucrats declare Food for Peace a success; they temporarily reduce their stored surpluses and win hosannas from a rogue's gallery of Third World thugs. As Uncle Sam's stored surpluses decline, support prices rise, and the surplus is rebuilt by increased production. Failure is success to the USDA. The taxpayer is milked in this and many other ways, including USDA's partial subsidy of advertising expenses for foreign advertising by Krogers, Blue Diamond almonds, Sunkist, and other large corporations and cooperatives. How any of this goes one whit toward the preservation of small family farms—whether in Iowa or the Ivory Coast—is a mystery.

Getting Farmers Hooked on Debt

Since the days of *Poor Richard's Almanack*, avoiding debt has been seen as wise policy. The yeoman farmer who was the backbone of the early republic eschewed—or was supposed to eschew—speculation. That backbone has developed crimps that no chiropractor could straighten. Egged on by the lure of cheap credit, many of America's farmers are so far in hock they'll never see solvency again.

The principal vehicle for granting subsidized loans to inefficient or incompetent farm businesses is the Farmers Home Administration (FmHA), which, according to economic journalist James Bovard,

> is a welfare agency that routinely destroys its clients' lives. Congress and the FmHA have effectively created tens of thousands of mini-Mexicos in rural America. By flooding America's least-competent farmers with easy credit and perpetual bailouts, Congress and the FmHA have spurred a boom-bust cycle in farmland values, helped bankrupt many farmers, created huge entry barriers for young farmers, driven up crop cost of production, and thereby undercut American exports. With each federal farm credit disaster, government dominance of agriculture credit has increased, and the federal government now effectively controls half of all farm debt.[30]

Bovard is not exaggerating.

The FmHA seeds failure by providing loans to farm businesses that are unable to secure private credit. The reason a farmer—or any businessperson—is unable to obtain credit is that lenders do not expect the farm will make enough profit to pay off the loan. By subsidizing such businesses, the FmHA virtually guarantees the perpetuation of relatively unproductive farms. Because resources are scarce and the government cannot subsidize everyone, its credit subsidies give favored farmers an unfair advantage and crowd other borrowers out of the market. The FmHA, in effect, reallocates farm resources from creditworthy to uncreditworthy farmers. Economist Clifton Luttrell writes:

> The natural process whereby competition weeds out the less efficient and preserves the more efficient is altered by the introduction of subsidized credit to those farmers who are failing. With a great advantage in capital cost through the use of such credit, even inefficient farmers can become successful. The overall competence of farm management suffers in the process.[31]

Henry Hazlitt, in his classic *Economics in One Lesson*, emphasized the "unseen consequences" of government intervention. The FmHA's victims aren't so unseen: they're the marginally profitable farmers squeezed out of the credit market, their fields fallow. Every dollar that is lent to a subsidized farmer is a dollar that is unavailable to the family that wants to purchase a home, the small businessperson who'd like to open a new shop, the local government that maintains the city park. Perhaps those huge billboards that declare "Your Tax Dollars at Work" wherever a pothole is being filled by forty workers should also adorn these unbought homes and untended parks.[32]

As agricultural land values rose during the 1970s, the FmHA actively encouraged farmers to take out low-interest subsidized loans to purchase vast landholdings with the expectation that skyrocketing land values would produce capital gains that could be used to pay off the loans. "Get big or get out," Nixon's Agriculture Secretary Earl Butz was credited with saying. When inflation sharply declined in the early 1980s and land values leveled (and in some regions plummeted), a new wave of farm bankruptcies swept over the Middle West. Third- and fourth-generation farmers who'd been suckered into profligacy went belly-up. The government's "solution" was to grant even more loans.

The FmHA, like virtually every other agricultural program, perpetuates the myth that it is the best friend the small family farmer ever had. Yes, the agency does loan money to farmers of moderate means, but large corporate farms are its real beneficiary. Among the "small family farmers" who have received subsidized FmHA loans are the lieutenant governor, former governor, nine state representatives, and two state circuit court judges from Mississippi, one of the most heavily subsidized states; a Mississippi real-estate speculator who used a $1 million FmHA loan to pay off his other debts; a large corporate farm whose chief officer was convicted of bank fraud; a sharpie who persuaded the FmHA that he could get rich quick by speculating on the futures market but who lost all of his $1 million loan; and John DeLorean's luxury automobile plant, to mention just a few egregious examples.[33]

The FmHA has made so many bad loans that in 1988 the U.S. General Accounting Office estimated that it had accumulated an operating deficit of $36 billion.[34] The agency itself admits that more than a quarter of its bankruptcies are the result of farmers "having received too many FmHA loans."[35] As a result, the FmHA is now the largest owner of farms in the country, with more than twenty thousand properties. No more voracious landlord has ever graced this land: the FmHA makes the early land barons look like pikers. All the while, it is inveigling more and more farmers into its indentured grip.

Loot the Treasury, Poison the Earth

Not only have farm programs busted farmers and taxpayers, they have also caused severe environmental degradation. Subsidies to expand grain production are a prime factor in soil erosion. For instance, the Great Plains have become vulnerable to devastating losses of topsoil as prairie grasses are plowed under. These grasses have evolved with the capacity to survive drought, and their roots anchor dry soil against high prairie winds.[36] They cannot, however, withstand the subsidy-driven onslaught of the plow. Chemical fertilizers are another destructive agent paid for by USDA checks; they are poisoning our lakes and streams. American farm policy is a fiasco. It scatters $30–40 billion per year to the four winds and reaps bankruptcy for the foolish midsize farmer; it damages the environment; it boosts food prices for shoppers; and it pours big bucks into the accounts of the corporate farmers who are driving this gravy train.

Clifton Luttrell estimates that price supports cost consumers $10 billion each year in added costs. Competition is effectively outlawed; for sixty years, U.S. agricultural policy has promoted blatant price fixing that benefits a few large corporations responsible for most of the country's farm output. (Alas, this cartel is not covered by antitrust laws.)

Yet the abysmal failure that is American agricultural policy maintains broad public support. Everyone (except perhaps Donald Trump) is against welfare for the rich, but if the millionaire charity-case is wearing overalls and has a pitchfork in one hand and a blade of grass strategically placed between his teeth, the opposition evaporates. Image, as tennis star Andre Agassi says, is everything. And the federal government has dressed up its farm program in image-enhancing—if deviously misleading—work clothes.

Image Versus Reality

A Tennessee real-estate developer recently told one of the authors of how he was having trouble raising an additional $1 million for one of his shopping-mall developments. Because local banks were balking at extending him additional credit, he decided to approach some independently wealthy individuals and offer them an investment opportunity. The first millionaire he approached was "the farmer who lives next door to my daddy." After a brief sales pitch, the farmer wrote the developer a personal check for $1 million.

We're not talking about the Joad family here. Such stories are not unusual, although farmers with humongous checking accounts aren't stock figures in the sob stories of ag-welfare crusaders such as Senators Tom Harkin (D-Iowa) and Bob Dole (R-Kan.). In modern political mythology, the farmer is a hard-working and beleaguered man of the soil hanging on to his ninety acres by the skin of his teeth. Some are middle class—you can spot them because they're the ones driving the '88 Ford pickups—but most are decent, honest, poor, and white. As one USDA official put it, "Farmers should recognize that they are all in the same boat. All must be helped."[37]

The middle-class farmer is the exception. Many farmers are quite wealthy, and most of the manna from government farm programs rains down on large corporate farms. According to the USDA's own figures, "30 percent of all U.S. farm and ranchland is owned by just 1 percent of the landholders. In the Pacific states, 5 percent of the owners control 70 percent of such land."[38] This is a long way from the Jeffersonian ideal. Moreover, as the *Christian Science Monitor* observes, government policy has helped create this situation: "What has given agribusiness the edge . . . is the tax benefits, [heavily regulated] marketing mechanisms, and subsidies. . . . Cheap water in California (subsidized by taxpayers) can increase land values $1,000 an acre and mean millions of dollars a year to individual corporations."[39] A 1983 study of the farm sector concluded that "one percent of the nation's farmers generated two-thirds of all farm profits in 1981," and "these farms have sales in excess of $500,000 each. The 25,000 farms in this category had average profits of $518,635."[40]

Thus, agricultural policy has led to a concentration of farm production in the hands of mostly large, wealthy, corporate farmers who, because farm-program benefits are generally proportionate to acreage or production, receive the lion's share of government largesse. More acreage means bigger subsidies. Statistics vary from year to year, but in one recent typical year the USDA reported that 3 percent of the producers consumed 46 percent of the federal government's agriculture subsidies.[41] Ever more appalling, in 1986 the Prince of Liechtenstein and his Texas business partners were paid more than $2 million in a program designed ostensibly to aid "distressed farmers."[42]

The dairy price-support program is a good example of how the government sees to it that the rich get richer. In return for taking 30 percent of their production off the market, about forty-two thousand dairy farmers were paid $22,700 each during a fifteen-month period in 1984 and 1985. One quarter of the payees, representing the largest dairy farms, received 62 percent of all the benefits. In Florida, 177 dairymen received an average of $226,700 for *not* producing milk. (This accounted for nearly all the dairy price-support payments in that state.) In California, 608 dairymen received $142,200 each, or 98.5 percent of all such payments.[43] In 1986 a group of 144 dairy farmers received government checks for more than $1 million each.[44] (If they're looking for investment opportunities, we know of a certain Tennessee shopping mall . . .) As one student of dairy programs concluded, "The dairy program serves to transfer large amounts of funds from less-wealthy taxpayers and milk consumers to more wealthy dairymen."[45]

As shown in table 5.1, more than two thirds of all direct payments to farmers in 1985 went to farms with sales in excess of $100,000. Farms with sales in excess of $500,000 received an average payment of $37,499; farms with sales between $250,000 and $499,999 received $21,783; and $12,845 in welfare was given to farms with sales between $100,000 and $249,999. Only 31 percent of the money went to relatively small farms.

The wealthiest farmers receive the highest individual subsidies and the majority of the total expenditures. These programs are welfare for the well-to-do; no amount of USDA gussying-up can hide the fact that a farmer

TABLE 5.1

DIRECT GOVERNMENT PAYMENTS TO FARMERS IN 1985 BY SALES CLASS

	$500,999 and Over	$250,999 to $499,999	$100,999 to $249,999	$40,000 to $99,999	Under $40,000	All Farms
Payments ($ millions)	1,024	1,437	2,834	1,667	732	7,704
Distribution of Payments (%)	13.3	18.7	36.8	21.8	9.5	100
Average Payment ($)	37,499	21,783	12,845	5,193	447	3,387
Distribution of Gross Income (%)	30.2	15.8	24.3	15.5	14.3	100

SOURCE: USDA, *Economic Indicators of the Farm Sector: National Financial Summary, 1985*, pp. 46, 52, cited in Clifton Luttrell, *The High Cost of Farm Welfare* (Washington, D.C.: Cato Institute, 1989), p. 118.

generally has a much higher income and net worth than the average taxpayer. In effect, U.S. farm policy is a regressive tax that redistributes income upward.

In 1987, for instance, the average farm-family income was 138.6 percent of the average income for all families.[46] The average net worth of farmers with sales exceeding $100,000 per year, those who receive more than two thirds of all direct farm subsidies, was $1,003,000—more than twelve times the net worth of the average nonfarm family.[47]

Imagine the uproar if Washington announced that lower- and middle-class Americans were to be taxed in order to subsidize investment bankers, stockbrokers, or insurance executives. There'd be revolt, and rightly so. But our gargantuan welfare program for large farm businesses draws nary a peep of protest. Sixty years of relentless government propaganda has paid off. As James Bovard points out, even during the Great Depression, when many farm subsidy programs were initiated, the average farm family had a net worth that far exceeded that of the average nonfarm family.[48] Republican and Democratic administrations alike have sold the American people a bill of goods. The price tag goes up every year, and we the taxpaying saps keep forking it over.

Parity

Another cornerstone of American agricultural policy is the curious concept of parity—that is, the ironclad principle that the ratio of farm prices to the prices of other goods should remain constant (or, if changed, should be changed in the farmers' favor). These ratios are based on the ratio of farm to nonfarm prices between 1910 and 1914, which were unusually fruitful years for American farmers, and they are, by now, one of the most venerable examples of protectionist law.

The whole notion of parity is a textbook case of economic ignorance. In any market—agricultural or otherwise—the costs of land, labor, and materials constantly change. Consumer demand fluctuates in response to changing relative prices worldwide, as well as to changes in income and in consumer tastes and preferences. In response to these constantly changing supply and demand conditions, relative prices of all goods and services are also in flux or "disequilibrium."

It is precisely the changes in relative prices that give producers and consumers the vital information they need to make economic decisions.

Changing relative prices of raw materials, for example, signal to producers to alter their mix of raw materials in order to economize on their resource use and improve their competitiveness. Higher relative prices for final goods signal to consumers that those goods have become more scarce and should be conserved. The law of demand dictates that consumers will reduce their consumption whenever the relative price of an item rises.

Parity tries to pretend that just as Peter Pan never grows up, so do markets never change. We're stuck in 1912, thanks to this state-sponsored time warp, and farmers and their USDA patrons blithely go about their business as the real world passes them by. But however much Congress huffs and puffs, the world never stands still. Consequently, government price-support programs informed by the concept of parity have been enormously counterproductive and have run afoul of the economic law of unintended consequences. Markets are always in a state of flux; therefore, ham-handed attempts to "control" markets with price floors, acreage reductions, or other schemes will inevitably cause economic distortions. A good example of this phenomenon is the way in which price supports cause surpluses, which lead to demands for higher price supports, which cause even greater surpluses, and on and on, forever and ever until the U.S. Treasury collapses into rubble.

Imagine if the automobile industry took a cue from farmers and organized a protest drive through Washington, D.C. Automobile executives and dealers from all over the country would cruise in Cadillacs, Mercedeses, and Buick Park Avenues around the Capitol, blocking traffic and honking their horns and blasting loud music. Their demand: that the government place price floors under automobiles to assure that auto-dealer income remains the same relative to the income of the average working American that it was in, say, 1955. The car-buying public, which in some parts of the country pays almost as much for certain models of automobiles as they do for a house, would be outraged.

Another contrast is with the personal-computer industry. Personal computers now sell for half or less of what they sold for ten years ago, to the delight of hackers everywhere. Stiff competition forced the industry to cut costs and improve quality. But what if the computer industry had instead hired slick lobbyists to push for parity prices based on conditions in 1980, when PCs were less sophisticated but far more expensive? The domestic industry would have become lethargic and been easily overtaken by foreign competitors. The hired guns then would have lobbied to erect tariff walls and quota barriers. If successful, there'd be a hell of a lot fewer personal computers in American homes and businesses today.

Computer protectionism and automobile parity are non-starters; our farm programs are never-enders. The myth of the poor farmer, so sedulously cultivated by the agriculture bureaucracy, has removed parity and price supports and cheap credit from the debate agenda. Public opposition to these welfare programs is rare. It is nothing less than bizarre that many Americans actually applauded the spectacle in 1982 of millionaire farmers flying to Washington, D.C., and renting or borrowing farm vehicles to drive around town in coveralls to demand that the government raise the price of food in order to make farmers even wealthier than they already are.

Farmers and policy bureaucrats are engaged in a price-fixing conspiracy against the public. Parity is cloaked in a shroud of almost religious impeccability. Heretics who dare criticize parity aren't burned at stakes, but they are derided as heartless skinflints. Turning the proverb on its head, America's farmers have decided that it is far nicer to receive than to give, and woe unto the giver who questions why things are the way they are.

Millions and Millions of Farmers

A "farmer," according to the Census Bureau, is anyone who sells at least $1,000 per year in commodities, including animals. Thus, the Beverly Hills nose-job specialist who keeps a horse at a rented stable and decides to sell it for $1,000 is deemed a plowboy by the head-counters in Washington. This allows the government to grossly overstate the size of the farm sector. As investigative journalist Bovard writes:

> The federal government says there are 2.2 million farms. Yet in the 1982 Census of Agriculture, one million of these so-called farmers denied that they were farmers, claiming some other occupation. Two-thirds of these so-called farmers lose money from farming most years; they are primarily gentleman farmers, hobby farmers, or tax farmers.[49]

In the early 1980s, off-farm income accounted for 99 percent of family income for 72 percent of all U.S. "farms"; in 1986, 55 percent of the income of "farmers" came from off the farm.[50] Clearly, most of the individuals the government designates as farmers earn their income in other occupations. According to economist Marvin Duncan, "One could almost disregard about 1.7 million farmers. . . . They have almost no impact on the food supply."[51]

Even counting farmers with sales of between $40,000 and $99,000, most of whom have other full-time occupations, "the total number of farmers is roughly 573,000," writes Bovard, "less than the number of postal workers, beauty and barbershop employees, or textile sewing-machine operators in the country. If we look only at subsidized farmers, we find fewer federally dependent farmers than there are bartenders, taxi and bus drivers, or social workers."[52]

Part-time farmers (or, more accurately, gardeners) make little money, which is fine for them—few of us have lucrative hobbies—but it enables the government to manufacture a "farm crisis" that can be solved only by throwing tons of welfare to corporate agribusiness.

Farm-state congressmen love to use the inflated numbers because federal subsidies depend on the number of farms within a state. We are told that millions of small family farmers—the "backbone of democracy"—are in trouble and need a bailout. It's not true, but since when did that stop a politician from talking?

Farm Subsidies: Stimulant or Depressant?

Some politicians actually assert that farm subsidies are good not only for the men who cash the checks but for the rest of us as well. President Franklin Roosevelt declared in 1933, "The two great barriers to a normal prosperity have been low farm prices and the creeping paralysis of unemployment."[53] The line of reasoning seems to be that by increasing the income of farmers, the rest of the economy will be stimulated by a "multiplier effect" as the farmers spend the money on goods and services. Congressman Tom Daschle (D-S.D.) recently claimed, for example, that "every American farm-generated dollar translates to five dollars of economic activity throughout the economy."[54]

This is absurd, preposterous, and idiotic, but when the boyishly handsome Daschle (now a senator) says it, and his colleagues of both parties repeat it loudly and earnestly, it starts to sound downright believable. By the same logic, economic recessions can be forever banished by simply having the government declare that all college professors should be paid 100 times what they currently earn. Or price floors can be placed under the housing market, so that anyone who rents an apartment or buys a house must pay five times what they are now paying in order to transfer wealth to landlords and mortgage bankers, who will presumably spend the money and create a huge multiplier effect. Similarly, the government of Bangladesh could end poverty in the blink of an eye by imposing farm price supports at one thousand times the current market prices.

What pie-in-the-sky politicians such as Daschle don't know (or don't say) is that the positive multiplier effect initiated by farm spending is more than offset by the negative multiplier effect on consumers, who pay higher food prices, and taxpayers, whose rising tax burden lowers their purchasing power, in turn depressing other sectors of the economy. Government farm subsidies cannot "create jobs" or economic growth because they amount to nothing more than robbing Peter to pay Paul. They take money out of the pockets of one group of citizens and give it to another. Agricultural subsidies cannot stimulate economic growth because of the economic law of opportunity cost: expanding government spending depresses private-sector growth. Government cannot create money and other resources out of thin air. FDR provided us with the perfect object lesson: despite massive government farm subsidies and myriad public-works programs during the Great Depression, the unemployment rate was higher in 1939 than it was in 1932. With due respect to Senator Daschle, the only thing subsidies are sure to multiply is the number of government employees.

Farmers and Food Stamps

Most Americans believe that the federal food-stamp program was established to combat a perceived "hunger crisis," but no mention was made of this crisis when food stamps were introduced in 1939. Rather than being a purely humanitarian gesture, " 'feeding the hungry' has been a primary means of disposing of agricultural surpluses and increasing farm incomes since the farm programs began in the early 1930s. . . . The aims and interests of the 'hunger lobby' have thus coalesced with those of farm subsidy supporters."[55]

Senator Bob Dole and George McGovern (Democratic ex-senator representing South Dakota) were for many years the tandem champions of the food-stamp programs. Dole and McGovern won fawning press coverage for their labors, but these two crafty pols understood well the real beneficiaries of food stamps: agribusiness. The annual cost of food-stamp programs exceeds $10 billion per year, or more than one third of annual net farm income. Obviously, some lower- and middle-income people are helped, but it is farmers who really reap the bounty. As Luttrell notes, "Evidence of this can be seen in the sources of the programs' [political] support, the specific commodities included in the [programs], and the fact that the distributions have been made through the Department of Agriculture, an agency designed primarily to aid farmers, rather than through other [i.e., welfare] agencies."[56]

The history of food-stamp programs demonstrates how producer (i.e., farmer) interests have dominated consumer interests. The Depression-era Federal Surplus Relief Corporation was placed in the USDA in 1935; it was generally regarded as "an organization to assist the department in its surplus removal programs rather than an organization for relief of the indigent."[57] Since the 1930s, a field full of similar programs, with liberalized eligibility, has sprung up: the national School Lunch Program; the Summer Feeding Program; the Child Care Food Program; the Supplemental Feeding Program for Women, Infants and Children; the Congregate Feeding Program for the Elderly; and the School Breakfast Program.

These manifold programs have helped reduce the USDA's embarrassing agricultural surpluses and have enriched many affluent corporate farmers, but there is scant evidence that they have improved the nutrition of lower-income Americans. Since the National Academy of Sciences concluded in 1975 that "little or no effective evaluation of the impact of these programs on the well being of the target groups has been carried out,"[58] the food-stamp industry has escaped close scrutiny. The U.S. Congressional Budget Office stated in 1980 that "ad hoc assessments have served as the major evaluations supporting the continued growth and expansion of the programs," and it admitted that "consistent and reliable data have not existed."[59] The scattered studies that have been done have found that nutrition levels of families receiving food stamps are not significantly different from those of families with similar incomes that do not receive food stamps.[60] The only folks whose nourishment can't be doubted are the farmers and the USDA bureaucrats.

Food-stamp programs may not combat hunger, but they have conquered a potentially formidable foe: urban congressmen whose constituents suffer from high food prices. These supposed champions of city dwellers faithfully support farm subsidies in exchange for rural support for food stamps. Besides busting the budget, this is a one-sided bit of logrolling, since

Kansans such as Dole would hurrah for food stamps anyway, as a means of disposing of the agricultural surplus.

The really fervid food-stamp advocates are those with both farm and urban constituencies. In 1975 Senator Hubert Humphrey (D-Minn.), a friend to every program that was ever proposed, from the Cold War to CETA, quoted a USDA propaganda sheet which claimed that

> $63.9 million in bonus food stamps provided in Texas . . . generated $232 million in new business in Texas and appeared to generate at least $89 million in business elsewhere in the United States. In addition, the $63.9 million provided in bonus food stamps created 5,031 jobs. Translated nationwide, this could mean that the food stamp program is now responsible for $27 billion in business in the United States each year and 425,000 jobs. . . . Furthermore, consider how much money we would have to spend to support those 425,000 workers and their dependents if they did not have the jobs that the food stamp program has apparently generated.[61]

The Happy Warrior had an oversized heart but not much of a head for economics. He fell prey to the same "multiplier effect" fallacy that Senator Daschle is in thrall to. The food-stamp program may rearrange the pattern of output and employment, but it does not increase it. We expect such prattle from Humphrey and his heirs. Unfortunately, American journalists have been silent partners in the USDA's campaign to delude the public about farm policy. Few journalists understand even the rudiments of economics; most are bored senseless (as are many sensible folk) by the numbing array of agricultural programs. It's easier to take the government's word for it than to bite the hand that feeds them information.

The populist firebrand Mary Ellen Lease told nineteenth-century farmers to raise "less corn and more hell." What we need today are fewer lazy journalists and more lively skeptics like the late H. L. Mencken, who spared no one's feelings when he wrote:

> Let the farmer, so far as I am concerned, be damned forever-more. . . . Any city man, not insane, who sheds tears for him is shedding tears of the crocodile.
>
> No more grasping, selfish and dishonest mammal, indeed, is known to students of the *Anthropoidea*. When the going is good for him he robs the rest of us to the extreme limit of our endurance;

when the going is bad he comes bawling for help out of the public till. Has anyone ever heard of a farmer making any sacrifice of his own interests, however slight, to the common good? Has anyone ever heard of a farmer practicing or advocating any political idea that was not absolutely self-seeking—that was not, in fact, deliberately designed to loot the rest of us to his gain?[62]

Mencken was a keen student of the reality, as opposed to the rhetoric, of American agricultural policy.

6

Fuel for the Propaganda Machine

It's fact. The latest U.S. Government figures indicate our proven [oil and gas] reserves will only last [12 years].

—American Electric Power Company, Inc.
The Wall Street Journal, January 21, 1976

ON SLOW NEWS DAYS—no tyrants are rattling sabers, no Kennedys are in the dock—the network anchors, in best unaccented stentorian voice, will announce the imminent arrival of some crisis. We're running out of timber! We're running out of gas! (Alas, we're never running out of meticulously coiffed models who can learn to read off cue cards.)

These scare stories kill a few minutes between commercials before drifting off to the netherworld of ephemeral stories, which we might call Donna Riceland. They're gone but not forgotten: they do have a cumulative effect. If repeated enough, they seep into the conventional wisdom. We start to accept them as fact, rather than the highly flawed products of biased research that they are. Worse, politicians make policy based on these fantastic claims; the upshot is more government control, more power concentrated in the hands of central bureaucracies, and *less* of the good that the policymakers are trying to preserve.

Bureaucratic control of economic activity displaces market mechanisms, distorts the information that prices provide, and reduces incentives to produce. How much more efficient are markets? In the old Soviet Union,

132

"private agricultural plots account[ed] for about 3 percent of the total arable land of the USSR and about *one third* of the agricultural output."[1] Indeed, the strips and parcels of private land were for many years all that stood between the Russian people and severe food shortages. Before the Communists collectivized Soviet agriculture, Russia had been a major exporter of wheat to Europe; the Ukraine was known as the "breadbasket of Europe." The expropriation of peasant and kulak land changed all that. The USSR became a net importer of grain and many other foodstuffs.

Ironically, as central planning wanes abroad, and Eastern Europe is busy codifying market systems within newborn constitutional democracies, American politicians and bureaucrats are conducting a propaganda campaign to convince the American public that unregulated markets do not work and that government's firm hand is required if the public weal is to be served. This is especially so with regard to the "renewable" resource of timber, which can be replenished, and petroleum and natural gas, which are "exhaustible."

Paul Bunyan, Despoiler

To the American colonists, forests were a blessing and a nuisance. They served as a primary source of building material and fuel, but they also competed with crops for agricultural land. No one owned the forest—it belonged to everyone. The big woods seemed as if they'd last forever. Inevitably, what economist Garret Hardin later dubbed "the tragedy of the commons" set in. (Hardin's point is that when land is held in common, with no clear rights to ownership, no one has any incentive to preserve, to replant, to tend. When everyone is responsible for upkeep, no upkeep gets done.)

The good old days were not always marked by wise stewardship of our resources. As the nation's population grew and westered, so did the demand for agricultural land and timber products. Extensive logging and land-clearing activities continued well into the twentieth century. Between 1850 and 1920, in excess of 270 million acres of forests in the United States were cleared, more than twice the area of forest that had been eliminated during the preceding 250 years. Between 1850 and 1920, the U.S. population grew from 23.2 million to 106.5 million, by a factor of 4.6; over the same period, the domestic annual production of wood increased from 5.4 billion board feet to 35 billion board feet, or by a factor of 6.5.[2] Railroads were among the nation's most voracious consumers of timber. One analyst reported:

> In the 1870s to the 1900s, railroads consumed between a fifth and a quarter of U.S. wood production—in 1890, 3 billion board feet annually, the equivalent of half a million acres of forest. In 1900 alone, U.S. railroads replaced 91 million crossties. The railroad industry, said Union Pacific general agent Howard Miller, was an "insatiable juggernaut of the vegetable world."[3]

Prices rose, providing incentives to economize on the use of wood. Railroads began to use coal for fuel and metals for trestles, and crossties were treated with creosote to extend their useful life. By 1890 "there were fourteen wood preservation plants; by 1915 there were 102. Eighty to 95 percent of the output of these plants went to the railroad industry." As a result of these measures (as well as the decline of the rail system), the railroads' consumption of timber fell from 20 to 25 percent of the annual harvest in 1909 to only 3 or 4 percent in the 1960s.[4]

The federal government's management of forests and timber began with the Timber Culture Act of 1873, which was passed in response to growing and legitimate popular concern about the depletion of our once-vast forest resources.

> By the 1860s and 1870s the widespread uncontrolled harvesting of timber on public lands had begun to attract national attention. An 1869 report of the Michigan legislature warned that "generations yet unborn will bless or curse our memory according as [sic] we preserve for them what the munificent past has so richly bestowed upon us, or as we lend our influence to continue and accelerate the wasteful destruction everywhere at work in our beautiful state." Commissioner Williamson of the General Land Office stated that "a national calamity is being rapidly and surely brought upon this country . . . the useless destruction of the forests. . . ." Reflecting such concerns, the Timber Culture Act of 1873 provided that settlers could acquire title to 160 acres by planting and sustaining trees for ten years on a quarter of this acreage.[5]

In 1891 President Benjamin Harrison signed into law legislation that enabled the president to designate lands as "forest reserves," or what we now call national forests. (Harrison's tiny band of defenders never tire of pointing out that the Indianapolis gentleman, and not the Rough Rider Teddy Roosevelt, is the real father of the parks.) Six years later, the Organic Administration Act declared that the goals of the reserves were to "improve and protect the forests . . . securing favorable conditions of water flows, and to furnish a continuous supply of timber." In 1905 a Bureau of Forestry was created in the Department of Agriculture, and management of the national forests was passed from the Department of Interior to what would become the Forest Service.[6] Since then, the USDA Forest Service has controlled the flow of the nation's timber reserves and issued a continuous supply of propaganda on behalf of government stewardship of the more than 100 million acres of forest in its bailiwick.

From the first, the Forest Service painted a desperate picture. In his June 1, 1920, report entitled, "Timber Depletion, Lumber Prices, Lumber Exports, and Concentration of Timber Ownership," U.S. Forester William B. Greeley warned:

> The virgin forests of the United States covered 822 million acres. They are now shrunk to one-sixth of that area. All classes of forest land . . . now aggregate 463 million acres, or a little more than one-half our original forests. Of the forest land remaining and not utilized for farming or any other purpose, approximately 81 million acres have been so severely cut and burned as to become unproductive waste. This area is equivalent to the combined forests of Germany, Denmark, Holland, Belgium, France, Switzerland, Spain, and Portugal. Upon an enormous additional area, the growth of timber is so small in amount or of such inferior character that its economic value is negligible.[7]

Greeley's dire report also noted that "three-fifths of the original timber of the United States is gone and . . . we are using timber four times as fast as we are growing it."[8]

The condition was severe. With stocks severely depleted and still being drawn down at four times the rate of replenishment through regrowth, U.S. forests were destined to disappear by 1945. Moreover, the prices of timber and wood products were becoming outrageously expensive, the result of short supplies and pent-up demand for home building and industrial material at the end of World War I.

The Forest Service proposed a solution: reforestation. Its June 1, 1920, report declared:

> A remedy for this appalling waste must be found in a concerted effort to stop the devastation of our remaining forests and to put our idle forest lands at work growing timber. It is inconceivable that the United States should forfeit the economic advantage of its enormous timber-growing resources and that it should go on using up its forests with no provision for growing more until wood products are priced on the basis of imported luxuries and their use is restricted to the lowest possible scale of civilized existence.[9]

Sound advice. But the Forest Service, like any new bureaucracy feeling its oats, was not about to restrict its own domain. Greeley insisted that private ownership of forests was the major impediment to his sensible remedy:

> The results needed can not be attained if timber production is left to the initiative of the private owner of land or is sought solely through compulsory regulation of private lands. Not only has the public very large interests at stake which justify an assumption of part of the burden; certain fundamental causes of forest devastation can be removed only by public action. Chief among these are the fire hazard of forest properties, particularly of growing forests, and a property tax system which discourages or may prevent the landowner from engaging in the business of growing timber.[10]

In that last clause, Greeley was on to something. An onerous tax system discouraged or prevented landowners from growing timber—and therefore from preventing or fighting forest fires. It is no surprise that the nation's forests were being depleted and not replanted. An overhaul of the government's pernicious tax system would've gone a long way toward solving our timber problems, but private remedies were not exactly what Greeley was looking for. Instead, he set forth a variation of the perennial policy of central authorities:

> One of the most direct and effective means of arresting devastation and offsetting the dangers arising from concentration of timber in private ownership is the extension of publicly owned forests. It is,

under present conditions, the only effective means for overcoming the depletion of old-growth timber of high quality and for restocking many denuded areas which require planting.

The public should own a half of the timber-growing land in the United States, well distributed through all the principal forest regions.[11]

By "public," Greeley meant his Forest Service. Bureaucratic control of private property was to replace market mechanisms. There were limits, however. The report conceded that "it is impractical to nationalize all of the forest land in the country or even the major portion of it."[12] No reason for the "impracticality" was given, nor was a distinction made between the "major portion" of forest land and the 50 percent that the Forest Service had its ravenous eyes on.

In 1920 the federal government already owned approximately one fifth of the nation's forests; roughly half was privately held by 250 large companies (many of them railroads that had finagled government land grants); and the remainder was distributed among smaller private owners, state forests, and municipal forestland. Under the Forest Service proposal, federal ownership would increase by 150 percent; so, too, presumably, would the Forest Service's budget, work force, and power. In addition, the plan required

a continuous study of the technical phases of reforestation . . . to carry the national policy forward to the best results. Recent cuts in congressional appropriations will necessitate closing the four experiment stations hitherto established in the Western States. Not only should those stations be restored, but provision should be made for additional experiment stations covering the other important forest regions of the country.[13]

This land-grab fell short. The Forest Service's recommendations were not adopted. The Sovietization of our forests was forestalled. Indeed, federal ownership of U.S. timberland today is roughly the same as it was in 1920. At last count, 483.3 million acres of land in the United States were classified as timberland; of this, 136.4 million acres (28.2 percent) were owned by the public sector and the remainder was privately owned. The federal government held 97 million acres, or 71.1 percent of the timberland held by the public sector and 20 percent of all timberland in the nation.

Among private owners, 276.4 million acres were held by individuals (almost 58 percent of the total) and another 70.6 million acres (14.6 percent of the total) were controlled by the timber industry.[14] There are also 242 million acres of parks, wilderness reserves, and nonworking forestlands from which timber is not extracted.

The dire consequences of private ownership foreseen in 1920 have not occurred. There are more trees growing now in the United States than in 1920. Much of this increase is thanks to the private sector, which began an aggressive program of planting new stands of trees. In 1930 about 139,000 acres were being replanted each year; by 1989, over 3 million acres were being replanted annually. Nearly one third of the land area of the United States—730 million acres—is now forested, and almost a half billion acres are commercial timber. The growth now exceeds the harvest.[15]

Each year, approximately 2.4 billion seedlings are planted and thousands of additional acres are replanted by direct seeding. Although the forest industry owns less than 15 percent of the nation's timberland, in 1989 it accounted for 41.3 percent of the total acreage replanted. Other private owners were responsible for 44 percent of the replanting, and the federal government's share amounted to just 12.2 percent. (Of course, millions of acres are reseeded naturally each year.)[16]

Private researchers, whose companies are driven by the profit motive, have developed higher-quality, faster-growing trees. Improved forest management, which recommends such techniques as removing vegetation that competes with trees for nutrients and water, promotes more rapid growth. In 1944 the net growth of trees was just over 13 billion cubic feet; by 1986, net growth exceeded 22 billion cubic feet. Better management has also reduced the annual losses of timber from forest fires. During the 1920s about 8.5 million acres burned each year; by the late 1980s, losses due to fire were cut almost in half.[17] This happy reduction is due less to Smokey the Bear than it is to Irv the Scientist.

Meanwhile, the demand for timber has been reduced in a variety of ingenious ways, most notably recycling. More than one third of the newspapers printed and more than half of the corrugated packaging used in the United States are recycled, which sharply lessens the demand for virgin timber. So at the same time that the nation's timber supply is expanding, technological changes fostered by market competition are reducing demand.

Yet the doomsayers still issue their dark portentous warnings. Marion

Clawson, a natural-resource economist, concluded in the august pages of *Science* that "timber growth potential has been repeatedly and seriously underestimated" by the Forest Service. He charged that the Forest Service has failed to recognize that ongoing harvests have a beneficial effect on future growth, because the "great increase in annual net growth of timber was a direct consequence of the decline in standing volume. . . . Net growth was only possible as original stands of timber were opened up by harvest."[18] That is, old timber grows very slowly; when it is cut down and the land replanted, the young stands of trees grow rapidly.

The Forest Service has been roundly criticized by numerous economists for its gloomy predictions—predictions that serve the interests of the agency but bear little relationship to reality. Robert Nelson observed that "the agency's tendency to overstate projected timber shortages . . . displayed its weak understanding of economic forces. Price changes operate to bring demand and supply into equilibrium; an impending shortage calls forth a higher price, which both reduces demand and stimulates additional supply."[19] This may be simple obtuseness, or a more sinister explanation may be needed. Perhaps the Forest Service bureaucrats *do* understand how markets work, but they choose to ignore them. After all, functioning markets leave no role for government bureaucrats to play.

Nelson contends:

> The Forest Service for years issued dire warnings about timber famines that in every case proved to be false alarms. It warned that public regulation of private harvests was the only way to achieve forest regeneration, only to see parts of industry exceed the Forest Service itself a few years later in regeneration success. The Forest Service persisted for years in promoting scientifically inaccurate and misguided information.[20]

For decades, the Forest Service has predicted timber famines and shortages. It has systematically underestimated future growth and overestimated consumption. These forecasts are not born of incompetence, but of self-preservation. The role of the Forest Service would be diminished—indeed, its existence would be threatened—if private ownership and a market system were seen as the answers to whatever timber problems we face.

Petroleum and Natural Gas

Petroleum, unlike timber, is an exhaustible resource. Whereas more timber can be produced by the simple expedient of planting trees, the supply of petroleum seems to be finite; replenishment is impossible. Once extracted, petroleum is irreplaceable. The process of exploration, development, and production of petroleum is far less understood by most people than is the growth and harvesting of trees. Moreover, our modern way of life is based on energy consumption, and the exhaustion of petroleum supplies would have more serious and far-reaching ramifications than would a shortfall of timber. For these reasons, the federal government's propaganda campaign against the petroleum market has been shrill and unrelenting. In 1909 the U.S. Geological Survey (USGS) of the Department of Interior forewarned:

> It is clear that considering the minimum quantity of petroleum in the United States as 15,000,000,000 barrels, and continuing the present rate of increase in production, the supply would be exhausted by about 1935. . . . Within a very few years a marked decline will be noted, and this will continue with increasing value for the oil product and an insufficient quantity for the legitimate demands of the industry after another decade, and . . . the production, on a reduced scale, will continue for a long time, but in an amount unsatisfactory to industrial necessity.[21]

The USGS made a similar forecast in 1922:

> The estimated reserves [in the U.S.] are enough to satisfy the present requirements of the United States for only 20 years, if the oil could be taken out of the ground as fast as it is wanted. Should these estimates fall even so much as 2 billion barrels short of the actual recovery, that error of 22 percent would be equivalent to but 4 years' supply, a relatively short extension of life.[22]

Of course these prophecies went unfulfilled. But then, errant forecasts were nothing new to Washington. The first commercial oil well in the United States was drilled in Titusville, Pennsylvania, in 1859; seven years later, the federal government scratched its regulatory itch by predicting imminent oil shortages. The rate of domestic production of crude oil rose, and its trusty concomitant was the annual prediction by government officials and agencies that reserves were being depleted and additional supplies were unavailable (see table 6.1 on the following page).

In retrospect, these forecasts are so wrong-headed that they seem almost comical. Behind the risible mask, however, is an unequivocal message: petroleum is too important to the nation's economic well-being to entrust to the marketplace. Therefore, government intervention and planning are essential to the nation's future.

These false forecasts were like the timber alarms: both were the products of self-interested government officials who had an incentive (namely, the accumulation of professional power) to discount the ability of markets to send the appropriate signals through prices to producers and consumers. Since the first bubblin' crude came up from the ground, proven reserves have always been sufficient to supply the nation's needs for only one or two decades. The reason for this is simple: proven reserves, by definition, are resources that are economically extractable with available technology at the time of the assessment. As prices rise to reflect increasing scarcity, it becomes economically feasible to use more intensive (and more costly) methods of extraction. Moreover, extraction technology is constantly improving, which makes it feasible to exploit marginal sources of petroleum.

Known reserves of natural resources, including oil, can change rapidly as technology improves and as prices rise (see table 6.2 on page 144).

The availability of large reserves discourages the exploration for new sources. If, for example, zinc reserves are adequate for the next 100 years, why would anyone begin searching for new supplies? But, as economists Herman Kahn, William Brown, and Leon Martel note:

> If current ore reserves were down to 10 years or less, then the marketplace would reflect that condition with increased prices until new mines are opened and reserves expanded to higher levels. Because of these economic considerations, there is little reason for known reserves to exceed the expected demand by more than a few decades. It does happen occasionally but *not* because shortages have prompted a search for new supplies. Thus, if we have stumbled upon coal reserves sufficient for more than 200 years and iron ore for more than 1,000, we can hardly expect private investors to be excited about a proposal to look for still more. As a result, those who make conservative predictions about the future availability of materials based upon such data naturally tend to underestimate future production capability. The literature

TABLE 6.1

RHETORIC AND REALITY: FEDERAL GOVERNMENT PETROLEUM PREDICTIONS, 1866–1951

Year	U.S. Daily Oil Production Rate (Billion bbls)	Agency Making Prediction	Rhetoric	Reality
1866	.005	U.S. Revenue Commission	Synthetics available if oil production ends	Synthetics not needed; 37 billion bbls. pumped in next 82 years
1885	.02	U.S. Geological Survey	Little or no chance of oil in California	8 billion bbls. pumped since that date; important new findings in 1948
1891	.05	U.S. Geological Survey	Little or no chance of oil in Texas or Kansas	14 billion bbls. pumped in these states since that prediction
1908	.18	U.S. Geological Survey	Maximum future domestic supply of 22.5 billion bbls.	35 billion bbls. pumped since 1908; 26.8 billion bbls. proven reserves on January 1, 1949
1914	.27	U.S. Bureau of Mines	Total future domestic production only 5.7 billion bbls.	34 billions bbls. pumped since 1914—6 times this prediction

142

Year		Agency	Prediction	Outcome
1920	.45	U.S. Geological Survey	U.S. needs foreign oil and synthetics; peak domestic production almost reached	1948 U.S. production exceeds U.S. consumption and is 4 times greater than in 1920
1931	.85	Secretary of the Interior	Must import as much oil as possible to conserve domestic oil supplies	During next 8 years, imports were discouraged and 14 billion bbls. were discovered in U.S.
1939	1.3	Department of the Interior	U.S. oil supplies will last only 13 more years	New oil found since 1939 exceeds the 13 years' supply known at that time
1947	1.9	Department of State (Petroleum Division)	Sufficient oil cannot be found in the U.S.	4.3 billion bbls. found in 1948, the largest volume in history and twice U.S. consumption
1949	2.0	Secretary of the Interior	End of U.S. oil supplies in sight	U.S. production rose by more than one million bbls. daily in the next 5 years
1951	2.0	Department of the Interior (Oil and Gas Division)	Reserves will last only 13 years	Reserves not exhausted

SOURCE: U.S. Congress, House Committee on Interstate and Foreign Commerce, *Presidential Energy Program, Hearings before the Subcommittee on Energy and Power*, House of Representatives, on The Implications of the President's Proposals in the Energy Independence Act of 1975, 94th Cong., 1st sess., 1975, p. 643. The 1951 prediction is from "Fear Is Expressed of U.S. Oil Scarcity," *New York Times*, June 11, 1950.

TABLE 6.2
CHANGES IN KNOWN RESERVES OF VARIOUS RESOURCES, 1950–1970
(MILLIONS OF METRIC TONS)

Resource	Known Reserves in 1950	Known Reserves in 1970	Percent Increase
Iron	19,000	251,000	1,321
Manganese	500	635	27
Chromite	100	775	675
Tungsten	1.9	1.3	−30
Copper	100	279	179
Lead	40	86	115
Zinc	70	113	61
Tin	6	6.6	10
Bauxite	1,400	5,300	279
Potash	5,000	118,000	2,360
Phosphates	26,000	1,178,000	4,430
Oil	75,000	455,000	507

SOURCE: Council on International Economic Policy, Executive Office of the President, *Special Report, Critical Imported Materials* (Washington, D.C.: Government Printing Office, December 1974), as quoted in Herman Kahn, William Brown, and Leon Martel, *The Next Two Hundred Years: A Scenario for America and the World* (New York: William Morrow, 1974), p. 92.

is full of such predictions. As one example, the prestigious Paley Report of 1952 stated that by the mid-1970s, U.S. copper production would not exceed 800,000 tons; in fact, it was 1.7 million tons in 1973. The report also said the *maximum* lead production would be 300,000 tons; yet it actually exceeded 600,000 tons. This tendency to underestimate future production is so strong that similar mistakes have been made over and over again.[23]

Bureaucrats love dire forecasts; they want apocalypse, now! The specter of shortage breeds panic, and into the breach step government regulators. Thus, there are strong incentives for bureaucrats and politicians to keep markets from operating properly.

Unnatural Gas Regulation

Like much regulatory activity, the roots of government intervention in energy markets can be traced to the Great Depression and the New Deal it spawned. The companies that owned natural-gas pipelines were on the edge of collapse; many had overbuilt and were reduced to furious price discounting. A 1935 Federal Trade Commission report surveyed the bankruptcies and concluded that "cutthroat competition" was the culprit. Congress responded with the Natural Gas Act of 1938, which extended the jurisdiction of the Federal Power Commission (FPC) from its original realm of the interstate sale of hydroelectric power to include the interstate sale of natural gas. The FPC's authority was limited, at first; it did not apply "to the production or gathering of natural gas." But court rulings broadened the FPC's mandate until natural gas came to be treated very much in the manner of public utilities.[24]

The dam break occurred in 1954, when the U.S. Supreme Court's decision in *Phillips* v. *Wisconsin* delivered unto the FPC's jurisdiction the regulation of the wellhead price for natural gas sold in interstate commerce. A dual market for gas was created: gas sold in interstate commerce was subject to a federal price ceiling, and gas produced and consumed within a single state was unregulated. The artificially low price of interstate gas encouraged consumption and discouraged production. As even the most obtuse Econ 101 student could have predicted, the supply of price-controlled gas dwindled while a surplus appeared on the intrastate market. In short, federal regulation *created* shortages in the energy market where "cutthroat competition" had previously guaranteed an ample supply.

Congress tried to straighten out this convoluted mess by passing the Natural Gas Policy Act of 1978. Though prominently sporting the then-fashionable "decontrol" designer tag, the law actually brought intrastate gas sales under FPC authority while liberalizing, in a modest way, interstate controls. The market became more tangled and coiled than ever before. FPC pencil-pushers devised more than thirty classifications for gas wells. Even though the gas flowing from all wells was chemically indistinguishable, the price received by producers depended on when, how, and where the wells were drilled. Except for "deep gas" wells, every category was surmounted by a price ceiling below market levels—a surefire prescription for shortages. The price ceilings, which ranged from 21 cents per 1,000 cubic feet (mcf) of natural gas to $11 per mcf,[25] threw the natural-gas market into a state of hopeless confusion. Producers were faced with enormous disincentives to develop new supplies of low-cost gas and powerful incentives to develop high-cost sources of supply from deregulated deep wells. All was chaos; only the FPC remained serene.

That rosy analysis was gainsaid by one expert, who opined:

> The Federal Power Commission failed to read the implicit message
> . . . where controls did not impede the market, supplies were
> increasing; but where controls were in place supplies were declin-
> ing. Instead, the FPC saw the dwindling interstate supplies as a
> "crisis," which required regulatory action to "share the shortage"
> by forcing large natural gas users to reduce their consumption.[26]

This rather charitable view suggests that the basic economic theory of supply and demand was beyond the ken of the FPC bureaucrats. Perhaps, but this interpretation seems disingenuous, for the effects of price controls are well known. Robert Schuettinger and Eamonn Butler, in *Forty Centuries of Wage and Price Controls*, demonstrate convincingly that such measures are doomed to failure:

> What, then, have wage and price controls achieved in the recurrent
> struggle to restrain inflation and overcome shortages? The histori-
> cal record is a grimly uniform sequence of repeated failure. In-
> deed, there is not a single episode where price controls have
> worked to stop inflation or cure shortages. . . . Instead of eliminat-
> ing shortages, price controls cause or worsen shortages. By giving
> producers and consumers the wrong signals because "low" prices
> to producers limit supply and "low" prices to consumers stimulate
> demand, price controls widen the gap between supply and de-
> mand.[27]

The FPC may very well have been aware of how its actions would affect the markets for natural gas, but it also knew that the agency's budgets and power would thrive in the climate of regulation-induced crisis. It wisely created a muscular client group—those few producers and consumers who made handsome profits in the new order—that howled with great wounded vigor anytime the FPC's fiefdom was threatened by unbought reformers.[28]

Although many controls on natural gas were phased out on January 1, 1985, under the provisions of the Natural Gas Policy Act, other controls remained in place, with pernicious consequences. As analyst Milton R. Copulos notes:

Continued federal rules . . . have kept large quantities of gas from the market, because the gas is in areas where the permissible price is less than the cost of developing the resource. As a consequence, many natural gas reserves that are far more expensive to develop have been brought to market because the price ceilings that determine what its producers can charge made it possible to do so. The result: the price controls intended to keep prices low have raised them to levels higher than otherwise would be the case.[29]

Just as the remaining price controls can be in part responsible for dwindling natural-gas reserves, so has the implicit—and in some quarters, explicit—threat of reregulation discouraged exploration.

Petroleum

The petroleum market has been just as bollixed up by the regulators. As economic historian Dominick T. Armentano writes:

Increasingly after 1911, there was active governmental intervention in the petroleum industry, and the industry itself, as well as the state, must bear a responsibility for that interventionism. Historically a substantial amount of petroleum regulation and legislation was supported, in whole or in part, by various segments of the industry in an attempt to further short-run business objectives. Unable to achieve monopoly power in a free market, various industry representatives and trade associations sought to transform the free petroleum market into a regulated and controlled market. . . . It is not at all unexpected to economists that just such continued intervention eventually produced the energy crisis of the 1970s and 1980s.[30]

Armentano's indictment of the industry is no surprise to those familiar with the history of regulation. As economists of the "right" (Sam Peltzman) and historians of the "left" (Gabriel Kolko) have made clear, the largest firms in regulated industries often "capture" the regulatory agency and virtually write their own tickets. Output is restricted, prices rise, consumers are gouged, and the industry basks in a warm (and profitable) regulated glow.[31]

In 1971 the Nixon administration imposed wage and price controls to combat inflation. These supposedly temporary controls were lifted in early 1974 on everything *except* crude oil and petroleum products. Meanwhile, world petroleum markets were jolted in October 1973 when members of the OPEC (Organization of Petroleum Exporting Countries) cartel suspended the shipment of crude oil to the United States and to other nations regarded as sympathetic to Israel.

Rather than allow market forces to allocate the diminished supply, Congress enacted a complex set of price controls and allocation rules for petroleum and refined products. These powers were vested in the Federal Energy Office, which burst its buttons and was refitted as the Federal Energy Administration. Growing by leaps and bounds, the FEA swelled into a cabinet-level Department of Energy in 1977.

All the schemes and dreams of the energy planners have been dismal failures. William E. Simon, the nation's first "energy czar," measured the magnitude of the calamity:

> As for the centralized allocation process itself, the kindest thing I can say about it is that it was a disaster. Even with a stack of sensible-sounding plans for evenhanded allocation all over the country, the system kept falling apart, and chunks of the populace suddenly found themselves without gas. There was no logic to the pattern of failures. In Palm Beach suddenly there was no gas, while 10 miles away gas was plentiful. Parts of New Jersey suddenly went dry, while other parts of New Jersey were well supplied. Every day, in different parts of the country, people waited in line for gasoline for two, three, and four hours. The normal market distribution system is so complex, yet so smooth that no government mechanism could simulate it. All we were actually doing with our so-called bureaucratic efficiency was damaging the existent distribution system. As the shortages became more erratic and unpredictable, people began to "top off" their tanks. Instead of waiting, as is customary, to refill the tank when it is about one-quarter full, all over the country people started buying 50 cents' worth of gas, a dollar's worth of gas, using every opportunity to keep their tanks full at all times. And that fiercely compounded the

shortages and expanded the queues. The psychology of hysteria took over.

Essentially the allocation plan had failed because there had been a ludicrous reliance on a little legion of government lawyers, who drafted regulations in indecipherable language, and bureaucratic technocrats, who imagined that they could simulate the complex free-market processes by pushing computer buttons. In fact, they couldn't.[32]

When crude bullying failed, politicians fell back on exhortation (dressed up, of course, in the rhetoric of patriotism, that last refuge of the scoundrel). President Jimmy Carter, borrowing from philosopher William James, called the energy crisis the "moral equivalent of war." Citizens were hectored by limousine-riding mandarins to reduce their driving and to lower their thermostats in winter and raise them in summer.

Various ineffectual rationing schemes were employed to reduce lines at gasoline stations. For example, drivers were allowed to fill their automobile gasoline tanks on either odd or even days of the month, depending on their license-plate numbers. Wild predictions were made: "Projections of future oil prices commonly accepted during the Carter years indicated that by 1990 the nominal price of a barrel of oil would be around $115, and the real (constant dollar) price would be at least $45."[33]

These forecasts assumed that demand would continue to grow and supply would continue to decline—in other words, that the laws of supply and demand would not operate in the energy market. The bureaucrats and the politicians labored long and hard to limit supply: the Department of the Interior restricted exploration for oil and gas on its land and on the offshore continental shelf; the Nuclear Regulatory Commission threw roadblocks in the way of the construction of new nuclear-power stations and delayed the completion of plants already under construction; and Congress, via the "windfall profits" tax and sharp reductions in the depletion allowance for petroleum companies, dried up the financial resources available for and the incentives of domestic companies to develop new oil fields.

The world price of petroleum had risen dramatically; in 1979 foreign producers were charging Americans an average of $20.19 per barrel of crude, while domestic producers were allowed to charge a per-barrel average of only $12.64. Had domestic prices been brought into line with world prices, and assuming that the oil companies were as greedy as all and sundry believed them to be, the additional funds would have been used to explore for more oil—thus increasing the supply and bringing down prices. But the politicians had other ideas. One of the most egregious, the politically popular Windfall Profits Tax of 1979, siphoned off more than $72 billion over five years from the oil industry into federal coffers.[34] Energy czar Simon concluded that the tax was unjustified:

> An increase in profits for the suppliers (and potential suppliers) of a suddenly scarce commodity should be welcomed. Only when profits rise can companies amass the immense amounts of capital necessary for new exploration. Only then will outsiders be given the incentive to undertake the substantial costs of entering the oil business. So, the faster profits rise, the faster new oil will come into the market and the faster OPEC's stranglehold will be removed. A tax will hinder this beneficial process, either slowing down energy independence or making the consumer pay more for it. In other words, it is Big Government which is ripping us off, not Big Oil.[35]

Few bureaucrats shared Simon's view. The evidence may suggest that the Windfall Profits Tax discouraged new firms from entering the oil industry and existing firms from finding new sources of supply, but when does mere evidence ever carry the day in political discourse?

After hamstringing the ability of market forces to solve the nation's energy problems, the DOE and its allies embarked on an ambitious program that they dubbed "Project Independence." The program's objective was to give the nation "the capacity for self-sufficiency" in energy by 1980—and who could be against that? The eight hundred-page Project Independence report was prepared by a phalanx of 750 policy wonks and consultants and well-meaning energy specialists. Ten hearings were conducted around the country; almost a thousand witnesses testified.[36] All this sound and fury produced, in the end, just four possible remedies to what ailed us. The *Wall Street Journal* summarized the menu:

1. Subsidize new synthetic-fuel industries. Uncle Sam would purchase their high-cost output, or support their prices, and stand ready to bail them out if they fail.

2. Erect an oil-tariff wall around the U.S. to protect new high-cost domestic energy industries from being undercut in the future

by cheaper foreign oil . . . even though it is the sort of trade protectionism that the U.S. has criticized Europe's Common Market for practicing.

3. Store huge quantities of crude oil against a future cutoff of foreign supplies.

4. Concentrate on long-range conservation measures. Huge investments in mass transit and renewal of inner cities would "balance the energy budget" by cutting demand instead of boosting supply.[37]

Notice that each and every option would enhance the power of the very government that commissioned the study. And except for the tariff wall, which was never given serious consideration, these schemes promised a whole tub of pork for pols to parcel out.

Synthetic Fuels. The first synthetic-fuels legislation, introduced in the House of Representatives in 1979, envisioned a $3 billion program of price supports and purchase guarantees. Under this bill, taxpayers took on no liability unless the price of petroleum products fell below the price of synthetic fuels; the synfuels plants were to be constructed with private money. But in the Senate, this $3 billion contingent commitment ballooned into an $88 billion boondoggle with the pregnant title of the Energy Security Act of 1980. The act created a quasi-governmental agency, the Synthetic Fuels Corporation (SFC), which was empowered to make loan guarantees to firms developing synthetic fuels and to construct and operate three synthetic-fuel plants of its own. The final version also included price guarantees and purchase commitments.

To spread the pork like jelly across the nation, the act required synfuel projects to demonstrate a diversity of technologies and geographic locations. The SFC was instructed to produce 500,000 barrels of synthetic fuels per day by 1987 and 1.5 million barrels per day by 1992—alack, it never accounted for as much as 2 percent of those 500,000 barrels. By that bizarre logic that passes for modern-day statesmanship, the SFC was permitted to only fund those projects that could not, by hook or crook or bribe, obtain private financing. In other words, the taxpayers were forced to pump money into risky ventures that professional lenders wanted no part of. Making things even dicier, the SFC was forbidden from investing in the technology of transforming coal into petroleum products (done with some success by Germany in World War II) and instead required to fund highly dubious shale-oil projects.

The SFC was doomed to failure from the start. It was, above all, a tub of pork in which hoggish pols feasted. There were exceptions, notably Senator William Proxmire (D-Wisc.) and Congressman-turned-Office of Management and Budget Chief David Stockman (R-Mich.), who pilloried what columnist Jack Anderson called "one of the biggest boondoggles of all times."[38] Another critic, Representative Jim Leach (R-Iowa), said of the SFC's muckamucks: "These are the only guys in the world who make the Pentagon look streamlined."[39] Analyst Copulos explained how this bungling entity retarded what it was supposed to encourage:

> The federal government established a huge fund to subsidize construction of alcohol stills to provide motor fuel. Loan guarantees and in some cases direct loans were to be made available for the construction of "small stills." The program was an economic disaster. The limitations on size and capacity under the federal programs were so stringent that the units were never likely to be self-supporting. At the same time, the very existence of a federal loan guarantee program caused investment bankers to require prospective borrowers to seek such federal assistance regardless of the risk associated with their particular project. The result was that virtually all lending for alcohol fuels plant construction came to a halt as the banking community waited to see what the federal programs would eventually include. Needless to say, construction of alcohol plants came to a virtual halt as well.
>
> In short, as long as the market was allowed to function without federal interference, the alcohol fuel development progressed at a pace commensurate with its true potential. Once the government entered the picture, false signals were sent to the marketplace, leading to misallocation of resources and waste of manpower and materials.[40]

Mercifully, in 1986 the Synthetic Fuels Corporation was snuffed. A few politicos and favored businessmen kicked, but the sun rose the next morning, and the next one, too.

Tariffs. The oil tariff option never stood a chance. Although it would have generated billions for federal coffers, consumers would have suffered because tariffs discourage protected domestic producers from reducing costs. This approach also would have been the apex of hypocrisy; since the end of World War II, the United States has castigated other nations for gross acts of protectionism.

The Strategic Petroleum Reserve. In 1977 the federal government began spending billions of dollars to store crude oil in salt caverns on the Gulf Coast as insurance against an embargo or some other unexpected interruption in the flow of oil. Clad in the language of military security, the Strategic Petroleum Reserve attracted little opposition.

Yet there were snags. By March 1979, only 88 million barrels were held in storage, far below the 250 million barrels that the Department of Energy had set as a target. And—as with so many government schemes—the costs were much greater than anticipated. Storing the oil was supposed to cost $1.50 per barrel, but by 1979 the estimated cost was $3 per barrel and rising.[41]

But the political turmoil in Iran looked as if it would vindicate the SPR's existence. Shipments of crude oil to the United States were reduced by about 500,000 barrels per day in 1979, and the shortages and gasoline lines that accompanied the 1973 OPEC embargo appeared ready for a return engagement. Flacks in the DOE trumpeted the petroleum reserve as a splendid example of government foresight and planning—except for one little detail. By design, the Department of Energy had failed to install pumps to get the oil out! As the *Wall Street Journal* reported: "Things were planned this way. Energy officials assumed that an oil emergency wouldn't strike before next year, so their plan was to delay installing the pumping system until next autumn." Without pumps to extract the oil, the reserve was useless. Red-faced and under fire from Congress, the Department of Energy hastily devised a temporary pumping system that would later have to be torn out. But even this stopgap measure was inadequate:

> Complications abound. Both the permanent and temporary pumps would work by forcing water into the caverns to drive the oil out. But the temporary system is designed to draw water from small nearby lakes, requiring emergency waivers of certain environmental rules. Part of the extra cost of the temporary system is for eventual rerouting of water pipes from these lakes to larger, more suitable bodies of water.
>
> Even if the oil can be withdrawn sooner than originally planned, the problems of the emergency reserve won't be over. For one

thing, the government hasn't yet negotiated contingency arrangements with operators of three adjacent commercial pipelines for
moving oil from the caverns. Nor has there been any discussion of
prices to be paid to pipeline companies.

And the planners haven't made the essential detailed decisions
on which users would get what share of the oil and when.[42]

Even if the oil could have been pumped to the surface, there were still no
arrangements for transporting it to refiners. So much for strategic planning
by the less than prescient bureaucrats of the DOE.

Conservation. Individualist Americans were slow to get with the conservation program; they needed prodding. So the Carter administration engineered a Central Intelligence Agency report in April 1977 predicting
severe world energy shortages by 1985. The *Wall Street Journal* reported:
"White House officials released the report in the hope that hearing the grim
warning from the CIA would startle Americans into a new willingness to
conserve energy now."[43] The "Cold War" was acquiring an entirely new
meaning.

To put teeth in the conservation message, Congress twice authorized the
Department of Energy to mandate thermostat settings in private homes and
businesses. The department proposed that thermostats be set at 78 degrees
during the summer and at 65 degrees during the winter, and consideration
was actually given to deputizing federal "thermostat inspectors" to inspect
homes and businesses for compliance, with fines and penalties for vio-
lators. Public derision kept the proposal from being implemented.[44] On a
greater scale, the federally mandated 55-miles-per-hour speed limit met
widespread resistance. Not since Prohibition had a law been disobeyed with
such impunity. Reams of pro-55 propaganda were churned out by the the
Department of Transportation, but the law was such an affront to the sense
(not to mention patience) of drivers that it was repealed in 1987. American drivers, it seems, were conscientious objectors in the moral equivalent
of war.

A Few Honest Men

To paraphrase Motown's Jimmy Ruffin, what becomes of the honest bureaucrat? In 1977 a task force within the Energy Research and Development Administration (ERDA) discovered the unhappy answer. Its report on

potential natural-gas reserves, "Market Oriented Program Planning Study," or MOPPS, concluded that if prices were allowed to rise above the price-controlled level of $1.75 per mcf to $3.25 per mcf, potential reserves from conventional sources would double. Indeed, because the first geopressured methane well had just been developed, the final MOPPS report estimated that a price of $3.25 per mcf would give the United States some 600 trillion cubic feet of natural gas reserves, enough to supply the nation for fifty-five years.

The MOPPS report was actually issued three separate times: on April 1, April 6, and June 3, 1977.[45] With each version, the volume of estimated potential reserves under a market scenario shrunk. This was no accident; ERDA officials were peeved by the findings of the MOPPS task force, and let the honest bureaucrats know it. "So affirmative a prediction, right or wrong, dismayed ERDA. It cancelled the MOPPS study and reassigned those who had participated in it."[46] Like whistle-blowers in the Department of Defense, the MOPPS team learned that candor and independence have their price. The simple expedient of letting prices rise to free-market levels would alleviate the much-ballyhooed natural-gas shortage, but some agencies, it seems, are addicted to the myth of an energy crisis.

This crisis began to ease during the late 1970s, no thanks to Uncle Sam. Higher world prices for crude oil encouraged exploration and development as well as conservation; consequently, supplies increased and demand diminished. The gloom-and-doom scenario failed to materialize, and by 1980 the panic had dissipated to such an extent that Ronald Reagan was elected president on a platform that called for dismantling the Department of Energy. In his first week in office, Reagan eliminated the price controls on crude oil that Nixon had clamped on in 1971. In time, the natural-gas market was largely deregulated as well, although Reagan reneged on his promise to abolish the DOE. (In fact, he increased its budget to appease his favorite charities, the military and the nuclear industry.)

The apocalyptic forecasts of the FEO/FEA/DOE/CIA and the alphabet soup of energy agencies and bureaus turned out to be balderdash. Falling oil prices in the 1980s indicated a glut of crude and abundant natural gas, not severe shortages. Not to worry: the Department of Energy rewrote its pamphlets and dug in its heels. The department's Energy Information Agency managed to have Congress declare October "Energy Awareness Month," and the EIA floods the nation's schools and helpless bystanders with cutesy materials emphasizing—News Flash—the importance of energy and the need to conserve. Like all propagandists, the EIA claims that its function is, innocuously, "education"—as if Americans aren't constantly reminded of the cost and importance of energy every time they pay a utility bill or fill 'er up at a gasoline station. Perhaps the best way to look at the EIA is as an agency engaged in a holding pattern, excreting pap until another "crisis" can be generated to justify a bigger, fatter, more intrusive energy bureaucracy.

Failure Is Success

These crises, whether real or contrived, teach us an important lesson. Government propaganda is usually—if not always—directed at non-government institutions. Markets are said to "fail," according to the propagandists: sometimes they produce surpluses, sometimes shortages. The cure is advertised to be additional government intervention. Yet what if the cure is worse than the disease? It is, after all, in the self-interests of politicians and bureaucrats to exacerbate problems, not to solve them. A successful program would work itself right out of existence. Even high-ranking bureaucrats would be in the unemployment line; pork-ladling pols would disappoint plenty of friends and supporters. Pet projects back in the district would starve to death.

Failure is success to those in government who benefit from crises. Just as the Trojans were warned against Greeks bearing gifts, Americans ought to be suspicious of pinstripers demanding authority to solve national "crises" in the public interest.

7

The Sky Is Falling!

*Human happiness, and certainly human fecundity, are not as impor-
tant as a wild and healthy planet. I know social scientists who remind
me that people are part of nature, but it isn't true. Somewhere along
the line—at about a billion years ago, maybe half that—we quit the
contract and became a cancer. We have become a plague upon our-
selves and upon the Earth. It is cosmically unlikely that the developed
world will choose to end its orgy of fossil-energy consumption, and the
Third World its suicidal consumption of landscape. Until such time as
Homo sapiens should decide to rejoin nature, some of us can only hope
for the right virus to come along.*

—DAVID M. GRABER
National Park Service

STEVEN SCHNEIDER of the National Center for Atmospheric Research
knows firsthand the truth of the ancient joke: everybody talks about the
weather but nobody does anything about it. In the 1970s he was predicting
a coming ice age. But temperatures rose. Today he is predicting the opposite: global warming. Given his track record, you needn't buy a plot in
Nome just yet. The computer models from which Schneider spins his
frightening yarns are the basis of many of the Chicken Little forecasts of
recent years. He makes no pretense of even-handedness: Schneider has
said, "We have to offer up scary scenarios, make simplified, dramatic
statements, and make little mention of any doubts we may have. Each of us

157

has to decide what the right balance is between being effective and being honest."[1]

Another government scientist, James Hansen of the National Aeronautics and Space Administration (NASA), foresees catastrophic consequences from the "greenhouse effect." Senator Al Gore (D-Tenn.), the barefoot boy from St. Albans prep school who threatens to run unsuccessfully for president from now unto the twenty-third century, predicts "an environmental holocaust without precedent."[2]

The political response to the threat of global warming has been hysterical. In 1989 forty-nine U.S. senators cosponsored a "Global Warming Prevention Act" that would have enabled the federal government to take extensive tracts of land out of food production and cultivate sugar cane to make ethanol, a replacement for gasoline. The bill also proposed subsidies for "low-cost vehicles," such as bicycles and even pack animals, for lower-income Americans.[3] Yes, that's right: government would give away bicycles. Members of the congressional leadership would not, of course, have traded in their gas-guzzling government limousines for burros. (Fortunately, the bill did not pass.)

The fevers—and the globe—have cooled of late. Evidence of global warming has become shakier almost by the month. If anything, a global cooling seems likely. (Back to the ice-age hypothesis, Steve?)

The fuss over global warming, which we shall discuss at length later in this chapter, is all too typical of the strategy used by advocates of greater governmental control over resources. In the absence of a genuine catastrophe, *hypothetical* catastrophes are fabricated on computer "models," which can rarely even explain the past, let alone predict the future. But impending doom sells, as Stephen King knows, and when the dark prophecies are issued by scientists at distinguished research institutes, public opinion proves to be extremely malleable. Since the average citizen is "rationally ignorant" of advanced scientific methods—especially sophisticated computer-modelling techniques—he or she is vulnerable to catastrophe stories, especially those with the imprimatur of NASA or other prestigious government agencies.

The following discussion is by no means meant to imply that there are no serious environmental problems; clearly there are. But a large and growing body of knowledge indicates that many of these problems are not caused by "progress" or capitalism, as many political environmentalists insist, but by the failure of governments to properly define and enforce private-property rights in natural resources. The "tragedy of the commons" has been played out worldwide: we see, in the newly open societies of Russia and her sister republics, the disastrous results of "common"—read: government—ownership of virtually all resources.[4] The absence of well-defined and protected property rights leads to horrifying levels of pollution of the air and water and a barren, blasted landscape.

The free market is the better alternative. Voluntary, market-oriented solutions to environmental problems deprive government of a large measure of its power. As is the case with timber and petroleum, air and water are tempting targets for the controllers. Predictably, the virtually endless stream of government-generated propaganda on environmental matters flows from a familiar source: the turf-grabbing baronies of the Leviathan state.

The Environmental Propaganda Machine

An early and notorious attempt at global modelling was the work of the "Club of Rome," an international association of academics, industrialists, and government bureaucrats. The Club's 1972 book *The Limits to Growth* described its origin: "In April 1968, a group of thirty individuals from ten countries—scientists, educators, economists, humanists, industrialists, and national and international civil servants—gathered . . . in Rome . . . to discuss . . . the present and future predicament of man."[5] Philosophically, the group ran the constricted spectrum from neo-Malthusians to socialists. Like Malthus, they doubted the capacity of the planet to support many people; like Marx, they desired state control of much of the economy. They were blissfully ignorant of the historical fact that human ingenuity and market-price adjustments have enabled human beings to adapt to changes caused by population growth. Socialist and misanthropic—clinging to the long-discredited view that population increases necessarily lead to massive worldwide starvation—the Club of Rome advocated extensive income redistribution around the globe as the best way to defuse the ticking bombs of progress and population. A linchpin of any such redistribution would be an enormous increase in the power and budgets of international governmental bodies such as the World Bank, International Monetary Fund, and United Nations: no wonder why "international civil servants" were present at the creation in April 1968.

The incendiary conclusions of the book were camouflaged in scientific language and deliberate understatement:

> If the present growth trends in world population, industrialization, pollution, food production, and resource depletion continue unchanged, the limits to growth on this planet will be reached sometime within the next one hundred years. The most probable result will be a rather sudden and uncontrollable decline in both population [by death and starvation] and industrial capacity.[6]

To prevent this dreadful future, the Club of Rome called for an immediate halt to economic growth, which was supposedly using up "finite" resources, and a redistribution of "world wealth." In a paean to nineteenth-century Marxism, *Limits to Growth* called for a "fundamental revision of human behavior and, by implication, the entire fabric of present-day society."[7] Nothing less than a comprehensive worldwide experiment in social engineering could avert catastrophe; the Club of Rome, no less than the early Bolsheviks, wanted to remold the nature of man.

Without worldwide central planning by international bureaucrats, the report ominously warned, "today's already explosive gaps and inequalities" will "continue to grow larger. The outcome can only be disaster, whether due to the selfishness of individual countries that continue to act purely in their own interests, or to a power struggle between the developing and developed nations."[8] The authors went on to endorse "radical reform of institutions and political processes at all levels" and argued that "concerted international measures and joint long-term planning will be necessary on a scale and scope without precedent."[9]

The Limitations of Limits to Growth

Despite the imprimatur of the Massachusetts Institute of Technology and many other prominent academic and scientific institutions, the unsubstantiated claims made in *Limits to Growth* were so outrageous that they provoked an immediate hailstorm of criticism. The fatal flaw in the study—which betrayed its essential misanthropy—was that it assumed no human response to admittedly disturbing trends. The Club thus cast aside a central lesson of history: human beings and their technology adapt to change. Even those who were sympathetic to the Club of Rome's political bent denounced the study. Socialist economist Gunnar Myrdal was infuriated by the "inexcusably careless" nature of the study, which he referred to as "quasi-learnedness."[10] The chief scientific adviser to the British government said the study was only praised by the "scientifically uninitiated" and that the only "kind of exponential growth with which the book does not deal . . . is the growth of human knowledge."[11]

Limits to Growth called for a worldwide economic restructuring, but its analysis was all but devoid of the most elementary economic analysis. For example, it predicted worldwide oil shortages by extrapolating world demand for oil, which at a point, was shown to exceed the known reserves. Unmentioned was the simple fact that if demand exceeds supply, price will increase, inducing conservation while creating economic incentives to discover additional sources of petroleum and petroleum substitutes. This dominant theme of the entire history of the energy industries was inexplicably—and inexcusably—ignored.

Limits to Growth was shoddy, mendacious, and had less redeeming social value than the oeuvre of Jackie Collins. Just four years after its publication, it was even repudiated by the Club of Rome, which grudgingly endorsed "more growth." This reversal went unnoticed in the popular media; certainly the four million extant copies of the book were never recalled, General Motors–style. The Club's explanation of its reversal was termed by economist Julian Simon as a "masterpiece of face-saving double-talk":[12]

> The Club's founder, Italian industrialist Aurelio Peccei, says that *Limits* was intended to jolt people from the comfortable idea that present growth trends could continue indefinitely. That done, he says, the Club could then seek ways to close the widening gap between rich and poor nations—inequities that, if they continue, could all too easily lead to famine, pollution and war.
>
> The Club's shift, Peccei says, is thus not so much a turnabout as part of an evolving [political] strategy.[13]

In an exceptionally candid statement, Peccei conceded to the *New York Times* in 1976 that "the *Limits to Growth* report had served its purpose of getting the world's attention focused on the ecological dangers of unplanned and uncontrolled population and industrial expansion."[14] If a lie helps the unenlightened glimpse the truth, so much the better.

The Club's report, unfounded as it was in science and economics, taught governments the world over that whipping up fear, even hysteria, over the fate of the planet provides an excellent excuse to enact myriad controls over the private use of natural resources. The meager publicity given to the

Club's recantation demonstrates that playing fast and loose with phantom numbers carries no real penalty. The original message of *Limits to Growth* was widely believed by a public that remained unaware of the devastating critiques of the study and of the Club of Rome's reversal.

Global 2000: *Same Old Same Old*

Just when the scientific community thought the final nail had been driven into the coffin of *Limits to Growth*, the corpse sat up and smiled. One year after the Club of Rome's renunciation of the conclusions of *Limits to Growth*, the Carter administration employed, under the auspices of the federal government, many of the *exact same people* who had worked on *Limits to Growth*, including Dennis and Donella Meadows, editors of the book, and Jay Forrester of MIT, who had done much of the modelling in the previous report. These thoroughly discredited retreads were given three years to prepare a *Global 2000 Report to the President* that would, in effect, be a government-sanctioned clone of *Limits to Growth*.

Also associated with the project were many lobbies and political organizations that had demonstrated passionate enthusiasm for federal-government control of land and resources: the Natural Resources Defense Council, Friends of the Earth, WorldWatch Institute, Environmental Action, National Wildlife Federation, World Wildlife Federation, Zero Population Growth, and the Nature Conservancy, among others. An appendix in *Global 2000* proudly claims *Limits to Growth* as an intellectual forebear; Aurelio Peccei is cited and praised in the opening passages of several chapters.

Work commenced on *Global 2000* in May 1977, barely months after the organizers of the Club of Rome project admitted publicly that science and economic forecasting had taken a back seat to the generation of propaganda in support of worldwide economic and social planning. Every bloated bureaucracy within the Beltway had its paws on the project: the Departments of Energy, Agriculture, Interior, State, and Commerce; the National Science Foundation; Environmental Protection Agency; NASA; the White House Office of Science and Technology; Federal Emergency Management Agency; and the CIA. These agencies—not all of them renowned for veracity and scrupulous honesty—could greatly expand their domains (and budgets) by convincing Americans that only Washington stood between the planet and catastrophe. The catastrophe didn't have to be real; it just had to be believed by enough people.

Predictably, *Global 2000*'s conclusions were just as stark as those of the discredited *Limits to Growth*. Completed in 1980, it asserted:

> If present trends continue, the world in 2000 will be more crowded, more polluted, less stable ecologically, and more vulnerable to disruption than the world we live in now. Serious stresses involving population, resources, and environment are clearly visible ahead. . . . Barring revolutionary advances in technology, life for most people on earth will be more precarious in 2000 than it is now . . . unless the nations of the world act decisively to alter current trends.[15]

"Decisively"—how many acts of cruelty and oppression have been committed under cover of that adverb? As a means of acting "decisively," the report recommended "the establishment by law of a permanent group in the Executive Office of the President to institutionalize the coordination of long-term global and holistic considerations of population, resources, environment, and their related issues."[16] Bland stuff, you say? In fact, such an office would become a permanent central economic planning board that would gather data on population, resources, etc., and then "plan" the economy on the basis of *Limits to Growth*-type analyses. Tyranny is no less so just because the tyrants claim to like fishes and trees and water. (Curious, though, isn't it, that most political environmentalists live in dirty, crowded Washington, D.C., or New York City rather than under Wyoming's open skies?)

In hindsight, *Global 2000*'s love affair with planning seems almost funny given the subsequent collapse of the planned economies of Eastern Europe and the Soviet Union. Nevertheless, as we'll discuss later, self-proclaimed global thinkers are still making grandiose—withal coercive—proposals to solve ecological problems. The impulse on the part of some to plan the lives and activities of others—to "perfect" human behavior—will likely never die.

Global 2000 garnered a tremendous amount of publicity: it was an "official" federal-government document prepared at the request of President Carter and given a lavish send-off. The propaganda barrage hit major newspapers, magazines, television, radio, and even the nation's schools, where the report was used as an "educational" tool. As two observers noted, "As far as published comment is concerned, *Global 2000* [was] almost universally accepted at face value, and accorded great respect."[17]

For all the hype and hoopla, *Global 2000* was no more credible than *Limits to Growth*. In his meticulous study of the report, economist Julian Simon concluded: "The facts . . . point in quite the opposite direction on every single important aspect of their prediction for which I could find any data at all."[18] Although *Global 2000* claimed to plot trends using "the long-term global data and models routinely employed by the federal agencies,"[19] in fact "the most striking aspect of the report is the absence of these very trend data."[20] The nightmarish projections of *Global 2000* turned out to bear not the stamp of objective science but were instead the prejudiced opinions or even the hunches of a small number of government employees.[21]

Simon did what the authors of *Global 2000* apparently did not take the time to do: he examined the trend data upon which the report's projections were supposed to be made. Simon found that any similarities between the projections and the data were strictly coincidental (see table 7.1).

Data were often ignored or fabricated. When questioned about *Global 2000*'s crucial projection of slow or negative income growth, one of the study's authors confessed: "I doubt that anyone knows where those income estimates come from."[22] *Global 2000*, like *Limits to Growth*, relied almost entirely on computer simulations even though decades, if not centuries, of real data were available. Quotes from political activists such as Paul Ehrlich, whose prediction track record is roughly equal to that of Jeanne Dixon, pepper the report.

Even a cursory examination of available data indicates that, contrary to the report, the United States is not becoming more polluted; life expectancy is not declining; energy prices are not rising; food is becoming more plentiful and cheaper; arable land continues to increase; and neither logic nor evidence supports the conjecture that population growth *per se* is necessarily a bad thing.

How can the government get away with passing off such shoddy work and patent nonsense as gospel truth? Simon answers this with another question: Who is to stop them? The government can publish whatever it wants. It faces no censor or panel of unbiased peer reviewers. Unlike private publishers, it is unconstrained by market forces; even a work of execrable quality can be hawked by its public-relations staffs. Simon relates, from personal experience:

TABLE 7.1
GLOBAL 2000 PROJECTIONS VS. REALITY

Projection	Reality
The U.S. will become more polluted	Both water and air quality have been improving
Life-expectancy growth rate will decline	Actual rate has increased at an increasing rate
Environment becoming "less stable"	No data offered in the study to support this claim
"Serious stresses" on resources	Long-run trends are all toward less scarcity or "stress" as reflected by lower resource prices
Energy prices will increase	Long-run trend is for lower prices and less scarcity
Food availability will grow slowly	Per capita food production had been growing twice as fast as projected
Food prices will double	Historical trend shows a two-century declining trend in real food prices
Significant loss of forests	*Global 2000* offered no data on forests
Overpopulation is catastrophic	No logic or evidence offered that population growth *per se* adversely affects net human welfare
Arable land will increase slowly	Arable land has continued to increase since Biblical times

SOURCE: Julian Simon, "Global Confusion, 1980: A Hard Look at the *Global 2000* Report," *Public Interest* 62 (Winter 1981), pp. 3–20.

An individual outside the government must have the stomach to get into a long-odds fight against an opposition that is widely presumed to be in the right because it is "official." He or she must also be willing to invest the time and energy knowing that the probability of reaching a wide audience is exceedingly slim, especially if the government report says things that are already widely believed. The very best scholar is likely to judge that it is more important to get on with his or her own work rather than try to act as a one-person truth squad.[23]

The iconoclastic Simon has performed that thankless role in much of his own research.[24] Most recently, he won a $10,000 wager with insect biologist and "no-growth" polemicist Paul Ehrlich, who bet that the real price of five important resources would increase over the decade of the 1980s. The price of all five resources actually declined, continuing a decades-long trend reflecting increasing resource abundance. Ehrlich, of course, is unfazed. Zealots always are. Like the Millerites, who predicted the Second Coming in 1843—then hastily revised that to 1844 once 1843 had passed uneventfully—Ehrlich is now warning that the U.S. population will shrink from 250 million to about 22.5 million before 1999 because of famine and "global warming."[25]

Global 2000: *Global Warming and Globaloney*

No sooner did the controversy over the claims of *Global 2000* scatter to the winds than many of the same eco-catastrophe theorists—in and out of government—began building a new series of models. This time the apocalypse-wreaking bogeyman was global warming. Among the things we could look forward to: palm trees would grow in Canada, tropical rain forests would become deserts, the ice caps would melt, coastal regions would be flooded, major crop-growing regions would experience recurrent droughts, and hurricanes would become more frequent and destructive.[26] The planet would be on the verge of environmental collapse, beyond even the ministrations of Superman.

Ambitious pols, eager to harvest the affluent green vote, gave grave speeches: Senators Al Gore (D-Tenn.) and Tim Wirth (D-Colo.) had their ghostwriters working overtime. The Environmental Protection Agency (EPA), reeling from the Anne Gorsuch-Burford scandal of the Reagan years, latched on to global warming. Perhaps the EPA's minions were motivated by genuine concern, but as the late economic journalist Warren Brookes pointed out, "Under a global warming scenario, the EPA would become the most powerful government agency on earth, involved in massive levels of economic, social, scientific and political spending and interference."[27] One needn't be a deep-dyed cynic to imagine how easy it would be for EPA bureaucrats to convince themselves that they could do well by doing good: if "protecting" the public from global warming meant expansion of one's own power and prestige, who could complain?

Global Warming Heats Up

Global warming centers around the climactic consequences of the "green-house effect." As explained in layman's terms by Warren Brookes:

> The earth's atmosphere does operate as a greenhouse. In addition to oxygen, nitrogen and water vapor, the atmosphere contains several gases that trap radiated heat, including methane and [carbon dioxide]. Carbon dioxide is essential not only to warmth but to vegetation. It is also essential to life in another way: Without its heat-containing effect the planet would freeze, like the atmospherically naked moon.[28]

For at least a century we have known that burning fossil fuels—coal, oil, and gas—increases the normal atmospheric content of carbon dioxide. This enhances the natural greenhouse effect and leads to a warming of the global climate. The "greenhouse effect" is nothing new: it has long been part of common knowledge.

Since carbon dioxide absorbs infrared radiation, its buildup impedes the escape of heat radiation from the earth's surface.[29] The greenhouse effect from *naturally occurring* carbon dioxide and water vapor has warmed the earth's surface for millions of years. The controversy concerns whether the nearly 30 percent increase in carbon dioxide that has occurred since the end of World War II calls for drastic action, that is, a sharp reduction in fossil-fuel use. The political environmentalists say so; they point to the dire consequences of rising planetary temperatures.

The postwar increase in carbon dioxide is due in about even measure to natural and man-made causes. The natural causes are the respiration of all living organisms and decaying vegetation, which is injected into the atmosphere by volcanoes and forest and grass fires.[30] The primary man-made source of carbon dioxide is the burning of fossil fuels.

Yet carbon dioxide is not the only (or even most important) greenhouse gas. Hydrocarbons and methane gas, also prevalent in the atmosphere, are derived from many sources. The largest source of greenhouse gases may well be termites, whose digestive activities "are responsible for about 50 billion tons of [carbon dioxide] and methane annually. This is 10 times more than the present world production of [carbon dioxide] from burning fossil fuel."[31]

Methane is produced largely by the odd troika of rice paddies, cattle, and oil-field operations. Another greenhouse gas is nitrous oxide, whose increased presence is mostly due to soil bacterial action promoted by the use of nitrogen fertilizers. Ozone from air pollution also contributes to the greenhouse effect, as do chlorofluorocarbons manufactured for use in refrigeration, air-conditioning, and industrial processes. Water vapor is by far the most prevalent greenhouse gas.[32] The large volume of natural greenhouse gases should make us pause before leaping onto the bandwagon of the global-warming theorists. Even if we gave EPA the guns and money to dictate a sharp reduction in the use of fossil fuels, there may not necessarily be a significant overall decline in greenhouse gases. The reduction would cost consumers and industries billions of dollars in return for . . . well, nothing measurable.[33] (Except a fattened campaign kitty for Senator Gore and his ilk.)

Is It Hot in Here, or Is It Just Me?

Opinion polls ought never to determine a scientific truth. Copernicus, after all, was not deterred by the consensus on the streets of Warsaw that the sun traveled around the earth. So we shouldn't be overly impressed that six in ten Americans believe that global warming is already occurring and will worsen. This doesn't make it so, but it is remarkable, given that before 1988 virtually no one but atmospheric scientists knew what on earth a greenhouse effect was. A well-orchestrated campaign by a number of (usually government-sponsored) scientists, activists, and politicians changed all that. The public came to believe, almost overnight, that a global environmental crisis impends and that the best way to head it off at the pass is to commission a federal-government posse and arm it with vast powers and unlimited money. A crucial moment in this climatic campaign occurred when NASA scientist James Hansen held court at a congressional hearing sponsored by Senator Al Gore in June 1988—smack in the middle of a nationwide summer heatwave.

Hansen, shrouded in the celestial glow of the beloved NASA, the one government agency that is admired by the citizenry, averred that he was "99 percent confident" that the greenhouse effect is already here. Global-warming modeller Steven Schneider, who in his 1976 book *The Genesis Strategy* predicted a coming ice age, thrilled to Hansen's testimony. A gleeful Schneider enthused: "Environmentalists loved it. Jim [Hansen] appeared on a dozen or more national television news programs."[34] The publicity-mongering Senator Gore knew he had a hot one on his hands: he and his staff on the Subcommittee on Science and Technology fed the media a savory if un-nutritious diet of scare stories for weeks. Famine, drought, mass death: the TV boys loved it. We weren't experiencing just another hot spell: we were suffering from global warming. It was like taking part in our very own science-fiction movie.

Eventually, the cameras moved on. The sweltering Washington summer ended. A few spoilsports reminded Hansen and Gore that we'd had harshly cold winters in 1978 and 1982. Then—as if Mother Nature was angry at *Time* magazine for deeming an "overheated" earth as its "Man of the Year"—Alaska froze through its worst cold in history. Temperature records were set in more than twenty locations; in Fairbanks, the mercury dipped to a numbing −75 degrees Fahrenheit. The severe cold snap soon covered the entire nation, breaking temperature records in Texas, Florida, and most other states. Senator Gore clammed up till the snow melted.

Scientific Déjà Vu

As with *Limits to Growth* and *Global 2000*, the wild claims made by some of the global-warming modellers drew immediate and fierce criticism by the scientific community, the vast majority of which was "outraged" by Hansen's testimony.[35] Reluctantly, many scientists emerged from their research labs and into the messy, fractious world of public-policy debate. Science would not be further politicized without a fight.

The subsequent examination of actual temperature records, as opposed to easily manipulated computer models, showed no evidence of global warming; indeed, a global cooling may even be taking place. (Historically, ice ages have occurred about every eleven thousand years; we're due for another any century now.)

Hansen predicted to the rapt Gore committee that "1988 would be the warmest year on record, unless there is some remarkable, improbable cooling in the remainder of the year."[36] The record books were safe. At the very moment Hansen was sweating through his remarks, the eastern tropical Pacific Ocean underwent a sharp cooling of seven degrees, courtesy of a mysterious, yet to be understood phenomenon called "La Niña" (not to be confused with "El Niño," or warming). La Niña caused a slight reduction in global temperatures, but, alas, Hansen's computer models do not take sea temperatures into account. This raises an interesting question: how can a computer model predict a "global" temperature change while ignoring 73 percent of the globe? Hansen's theatrical presentation was deemed by most scientists to be far less valuable as a predictive tool—not to mention less entertaining—than the Channel Seven Accu-Weather forecast.

Confronted by a large and growing body of climatic temperature data and analysis by reputable scientists, the global-warming theorists revised their forecasts downward. Whereas in 1988 they foresaw a temperature rise of between 4.5 and 6.0 degrees Celcius, they are now somewhat timorously projecting an increase of between 0.7 and 1.5 degrees. Other scientists—the ones who were right the first time—are skeptical about the possibility of *any* temperature rise.

A new study of worldwide ocean temperatures since 1850 by MIT climatologists Reginald Newell, Jane Hsiung, and Wu Zhongxiang concludes that "there appears to have been little or no global warming over the past century."[37] Oceans, which cover three fourths of the earth, are a preponderant influence on global climate conditions. These researchers found that the average ocean temperature in the 1980s—a relatively warm decade—was only an eighth of a degree centigrade higher than the average ocean temperature of the 1860s. Ocean temperatures are virtually unchanged since the 1940s. Since most of the buildup in carbon dioxide has taken place over the last half century, the global-warming hypothesis is cast in serious doubt.

Three of the world's most respected climatologists (Thomas Karl, Kirby Hanson, and George Maul of the National Oceanographic and Atmospheric Administration) recently reviewed the best climate data available anywhere in the world—that for the contiguous United States. They concluded that "there is no statistically significant evidence of an . . . increase in annual temperature or change in annual precipitation for the contiguous U.S. 1895–1987." The researchers continued, "If there is a greenhouse effect, you can't find it in the U.S. records."[38] Temperature data from other parts of the world are incomplete and fragmentary, but the law of large numbers[39] suggests a sample as large as the continental U.S. may accurately reflect global temperature trends.

Also contradicting the global-warming theory is the fact that most of the twentieth-century's warming occurred by 1938, well before the steep rise in carbon-dioxide concentration. From 1938 to 1970 temperatures *plunged* so sharply that a new ice age was being widely forecast, even by Steven Schneider, father—or at least chief guru—of global warming.[40]

Perhaps most significant are studies that document a relative rise in *nocturnal* temperatures in the United States over the past sixty years, even while daytime temperatures remained constant or declined.[41] The consequences of this, environmental scientist Patrick Michaels of the University of Virginia has pointed out, are actually beneficial: a longer growing season, fewer frosts, and no increase in soil evaporation.[42]

Global Warming: A Word on Its Behalf?!

Few scientists have completely dismissed the global-warming thesis: a warming could conceivably be taking place, and perhaps it will be verified by better data at some future date.

But let's consider a startling possibility: might global warming be a mixed, or even substantial, *blessing*? Agriculturalists believe that an increase in atmospheric carbon dioxide (which is, after all, plant food) will cause plants to grow for longer periods of time and require less water. Warmer nights will lengthen growing seasons; heavier precipitation will foster plant growth. (Of course it would also boost the number of baseball rainouts, pushing more teams indoors, to domed stadia, effectively killing the national pastime.) New research has revealed that warmer temperatures are even likely to make hurricanes less severe.[43]

The Intergovernmental Panel on Climate Change, a United Nations affiliate, recently calculated the effects of a doubling of carbon dioxide in the atmosphere and the subsequent raising of temperatures by two degrees centigrade.[44] The results? Food output in the United States would increase by 15 percent, or nearly $2 billion per year; U.S. water resources would rise by 9 percent, or $30 billion to $50 billion per year; and U.S. forest volume would increase by approximately 10 percent, adding a potential value of more than $500 billion. On the debit side, a doubling of atmospheric carbon dioxide (and a resultant twenty-inch sea rise) could cost us $25 billion per year in damage or destruction of shorelines. By the panel's admittedly rough utilitarian reckoning, the net benefits of global warming for the ex-Soviet Union, China, Europe, Australia, and South America were comparable.

We are not being Pollyannaish. Only the most hubristic fool would advocate the artificial heating of the earth's surface as some kind of grand climatological experiment. Nevertheless, the rapidity with which political environmentalists painted, in nightmarish hues, what appears to be a confoundingly complex—perhaps even beneficial—phenomenon is alarming.

Lost in the Masquerade

The threatening specter of global warming gives interest groups effective rhetorical cover as they promote their same old agendas. These groups are legion; they range from Luddite to techno-freak, from the hardest-nosed businessman to the bleedingest heart. For example, proponents of nuclear energy see a chance to refurbish their Chernobyl-tainted public image; natural-gas producers see an opportunity to gain market share over coal; grant-grubbing scientists see it as the key that unlocks foundation budgets; supranational civil servants and New World Orderlies believe it may grease the channels of foreign aid; and last and never least are the politicians, who will bend, fold, spindle, and mutilate anything or anybody in the quest for votes. Warren Brookes assayed one such specimen:

> Senator Albert Gore . . . seems determined to run his next presidential campaign at least in part on climate change, saving Mother Earth. Every year, at least one-sixth of the U.S. is classified by the government's Palmer Index as being in drought. Even though that index overstates the case, Gore could be looking at some very big political states—maybe California or Texas or Iowa—where his message will resonate with farmers and business. All he has to do is wait for a warm spell, and capitalize on what mathematicians call noise in the statistics.[45]

Not only did government promote, subsidize, and flack for the dubious global-warming theory, it has also actively prevented the American public from gaining access to information that might contradict the theory. Consider the British television producer Hilary Lawson and his 1990 documentary "The Greenhouse Conspiracy." Lawson, a self-professed layman, set out to do a program on the threat global warming poses to mankind. He had no reason to doubt the conventional wisdom; he took the government scientists and their magpies in the media at their word. But after interviewing the world's leading climatologists, Lawson reversed the message of his documentary: "I learned that the only problem with the theory of global warming is that there is mounting evidence that it is untrue."[46]

"The Greenhouse Conspiracy" presented each claim of the global-warming theorists and stacked it up against the evidence. The verdict was a clear "not proven"; indeed, for the first time television viewers heard leading scientists explain why they thought global warming was at best a flawed theory and at worst bunk.

"The Greenhouse Conspiracy" won rave reviews in Britain. Lawson, knowing of the transatlantic Public Broadcasting Service's fondness for British imports, offered the program to PBS. The government-funded network rejected "The Greenhouse Conspiracy" because it was "too one-sided." Shortly thereafter, PBS aired "After the Warming," a breathless strip of celluloid advocacy that the *Wall Street Journal* charged "more resembled science fiction than fact."[47] In "After the Warming," global warming was taken as a given; the only issue was how devastating it would be. It taught the "lesson" that only a radical disruption of industrial production could avert catastrophe.

The Public Broadcasting Service, a government-funded and -controlled television network, rarely carries programs that argue—or even hint—that PBS's benefactors in Washington should be stripped, or even pruned, of power. So it's no surprise that it rejected a program presenting in lay terms state-of-the-art knowledge about global warming by the world's top climatologists. Nor is it surprising that it carried a hackneyed fable setting forth the crumbling theory that global warming is inevitable unless we delegate more responsibilities to large governmental organizations. The people at PBS are no fools; they'll not bite the hand that feeds them. What is dismaying is the way in which ostensibly *private* news gatherers fall into line without government ever cracking the whip. *Time* magazine has gone so far as to assure its journalists that it is all right to become environmental activists, even if it means ignoring scientific facts.[48] The press seems to have lost the biting, skeptical edge it developed in the wake of Watergate and Vietnam; where once the Fourth Estate harbored lions, today it is the domain of pussycats.

The Ozone Hole Panic

In April 1991, EPA Administrator William Reilly announced that a NASA satellite had observed the rapid depletion of stratospheric ozone—the result, in his opinion, of continued use of man-made chlorofluorocarbons. The complaisant cheerleaders of the media gave Reilly good headlines:

"Ozone Loss Over U.S. is Found to be Twice as Bad as Predicted: EPA Chief Says Rate is Stunning and Disturbing" (*New York Times*); "Discovery of Faster Depletion of Ozone Sparks New Worry on Use of Chemicals" (*Wall Street Journal*); "Ozone Layer Over U.S. Thinning Swiftly: Study Indicates Skin Cancer Deaths Could Double in 40 Years" (*Washington Post*).

Journalistic ejaculations over the supposed depletion of the earth's ozone layer—and a subsequent outbreak of skin cancer—have become drearily commonplace. The reporters and editors who work on these stories seldom have the background to judge their accuracy: the press releases of government science officials are treated as incontestable truths.

Reilly's ghostwriters appear to have mistaken the natural variation in the global ozone layer (a correlative of the eleven-year sunspot cycle) for a permanent depletion. As two scientists noted, "Global ozone has large and irregular natural variations, ranging from seasonal swings of some 10 percent to 50 percent within a few weeks' time to an eleven-year variation of up to 5 percent associated with sunspot activity. These fluctuations make it extremely difficult to extract a long-term trend of only a few tenths of a percent per year."[49] Moreover, the total ozone produced within each eleven-year sunspot cycle is different, and the NASA satellite data cover only *one* sunspot cycle. Espying a "trend" of any kind from this changeable data is nigh impossible.

The ozone hole keeps widening in the public mind; it stretches every time a Reilly faces a battery of microphones and fuels gloomy speculation about cancer epidemics and other unpleasant effects. But as Dixy Lee Ray, former chairman of the Atomic Energy Commission and past Democratic governor of Washington, has stated, "the term ozone 'hole' is misleading, since it persists for only a few weeks. The Antarctic ozone 'hole' grew during the early 1980s, becoming large in 1985, smaller in 1986, and reaching its greatest size in 1987. In 1988 the 'hole' did not appear as expected. It was finally discovered—only 15 percent as large as predicted and displaced over the ocean."[50]

Taking a snapshot satellite photograph of the ozone "hole" at a point in time and basing predictions on that photo alone is irresponsible. Basing a forecast of a worldwide skin-cancer epidemic on such a photograph would be the scientific equivalent of prophesying forty days of continuous rain just because the last time you looked outside it was raining.

There are many other uncertainties above and beyond the natural fluctuation in ozone levels. As Governor Ray explains:

The changes in the amount of ozone appear to be related to complex chloride chemistry and the presence of nitrous oxide. Although there is widespread belief that the necessary chloride ion comes from chlorofluorocarbons (CFCs) this has not been unequivocally established. . . . Since . . . 300 million tons of chlorine reach the atmosphere each year through evaporation of sea water alone [world production of CFCs peaked at 1.1 million tons per year] we cannot be sure where the stratospheric chloride comes from, and whether humans have any effect on it.[51]

As far as we know, there is not a cancerous hole eating away at the earth's ozone layer and opening the floodgate for a tidal wave of excessive ultraviolet radiation. However, no sense of uncertainty restrains the eco-catastrophe theorists, ever ready to prey on the rational scientific ignorance of the general public. In the immortal (and perhaps immoral) words of Steven Schneider, "We have to offer up scary scenarios, make simplified, dramatic statements, and make little mention of any doubts we may have."

While the Schneiders dissemble, momentum builds toward a regulated economy in the holy name of the environment. Government-mandated reductions in the use of chlorofluorocarbons, for instance, would cost businesses tens of billions of dollars to change or replace capital equipment that is associated with the creation of CFCs. And to what end? To defeat what may very well be a chimera?

As with global warming, the data lend themselves to a multitude of often contradictory interpretations. Hugh W. Ellsaesser of the Lawrence Livermore National Laboratory even suggests that increased exposure to ultraviolet radiation has benefits as well as the indisputable dangers:

Ultraviolet light converts oils in the outer covering of most air-breathing vertebrates into . . . vitamin D . . . which is essential for the assimilation of calcium into skeletal bones. Vitamin D deficiency in the growing years leads to rickets . . . [or] may result in a light skeleton leading to . . . bone fractures as calcium loss occurs in life's later years. . . . Since exposure to higher levels of ultraviolet would presumably lead to stronger bones . . . a decrease in ozone and an increase in ultraviolet flux may well constitute a net health benefit.[52]

Further confusing the situation is the fact that measurements taken at the surface of the earth indicate that the total amount of ozone in the atmosphere may be *increasing* while ultraviolet light reaching the earth's surface has *decreased* each year for the last few years.[53] If the ozone-catastrophe theorists were correct, the opposite would be true.[54]

Scientists can and should have vigorous, honest disagreements; science demands intellectual rigor and challenges to orthodoxy. But the usual give-and-take of scientific dispute is corrupted when government becomes involved. When the EPA administrator relies on ambiguous data to forecast 200,000 additional deaths from skin cancer over the next half century, his message is splashed across the front pages of the nation's newspapers. Handsome newsreading anchorpeople give his alarmist projections just the right intonation. (Or in Peter Jennings's case, that irritating arched eyebrow.) Is it coincidental that Reilly's fiefdom will benefit from his forecasts? Is it ignorance or something more sinister that motivates him to ignore several well-established scientific facts: measured ozone concentrations have *decreased*, as has measured ultraviolet radiation; the amount of time spent in the sun, rather than the mere intensity of ultraviolet radiation, accounts for increased skin-cancer rates; and the increased risk of skin cancer from a 5 percent depletion of stratospheric ozone, which causes (in theory) a 10 percent increase in ultraviolet intensity, is equivalent to moving sixty miles south.

That Reilly is unmoved to mention these facts is hardly shocking. The failure of our vaunted free press to do so should disturb every independent American.

Acid Rain and Fish: The One That Won't Go Away

There are plenty of good reasons to cut down on the amount of sulfur and other pollutants that pour into the atmosphere, but to use acid rain as an excuse and to intimate that if [sulfur dioxide] is eliminated then acid rain will disappear is not only simplistic and unscientific, it is grossly misleading as well. Yet that is what the federal government has done.
    —DIXY LEE RAY[55]

The acid-rain provisions of the 1990 Clean Air Act Amendments forced the electric-power industry to reduce sulfur-dioxide emissions by investing more heavily than it already has in smokestack scrubbers.[56] By even the most conservative estimates, this mandate will cost at least $7 billion per year in higher electricity rates, which the utility monopolies will cheerfully pass on to consumers. The Tennessee Valley Authority alone will spend over $1.2 billion; TVA bills are expected to increase by more than 25 percent, crippling many manufacturers in a region that is not exactly El Dorado.

"Acid rain" entered the political vocabulary in the 1970s; by the early 1980s, it had become an almost deific locution. President Carter called it one of the two most serious environmental problems of this century; it was blamed for the depletion of game fisheries in the Adirondacks and Nova Scotia and for damage to forests and buildings. Acid rain poisoned U.S.-Canadian relations; the Canadian government insisted that emissions from Midwestern power plants were destroying Canadian lakes and forests. Although evidence linking smokestack emissions from Ohio to dying lakes in New England and northern New York was on the scant side, many government environmentalists were swollen with certitude. Senator Robert T. Stafford (R-Vt.), chairman of the Committee on Environment and Public Works (and the most powerful Senate player on the issue), opened a 1984 hearing with this declamation:

> I believe that acid rain exists because dozens of highly regarded scientists have told this committee that acid rain is real.
>
> I believe that emissions from polluting smokestacks in the Midwest contribute to the acid rain that falls in New England and other parts of the Northeast because study after study has demonstrated that is the fact to be true beyond a reasonable doubt.
>
> I believe that lakes and streams are, without any question, being damaged by acid rain because there is no longer any genuine scientific dispute over that circumstance.
>
> Scientist after scientist and study after study have all come to the same conclusion.[57]

Senator Stafford turned out to be wrong. And therein lies one of the great unreported stories of our day.

The acid-rain issue germinated for about fifteen years before President Bush's Clean Air Act legislation called for a 50-percent reduction in sulfur-dioxide emissions by the year 2000. This time and effort was not completely wasted: the concerns that acid-rain legislation is intended to address are legitimate. Hundreds of lakes and streams in the Northeast and Canada have lost most or all of their fish over the past half century. Red spruce and other trees are dying in Vermont and North Carolina. Many fisheries in the Adirondacks are in very poor condition and getting worse.

But government's cure for these ills is disastrously wrong. Acid rain may not even be the culprit. So determined a blue-ribbon, ten-year, $600 million study commissioned by Congress and described by some as the most extensive scientific study ever.[58] According to Dr. Edward C. Krug, a soil chemist who participated in this National Acid Precipitation Assessment Project (NAPAP),

> Surveys of lakes in New England and New York show much less acidity than anticipated, while other studies show that acid rain has very little effect on surface water acidity. Perhaps most intriguing, studies of the fossil records in lake sediments reveal that many lakes that are acidic today have been highly acidic for centuries, except for several decades in the late 19th century and early 20th century when they were unnaturally alkaline.[59]

Memories of plentiful trout and salmon in Northeastern lakes and streams that are now fishless, Krug argues, date back to a "period of ecological aberration."[60] Numerous lakes and streams in the Adirondacks and Nova Scotia that are naturally acidic became more alkaline for several decades in the late nineteenth and early twentieth centuries due to the widespread cutting of trees and the burning of stumps by the lumber industry. Such cutting and burning reduced the acidity of the forest floor; the less acidic soil runoff made it possible for species of trout and salmon to survive. (What a grand irony: the despoiling timber industry was a godsend to Northeastern fish!) When the forests grew back, the land—and eventually the lakes and streams—returned to their naturally acidic condition; the fish population died off and these bodies of water remain to this day crystal clear because they are so void of life.

Most of the lakes in the Northeast are not particularly acidic, even though rain and snow in these areas are substantially more acidic than in other regions. Krug notes, "Rain over the Ohio Valley and Adirondacks has a pH of 4.2, while that over Nova Scotia has a pH of 4.6 to 4.8— compared with a pH of 5.0 for normal rainfall over forested areas" (a lower pH indicates higher acidity).[61]

Few American lakes are acidic, and very few—if any—got that way because of acid rain. The NAPAP study found that only 240 of New England's and New York's more than 7,000 lakes were "acid dead," which means they had a pH of 5.0 or lower. In the whole Eastern United States there are only 630 acid lakes, constituting 35,000 of the approximately 200 million acres of water in the East, or less than one fiftieth of one percent. More than half of those 35,000 acres are in Florida, where the phenomenon labeled "acid rain" is, all admit, rare.[62]

Both acid and alkaline lakes are natural phenomena; they were created and persist quite without human intervention.[63] The defiling hand of man is a far less likely cause of acidity in Adirondack lakes than is Mother Nature:

> The Adirondack lakes in question are in poorly buffered and, therefore, naturally acidic watersheds. Their rocks are poor in lime-like substances; their watersheds are mantled by highly acidic, very thick peaty forest floors, and leaching of water through the soil produces a low-nutrient environment where acid-producing trees and plants, such as sphagnum mosses, are common.[64]

The relationship between acid rain and acidic lakes and streams is thrown further into doubt by the existence of highly acidic bodies of water in regions with *no* acid precipitation. NAPAP found that in areas of Tasmania and Australia, blessedly unvisited by acid rain, highly acidic lakes and streams abound. "Indeed the magnitude of acidic surface waters in areas without acid rain dwarfs that of areas supposedly 'devastated' by acid rain," writes Dr. Krug.[65]

Nor is there evidence of widespread damage to Northeastern forests. The U.S. Forest Service's own statistics pronounce these forests to be the most robust in the country, acid rain notwithstanding. There is a very real possibility that acid rain may have damaged red spruce trees in high altitudes, but these trees represent less than 1 percent of Eastern forests, and even in this case there is an element of uncertainty. According to professors Arthur H. Johnson and Samuel B. McLaughlin, who have studied red spruce forest decline, "There is no indication now that acidic decomposition is an important factor in red spruce decline. . . . The abrupt and synchronous changes in ring width and wood density patterns across such a wide area seem more likely to be related to climate than to air pollution."[66]

The NAPAP Cover-up

You'll note that the NAPAP study to which we've adverted was financed by the federal government. Does this gainsay our thesis? Is government really an intrepid seeker of the truth? Not really. The NAPAP scientists, unbought and unbossed, committed the glorious sin of independence.

Congress, the EPA, and President Bush ("the Environmental President," said his lips) assumed that the study would duly and dully endorse the inevitable acid-rain provisions they were about to pass in the revised Clean Air Act. When the initial findings of the study were published, the project's director was pressured to resign. A decade of scientific study, calling on the expertise of seven hundred scientists, had produced results that were politically incorrect. Congress, which had commissioned the study ten years earlier, had expected the world's finest soil, water, and forest scientists from Yale, Dartmouth, University of Pennsylvania, Oak Ridge National Laboratory, and other distinguished institutions to give their credentialed stamp of approval to new regulatory schemes. When NAPAP refused to play the rubber stamp, it was virtually ignored, even by journalists who love to apply to their craft the adjective "investigative." *Washington Post* reporter Howard Kurtz, curious as to why this major story was being all but ignored, asked his *Post* colleague Michael Weisskopf to explain. Kurtz wrote, "He said many people involved in the acid rain debate told him it had little news value."[67]

Senator Daniel Patrick Moynihan (D-N.Y.), the original sponsor of the bill that gave birth to NAPAP, responded with characteristic integrity. "It's good news to know you don't have a devastating problem," he told CBS-TV's "60 Minutes."[68] Moynihan's Senate chums, however, were crestfallen. A "devastating problem" would be license to legislate, to spend, to order other peoples' lives for them. But without the public *perception* of a problem, passing major pieces of legislation is much more difficult. For its part, the EPA did its best to undermine the NAPAP study. According to press critic Terry Eastland, agency officials tried to smear the reputation of Dr. Krug, claiming that he was "on the fringes of environmental science and policy making" and that he possessed "limited scientific credibility even in the limited area of surface water acidification."[69]

The NAPAP study was completed before passage of the 1990 Clean Air Act Amendments, but it received only a one-hour hearing before a small subcommittee. The media virtually ignored it. The exception, "60 Minutes," aired its segment *after* the Clean Air Act Amendments had already been passed. The possibility that the acid-rain provisions will dirty the environment and cost thousands of Americans their jobs went unexplored by the kept poodles of the Fourth Estate. So did the prospect of mitigating the effects of acid rain by an annual expenditure of $500,000, as opposed to the $10 billion per year the Clean Air Act Amendments will cost. The NAPAP scientists determined that

> a much less expensive and more effective solution is to do what farmers and gardeners do with acid soil: add lime. . . . A NAPAP study estimates that all Adirondack lakes and ponds more acidic than pH 5.7 can be limed for $170,000 per year. Extrapolating this study to the entire Northeast, all acid lakes in New England and New York could be limed for under $500,000 per year.[70]

Of course this solution has a problem, at least from a politician's point of view: it works. It obviates the need for further legislation, further tax revenues, and further powers bestowed upon what is already a bureaucracy of frightful corpulence, the Environmental Protection Agency.

The Toxic Terror

Few government press releases are such surefire attention-grabbers as Official Reports declaring that something we eat, drink, or breathe causes cancer. Savvy activists—humorist P. J. O'Rourke calls them "health Nazis"—learned years ago that scare stories lead off the evening news and become a staple on the midafternoon talk shows. People fear cancer as they fear no other disease: environmental bills are best sold in the guise of anti-cancer legislation.

For twenty years there has been a political assault on uncountable man-made chemicals and substances, an assault the distinguished epidemiologist Elizabeth Whelan calls "toxic terrorism."[71] "The promoters of toxic terrorism," writes Dr. Whelan, "seem to imply that we must go back to methods of the good old days of the early 1930s, before the use of chemical fertilizers, pesticides, synthetic fibers, and plastics, etc., came into being."[72]

This assault on modern technology and medicine rests upon six contentions that have almost attained the status of conventional wisdom:

1. America is being poisoned by chemicals and radioactivity.

2. Our country's health has never been worse and is threatening to deteriorate even further.

3. Big business is responsible for the environmental nightmare and cares not at all about what it is doing, concerned only with its short-term profit margin.

4. Little people (like you and me) are the victims of this corporate greed and toxic crime.

5. This current and future wave of disease and death is the ultimate price we pay for technology and the "good life."

6. New and complex chemicals are poisons and must be either eliminated or highly regulated. The death-dealing technology must be stopped *at any cost*.[73]

Dr. Whelan laments that the purveyors of this crackpot wisdom "have managed to convince the American public that there is nothing but bad news about health and the environment in this country and that American industry is the culprit."[74]

Pollution and other environmental contaminations can certainly cause severe public-health problems. But politicized health-science professionals have exaggerated or fabricated the health threats of man-made substances while virtually ignoring many of the far more dangerous *natural* carcinogens and harmful substances. The "America is poisoned" movement seems less interested in protecting public health than in condemning capitalism. By deception and the dishonest use of science, a cadre of activists has secured the restriction or banning of many substances whose benefits far exceed their potential hazards—if there are any hazards at all.

Volumes have been written on the subject of misguided regulation of toxic substances, but two striking examples will illustrate how government has manipulated the public perception of the health hazards associated with certain man-made substances.[75]

The Asbestos Scare

In 1978 the government-funded National Cancer Institute and the National Institute of Environmental Health Sciences issued a mimeographed report with no listed authors entitled "Estimates of the Fraction of Cancer Incidence in the United States Attributable to Occupational Factors."[76] Among the occupational carcinogens listed was asbestos, which the report claimed would be responsible for a remarkable two million premature cancer deaths over the coming three decades; previous estimates put the number at two thousand. Joseph Califano, who was then the Secretary of Health, Education and Welfare, extrapolated (in a mysterious way) from the report that "17 percent of all cancer deaths in the U.S. every year will be associated with previous exposure to asbestos."[77] Califano's baseless prediction, made at an AFL-CIO convention, was a boon to the Occupational Safety and Health Administration (OSHA), which had been the object of widespread ridicule for its nosy inspections of toilets in the workplace. Now that a *real* danger had been found, OSHA might finally take its rightful place in the regulatory sun.

Paranoia struck deep. Asbestos panic swept the land. The Manville Corporation, the nation's largest producer of asbestos, went bankrupt after establishing a "settlement trust" that was expected to pay out over $2.5 billion over the next twenty years. In 1990 EPA Administrator William Reilly signed the industry's death warrant by banning virtually all uses of asbestos by 1997 (and many of them by 1993). The EPA has also ordered that asbestos be removed from all public buildings, including over forty-five thousand public schools. Again, Washington acts as judge, jury, and executioner. Its minions do the research, publish the results, and then it bases coercive laws on its own findings. This is quite different from the situation of any other scientific publisher in the land.

These bans were obviously motivated by concern for public health. But we are not being unduly cynical to point out that powerful interests not heretofore noted for their solicitude for public health also benefitted. As *Forbes* comments: "Fear of asbestos has created a $3 billion-a-year industry for lawyers, consultants, smart real estate developers—and especially for the so-called asbestos abatement contractors who get paid a lot of money to rip asbestos out of buildings and bury it in landfills."[78]

Asbestos occupies a prominent spot on the federal government's "Official List" of poisonous substances; American taxpayers are paying tens of billions of dollars to have it removed from schools and other buildings. And yet a nagging question persists: was the 1978 report that led to the ban unfounded?

The anonymous report was never published and never peer-reviewed; it went straight from the nether regions of the government bureaucracy to the rouged lips of Tom Brokaw. It was accepted without demurral by the tabby cats of the press, who've since been slow to catch on to the powerful critiques—if not condemnations—of the study by some of the world's top epidemiologists. Cancer researchers Richard Doll and Richard Peto have written that the 1978 report was "so grossly in error that no argument based on [it], even loosely, should be taken seriously." Doll and Peto conclude that the unknown authors of the study probably wrote it "for political, rather than for scientific, purposes."[79] Mr. Califano's OSHA-pleasing bombshell at the AFL-CIO convention lends credence to this charge.

Dr. Richard Gee, a professor of medicine at Yale, has written in the *New England Journal of Medicine* that "the basis for this fear [of exposure to asbestos] is unreal, not founded in reality, a gross overreaction that's high in emotional content." Dr. Gee continues, "There is no evidence that environmental exposure to asbestos is a public health hazard."[80] Readily available statistics support these contentions: the risk of dying prematurely because of exposure to asbestos is less than the risk of being hit by lightning or swept away by a hurricane.[81] But cancer, and the fear thereof, remain a superb bogeyman.

There is good reason to fear asbestos, but not the kind that the average person ever comes into contact with. There are two different types of asbestos: chrysotile, found naturally in the United States, which accounts for 95 percent of all asbestos used; and crocodolite, found only in South Africa. Crocodolite is extremely dangerous. It has fibers that are small enough to penetrate the air sacs of the lungs and, once taken in, cannot be eliminated. They are truly deadly.[82]

Diseases such as asbestosis and mesothelioma are generally caused by breathing crocodolite fibers; chrysotile is benign. As Dixy Lee Ray writes:

> This is amply illustrated by the lack of asbestosis and lung cancer among Canadian asbestos miners and their families. Similarly, near San Francisco . . . there exists about 16 square miles of bare rock containing 50 percent chrysotile asbestos. Although the local people have been drinking chrysotile-rich water and breathing chrysotile-rich air for lifetimes, there is no heightened lung cancer incidence and certainly no cancer epidemic in that area of California.[83]

In 1990 the same year that Administrator Reilly announced a ban on asbestos, the EPA released a major study of the health effects of asbestos that confirms what much of the scientific community has known all along: "The asbestos fiber levels indoors were no more dangerous than the outdoor levels."[84] And there is no evidence that the outdoor levels are dangerous to one's health. Despite this admission, the EPA plunges on with its asbestos-banning policies; school boards across the country keep ripping asbestos out of their buildings. The cost of asbestos removal in California schools alone will exceed $1 billion; to rid our country's offices of this substance may cost $200 billion.[85]

Ironically, this policy of asbestos removal is likely to cause real health problems. The air in school rooms measured before asbestos removal contains about .00009 fibers per cubic centimeter; after removal there is typically a forty-thousand-fold increase, to twenty to forty fibers per cubic centimeter. This higher level may persist for years.[86] What's worse, the asbestos may be replaced by fiberglass or rock wool, both of which are more carcinogenic than chrysotile asbestos.

The best solution would appear to be to just leave the asbestos alone, perhaps covering it with a good coat of paint. "But we can't expect OSHA or the EPA to know that," says Dixy Lee Ray, for "our government agencies have to create crises and interfere in our lives to feel needed."[87] Indeed, EPA and its Administrator Reilly seem utterly unaffected by the mounting evidence that the asbestos scare was as baseless a panic as the one that followed Orson Welles's 1930s radio play "War of the Worlds." The agency line is expressed by Charles Elkins, director of the Office of Toxic Substances: "I would agree that in many cases removal is the wrong thing to do. It is a mistake for people to overreact. But it is also a mistake to say that asbestos is not a problem."[88] How's that for a mealy-mouthed mea culpa?

The Great Alar Scam

Nature produces far more pesticides than are manufactured by man. According to the renowned University of California at Berkeley biochemist Dr. Bruce Ames, author of the famed Ames Test for measuring carcinogens, "We are ingesting about 10,000 times more natural than synthetic pesticides."[89] Dr. Robert Scheuplein, head of the U.S. Food and Drug Administration's Office of Toxicological Sciences, adds that "about 98 percent of the cancer risk in foods occurs naturally."[90] Less than one tenth of one percent of all cancer risks from food can be traced to synthetic pesticides. Toxicologists know this. So do most other scientists. Yet political environmentalists and their allies in government resolutely ignore these incontrovertible facts while waging a fierce campaign to ban synthetic pesticides. In their view, anything man-made is suspect if not lethal, while everything natural is benign. This is more than misanthropy—it is downright life-threatening.

Synthetic pesticides have increased crop yields enormously, made our food substantially disease-free, and helped our agriculture industry thrive. Yet in the popular mind, they poison the food we eat and the children we raise. Why the misconception?

Consider what *Reader's Digest* called "the great apple scare" of 1990. In February 1990, CBS-TV's "60 Minutes" broadcast a shocking exposé of how cancer-causing chemicals sprayed on fruits and vegetables were "putting all of us—particularly our children—at risk."[91] The show, traditionally a fixture in Nielsen's Top Ten, was seen by tens of millions of Americans; parents were understandably alarmed. Why hadn't they been told about this before letting their kids eat apples?

They hadn't been told about it because the report was based on an unpublished, non-peer-reviewed study by the Natural Resources Defense Council. The NRDC had previously announced its long-term objective of eliminating *all* man-made pesticides. As part of that campaign, it claimed that Alar, a growth-enhancing substance applied mainly to apple trees, was causing "as many as 5,300 children to contract cancer from their preschool exposure" to the chemical. Ed Bradley of "60 Minutes" fell for this hook, line, and sinker, announcing on the air that Alar is "the most potent cancer-causing agent in our food supply."[92]

Again, the media's credulity was astonishing. The *Los Angeles Times*'s headline blared: "Preschoolers Face Intolerable Risk from Pesticides," while *USA Today*'s front-page story was "Fear: Are We Poisoning Our Children?" Meryl Streep and other Hollywood celebrities not theretofore acknowledged as toxicologists made the talk-show circuit, appearing on "Donahue" and "Today" and, finally, before the klieg lights of a publicity-hungry congressional committee.

Panic set in. Apples and apple products were taken off grocery-store shelves as though they were bottles of strychnine. Concerned parents flooded doctors' offices. One distraught mother even inquired if it was safe to pour apple juice down the sink. Sales of apples plummeted as the industry lost over $100 million. All of this without a shred of evidence that Alar was the least bit hazardous.

How Alar Became Alarming

How did we reach that preposterous point? In the early 1980s the NRDC began its crusade against farm chemicals. It found a sympathetic ear in William Ruckelshaus, who took the agency's helm in 1983 and was eager to burnish the EPA's image. Under Ruckelshaus, Alar was put up for "special review," meaning that the EPA regarded it as potentially dangerous. In August 1985 the EPA abruptly announced that the cancer risk of Alar was so great that it should be banned.

This was *before* the EPA's own panel of scientific experts, composed of distinguished scientists nominated by the National Science Foundation and the National Institutes of Health, had even reviewed Alar. When the Scientific Advisory Panel finally met, and the EPA presented its case, the panel decided *unanimously* that there was no scientific basis for believing that Alar posed a health hazard to anyone. The EPA tried to intimidate the panel into reconsidering, unsuccessfully.[93] So the agency commissioned tests in which doses of daminozide (Alar) were injected into mice. When *all* the tests failed to produce tumors in the mice, the EPA ordered the researchers to quadruple the "maximum dose levels" of the chemical.

The massive doses were so toxic that 80 percent of the mice died before developing any tumors. The mice had been injected with twenty-two thousand times the normal amount of Alar ingested by children. When, finally, a single mouse developed a tumor, the EPA declared victory. The agency announced in February 1989 that it would ban Alar within a year. The "60 Minutes" story aired a few weeks later, after which all hell broke loose.

In the midst of the hysteria, independent scientists began to investigate Alar. They found that the EPA had greatly exaggerated the amount of chemical residue that is ingested. The Advisory Committee on Pesticides for the British government concluded: "Even for children consuming the maximum quantities of apples and apple juice, subjected to the maximum treatment with daminozide, there is *no* risk."[94]

In fact, an Alar ban would actually *harm* public health. While the Alar fight was raging, the National Research Council issued a seventeen-hundred-page dietary study concluding that the best way to fight cancer by dietary means is to increase consumption of all fruits and vegetables. "The small potential risk of increased ingestion of pesticide residues," the Council declared, "would be greatly outweighed by the potential benefits [i.e., reduced risk of cancers] to be expected from greater fruit and vegetable consumption."[95]

Alar is off the market. Uniroyal, its manufacturer, has ceased sales. Nevertheless, lurking in the back of many minds will always be the suspicion that the apples on sale at the corner grocery are poisoned. Dr. Elizabeth Whelan's observation that "there has never been a documented case of human illness or death in the United States as the result of the standard and accepted use of pesticides"[96] is eye-opening—but one wonders how many eyes will ever come across it.

Ecos in the Dark

The decline of America's manufacturing industries has devastated numerous cities over the last two decades: Youngstown, Ohio; Wheeling, West Virginia; Lackawanna, New York. Yet one industry in one city has thrived: the eco-catastrophists of Washington, D.C. This anti-industry industry comprises activists ever searching for a new cause, politicized scientists seeking research grants, and politicians and bureaucrats eager to take credit for "saving" the public from mostly nonexistent dangers. A central tenet of this industry is that modern civilization is poisonous, wasteful, and on the verge of collapse. Only a gigantic supranational bureaucracy with police powers rivaling the Iron Heel can preserve Mother Earth. The benighted (i.e., the rest of us) are to be told what to eat and drink and smoke, how many children we may have, and what we may produce. Science is useful to this new order only insofar as its findings can be used (and distorted) in political polemics.

Most scientists, like most economists, both in and outside of government, read and research and teach and keep a healthy distance from public-policy debates, which they find tawdry and often dishonest. The field has been left to catastrophe theorists, many of whom do not scruple to misrepresent facts. The legitimate scientists typically become involved in the public debate only after being shocked and disgusted by the mendacities and the abuses of science that command media attention.

Scientists, economists, and other professionals who prefer labs to committee rooms must enter the public debate. The propagandists cannot go unchecked. Their agenda is explicitly anti-science, anti-technology, anti-growth, anti-free enterprise, and even anti-human, characterizing man as a "cancer" on nature. They are opposed to virtually all forms of economic progress, for they wish to use the power of the state to force a return back to the "good old days" before modern technology began to make life so much easier to enjoy.

Dixy Lee Ray provides some insight into just how good the "good old days" of environmentalist myth were:

> The world in which I spent my early years [75 years ago] was a very smelly place. The prevailing odors were of horse manure, human sweat, and unwashed bodies. A daily shower was unknown. . . . Indoors the air was generally musty and permeated by the sweetly acrid stench of kerosene lamps and coal fires. It was the era of the horse and buggy, the outhouse, and dirt. . . . Only a few urban streets were paved—with cobblestones or brick. . . . Automobiles . . . were few in number . . . and expensive. . . . Long distance travel was by steam-driven train or boat. . . . Most people did not venture far from home. . . . Electricity in the home usually meant a single 15 or 25 watt light bulb hanging from a wire in the center of a room.[97]

Along the same lines, the socialist C. P. Snow once wrote, "It is all very well for one, as a personal choice, to reject industrialisation—do a modern Walden, if you like, and if you go without much food, see most of your children die in infancy, despise the comforts of literacy, accept twenty years off your own life, then I respect you for the strength of your aesthetic revulsion. But I don't respect you in the slightest if, even passively, you try to impose the same choice on others who are not free to choose."[98]

The expected life span of a child born in 1915 was 54.5 years; today it is 75.4 years. The infant mortality rate has tumbled over that same period, from 99.9 to fewer than 20 deaths per 1,000 births. Illiteracy was seven times greater then than now. True, there was no Paula Abdul or "Rescue 911," but nor were there radios on which to hear Placido Domingo or Garrison Keillor, televisions on which to watch the World Series, or VCRs on which to enjoy *Citizen Kane* or *It's a Wonderful Life*.

The real threat from the environmental propaganda machine is that sooner or later the public will grow sick and tired of its scary (and always unrealized) scenarios and become cynical about genuine environmental problems. Alar didn't poison apples, but Alar-type hoaxes are poisoning our political discourse.

8

Compelling Belief

Great care must be taken to inform and regulate the will of the people.

—HORACE MANN, 1848

THE FERVENT MR. MANN was involved in countless reform causes of the day—temperance, abolitionism, hospitals for the insane—but none so occupied his considerable talents as did compulsory public schooling. A century and a half later, "taking the pledge" of abstention has fallen by the wayside, but public schools are the dominant, indeed in many areas the *only*, educational institution. The motivations of Mann and his conferees were many and complex: the assimilation of immigrants; the provision of opportunity for the poor; and, not least, the regulation if not manufacturing of "the will of the people."

Massachusetts pioneered compulsory public schooling in the late eighteenth century; one of its leading proponents explained that "the people must be taught to confide in and reverence their rulers."[1] Another early supporter, Boston merchant Jonathan Jackson, saw public schooling as a means of inculcating "habits of subordination" to government.[2]

An equally troubling assumption shared by certain of these men (and by many contemporary educational administrators) is that government ought to take on many of the roles traditionally performed by parents. Schools are to act *in loco parentis*—in the place of parents—in matters great and small, from hygiene to morals. Compulsory-education advocate Newton Bateman wrote in the late nineteenth century that government has a "right of eminent domain" over the "minds and souls and bodies" of us all; therefore education "cannot be left to the caprices and contingencies of individuals."[3] This philosophy manifests itself today in those public-school administrators' and teachers' unions that plump for earlier and earlier public schooling: some want children to be taken from their parents as early as age three. The Huxleian nightmare of women forfeiting their issue almost as they emerge from the womb is no longer quite so far-fetched. The National Education Association (NEA), for example, has long advocated mandatory kindergarten. Of course the NEA's chief motive is to increase the demand for teachers, but there is an ideological faction within the union that makes Newton Baker look like a homeschooler. They hold with Horace Mann that "men are cast-iron; but children are wax."[4]

Foes of compulsory education were hardly mossbacks. The Transcendentalists, for instance, feared that Mann & Co. wanted to suck the individuality out of American youth. Writes historian Maxine Greene:

> In 1839, after hearing Horace Mann deliver one of his talks, Ralph Waldo Emerson wrote in his journal: "We are shut in schools . . . for ten or fifteen years, and come out at last with a bellyful of words and do not know a thing." To know, for Emerson, meant to feel his poetic imagination soar. It meant to open his soul to the "Oversoul," to see by the "Divine light of reason" with which every human being was endowed. The Common School, teaching conventional or "common" habits of thought and perception, seemed to him a barrier against authenticity. The school reformers, he believed, would make impossible the "self-reliance" which alone permitted God to enter through the "private door."[5]

Since Mann's time, the distillation of certain "common values" has been a rationale for public schooling. Indeed, in the Reagan-Bush years, in which federal involvement in formerly local educational matters has reached new levels of intrusiveness, the teaching—no, the virtual enshrinement—of "Democracy" has replaced readin', writin', and 'rithmetic as the central mission of our schools. William Bennett, Reagan's Secretary of Education, used the powers of his office to teach "students the differences between democracy and other, less worthy forms of government."[6] There is a fine line, quite invisible to Bennett and the Reaganauts, that divides the *communication* of values from the *imposition* of values.

"To show how easily governments overstep the mark in favor of a particular ideology," economic historian E. G. West has written, "it is common to point to the examples of indoctrination in Hitler's Germany, or to the educational 'brainwashing' of Stalin's Russia."[7] What is not so commonly recognized, says West, is that "many other, more ostensibly democratic governments, in their haste to erect 'national systems of education,' have also been guilty, not so much of imposing their own values, as of standing in the way of those common to minority groups."[8]

West's point is grounded in history and practical experience. Centralized control of education by government stifles diversity. A national curriculum—an idea promoted by William Bennett and Bush Secretary of Education Lamar Alexander—will not (indeed, cannot) be tailored to the special needs of our multitudinous regions and cultures and ethnic groups. Students in Nebraska, for instance, should probably spend a good deal of time learning about the peculiar history and culture of Nebraska; Armenian Americans in Glendale, California, should probably read Saroyan and listen to Khachaturian and learn of the Armenian holocaust of the first two decades of this century. This healthy particularism is not possible in a centralized system, under which a farm boy in De Smet, South Dakota, learns exactly the same things as a Vietnamese immigrant girl in the Bronx.

Even the option of "voting with your feet" by moving to another school district has been foreclosed in many areas by school consolidation, a euphemism for "merger." Consolidation has left many metropolitan areas with but one large monopoly public-school system. The ravages of consolidation are suggested by the fact that in 1950 there were more than fifty thousand school districts in the United States; today there are fewer than sixteen thousand.

Rather than enjoying the healthy ferment of "the marketplace of ideas," public schooling tends to promote conformity of thought. What is a parent to do, education theorist William Rickenbacker has asked, if: You are Amish and believe that most education offends God? You are a Christian Scientist and the public schools require your child to be vaccinated before he or she can attend classes? You believe in the Biblical version of the Creation, and your children are taught Darwinian ideas? Your school is mediocre and you wish to teach your gifted child at home? Your education bureaucracy forces ever-increasing taxes and ever-inferior schooling on you? Or you desire to withdraw your child from public school one day a week for religious instruction?[9]

The answer to all these questions is "not much," unless parents are wealthy enough to send their children to private schools while continuing to pay property taxes to support public schools. The one-size-fits-all approach of the public schools is frustrating in the extreme. For instance, black youth have in recent years rediscovered Malcolm X, thanks largely to a generation of rappers who preach Malcolm X's message of black pride and self-sufficiency. Yet he is barely mentioned in the classrooms of predominately black public schools. "If you want to learn about him, you're going to have to do it on your own," fifteen-year-old Ray Causly told the *Los Angeles Times*. "I don't know, maybe [the schools] are afraid of him."[10] (The thought police stifle unsettling speech on the Left *and* the Right—as collegiate victims of "political correctness" have learned.)

Young Mr. Causly is learning early how dissenting views are squelched (or ignored) in the government's quest to instill "common values" in the citizenry. Much of the public-school curriculum is used as it was originally intended—to preach confidence in and reverence for our "rulers."

The Public-School Monopoly

Public schools in America are essentially monopolies. They are financed by compulsory taxation, enjoy a captive audience of students thanks to compulsory-attendance laws, and—in most cities—assign students to schools according to where they live. Parents who are dissatisfied with the quality of education their children are receiving must either move to an affluent area, where schools are often better, or send their children to private schools. If they choose the latter, parents must pay twice for their children's education: once in property taxes and again in tuition. As legal scholars Stephen Arons and Charles Lawrence III write:

> We have in effect created a system of school finance which provides free choice for the rich and compulsory socialization for the poor and working class. The present structure of American schooling—its method of finance and control—discriminates against the poor and working class and even a large part of the middle class by conditioning the exercise of First Amendment rights of school choice upon an ability to pay while simultaneously eroding that ability to pay through the retrogressive collection of

taxes used for public schools only. The arrangement seems no
more defensible than denying a man the right to vote because he
cannot afford the poll tax.[11]

Arons and Lawrence make a telling point, one to which the educrats
seem oblivious. There are few more tenacious defenders of the status quo
than the education bureaucracy, and that leads to some glaring inconsisten-
cies. For example, in 1991 President Bush eliminated federal funding for
family-planning clinics (such as those run by Planned Parenthood) if they
provided abortion counseling. Gale-force winds of outrage greeted this act;
"Choice!" "Choice!" "Choice!" became the slogan of those who argued
that it is unfair to deny low-income women access to information about
abortion. (As columnist Stephen Chapman has noted, "choice" has become a virtual synonym for the pro-abortion rights position; seldom is the
A-word mentioned anymore.)

Ironically, many of the groups that scream "Choice!" when the issue is
the right of women to receive abortion counseling (or an abortion) are
knee-jerk foes of measures that would allow the same women the freedom
to choose which schools their children will attend. At the July 1991
convention of the National Education Association, the union endorsed one
resolution supporting government funding of abortion (not just abortion
counseling) and another resolution instructing members to "work for the
defeat" of tuition-tax credits or school-voucher plans.[12] The NEA, it
seems, supports "choice" not as a matter of principle but as a simple
expedient; the minute "choice" threatens the public-school monopoly, out
the window it goes.

Lemon Socialism?

The American primary and secondary education system is organized in
essentially the same way as all industries were in the defunct communist
countries: they are heavily bureaucratized government monopolies kept
afloat by endless subsidies. Like any socialized industry, its product grows
worse by the year. Even dedicated employees suffer from low morale and
the lack of built-in incentives to better performance. Yet just as grossly
inefficient Russian tractor-parts factories lumbered on for decades, potential competitors outlawed by the state, so is our public-school monolith
seemingly eternal. Few parents can afford to pay double tuition, making it

very difficult for alternative suppliers of education to exist. Insidiously, the public-school monopoly can be used to teach fealty (or submission) to the regnant government and its orthodoxies. As educational historian Joel Spring has written, "Those who control the schools control a character-producing institution."[13]

The real danger to democracy, according to Spring, is

> the establishment of a system of mass, compulsory, and state regulated schooling. This does not mean that learning, knowledge, and intellectual skills are not beneficial to a democratic system. What is dangerous is a compulsory regulated institution whose purpose is to create something called democratic character. It is through this institution that an elite in a democracy can bend the character of the population to accept the status quo and the power of the ruling institutions, that citizens are led to believe that they should serve their government and not that their government should serve them.[14]

They Told Us It Was Gonna Be Like This

Spring's vision of a vast propaganda machine was foreseen by numerous nineteenth-century opponents of compulsory public schooling. English philosopher William Godwin wrote in 1843 that it is "the height of folly, the mere vapouring of credulity, to imagine that the educational system, if entrusted to the minister of the day, will not be employed to diffuse amongst the rising generation, that spirit and those views which are most friendly to his policy."[15] Godwin further warned that government control of education would "cover the land with a new class of officials, whose dependence on [government] patronage will render them the ready instruments of [government's] pleasure."[16]

He went on to condemn the "criminal attempt of short-sighted or wicked politicians to mold the intellect of the people to their pleasure."[17] Public-school teachers would inevitably, Godwin believed, become propagandists for the government:

> What a host of stipendiaries will thus be created! And who shall say what will be their influence in the course of two generations? All their sympathies will be with the powers by whom they are

paid, on whose favor they live, and from whose growing patronage their hopes of improving their condition are derived.[18]

Herbert Spencer, the brilliant English philosopher two generations removed from Godwin, seconded the old radical's point about political indoctrination. Government, Spencer said, would "mold children into good citizens, using its own discretion in settling what a good citizen is and how the child may be molded into one."[19] John Stuart Mill concurred: "A general State education is a mere contrivance for molding people to be exactly like one another; and as the mold in which it casts them is that which pleases the predominant power in the government . . . in proportion as it is efficient and successful, it establishes a despotism over the mind, leading by natural tendency to one over the body."[20]

See Dick Run. See Dick Win. See Dick Legislate.

Textbooks shall not contain certain material which serves to undermine authority.
—Texas law

The wisdom of William Godwin, Herbert Spencer, and John Stuart Mill is verified every single school day in American classrooms. Every state requires at least one high-school course in "Civics" or "American Government." Course materials are screened, censored, and chosen by government education officials. How likely is it that an agent of government will approve a text that is critical of that same government? What emerge from the messy process of textbook selection are books that emphasize a *theoretical* vision of the U.S. government that bears only incidental resemblance to reality.

The promoters of textbooks and standardized texts convey the idea that what is taught in public schools is neutral, but as Joel Spring has remarked, "nothing could be further from the truth."[21] These publications are less the result of Olympian detachment than of grubby coupling in the muck. They are conceived, gestated, and born in impure politics. At least fifteen states empower a state textbook board, usually staffed by political appointees, to judge what truths (or versions of truth) may be taught. The remaining states place the decision at the school-district level. In either case, uniformity prevails, and that uniformity is defined by politics. Government is a political institution; public schools are part of government. Thus, what is taught in those schools is largely determined by the dominant political forces in a particular place at a particular time.

Science and mathematics books are usually neutral in their presentation of knowledge, but the same cannot be said for texts in other areas, especially social studies. Controversy and disagreement are the lifeblood of the humanities and arts; debate and contention strengthen those disciplines. Alas, the excitement of intellectual discussion and give-and-take is missing from most current textbooks. It's not that the texts are necessarily pro-Democratic or pro-Republican; it's that they're *boring*. "The public schools present a smaller variety of books and ideas than do commercial bookstores,"[22] Joel Spring has written. In their mission to offend as few textbook boards as possible, publishers present American politics and government in terms that are, at best, bland and misleading. Parents who hold social, political, religious, or economic views contrary to the state-sanctioned versions are out of luck, unless they can scratch together the tuition for private schools.

Fables for the Kiddies

There is a long history of litigation over textbook adoption, although most of it focuses on only one aspect: religion. Legal disputes over the economic and political content of public-school texts are rare. But a survey of what is taught about government itself in America's public schools reveals a tangle of incomplete, misleading, or simply incorrect assertions that are being passed off as fact to our children.

Since the textbook industry strives to meet the uniform standards established by state and local governments, there are remarkable similarities between virtually all Civics or American Government texts. Most portray government in saintly hues. Its servants are selfless, public-spirited politicians and bureaucrats whose greatest desire is to serve others. Mother Teresa would not be out of place in its employ. There are undoubtedly many honest, hard-working, and charitable people who work in government, but real-world politics is vastly different from the fairyland depicted in our children's texts.

For example, in the widely used *American Government* by Mary Turner, Kenneth Switzer, and Charlotte Redden, Congress is an "effective" institution whose hallmarks are diligence and sobriety. The authors write:

"Congress tries to assure that the rules set by [regulatory] agencies are reasonable. It does this through its powers of oversight."[23] Thanks to Congress, all regulations "must be reasonable in what they require of the public."[24]

Does the word "reasonable" describe the Congress that actually exists in the observable world? Do its members approach regulatory agencies with the magic word "reasonable" on their lips? Recall that it was congressional oversight that led to the savings-and-loan debacle of the 1980s, which will end up costing American taxpayers hundreds of billions of dollars. A group of U.S. senators later dubbed the "Keating Five" interfered with bank regulators to obtain preferential treatment for their sugar daddy Charles Keating, former chairman of the now-bankrupt Lincoln Savings and Loan, who had made enormous campaign contributions to each of the five senators.

Contra Turner, Switzer, and Redden, Congress is often the main road-block to "reasonableness" in regulatory policy. Take the sorry case of the Office of Information of Regulatory Affairs (OIRA), a division of the Office of Management and Budget that was established during the Carter administration to review federal regulations to ensure that the social costs they impose do not exceed their social benefits. The OIRA operates, in effect, as a regulatory sanity check. In a city in which the EPA, for instance, has issued regulations with cost over benefit ratios as high as ten thousand to one, OIRA probably isn't a bad idea.

Members of Congress are less then enthralled; their frequent and petty interferences with OIRA on behalf of special interests have been some-where short of "reasonable." For example, in 1991 the *Wall Street Journal* reported a "political hostage taking" whereby Senator John Glenn (D-Ohio) had "put a hold on a planned Bush appointee in the hope of extorting a compromise from the White House that would gut OIRA."[25] Senator Glenn "held Vanderbilt Professor James Blumstein hostage for so long that he finally gave up trying to come to Washington to run OIRA."[26] Senator Glenn, coincidentally, was also one of the Keating Five. His actions in this regard, as reported by the *Wall Street Journal*, were not the Right Stuff of which heroes are made:

> Senator Glenn solicited $200,000 in contributions from Mr. Keat-
> ing for a committee he controlled that paid him to travel around the
> country and otherwise subsidized his political activities. On the
> tenuous grounds that Mr. Keating grew up in Ohio, Senator Glenn

decided it was part of his "constituent service" duties to join the rest of the Keating Five in lobbying regulators on behalf of Lincoln Savings. At one meeting, Ed Gray, the top thrift regulator, was pressured to drop a key regulation harmful to Lincoln.[27]

This is not to suggest that all congressional oversight is unreasonable; it can be vigorous and even salubrious. But the picture presented in the textbooks is incomplete if not downright deceptive. It ignores the well-established fact that oversight is often the *cause*, not the preventative, of policy failures, as with the savings-and-loan debacle.

Regulators from Heaven

Public-school texts typically explain to students that regulations are implemented to serve the public interest by curbing avarice. As Alan Kownslar and Terry Smart explain in *Civics*, "the Environmental Protection Agency was instructed to set up rules to make sure that the country's air and water supplies did not harm people."[28] Well, maybe this was the intention of certain of EPA's progenitors, but two-plus decades of experience have shown that the *effect* of EPA regulation, as with all regulation, often diverges from its intention. The large body of research detailing the failures of regulation is conspicuously absent from almost all civics texts.

For example: the 1977 Clean Air Act Amendments actually made the air *dirtier* while imposing billions of dollars of costs on consumers and businesses. The amendments allowed the EPA to require new plants to use the "best available technology" to remove sulfur dioxides from waste gases. The phrasing was crucial; it explicitly prohibited the use of low-sulfur coal, which is much less polluting, as a way of complying with the law.

Brookings Institution economist Robert Crandall explains how this environmentally destructive regulation came about:

> Eastern coal producers feared that a sensible environmental policy would lead electric utilities to buy increasing amounts of low-sulfur Western coal. Since much of the Appalachian and Midwestern coal is high in sulfur content, it would eventually lose market share to the cleaner Western coal. Requiring stack-gas scrubbers for all new plants, regardless of the sulfur content of the

coal burned, would eliminate the incentive for Eastern and Mid-western utilities to import low-sulfur Western coal.[29]

The polluters won because in 1977 the chairmen of both authorizing committees for the EPA were from West Virginia; the majority leader of the president's party in the Senate was from West Virginia; and the United Mineworkers Union, which only organizes Eastern (high-sulfur) coal miners, was a key supporter of the Carter White House and the Democratic-controlled Congress.

Consequently, the Clean Air Act Amendments were subversive of their name. They gave us dirtier air by protecting the high-sulfur coal industry. "To require many billion dollars in annual control costs to *increase* regional air pollution cannot be defended as sensible 'clean' air policy," Crandall concluded.[30] One can look far and wide and futilely through civics texts for the instructive example of the Clean Air Act Amendments of 1977—or any of a score of similar cases.

Kownslar and Smart's popular text, McGraw-Hill's *Civics: Citizens and Society*, is also filled with Pollyannaish paeans to government regulation. The text does note that there are critics of regulation, but emphasizes that regulations are "needed to protect the health and safety of the public" and to "keep large businesses from cheating the average person."[31] The next paragraph identifies one such wonderful prophylactic, the Interstate Commerce Commission, which is said to protect consumers from being cheated. "The services and schedules of shippers are . . . watched over by the ICC,"[32] Kownslar and Smart assure a nation's school kids.

Unmentioned is the ICC's notorious role as a cartel-enforcement agency for the trucking industry. Its role in boosting rates and restricting entry into the market earned it the enmity of many self-styled consumer advocates; Senator Ted Kennedy and Ralph Nader, who are not known as passionate deregulators, were the principal forces behind the deregulation of trucking in the late 1970s, when the powers of the ICC were curtailed.

Kownslar and Smart are no less gullible when it comes to other pieces of the regulatory apparatus. They describe the Federal Communications Commission (FCC) as "the regulatory agency that protects . . . public airspace. Radio and television stations must get licenses from the FCC before they can broadcast."[33] The FCC is thus cast in its favorite role: fearless defender of the public's airwaves. Students are not told that at the behest of the powerful television networks, the FCC retarded the development of cable television for decades. The moronic trash spewed over the networks had little real competition until the 1980s, thanks to our champion, the FCC.[34]

The next entry in the Kownslar and Smart regulatory Hall of Fame is the Federal Trade Commission (FTC), which is said to ensure "free and fair trade" by prohibiting "deals that unfairly hurt other businesses."[35] A company "should not have an unfair edge on its competition," the authors nebulously proclaim.[36]

Far from being a pro-consumer watchdog, the FTC has more often than not acted as an agent of protectionism, as has long been known by students of antitrust regulation. Economist Dominick Armentano has documented how, for over a century, antitrust has been used as an anticompetitive weapon against business firms that cut their prices, expand their production, or diversify their product line in a way that allows them to increase their market share.[37] Economist William Baumol argues that antitrust laws are typically used "to subvert competition."[38] The bogus rationales for antitrust cooked up by big business and FTC propagandists have been swallowed wholesale by most textbook authors, ever willing to take government at its word.

These examples are typical. The textbooks our children read in public school are filled with uncritical puffery when it comes to virtually any act of government regulation. The private sector, by contrast, will, if unchecked by the wise hand of regulation, breed monopolies, crime, greed, and just plain unfairness. James Madison's formulation, "If men were angels. . . ," is evidently out of date; the public servants who glide through these texts in search of demons to slay *are* angels.

The effects of regulation have been studied extensively for decades. Economist Ronald Coase, a Nobel laureate, concluded in 1975:

> There have been more serious studies made of government regulation of industry in the last fifteen years or so, particularly in the United States, than in the whole preceding period. These studies have been both quantitative and nonquantitative. . . . The main lesson to be drawn from these studies is clear: they all tend to suggest that the regulation is either ineffective or that when it has a noticeable impact, on balance the effect is bad, so that consumers obtain a worse product or a higher-priced product or both as a result of the regulation. Indeed, this result is found so uniformly as to create a puzzle: one would expect to find, in all these studies, at least some government programs that do more good than harm.[39]

Coase's summation is rarely presented to public-school students. This should come as no surprise: who would expect government to give students anything but an unrealistic and flattering vision of government? The textbook-selection boards are hardly likely to approve content that looks with disfavor—as, say, our Forefathers did in 1776—on centralized power.

No Greater Love: One Bureaucracy Looks at Another

The typical public-school textbook coats bureaucracy with the same Panglossian gloss as it does regulation. Agencies and bureaus and departments are bathed in noble colors; high-minded sentiments substitute for actual descriptions of how government's massive administrative sector works. The U.S. Department of Agriculture "works with farmers to improve crops, . . . studies new farming methods," and "helps landowners protect soil, water, and other resources,"[40] says *Civics: Citizens in Action* by Mary Turner, Cathryn Long, John Bower, and Elizabeth Lott. The aforementioned *American Government* lauds the department for fighting "hunger and malnutrition through the food stamp program and school lunch program."[41]

Turner, Long, Bower, and Lott explain that "the Department of Agriculture provides many services for farmers." Among these good deeds are seeing to it that "farmers . . . have an adequate income to buy the same variety of goods as urban workers" and "assur[ing] that farm products would be available in a steady supply."[42] As if that wasn't enough, the USDA also guarantees "reasonable prices for both farmers and consumers."[43] (What is it about that word "reasonable" that so attracts civics-text authors?)

The notion that American agricultural policy results in "reasonable prices" for consumers is ludicrous. As discussed in chapter 5, price-support programs are a price-fixing conspiracy that rips off taxpayers and shoppers and benefits, above all, wealthy corporate farmers and their political sponsors. To claim that agricultural policy fights "hunger and malnutrition" is equally absurd. For over half a century price supports have made food *more* expensive than it otherwise would have been. Since higher food prices impose a disproportionately large burden on lower-income families, price supports operate as a regressive tax. They are an enemy of the poor and a friend to malnutrition. It is hardly consolation that after the government buys votes from farmers by mandating higher prices, it throws a few crumbs, in the form of food stamps, to struggling families.

The claim that agricultural policy protects soil, water, and other resources is another howler. Farm policy has degraded the environment. Government subsidies for fertilizer, for example, have been a major source of water pollution in the United States; subsidized water for affluent farmers has caused gross resource misallocations, particularly in the West. These pernicious environmental effects of agricultural policy have been widely known and discussed for decades by scholars—except, apparently, those who write textbooks for our children.

Nor do textbooks display much awareness of the federal government's disastrous experiments in central planning as a means of dealing with various energy crises. In this the textbook writers are similar to many journalists: they bemoan our lack of a "national energy policy," blissfully unaware that Uncle Sam's byzantine system of controls and allocation schemes caused whatever crises arose.

The claims in *American Government* are typical: "In spite of the repeated threat of energy emergencies, the [U.S. Department of Energy] has failed to develop a clear national energy policy."[44] The absence of central planning in the energy industry is termed a "failure"[45] whose consequences are truly terrifying: for example, because "the nation experienced an energy surplus in the early 1980s . . . many government officials felt it was less urgent for the department to act strongly."[46] Lulled into this false sense of security, Washington relaxed its grip on energy producers, leading to . . . well, nothing bad yet, but the implication is that catastrophe, like a brass-knuckled mugger, waits just around the corner.

The reason there were energy surpluses in the early 1980s is that the price of oil was deregulated and the federal government (temporarily) abandoned its attempts at central planning. What students learn was a "failure" was really a success: the federal government acknowledged that markets do a much better job—in terms of both efficiency and equity—of allocating resources than bureaucrats do. *American Government* does not conclude that government planning has failed, or even that reasonable (if we may borrow the word) people disagree on the need for a national energy bureaucracy; rather, the authors emphasize the need for the federal government, through its energy policies, to "plan for a crisis"—which is, of course, the best way to ensure a crisis![47]

Monopoly Love Affair

The federal government operates dozens of "public corporations" that are similar to their private-sector namesakes, although only in a very limited sense. The U.S. Postal Service is the most familiar—and, by school children who thrill to receive cards, loved. If only the kiddies knew. . . .

The Postal Service, like many other public corporations, is granted monopolistic privileges by law.[48] It has a legal monopoly on first-class mail delivery that it enforces with maniacal zeal; the federal government has gone so far as to bring charges against elementary school children who hand-delivered Christmas cards to their classmates. This was a public-relations man's nightmare, but monopolists are free to say, in the immortal words of William Henry Vanderbilt, "the public be damned." The Postal Service wasn't cowering in fear of any competitive threat the children might have posed; rather, it was the *precedent* that was dangerous.[49]

Nothing scares the U.S. Postal Service more than the threat of competition. Its record is what one might expect from any enterprise shielded from the market: its prices have increased in excess of inflation while its service has declined. It has cut back on the frequency of delivery, has eliminated door-to-door delivery in many areas (relying instead on street boxes), and is notorious for losing and destroying mail. As one can glean from reading the papers, an amazingly disproportionate percentage of postal workers goes on shooting sprees in the workplace.

Few public-school texts even mention the obviously monopolistic nature of the U.S. Postal Service (not to mention those shooting sprees). *American Government* acknowledges its inefficiencies but makes a weak (or disingenuous) excuse: "There are some government corporations—just as there are some private ones—that do not make a profit. For example, Congress has complained about the poor profit and service of . . . the Postal Service."[50]

Yes, some private corporations do not make a profit, but what the authors neglect to tell the students is that in a competitive market a business that does not make a profit must cut its costs, improve the quality of its product, or go out of business. Public corporations face no such discipline. Heavy losses by a government monopoly like the U.S. Postal Service are simply compensated for by larger appropriations from the federal treasury or government-mandated price increases. Since there is no legal competition, the postal monopoly need not worry about losing "market share" if it jacks up the price of a stamp. The consumer has no alternative. An even more naive text, *American Civics* by William Hartley and William Vincent, states with what we assume is tongue firmly planted in cheek that the aim of the U.S. Postal Service is "to make the mail service self-supporting and more efficient."[51] It's a wonder the authors didn't include a chapter asserting the existence of the Easter Bunny.

The naive and unrealistic view of government that appears in most public-school texts is a disgrace. Most writers simply state the official purpose of a federal entity; they're too lazy—or biased—to scrutinize an agency's actual operations and its effectiveness. Since all organizations—governmental or private—accentuate the positive in their public pronouncements, students are shown a distorted picture and told it is lifelike.

Any scholar who wrote about the role of corporations in America by simply quoting the self-serving rhetoric found in corporate annual reports would be laughed out of his field. But when it comes to civics texts, a double standard applies, in spades.

Ignoring American History

It's not as though the pool of knowledge about how government works is too shallow to draw from. From the Imperial Presidency to the Permanent Congress, the afflictions on our body politic have been studied (though not, alas, to death).

Nor is this information too fresh and new to have been incorporated into textbooks of recent vintage. All the authors need to do is consult *The Federalist Papers*, first published as a series of letters in New York City newspapers in 1787. Written by three keen students of political history—Alexander Hamilton, James Madison, and John Jay—*The Federalist Papers* were an astute analysis of the problems of democracy. The authors took a skeptical view of unchecked government power and promoted the Constitution as an ingenious system of limits upon the powers of special interests, which they believed led to the downfall of any democracy.

"Among the numerous advantages promised by a well-constructed Union," James Madison wrote in *Federalist* Number 10, "none deserves to be more accurately developed than its tendency to break and control the violence of faction."[52] Madison explained: "By a faction, I understand a number of citizens, whether amounting to a majority or minority of the whole, who are united and actuated by some common impulse of passion, or of interest, adverse to the rights of other citizens, or to the permanent and aggregate interests of the community."[53]

"Complaints are everywhere heard," Madison wrote in 1787, "that measures are too often decided, not according to the rules of justice and the rights of the minor party, but by the superior force of an interested and overbearing majority."[54] "The regulation of these various and interfering interests" by constitutional means "forms the principal task of modern legislation" and was the focus of *The Federalist Papers*.[55]

Madison and the other Founding Fathers understood that a government acting in "the public interest" was a rare occurrence indeed. Without workable constitutional constraints, government would inevitably be controlled by "factions." Madison realized: "It is in vain to say that enlightened statesmen will be able to adjust these clashing interests and render them all subservient to the public good. Enlightened statesmen will not always be at the helm."[56] (Boy, was he ever prescient.) The nature of politics is such, Madison believed, that the long-term "public interest" will "rarely prevail over the immediate interest which one party may find in disregarding the rights of another or the good of the whole."[57]

Such thinking, which formed the philosophical basis of the U.S. Constitution, is all but absent from contemporary public-school instruction. Most texts take an antithetical view: in their renderings, government routinely acts in the public interest to curb the crimes and peccadilloes of special interests. Madison's warnings about the "violence of faction" are accorded all the attention and respect that the public schools of Cambridge, Massachusetts, lavish on the Biblical story of Creation. The Founders' wisdom, sadly, is long lost.

Universities and Other Federal Agencies

In a survey of changes in university curricula over the past several decades, journalist Charles Sykes, a critic of the politicization of higher education, finds that courses in the humanities and social sciences are coming to emphasize "the political, the obfuscatory, and the silly." The modern university, writes Sykes,

> has engendered its own form of . . . academic ignorance, an agglomeration of prejudice, dogma, misinformation, and sophistry. . . . The modern student is schooled in the culture of universal

skepticism, but he is unarmed in any true confrontation of ideas. This is perhaps inevitable when we have students who take courses in the economic imperialism and oppression of the West, but have no background in economics; or who are indoctrinated in the . . . evils of American society, without ever studying its history or institutions. . . . [Today's students] are hollow men [and women] stuffed with the straw of academic confusion.[58]

It makes little difference whether the schools are public or private. For example, Stanford is ostensibly a "private" university but only in the nominal sense. Like virtually every university in the country, it is heavily dependent on research grants and other forms of government support. In 1991 the federal aid to all colleges and universities totaled $12.9 billion. So awash in federal lucre is Stanford that in 1991 its president, former Carter administration official Donald Kennedy, resigned in disgrace after it was revealed that the university had misused $232 million in research grants over the last decade. Among other things, this research money went toward flowers and bed sheets for Kennedy's home, a presidential yacht, and myriad other questionable expenses.

Federal involvement in higher education is so pervasive that there are almost no truly private colleges and universities left. As the *Village Voice* columnist Nat Hentoff writes, "There's no such thing as a free lunch—especially when government sets the table."[59] Universities have become vehicles of political indoctrination for the expansion of governmental power.

Walking the Line

The distinguished sociologist James S. Coleman makes a powerful case that government funding of academic research—which grew enormously during the Cold War years—has corrupted the integrity of the American professoriate. Coleman was employed by President Johnson in 1966 to direct a research project, mandated by the Civil Rights Act of 1964, studying disparities in educational opportunity among the races. Coleman's group arrived at some unexpected results. First, the study found that race had little to do with the quality of school facilities and resources. The principal differences occurred between regions and between rural and urban settings, not between blacks and whites.[60]

Second, the study found that the measurable quality of education was not significantly related to the amount of money that a school spends. Third, black children achieved far better in schools with student bodies that were predominantly middle class.

These findings greatly displeased the authorities. As Coleman writes: "The first two were strongly opposed within the Department of Health, Education, and Welfare [which funded the study], for they went against the conventional wisdom and against recently initiated federal policy of funding school physical facilities."[61] Political pressures prevented many follow-up research questions from being addressed. "We had many . . . battles to fight with agency officials who did not like the results we had achieved, many problems in merely maintaining the integrity of the research report in the face of attempts to rewrite it,"[62] recalls Coleman, who notes that a dispassionate researcher "concerned in finding facts relevant to the issues at hand, would have gone on to ask . . . [questions] we did not ask."[63] The impulse *not* to ask questions that might offend governmental funding sources, says Coleman, "prevents many relevant research questions from being raised."[64]

Similar cases are legion. Higher education has become so politicized that those who dissent from the "politically correct" regnant orthodoxy (which almost always supports the expansion of state power) are harassed or punished by being denied tenure or job opportunities. Coleman further explains:

> There are certain policies, certain public activities, that have the property that they stem from benevolent intentions toward others less fortunate or in some way oppressed—policies intended to aid the poor, or to aid blacks or Hispanics or women. Any research that would hinder these policies is subject to such disapproval and attack. These are policies intended to display, ostentatiously even, egalitarian objectives. For many academics they replace the patterns of conspicuous consumption that Thorstein Veblen attributed to the rich. They might be called policies of conspicuous benevolence. They display, conspicuously, the benevolent intentions of their supporters.[65]

Coleman may be too generous to his fellow academics; the word "paternalistic" may be more accurate than "benevolent" in describing the attitudes many intellectuals, in their exalted perches, take toward the benighted masses.

Coleman's point, nevertheless, is trenchant: It explains why so much of the public-policy research that evaluates the actual effects, as opposed to the stated intentions, of government policies has come not from universities but from independent think tanks, such as the Hoover Institution, American Enterprise Institute, Brookings Institution, Cato Institute, and the Heritage Foundation, none of which accept direct government aid. On many issues these nonprofit communities of scholars have taken the lead in "extending the range of questions examined, and questioning the consequences of the policies of conspicuous benevolence."[66]

A large and still-swelling body of evidence highlights gaps—no, veritable canyons—separating stated intentions from actual effects. Welfare, for instance, has only made life worse for the poor by fostering dependency. Public housing has everywhere degenerated into drug- and crime-infested slums. Rent control has caused massive housing shortages. Taxes and regulation have stifled economic development in every city in America. The public-school monopoly is responsible for something less than an American intellectual renaissance. In short, the Great Society has been a Great Disaster.

Genuine social reform would include expanding private property, unshackling free enterprise, and limiting government intervention. These policies, we believe, would make better (and more prosperous) the lives of the poor, but their implementation would face powerful intellectual opposition from the "elite" universities whose faculty cling to the theory of benevolent intentions, by which public policy is not judged according to its actual consequences, but rather by the declared good intentions of the intellectuals who design and propagandize (often at taxpayer expense) for these schemes.

Unless they take an economics course—and not always then—today's students are much more likely to study economic and social policy in the context of what the policies "should" do rather than what they actually do. They are taught that the minimum wage and rent control, for instance, enhance the lives of the poor, although no evidence is presented. They are taught that the welfare state is underfunded, else it would bring us nirvana, and that the market system is "imperfect" and sorely in need of regulation by benevolent government bureaucrats. Economics, to the extent that it intrudes into these classroom fables, is derisively dismissed as "the dismal science," a handy way of relegating inconvenient facts and studies to the dungeon of gloom.

Massaging the Hand That Feeds You

It takes a brave person to denounce the politicization of her own discipline. Retribution—in the form of tenure denial or professional ostracism—is a very real possibility. One such heroic figure is agricultural economist E. C. Pasour of North Carolina State University. Professor Pasour has studied the link between government funding of academic research and academic support for federal agricultural policy and has concluded that "agricultural economists have played an important role in legitimating the complicated programs of agricultural cartels that have persisted in the United States for the past 50 years."[67]

The field of agricultural economics originated as part of the land-grant system of universities in the nineteenth century. As such, it has been financed and entwined with the federal government to a greater extent than almost any other academic discipline. As Pasour writes, "There is relatively little agricultural economics research in the United States that is not governmentally supported."[68] The field contains, undoubtedly, many honest and objective scholars. But it is no slur on their integrity to point out that when so much of their financial support comes from Washington and state governments, they are unlikely to ask certain hard questions that one might expect of an objective researcher. In some worst cases, as Pasour documents, agricultural economists have served as paid propagandists for the U.S. Department of Agriculture.

The New Deal farm programs (see chapter 5), which sought to arrange the farm economy into a series of monopolies and cartels, "were [and are] defended by agricultural economists," historian M. R. Benedict wrote in 1953.[69] "Agriculture has been the victim of more than its share of faulty economic analysis and of faulty programs based on that analysis," according to Pasour, who charges that "agricultural economists have played an important role in providing the rationale for these programs."[70] Supply controls, price supports, and parity are just a few of the monumentally wrong-headed ideas hatched by agricultural economists. And don't count on the parents to give a fair evaluation of their children. Agricultural economists seldom offer vigorous criticism of farm programs; their dependence on federal support "is not conducive to the objective analysis of the effects of [farm] programs," writes Pasour, for "political pressures affecting the agricultural economists . . . have been very strong."[71]

As government has made higher education a virtual ward of the state over the last forty-five years, university coffers have fattened while freedom of inquiry has been compromised. The sorry case of agricultural economics demonstrates how scholars in subsidized disciplines produce work that justifies, even glorifies, their bureaucratic benefactors. "He who takes the king's shilling becomes the king's man," is an old proverb that has acquired disturbing new relevance.

The Cult of Political Correctness

In the fall of 1990, a spate of stories in the popular press exposed the cult of "political correctness" (PC) that had swept college and university campuses. From New Haven to Austin, students and professors who challenged the assumptions of democratic socialism, feminism, or affirmative action were being punished for expressing their views. The first pimples of the PC rash were spotted in the early 1980s, when conservative political figures such as U.N. Ambassador Jeane Kirkpatrick, Secretary of Education William Bennett, and Attorney General Edwin Meese III were shouted down, physically threatened, or otherwise barred from speaking on various campuses because the things they might say upset the PC Ministers of Information. A more recent example of this contempt for the free exchange of ideas occurred in 1990, when hundreds of women at Wellesley College protested First Lady Barbara Bush's selection as commencement speaker on the grounds that her roles as wife and mother made her a poor role model.

(Lest we forget, the U.S. State Department, through the McCarran-Walter Act, is an even sterner policeman: it regularly forbids foreign intellectuals and activists, from Salvadoran rebel Ruben Zamora to Canadian writer Farley Mowat, from entering this country to go on college speaking tours.)

Why have our campuses become havens of intolerance? According to Nobel laureate Milton Friedman, many of the PC zealots are professors who "went to colleges and universities during [the Vietnam war] period who would not ordinarily have gone there, in order to stay out of the war."[72] These people, says Friedman, "who would otherwise have been businessmen or something, became instead academics. But they are not intellectuals fundamentally, they are really activists."[73] Former Berkeley student protester Annette Kolodny, now dean of the humanities at the University of Arizona, seems to confirm Friedman's perception: "I see my scholarship as an extension of my political activism," Kolodny told *U.S. News & World Report* in 1989.[74]

The marriage of scholarship and political activism has engendered a "mood of ideological conformity" within numerous academic departments.[75] Of course, the presence of ideology is nothing new in American universities. What is new is the creation of academic disciplines, such as *certain* aspects of African Studies, "that were in actuality political movements. . . . [T]he politicization of academia has meant that much of what passes for scholarship is no longer a search for 'truth,' but rather an inquiry into political loyalties and ideological usefulness," Charles Sykes asserts.[76]

The lengths to which some universities have gone to enforce ideological conformity range from hilarious to Stalinist. As of early 1991, at least 125 colleges and universities had enacted "speech codes" designed to limit "offensive" speech—that is, politically incorrect speech—on campuses. The University of Connecticut even banned "inappropriate laughter," "inconsiderate jokes," and "conspicuous exclusion [of another student] from conversation"—the penalty for jokesters (or their insensitive auditors) is expulsion.[77]

A typical document, the "Statement Regarding Intellectual Freedom, Tolerance and Political Harassment" by the law faculty at the State University of New York at Buffalo, asserts that free speech must be subordinated to "the responsibility to promote equality and justice."[78] "No totalitarian could have put it better," remarks sociologist Paul Hollander, for "it would be interesting to know who will be authorized to define what constitutes equality and justice and just how they are to be promoted."[79]

A Harvard professor has openly called for "self censorship" in both research and teaching for fear that complete freedom of inquiry "might hurt a group."[80] Student journalists have been censored or harassed at Vassar, Brown, Berkeley, UCLA, Dartmouth, and elsewhere. At UCLA, a student editor was suspended in 1991 after publishing a cartoon featuring a rooster who crowed that he'd gotten into UCLA "because of affirmative action." When another student editor at the University of California at Northridge protested the suspension by publishing the cartoon in his own paper, he, too, was suspended by his university.[81] The granddaddy of all conservative student newspapers, the fiery *Dartmouth Review*, has been attacked for more than a decade by the university administration. *Review* editors and staffers have been suspended, the paper was once sabotaged by someone who inserted a quotation from *Mein Kampf* on the paper's masthead the night before publication, and hostile students and faculty have repeatedly called for censoring the paper.

The three areas in which ideological conformity is most ruthlessly enforced are race, sex, and Western culture, broadly defined. Honest people can disagree over the best ways to improve black-white relations, but at many universities anyone who criticizes the use of racial quotas is labeled a racist. End of argument.

The same is true of feminist and homosexual politics on university campuses. Those who take issue with any of the scholarship produced in these areas—even if they are not intolerant in any way of feminists or gays or lesbians—risk being slandered as sexist or homophobic. To criticize "equal pay for comparable worth" proposals, as most economists do, is to earn opprobrium as a "sexist"—or worse. To advocate traditional family stability as a partial antidote to poverty, as many social scientists do, is coming perilously close to committing the most heinous of anti-PC crimes: "insensitivity." This is the language of bullies and tyrants, not men— excuse us, persons—of honor.[82]

Multicultural Myths

The buzzword upon which the entire edifice of PC is built is multicultural-ism. If the word meant learning about and respecting the peoples and histories of lands far removed from our own, then no one would quarrel with it. Indeed, many universities have long offered courses on non-Western cultures. It is especially important today, in an increasingly inter-dependent world economy, that students are exposed to the philosophies and practices of those who live in Africa and Asia and South America.

But "multiculturalism" as practiced at many universities does not mean the teaching of non-Western cultures. It means diminishing, distorting, or denouncing Western culture—particularly such Western institutions as private property and limited constitutional government. A particularly bizarre moment in the life of multiculturalism occurred during a 1988 protest at Stanford University, led by the Reverend Jesse Jackson, in which marchers chanted "Hey, Hey, Ho, Ho, Western Culture's Got to Go." Jackson led the protest while running for president, an office that would have required him to uphold one of the pinnacles of Western culture, the U.S. Constitution.

Taking Western culture's place at many universities is not non-Western culture *per se*, but left-wing political tracts by authors who happen to live in non-Western countries. Bearing the scars of Western imperialism, these authors are celebrated by the Politically Correct:

> At Mount Holyoke and Dartmouth students must now take a course in Third World culture although there is no Western culture requirement. The University of Wisconsin recently instituted a mandatory non-Western and ethnic studies course, although students need not study the classics, American politics, or American history. Berkeley's newly adopted ethnic course requirement is the only undergraduate course that all students must take. . . . Meanwhile, the bastions of core curricula in Western classics, such as Columbia and the University of Chicago, are under pressure to climb on the multicultural bandwagon.[83]

The material being taught at many American universities under the rubric of multiculturalism would "produce puzzlement, if not disbelief, among many educated citizens of Asia, Africa, Latin America, and the Middle East," comments writer Dinesh D'Souza.[84] The teachings "bear virtually no resemblance to the ideas most deeply cherished in their culture."[85] Instead, writes D'Souza, "American students receive a selective polemical interpretation of non-Western societies, revealing less about those societies than about the ideological prejudices of those who manage multicultural education."[86]

For example, in a course at Stanford, Euripedes and Shakespeare are reduced to case studies of colonialism and racial and sexual stereotypes. "Latin culture" is taught at Stanford through the book *I, Rigoberta Menchu* about an Indian woman from Guatemala who speaks "for all the Indians of the American continent." Sure she does. The book's translator, feminist author Elisabeth Burgos-Debray, met Menchu at a socialist scholars' conference in Paris. Menchu does not write about the real lives of Mayan villagers; she prefers to essay "a projection of Western radical and feminist views onto Latin Indian culture."[87] She is used by her American translator as a mouthpiece for promoting socialist and feminist ideology in a peasant dress.

The PC zealots' hatred of Western culture has blinded them to the truly appalling injustices of many non-Western cultures. The idea of equality is foreign to many of them; for better or worse, few Islamic marriages are modeled on the union of Phil Donahue and Marlo Thomas. The Koran, for example, stipulates that "men have authority over women."[88] The Confucian maxim, "If you care for your daughter, you don't go easy on foot binding," must offend feminist ears, while wife-burning and clitoral mutilation are still widespread in some non-Western cultures.[89] In Cuba, homosexuals are jailed; in China they are subjected to electric shock treatment. In parts of Africa, homosexuality is regarded as a sickness caused by witchcraft.[90]

The ideology of multiculturalism is not derived from a genuine concern about multicultural education. If it was, the Politically Correct would probably be denouncing Islamic and Zulu peoples with the fanatical venom they now train on middle-aged white men from Iowa. At many schools, multicultural education has been perverted into a propaganda tool. The richness and complexity of non-Western cultures are largely ignored in favor of "representative figures who are congenial to the [professor's] propaganda agenda—then, like Rigoberta Menchu, they are triumphantly presented as the 'repressed voices' of diversity, fit for solemn admiration and emulation of American undergraduates."[91]

School Daze

William Godwin saw it all coming. He understood that government control of education made inevitable a bureaucratized system of public schools that serve "the minister of the day." At the primary and secondary levels, American students are taught to revere government; its interventions in the economy are said to be wholesome and necessary. Jefferson may have said "the merchants will manage commerce the better, the more they are left free to manage for themselves," but like his brother Founders, he makes but a cameo appearance in today's classrooms.

On the heels of the dramatic increase in federal funding of academic research has come a thoroughgoing politicization of higher education. The result is a powerful bias in research and teaching in favor of bigger government and against free markets and limited government. The silly but dangerous cult of political correctness is a vivid manifestation of the state's attempt to impose ideological uniformity in the schools. Students are not being taught to think, to question, to challenge; they're force-fed propaganda and threatened with punishment if they retch. As long as government is in the business of education, it can be expected to do what Horace Mann hoped it would do: "Inform and regulate the will of the people."

9

Dope, Booze, Smokes, and Sex

Mighty reformer! Of the trump of Fame,
Blown by thyself, has sent abroad thy name!
Sublime Fanatic! who to aid thy cause,
Slights trifles such as Constitutions, Laws!
O Pimp Majestic! whose sharp gimlet eye,
All jugs conceal'd and demijohns can spy!
Astute smell-fungus! Striving as a goal,
To poke thy nose in every dirty hole!
Pimp, Spy, Fanatic arrogant at heart!
Language would fail to draw thee as thou art!

—Anonymous

In one of the classic 1960s protest songs, Donovan said of The Man: "He can't even run his own life; I'll be damned if he'll run mine." A quarter-century later, the good news is that he still can't run his own life. The bad news is that he's thinking up new ways to run ours.

Around the globe and especially in the United States, governments are conducting well-orchestrated campaigns to "enlighten" citizens about their life-styles. Hardheads who refuse to be enlightened are harassed and taxed and sometimes even jailed. The state has determined that government officials know best; henceforth, citizens will diet and exercise and take care of themselves in ways that conform to standards set by Washington. The British and Australians call this phenomenon the "nanny state," which describes a system that treats citizens more like children than adults.

Offering citizens advice about their life-styles is not as innocuous as it might appear. When admonitions do not achieve the desired effect and "nanny" is thwarted, there is an almost irresistible urge for government to use its powers to compel people to live the "appropriate" life-style. This compulsion erodes individual liberties and turns citizens into serfs who haven't even a property right to their own bodies.

Nanny and the Professor

nan•ny . . . *n, pl* nannies [prob. of baby-talk origin] *chiefly Brit* (1795): a child's nurse; NURSEMAID
—*Webster's Ninth New Collegiate Dictionary*

Individuals often behave in ways that seem irrational, exposing themselves to harm. For example, shooting heroin into a vein or guzzling a case of beer in one evening are self-destructive acts that many of us find incomprehensible. There is no question that addicts and alcoholics harm themselves, their families, and society, but government interventions to stop them, while appealing on the surface, can backfire. In his classic 1949 book *Human Action*, economist Ludwig von Mises argued:

Opium and morphine are certainly· dangerous, habit-forming drugs. But once the principle is admitted that it is the duty of government to protect the individual from his own foolishness, no serious objections can be raised against further encroachments. A good case could be made out in favor of the prohibition of alcohol and nicotine. And why limit the government's benevolent providence to the protection of the individual's body only? Is not the harm a man can inflict on his mind and soul even more disastrous than any bodily evils? Why not prevent him from reading bad books and seeing bad plays, from looking at bad paintings and statues and from hearing bad music? The mischief done by bad ideologies, surely, is much more pernicious, both for the individual and for the whole society, than that done by narcotic drugs.

These fears are not merely imaginary specters terrifying secluded doctrinaires. It is a fact that no paternal government, whether ancient or modern, ever shrank from regimenting its subjects' minds, beliefs, and opinions. If one abolishes man's freedom to determine his own consumption, one takes all freedoms away. The naive advocates of government interference with consumption delude themselves when they neglect what they disdainfully call the philosophical aspect of the problem. They unwittingly support the cause of censorship, inquisition, intolerance, and the persecution of dissenters.[1]

Mises was prophetic. The censors are still busy. They were at work in Cincinnati, Ohio, in 1990, when the city government tried to shut down an exhibition of Robert Mapplethorpe's homoerotic photographs. They were at work in Broward County, Florida, prosecuting the profanity-spouting rap group 2 Live Crew. Whatever one thinks of Mapplethorpe and the Crew, these actions smacked of thought control. Once art is labeled "offensive" and is banned, books inevitably suffer the same fate. "Offensive" speech is next to be forbidden, as we have so vividly witnessed with the political correctness movement on college and university campuses.

Once it becomes legitimate for government to protect individuals from their own follies, there is no way to establish limits to this power. Anything can be banned. After all, taken in excess, virtually any substance may be abused. Vitamin A is essential for good health, but it becomes toxic in large doses. Physical exercise is wholesome, but if overdone it can result in bodily harm, as can all sports. Obesity contributes to health problems. If the principle of governmental control over the most pernicious substances and activities is established and accepted, then nothing prevents the state from regulating less pernicious activities. Fat people can be taxed—for their own good, of course. Twinkies can be outlawed. Mandatory sit-ups can be stipulated.

Mises predicted that banning substances such as opium and morphine would lead to the prohibition of nicotine and alcohol. The propaganda campaign now taking shape in the Congress against tobacco and the tobacco industry may eventually prove him correct; the Prohibition movement that raged over America in the last century shows that it can— indeed, it *did*—happen here.[2]

The Ignoble Experiment

There has always been a segment of the American populace that wants government to play nanny. In 1791 the College of Physicians of New York recommended to the U.S. Senate that it place high duties on imported alcohol to discourage consumption.

In the nineteenth century, prohibition became an organized mass political movement; reformers within bodies such as the American Temperance Society and the Women's Christian Temperance Union quickly tired of moral suasion and lobbied for laws restricting the sale and use of the demon rum. When in 1851 Maine enacted the first statewide prohibition act, the compulsory-education apostle Horace Mann declared it equal to "the discovery of the magnetic needle, the invention of printing, or any other great strides in the progress of civilization."[3]

Like our contemporary nannies, the prohibitionists lobbied politicians while propagandizing amongst the young. The WCTU's Department of Scientific Temperance Instruction bullied legislatures in every state and territory into mandating temperance education in the public schools. The WCTU set up a panel to give its imprimatur to school texts; it demanded that texts teach that "alcohol is a dangerous and seductive poison."[4] By 1906 this panel, which had pledged itself to "a prolonged struggle . . . to free our public-school system from the incubus which rests upon it," had endorsed forty texts for classroom use. The WCTU's Mrs. Mary Hannah Hunt saw a day "surely coming when from the school houses all over the land will come trained haters of alcohol to pour a whole Niagara of ballots upon the saloon."[5]

And what did these pint-sized haters imbibe in their classrooms? The WCTU's Department of Scientific Temperance Instruction taught the following as incontrovertible facts:

1. The majority of beer drinkers die from dropsy.

2. When [alcohol] passes down the throat it burns off the skin leaving it bare and burning.

3. It causes the heart to beat many unnecessary times, and after the first dose the heart is in danger of giving out so that it needs something to keep it up and, therefore, the person to whom the

heart belongs has to take drink after drink to keep his heart going.

4. It turns the blood to water.

5. A[n invalid] man who never drinks liquor will get well, where a drinking man would surely die.[6]

This sounds like sheer nonsense to modern ears, although we might well wonder how the pronouncements of our Drug Warriors will strike American sensibilities in the year 2090. At all events, the propaganda campaign in the schools was a smashing success. No less a personage than the U.S. Commissioner of Education said in 1920: "In the creation of a sentiment which has resulted first in local option, then in state prohibition, and now in national prohibition, the schools of the country have played a very important part; in fact probably a major part. . . . The instruction in physiology and hygiene with special reference to the effects of alcohol . . . has resulted first in clear thinking, and second in better and stronger sentiment in regard to the sale and use of alcoholic drinks."[7]

As with our modern Drug War, the mass media eagerly cooperated in the campaign for prohibition. The editor of *McClure's* wrote hogwash of this sort: "Every function of the normal human body is injured by the use of alcohol—even the moderate use; and that injury is both serious and permanent."[8]

To those who raised the hoary objection that prohibition violated personal liberties, the editor of the popular monthly *The Gospel of the Kingdom* retorted: " 'Personal liberty' is at last an uncrowned, dethroned King, with no one to do him reverence. The social consciousness is so far developed, and is becoming so autocratic, that institutions and governments must give their heed to its mandate and shape their life accordingly. We are no longer frightened by that ancient bogy—'paternalism in government.' We affirm boldly, it is the business of government to be just that—paternal."[9]

Just as our modern anti-tobacco, -alcohol, and -drug crusaders indict weeds and liquors for every little economic slump, so did their forebears. The *Manufacturer's Record* editorialized: "Drastic prohibition would increase the efficiency of the army. It would increase the efficiency of the workers in industrial plants and mining operations. It would increase the efficiency of men on the farms and add enormously to the potential power of the nation."[10] As for those sluggards who didn't want to shape up and make good soldiers or peons, one prohibitionist had a final solution for them: "It would be a saving to the Nation if we could kill off all its hard drinkers tomorrow. There are two and one-half million of these, and their first cost, at twenty-one years of age, was at least *five billion of dollars*."[11] (Similar estimates are made, though couched in more compassionate terms, for the "costs" that heavy smokers impose on us.)

Before we return to the present, let's look at one last argument of the prohibitionists, which we shall see has been revived by our new nannies. It is the racist claim that black men are beasts who are incapable of exercising self-restraint and discretion when close to a booze bottle or a white woman. Will Irwin in *Collier's Weekly* spoke for his generation of racists in 1908:

> The primitive negro field hand, a web of strong, sudden impulses, good and bad, comes into town or settlement on Saturday afternoon and pays his fifty cents for a pint of Mr. Levy's gin. He absorbs not only its toxic heat, but absorbs also the suggestion, subtly conveyed, that it contains aphrodisiacs. He sits in the road or in the alley at the height of his debauch, looking at that obscene picture of a white woman on the label, drinking in the invitation which it carries. And then comes—opportunity. There follows the hideous episode of the rope or the stake.[12]

Mr. Irwin's breed, alas, is still with us. We'll meet them later in this chapter.

Smoke Gets in Nanny's Eyes

Tobacco is harder to demonize than, say, opium. Tens of millions of Americans—mothers, sisters, beloved grandpas—are regular smokers. We are unwilling to relegate them to the same moral plane as drooling junkies and spaced-out potheads. While the health risks associated with smoking are well known, tobacco is deep-dyed in the American grain. From Bogart and Bacall to the pastel cops of "Miami Vice," pop culture is enveloped by the haze of smoke.

But nanny can no longer abide the acrid smell of burning tobacco. As cigarette smoking has lost its glamorous gloss and become a habit found primarily among the working class, government and its busybody allies in the nonprofit sector have intensified the anti-tobacco propaganda campaign. (The Big Three nonprofits—the American Cancer Society, the American Lung Association, and the American Heart Association—had combined assets of $1.157 billion in 1991, putting them in the same fiscal league as small countries.)

The principal goal of these voluntary health agencies (VHAs) is the alteration of the life-styles of American citizens in ways pleasing to the upper classes. Today's educated elite favors exercise, frowns on obesity, and disdains smoking as hopelessly déclassé. Smoking cigarettes and chewing tobacco are the vices of the lower-middle class, that pool of the tasteless and icky masses who are too stupid to make their own decisions. The VHAs are wealthy exponents of puritanism—defined by social critic H. L. Mencken as the "haunting fear that someone, somewhere, may be happy."

Smoke, Mirrors, and Deep Pockets

Through their political advocacy, VHAs seek to accomplish two goals: first, to shift the cost of disease research to taxpayers; and second, to use the coercive powers of government to enforce their idea of a healthy life-style. At the first, they have succeeded smashingly. The federally funded National Institutes of Health spends more than fifteen times as much each year for heart, cancer, and lung research than the ACS, ALA, and AHA combined.[13] Having saddled taxpayers with the cost for disease research, the VHAs are free to concentrate on political advocacy. They pursue their anti-smoking agenda through the Coalition on Smoking OR Health, which lobbies at the federal level, and Tobacco-Free America, a "legislative clearing house" that focuses on the state and local levels of government.

Unlike special interests that prefer their power plays to be stealthy, the VHAs are remarkably upfront about what they want. Their anti-tobacco political strategy is outlined in "Blueprint for Success: Countdown 2000—Ten Years to a Tobacco-Free America," a document drafted by lobbyists for the ACS, the ALA, and the AHA. The report calls for "severe limitations on sales and access of tobacco products, tobacco education, . . . tobacco-counter promotion for youth and minorities and the creation of state offices on tobacco and health."[14]

"Blueprint for Success" is a curious mixture of paternalism and paranoia. Unkind readers, catching the whiff of the jackboot, might rename it "Blueprint for Health Fascism." Constitutional protections for individuals—which extend to corporate entities because they are treated as individuals under the law—are dismissed by the VHAs as minor impediments, trifling nuisances. What's a Bill of Rights when there's a nation of obese, nicotine-stinking drunkards to be saved from themselves?

One of the most chilling goals of the VHAs is to "ban the advertising of tobacco products within each state."[15] Advertising is commercial speech, and the proposed restriction on advertising is a frontal attack on the constitutional guarantee of free speech. (Although, as U.S. Court of Appeals Judge Alex Kozinski has wryly noted, "Commercial speech is a stepchild of the First Amendment: Liberals don't much like it because it's commercial; conservatives mistrust it because it's speech."[16]) At all events, the First Amendment counts for little to the righteous. One is reminded of Carry Nation, the hatchet-wielding prohibitionist, who called herself "a bulldog, running along at the feet of Jesus, barking at what He doesn't like."[17]

It is one thing to use persuasion to urge people not to use tobacco (or any other product); it is altogether different to use the coercive powers of government to impose one's will on others. This second strategy, alas, is the one that the VHAs steadfastly pursue. They may not carry La Nation's trusty ax, but they share her contempt for the principle of individual liberty. (None of this is to suggest that tobacco deserves *subsidy*. Despite the praiseworthy efforts of Oregon Senator Mark Hatfield and Wisconsin Representative Tom Petri to abolish them, tobacco price supports enjoy overwhelming favor in Congress.)

A New Ministry of Propaganda?

Each year since 1989, Senator Edward M. Kennedy (D-Mass.), chairman of the Committee on Labor and Human Resources, has reported to the Senate the Tobacco Product Education and Health Protection Act (TPEHPA), which codifies the VHA trinity's "Blueprint for Success." This mammoth bill proposes to "establish a center for tobacco products, to inform the public concerning the hazards of tobacco use, to provide for the disclosure of additives to such products, and to require that information be provided concerning such products to the public."[18] Say this for Senator Kennedy: he doesn't lack gall. Under this legislation, taxpayers would be forced to *pay* for assaults on their own civil liberties.

The TPEHPA is based on these twenty-five "findings":

1. despite a steady decline in tobacco consumption, 52,000,000 Americans still use tobacco products annually;

2. tobacco use causes nearly 400,000 deaths each year in the United States, the equivalent of over 1,000 deaths per day;

3. tobacco use is the most important cause of death and illness in the United States today, causing one-sixth of all deaths annually;

4. in 1985 the private and public sectors in the United States spent approximately $22,000,000,000 on smoking-related illnesses and absorbed $43,000,000,000 in economic losses from such illnesses;

5. 50 percent of all smokers begin using tobacco by the age of 14, and 90 percent of all smokers begin using tobacco before the age of 20;

6. tobacco products contain nicotine and are addictive;

7. most young people initiate tobacco use and become addicted before they are sufficiently informed or mature enough to make an informed choice concerning such use;

8. the tobacco industry contributes significantly to the experimentation with tobacco and the initiation of regular tobacco use by children and young adults through its advertising and promotion practices;

9. in 1988 the tobacco industry spent $3,250,000,000 on the advertising and promotion of tobacco products, ranking such products among the most heavily advertised and promoted products in the United States;

10. the tobacco industry claims that the purpose of advertising is to influence consumer brand selection, but only 10 percent of tobacco users switch brands each year;

11. convincing evidence demonstrates that tobacco advertising is predominantly directed at market expansion or retention or both;

12. the tobacco industry must attract 6,000 new smokers daily to replace those who stop smoking or who die of smoking-related diseases and other causes, or who quit;

13. tobacco product advertising and promotion are intended to capture the youth market and seek to do so through advertisements that suggest a strong association between smoking and physical fitness, attractiveness, success, adventure, and independence, and advertisements that are designed to influence minors, who are more vulnerable to image-based advertising;

14. serious gaps in knowledge about the harmful effects of the use of tobacco products persist in both minors and the adult population, with surveys showing that large numbers of citizens are unaware that smoking causes lung cancer, heart disease and stillbirths in pregnancy;

15. education is effective in preventing and halting the use of tobacco products;

16. the proportion of smokers among the most educated adults is less than half that among the least educated adults;

17. the highest percentage of smoking is among those individuals with the least amount of education, including young citizens, blue-collar workers, high school drop-outs and minorities;

18. the total resources of the major voluntary organizations that sponsor educational activities on smoking have never exceeded 2 percent of tobacco industry expenditures for the promotion of tobacco;

19. children and teenagers should be informed about the dangers of smoking and be discouraged from initiating the use of tobacco products;

20. The American public and groups with high prevalences of tobacco use should be informed about the dangers of tobacco products;

21. although most States prohibit the sale of tobacco products to minors, such laws are not uniformly enforced;

22. in recent years, there have been efforts in some States to improve the enforcement of existing laws which prohibit the sale of tobacco products to minors;

23. cooperative Federal-State efforts will encourage more effective action to limit the sale of tobacco products to minors;

24. no Federal law currently requires public disclosure of the numerous additives in tobacco products; and

25. tobacco and tobacco products are in interstate commerce.[19]

"Nothing is new under the sun," Ecclesiastes tells us—not even the preambles to oppressive legislation. A spiritual ancestor of Senator Kennedy, another senatorial scion of wealth named Morris Sheppard, announced a similar set of findings in the constitutional amendment he introduced that later became the most hated law in American history: Prohibition. Sheppard's preamble read:

> *Whereas*, exact scientific research has demonstrated that alcohol is a narcotic poison, destructive and degenerating to the human organism, and that its distribution as a beverage or contained in foods, lays a staggering economic burden upon the shoulders of the people, lowers to an appalling degree the average standard of character of our citizenship, thereby undermining the public morals and the foundation of free institutions, produces widespread crime, pauperism and insanity, inflicts disease and untimely death upon hundreds of thousands of citizens, and blights with degeneracy their children unborn, threatening the future integrity and the very life of the nation. . . .[20]

Senator Kennedy's findings are just as shaky as Senator Sheppard's. More than fifty million adult Americans—about one in three—choose to use tobacco products. No one is forced to smoke or chew tobacco. The Orwellian claim that depriving people of choice will make them freer won't play here. Senator Kennedy and his VHA allies must, perforce, base their arguments on a series of dubious assertions, which we will now examine.

The Effects of Tobacco Use. Consider the two central claims made in the TPEHPA findings: "tobacco use is *the most important cause* of death and illness in the United States today, causing one-sixth of all deaths annually,"

and "smoking causes lung cancer, heart disease and stillbirths in pregnancy." Although no one can seriously champion smoking as a salubrious
habit, the assertion that smoking is "the most important cause" of lung
cancer, heart disease, and stillbirths cannot withstand even a cursory
examination.

An impressive body of research has been built on the connections
between smoking and disease, particularly lung cancer and heart disease.
Based on an exhaustive survey of this work, Hans J. Eysenck concluded:

> The received view—that smoking causes lung cancer and coro-
> nary heart disease and is responsible for the major portion of the
> deaths that occur from these two causes—has not been proven
> correct by existing research, but has encountered so many anoma-
> lies and difficulties, and is based on such insecure foundations
> (largely due to the lack of reliability of the data, and the incautious
> use of statistics based on these data) the only possible conclusion is
> a verdict of "not proven."[21]

Without question, the most dreaded disease associated with smoking is
lung cancer, which felled even the archetypal American hero John Wayne.
But lung cancer has other causes. As the *Washington Post* reports, "Exposure to low levels of radiation, such as that from X-rays or radon, is at least
three to four times—and under some assumptions, roughly 14 times—
more likely to cause fatal cancer than is commonly believed."[22] While
radon remains a subject of dispute, other known contributing factors to
cancer include exposure to carcinogens in the environment, diet, heredity,
genetic defects, stress, and even personality.[23] Then there is the puzzling
fact that the majority of the fifty-two million Americans who smoke *do not
get lung cancer*. Richard L. Stroup and John C. Goodman note:

> Despite the hundreds of experiments conducted and the enormous
> amounts of money spent on such tests (from $250,000 to $500,000
> per experiment), we still know very little about how cancer is
> caused. Even cigarette smoking, the most heavily studied of all
> carcinogenic risks, still remains much of a mystery. For example,
> two-thirds of all cigarette smokers do not get lung cancer and 25
> percent of the people who do get lung cancer do not get it from
> smoking. No one knows why.[24]

The Costs to Society of Tobacco Use. If tobacco is not the major cause of disease, then TPEHPA's cost estimates of $22 billion on smoking-related illnesses and $43 billion in economic losses from such illnesses become ridiculously exaggerated. Not that the VHAs have ever been sticklers for statistical accuracy: the ALA has claimed, at different times, that cigarette smoking causes 390,000; 350,000; and 300,000 deaths each year.

Politicians and publicists with a cause love high-cost estimates. The outrageously favorable cost-benefit ratios they produce make great talking points. If, by implementing a measly $2 billion program, the amorphous god "society" will at some unspecified point in the future save $400 billion, what obdurate slob could be opposed?

For purposes of argument, assume that medical research *has* proven a direct causal link between smoking and disease. Even then, it does not follow that society incurs costs because of tobacco consumption. One analyst reported:

> A 1989 study by the Rand Corporation found that the state and federal excise taxes on cigarettes—which together with sales taxes, represent 25 to 55 percent of the retail price—are sufficient to cover the net costs of smoking. The researchers noted that smokers tend to die early, thereby reducing the need for nursing-home care and demands on Social Security and pension funds.[25]

Tobacco users already more than pay their way through taxes; therefore, the cost to the taxpayers of reducing tobacco use will actually *exceed* the benefit to society. Ought a tribe of hardheaded utilitarians start passing out free smokes to teens on high-school campuses? The logic of the cost-benefit crew says so.

But a more fundamental issue underlies all. Does government—or a VHA acting at the behest of government—have a right to stop individuals from making bad or risky choices?

Many activities undertaken voluntarily are "risky" from a health perspective; indeed, the risk itself often adds to the appeal. Think of skydiving, football, skateboarding, skiing, mountain and rock climbing, bungee jumping, jogging, weight lifting, and other leisure pursuits. No one but a fool considers jumping from an airplane several thousand feet in the air to be hazard-free, yet government agencies are not engaged in expensive propaganda campaigns to "educate" skydivers in the error of their ways.

Of course, most skydivers are middle- or upper middle-class whites; interesting, isn't it, that the only dangerous sport that the safety commissars want to ban is boxing, which is dominated by skilled black and Hispanic athletes?

The anti-tobacco nannies respond to the charge of inconsistency with five arguments. First, they claim that the public is unaware of the risks of tobacco consumption. As finding 14 of the TPEHPA states, "serious gaps in knowledge about the harmful effects of the use of tobacco products persist." Second, they identify tobacco as an addictive substance (finding 6). Third, they claim that smokers impose health risks and costs on nonsmokers through "secondhand" smoke. Fourth, they appeal to our healthy paternal instincts by claiming in finding 7 that "most young people initiate tobacco use and become addicted before they are sufficiently informed or mature enough to make an informed choice." Finally, and revealingly, they identify smokers as less educated than nonsmokers, as blue-collar rather than white-collar workers, as high-school dropouts, and as minorities (findings 16 and 17). People who fall within these groupings (such as, say, Harriet Tubman, Lech Walesa, and H. L. Mencken) are deemed incapable of making informed decisions. This quintet of reasons deserves refutation.

Knowledge Gaps. Findings 14 and 15 claim that there are "serious gaps in knowledge" about the harmful effects of tobacco and that "education is effective" in filling these gaps and thereby halting the use of tobacco products. Yet in 1985 Surgeon General C. Everett Koop, an ardent anti-smoking activist, admitted, "The smoker today is well educated about the health hazards of smoking."[26] Gerald M. Goldhaber, chairman of the Department of Communication at the State University of New York at Buffalo, told a congressional subcommittee,

> in [1985] . . . the nationally-known consulting firm of Audits and Surveys, Inc. was commissioned to do a poll of the American public with respect to various smoking and health issues. When the pollsters asked whether, regardless of what they *believed*, people had *heard* that smoking was dangerous, an astonishing 99% responded in the affirmative. In that same year . . . a government-sponsored survey revealed that fully 95% of the American public *believe* that cigarettes and smoking increase the risk of lung cancer; that 92% of Americans *believe* that the risk of

emphysema is increased by smoking; and that 91% *believe* that the risk of getting heart disease is increased by smoking. Only 1% to 3% of Americans actively *disbelieve* these propositions.[27]

As background, Goldhaber reported polls showing that only 89 percent of Americans knew the name of the nation's first president and only 38 percent of Americans can name their congressional representative. Goldhaber concluded: "The American public seldom, if ever, reaches on any matter the awareness level that it has reached on cigarette smoking."[28]

Almost all Americans believe that smoking is hazardous to one's health. Yet more than fifty million Americans still touch the stuff. Which raises the question: what good is the further education recommended in findings 15, 19, and 20? The best way to stop that stubborn remnant of smokers is to handcuff them—or, as the fervent prohibitionist recommended a century ago, kill 'em off.

Addiction. Contrary to popular belief, the question of whether or not cigarette smoking is addictive has by no means been settled. As a philosopher has suggested:

> Someone might wish to argue that the allegedly "addictive" character of smoking makes the action substantially involuntary. The thesis that smoking is addictive, however, is thoroughly discredited by the large and ever growing number of people who quit smoking. Smoking is at most a habit (perhaps a strong one). But habits are not "substantially involuntary" actions. . . . All the term "habit" implies is a degree of difficulty in altering behavior.[29]

Many substances, including caffeine and alcohol, can produce physical or psychological dependence. In this age of Sally Jessy Raphael and psychobabble and the widespread disclamation of individual responsibility for one's own actions, having an addiction is becoming *de rigueur*. We have "chocoholics," "foodaholics," and of course that staple of tabloid television, nymphomaniacs. But the consumption of coffee, tea, chocolate, or sex (if practiced with discretion) is considered a private matter beyond the purview of the state—as smoking should be.

Environmental Tobacco Smoke. Children, always pictured as innocent little cherubim a world away from *Lord of the Flies*, are the ideal poster kids for supporters of the nanny state. In the tradition of their prohibitionist forebears, anti-tobacco crusaders try to demonstrate that smoking causes harm to innocent nonsmokers. The culprit is variously called "passive smoking," "secondhand smoke," "involuntary smoking," or "environmental tobacco smoke" (ETS). The concept of ETS is simple: exposure to the smoke exhaled by smokers or emitted by their cigarettes damages the health of nonsmokers. Therefore, smoking must be regulated so that innocent third parties—babes wrapped in swaddling clothing, new mothers in the pink of health—will not be harmed. Since the mid-1970s, the passage of "Clean Indoor Air" laws has been a prime objective of the VHAs.

The connection between ETS and disease, however, is far more tenuous than the link between smoking and disease. In December 1986 the U.S. Surgeon General issued a report that satisfied neither side of the debate. Although the VHAs seized upon it as evidence of the dangers of ETS to nonsmokers, one observer writes: "The Surgeon General's report does not provide irrefutable evidence of environmental tobacco smoke's mortal peril. In fact on no fewer than 147 occasions . . . the report demurs from making this claim and actually points out that it cannot conclusively establish such a claim."[30] Another analyst is more direct: "No one has shown that casual exposure to tobacco smoke is harmful."[31]

Whatever the health risks posed by ETS, banning smoking indoors will not result in "clean indoor air." Tobacco smoke is only one of a host of indoor pollutants; it stands out only because it is visible and has an acrid odor.

Polluted indoor air, the result of poor ventilation and filtration, dates to the mid-1970s. Spurred by skyrocketing energy prices caused by the oil embargo, building owners attempted to lower heating and air-conditioning costs by reducing the amount of ventilation. Tobacco smoke is easily apparent in inadequately ventilated buildings, but it is critical to recognize that a higher level of other pollutants is present as well. Put bluntly:

> Seducing the general public to ban smoking by having them vote for clean indoor air without addressing the ventilation rates and filtration standards leaves that same public in a fool's paradise. Indoor air pollution can still be rampant even where it is invisible. We cannot see carbon dioxide or monoxide, formaldehyde, ozone, ammonia, airborne fibers, bacteria, or fungi. Since these pollutants can make us sick and can even kill us, a clean indoor air act [banning only smoking indoors] cannot address these problems.[32]

Most nonsmokers are tolerant of those who light up; some are not. But where once common courtesy and decency ruled social intercourse— "Mind if I smoke?"—today these matters are adjudged by the state. And what a Pandora's box we open when government starts banning private action merely because it offends some people. After all, virtually all activities are offensive or annoying to *someone*. The list is endless, and includes offensive language, crude bumper stickers, rudeness, inebriation, slovenly or inappropriate dress, goofy hair styles, tardiness, stupidity, rank body odor, elevator music, punk rock, and obesity.[33] If the government regulates an activity simply because it imposes "external costs"—that is, because it annoys others—then there is no logical limit to the tyrannical powers the state can wield. Personal freedom, in all its many-splendored forms, would be lost.

Paternalism and Elitism The nannies are correct in saying that smokers tend to cluster at the lower end of the socioeconomic ladder in terms of education, income, and employment. And yes, minorities, particularly Hispanics, are more likely to use tobacco than are whites. So what? The use of such statistics as a rationale for government intervention is elitist paternalism of a high and nauseating order. No formal education is needed to understand that smoking may carry health risks. Moreover, there is no evidence that the public awareness of the risks of smoking varies widely by socioeconomic status. Consumers in the same socioeconomic profile as smokers are more likely to drink beer than white wine, but that preference does not indicate that they are somehow "vulnerable" to clever ad campaigns or incompetent to make their own judgments. Their taste for beer and tobacco sets them apart from—but does not make them "inferior" to—anti-smoking activists, who are typically college-educated, affluent whites, as are most politicians. Working-class Americans are not agitating for a ban on Evian; unfortunately, that tolerance is not reciprocated by the arrogant and presumptuous anti-tobacco crowd.

The flagrantly elitist and paternalistic nature of the anti-smoking crusade is clearly demonstrated by the reaction of the VHAs to the introduction of Uptown menthol cigarettes in 1990. The R. J. Reynolds Tobacco Company designed this new brand to appeal primarily to African Americans. Much of the advertising of this new brand was destined for inner-city billboards.

The VHAs' response to Uptown was vociferous and immediate: "This marketing strategy is outrageous and immoral," roared Harold P. Freeman, president of the American Cancer Society. "The cigarette industry just wants to make money because they know that poor and uneducated people are their main customers. And black people are disproportionately poor and uneducated."[34] One reporter wrote: "Critics, like the American Cancer Society, see the Uptown campaign as an alarming escalation in cigarette marketing. They believe the campaign exploits blacks, especially the ghetto poor."[35]

This is racist garbage. It differs little from the caricature of the debauched "primitive Negro field hand" related earlier in this chapter. Mr. Freeman and his conferees have set themselves up as white guardians of African Americans and Hispanics, whom they take to be too stupid to think for themselves. There is no reason for anyone but the most virulent racist to believe that African Americans are less capable than whites of judging the validity of advertising messages. Mr. Freeman must've lived an awfully sheltered life to assume that a sheepskin on the wall and a few bucks in your wallet are emblems of common sense and clear thinking.

African Americans, Hispanics, the poor, and the working class are not the only groups being herded into nanny's nursery. Even jarheads and leathernecks are the objects of VHA paternalism. In October 1990 tobacco companies donated thousands of cartons of cigarettes to American troops serving in Saudi Arabia. As the *Charlotte Observer* reported:

> When anti-smoking groups, such as the American Medical Association, the Cancer Society, and the American Lung Association, discovered this, they accused the tobacco companies of a thinly disguised marketing campaign designed to recruit new smokers. . . . [These groups] pressured the Pentagon and the Defense Department announced that it was against defense policy to accept and distribute free tobacco products, although the products could be bought by the troops if they desired.[36]

Evidently, the VHAs see the men and women in the armed services as immature, impressionable, callow tenderfeet unable to resist the temptation of free cigarettes. Never mind that virtually all members of the all-volunteer armed services have at least a high-school education, and many are trained to operate the most sophisticated military equipment in existence. When it comes to lighting up a Camel, these greenhorns are not to be trusted.

In 1990 the Philip Morris Company, a major producer of tobacco products, made a million-dollar education grant to the District of Columbia Board of Education to help inner-city schools. This was no isolated act: tobacco companies, like many other corporations, often make substantial grants to nonprofit organizations. Incredibly, the American Heart Association urged the D.C. school board to reject the grant.[37] By such contributions, the AHA charged, "the [tobacco] industry has bought the silence and complacency of the black community."[38]

Firing back at these haughty critics, Donald Hense, vice president for development of the National Urban League, asked, "Has anyone ever called Lincoln Center and asked why they haven't turned tobacco money down?"[39] Hense's point is sharp and cutting: there is not a shred of evidence that these donations buy "the silence and complacency of the black community." (As if African Americans are not distinct individuals but simply parts of one huge monolith.) What the VHAs seem to be saying is that while whites are sophisticated enough to avoid co-option, benighted African Americans are manipulable patsies.

In an act of supreme hypocrisy, the VHAs that condemn minority organizations for accepting "tainted" money have eagerly sought funding from every conceivable source, including corporations that have been vilified as polluters. Many VHAs, the American Cancer Society in particular, have agreements with the United Way, which receives contributions from tobacco companies. (Talk about biting the hand that feeds you!) Eugene Pendergrass, former president of the American Cancer Society, stated that the ACS will "take the devil's money to do the Lord's work."[40] The opposite is probably true as well.

The Advertising Issue. Findings 8 through 13 of the TPEHPA indict tobacco companies for irresponsible advertising. We are told that in 1988, the industry spent $3.25 billion on advertising, much of it—contrary to the industry's protestations of innocence—directed at young people who can replace the six thousand smokers who quit or die every day. The tobacconists' claim that "the purpose of advertising is to influence consumer brand selection" is said to be a lie. We are given to believe that there would be far fewer smokers if tobacco advertising did not exist. No evidence is offered to support these findings; they are axiomatic, and that's that.

Yet research does exist on the impact of advertising on cigarette consumption. At the Third World Conference on Smoking and Health, which was sponsored by the American Cancer Society and the National Cancer Institute of the National Institutes of Health "in cooperation with," among others, the ALA and AHA, James L. Hamilton reported on his investigation:

> Previous studies have indicated that cigarette advertising bans have had little effect on cigarette consumption in the United States. . . . For seven countries that have enacted bans, the evidence reveals that bans have not, in general, slowed consumption growth. . . . Countries that had banned broadcast cigarette advertising were compared with countries that had not and countries that never had permitted it. The growth of per capita cigarette consumption apparently was not slower in countries that had banned or had never permitted cigarette advertising. *A ban of cigarette advertising has not been an effective policy for reducing cigarette smoking.*[41]

At the same conference, Karl Warnberg concluded:

> There is no evidence to support the view that a ban on advertising would have a positive effect on smoking habits. No empirical research has been able to show that aggregate brand advertising leads to greater total tobacco consumption. Nor has anything been found to suggest that advertising entices nonsmokers, young people in particular, to become smokers. It follows, therefore, that there can be no evidence showing that a ban on advertising would result in reduced tobacco consumption and fewer new smokers.[42]

Thus, two experts at nanny's own conference threw cold water on her feverish fantasies. But, as we have seen, drawing conclusions from empirical research is not nanny's strong suit. Allison Smith of the Coalition on Smoking OR Health, an umbrella group made up of the AHA, ALA, and ACS, told a congressional subcommittee: "Congress could send this Nation's young people a powerful message by banning cigarette advertising and promotion altogether."[43]

Pace, Ms. Smith and TPEHPA, no one knows with certainty why people start smoking, but the empirical evidence shows that advertising entices neither old nor young to take up the habit. The principal goal of advertising really is to encourage smokers to switch brands. As with other products, advertising enhances competition within the industry. Newer firms tend to advertise heavily as a means of "breaking in"; like the upstart hotels discussed in chapter 2, new brands of cigarettes must advertise to survive. The restrictions and bans that nanny promotes would make the tobacco industry less competitive. Although prices would rise (and hit the poor especially hard), a significant reduction in smoking is unlikely. Research has demonstrated that the demand for cigarettes is "inelastic," that is, it is not very responsive to price changes.

An advertising ban might actually *worsen* the collective health of Americans. As competitive pressures ease, tobacco companies will either increase prices or reduce quality. In the past, competitive pressures have led to the development of healthier and safer products, such as low-tar or even no-tar and no-nicotine cigarettes, as tobacco companies competed for health-conscious consumers. Advertising restrictions, by weakening competitive pressures, will reduce the incentive to develop such products. Hence, one of nanny's pet causes will in the long run make smoking a more dangerous habit than it is now. The road to perdition has always been littered with good intentions.

Filtering Out the Truth

Since the risks associated with tobacco are better known than even George Washington, the education goals of TPEHPA seem an expensive redundancy. And given Uncle Sam's dismal record in presenting just the facts, ma'am, the likelihood of his meeting the TPEHPA's goal of "disclosure of accurate information to the public" is about as likely as Milton Berle's wedding Julia Roberts.

The issue here is far more important than the waste or abuse of taxpayers' dollars. A vital principle is at stake. When government attempts to control what citizens buy and restricts the advertising of goods it deems "unhealthy," greater and greater violations of liberty ensue. If it becomes legitimate for government to control the consumption of things that are viewed as "bad" for the body, it follows that it will also become legitimate for government to regulate things that are considered "bad" for the mind.

Once the precedent is established, there are no objective criteria that may be used to limit the powers of the state over its citizens—or, more accurately, its subjects.

Unlike narcotics and alcohol, tobacco has never been banned by federal law. But today we are somewhere along the road to prohibition, and our view of the point whence we started—liberty—grows dimmer by the hour.

Reefer Madness

The wars that governments wage often kill far more bystanders than enemies. A sterling case in point is the incessantly advertised War on Drugs, which has destroyed lives, wasted billions of dollars, besmirched the U.S. Constitution, and, incidentally, done very little to take dangerous drugs out of the hands (and noses and veins) of self-destructive fools.

The criminalization of drugs is a textbook case of bureaucratic aggrandizement. Take marijuana. Not until President Roosevelt signed the Marihuana [*sic*] Tax Act of 1937 did the federal government get around to making this mildest of drugs illegal. The problem, you see, was that marijuana was not a problem: few Americans smoked it, and those who did (mostly Mexican laborers in the Southwest and African Americans in New Orleans) didn't much bother anybody.

But the Federal Bureau of Narcotics, run by a turf-ravening commissioner named Harry J. Anslinger, wanted to extend its domain. Anslinger and the FBN launched a full-scale propaganda campaign against the wicked weed. They encountered little resistance: so few Americans smoked marijuana that the FBN's claims were accepted as truth.

And what were those claims? Marijuana causes insanity. It incites its users to rape. "Those who indulge in its habitual use," one FBN publication lied, "eventually develop a delirious rage after its administration, during which time they are, temporarily at least, irresponsible and prone to commit violent crimes."[44]

Commissioner Anslinger lectured: "But here we have a drug that is not like opium. Opium has all of the good of Dr. Jekyll and all of the evil of Mr. Hyde. This drug is entirely the monster Hyde."[45] What's more, as FBN flunkies frequently pointed out, many of its users were "Spanish-speaking."[46]

The lurid charges worked. The Marihuana Tax Act of 1937 encountered much ignorance and little opposition. As one historian writes: "[The Act] was the result of a publicity campaign staged by the Federal Bureau of Narcotics."[47]

Other drugs have similar histories. Heroin, once hailed for its medicinal and therapeutic qualities, underwent rapid demonization in the late teens and early 1920s. It was (theoretically) banished from American life in 1924, when an amendment to the Narcotic Drugs Import and Export Act of 1922 barred the import of opium.

As with marijuana, misinformation was mainlined into the public vein. During the landmark House of Representatives' hearings on the 1924 amendment, chief sponsor Stephen G. Porter was asked of heroin, "Does this drug produce insanity?" His terse reply: "Undoubtedly." To the same question U.S. Surgeon General Rupert Blue replied, "Oh, yes."[48] And the demonization was on.

Heroin users were accused of every imaginable act of turpitude. The deputy warden of New York City's Hart's Island Reformatory Prison told the House committee, "The man who uses heroin is a potential murderer, the same as the cocaine user; he loses all consciousness of moral responsibility, also fear of consequences."[49]

A new stock villain was entering the American ensemble: the dope fiend. Beady-eyed and foaming at the mouth, he'd just as soon kill you as look at you. His poisonous nectar—heroin—had to be stopped at all costs.

It made for sensational pulp magazine stories and entertaining B-movies, but it was mostly bunk. Scholar Arnold Trebach writes: "Virtually every 'fact' testified to under oath by the medical and criminological experts in 1924—including claims that heroin was no better than codeine in the treatment of the organically ill; that it produced insanity; that it was more poisonous than morphine and that its therapeutic dose was not much smaller than its toxic dose; that it propelled its users toward violent criminal activity; and that it destroyed the morals of its users—was unsupported by any sound evidence."[50]

The drug prohibitionists weren't above using racist appeals to further their cause. Cocaine dealers were often said to be "Jew peddlers." In 1910 a House committee was told that "the colored people seem to have a weakness for [cocaine]. . . . They would just as leave rape a woman as anything else and a great many of the Southern rape cases have been traced to cocaine."[51] (How eerily this echoes the "drunken Negroes rape white women" garbage quoted earlier in this chapter.) A typical Federal Bureau of Narcotics report read: "Colored students at the Univ. of Minn. partying with female students (white) smoking [marijuana] and getting their sympathies with stories of racial persecution. Result pregnancy."[52] Evidently when *they* aren't out robbing or looting or pillaging or killing under the influence of heroin, they're seducing our wimmin. The implicit message of all this is that those colored dope fiends need a good lynching—and that, alas, is exactly what they often got.

The propaganda campaign has modulated—not moderated, mind you, but modulated—over the last fifty years. Overwhelming evidence has been produced that drug users are *not* prone to violence. Historian Richard Lawrence Miller notes: "Few users of any illicit drug are arrested for violence. In the 1970s, a nationwide survey made for the U.S. Bureau of Narcotics and Dangerous Drugs found that burglary accounted for about 20 percent of offenses charged against drug users, robbery accounted for about 20 percent, automobile theft about five percent and drug law violations accounted for the rest. Murders, rapes, and assaults were so uncommon that they did not appear in the nearly 2,000 cases examined."[53]

Indeed, by 1958 the director of the Federal Bureau of Prisons was admitting, "The drug user does not commit serious crimes of violence— aggravated assault, bank robbery, kidnapping."[54]

Nevertheless, generations of propaganda have had their effect. Heroin, which induces passivity in its users, is still viewed by many as a stimulus to manic impulses. The government is mostly silent on marijuana these days, perhaps because the drug is so safe that a lethal dose has yet to be calculated. The Drug Abuse Warning Network, a warehouse of information on drug-related deaths, seldom reports more than a handful of marijuana-related deaths per year. Along the same lines, at the height of the Reaganite "Zero Tolerance" hysteria, the Network found cocaine in the corpses of just eleven children nationwide.[55]

Now of course even one drug-related death is one too many, as a politician would say, and cocaine, heroin, and even marijuana are to be avoided. Not because they are killers or inciters to violence, but because they retard ambition, creativity, and a joyous sense of life. But in its zeal to stamp out these drugs, the government is draining our Treasury and trashing our Bill of Rights.

In Our Enlightened Age . . .

The federal government appropriated approximately $12 billion in fiscal year 1992 on its "war" against illicit drugs.[56] The fifty states were no less bellicose: as Drug Czar William Bennett declared in a November 1990 report on state drug-control policies: "No strategy to combat illegal drug use can succeed without recognizing the crucial role played by the States."[57] He continued, "Well-crafted, effectively enforced State laws are important elements in the President's National Drug Control Strategy. . . . Leadership by State legislatures is crucial if States are to fulfill their critical role in reducing illegal drug use."[58]

Among the state policies recommended by Czar Bennett were military-style boot camps for convicted drug criminals, although he emphasized that such camps "cannot be a substitute for needed construction of regular prisons."[59] (This in a nation that recently passed South Africa and the ex-Soviet Union to gain the dubious distinction of imprisoning the highest percentage of its populace.)

These harsh policies are directed not only at drug kingpins—mustachioed Latinos, as the pop culture stereotype has it—but also the twenty-three million small-time users, who constitute nearly 10 percent of the population.[60] As of July 1990, there were at least sixteen states operating boot camps for drug offenders; more will surely follow. Meanwhile, the ironically named U.S. Justice Department has proposed doubling the nation's prison capacity to accommodate every last pot smoker in freedom's land.[61] Once they're in jail—or even merely awaiting trial—their families will be robbed blind: Bennett proposed to confiscate the "unexplained wealth" of accused drug users or traffickers. In his careless disregard for American liberties, Bennett reminds us of the early anti-narcotics crusader Harrison Wright, who complained, "the Constitution is constantly getting in the way" of his draconian schemes.[62]

As with the alcohol prohibitionists, the drug warriors are targeting innocent, gullible schoolchildren with their propaganda barrage. Formal training in "substance-abuse" education is required for teachers in sixteen states, and schools are now required to implement drug-prevention programs and policies as a condition of receiving federal funding "of any sort."[63]

Teacher training and education about drug abuse are certainly worthy objectives. However, serious questions have been raised about the accuracy and usefulness of much of the information about drug use provided by state governments.

These governments have formed an alliance with a nonprofit organization named the "Partnership for a Drug-Free America," which produces television and newspaper advertisements for use by the states.[64] Even

President Bush has appeared in some ads; in 1990 the Partnership's anti-drug crusade was the third-largest advertising campaign in the country, ranking just behind AT&T and McDonald's.[65]

Despite the labors of Madison Avenue's best and brightest, the ads are riddled with inaccuracies. For example, a 1989 print ad claimed that "15 million Americans used cocaine—and five million of those who survived needed medical help."[66] The May 1989 *Scientific American* corrected those numbers: the actual best estimate was 8.2 million users and 62,141 medical emergencies. The annual number of deaths attributable to *all* illicit drugs hovers around four thousand—or less than one tenth the number of annual highway fatalities. Yet automobiles remain legal.

Another ad depicted an electroencephalograph (EEG) monitor supposedly showing the brain wave of some poor fool smoking pot. The wave was flat, as if the machine was completely turned off. Pretty scary, huh? The *Hartford Courant* later discovered that the EEG was in fact turned off. The ad was a fake.

One ad claims that "one of every five people who try cocaine gets hooked."[67] But even the Office of National Drug Policy estimates the figure to be about 10 percent, the same as for alcohol.

Marijuana has "a lot more cancer-causing agents than cigarettes," declares the suave voice of Peter Jennings in another ad. But again, the Office of National Drug Policy admits that, although marijuana contains more than two hundred chemicals, "it is not clear which [if any] of them actually cause cancer or don't."[68] In fact, "there is no solid evidence linking marijuana to cancer."[69]

"If your kids have lost weight, if they seem lethargic, if their grades and attendance have dropped off at school, they're into drugs and they need your help," warns another ad sponsored by state governments in conjunction with the ubiquitous Partnership for a Drug-Free America.[70] Might not these symptoms also suggest the flu, a breakup with one's girlfriend, or a bad case of the blues? It seems a kid can't have a bad day anymore without being accused of juvenile delinquency. The Partnership's scare tactics recall the popular song by the rock band Suicidal Tendencies in which officious parents badger a listless boy with the question, "Are you on drugs?" while the frustrated youth screams back, "Mom, all I want is a Pepsi!"

There are countless examples of questionable or just plain wrong information passed off as "education" by governments. Ironically, such misinformation can *encourage* the use of harder drugs. Consider the following (entirely likely) scenario:

Ads about marijuana "scare the hell" out of a high-school senior. This student then goes off to college, where his roommate smokes marijuana, with no apparent adverse effects and without going on to shoot heroin. He begins to wonder if he's been lied to and winds up trying pot for himself. He lives. Having rejected . . . warnings about marijuana, he might subsequently reject more important warnings about riskier drugs such as cocaine or heroin.[71]

Drug-policy propaganda can have the same Chicken Little effect as the eco-catastrophe propaganda discussed in chapter 7.

The Crack-Baby Myth

Untold numbers of pregnant women have been scared out of their wits by public-service ads, sponsored by governments and nonprofits, depicting deformed babies with deep behavioral and developmental problems caused by the mothers' use of crack cocaine during pregnancy. So-called crack babies supposedly suffer from Alzheimer's-like symptoms: they are virtual zombies; they often cannot walk and when they do, they bump into walls and trip over their own feet; they are "learning disabled" in a way that Head Start can never remedy. They have been called our "lost generation," in a sense that Gertrude Stein never imagined.

Crack cocaine can kill its users. No argument there. The drug boosts the heart rate and blood pressure and can therefore, in some cases, cause heart attacks, strokes, and seizures. Crack is also thought to be extremely addictive. But there is mounting evidence that the stories of zombie infants—"crack babies"—are bogus. "Several new studies discount the adverse effects of prenatal cocaine use on the fetus and many scientists now believe that poverty, poor nutrition, alcohol, tobacco, and the use of other drugs do more to hurt the fetus than cocaine," writes Kathy Fackelmann in Washington's iconoclastic *City Paper*.[72] According to Dr. Gideon Koren, director of the Motherisk program at the Hospital for Sick Children in Toronto, Canada, "the media coined the term cocaine babies although there is no such syndrome."[73]

Although some early studies found evidence that mothers who use cocaine may pass the drug on to their unborn children, later studies dispute these findings. Some scientists have always been suspicious of the "crack baby" stories because of their understanding of basic physiology:

Fortunately, nature devised an elegant protection system for the developing baby. During a two-week period at the start of pregnancy, the tiny fertilized egg makes its way through the Fallopian tube to the uterus and remains virtually impervious to any damage from drug or alcohol exposure. . . . The danger to the developing baby starts soon after a woman misses her menstrual period. That's when the tiny embryo, which is attached to the mother via the umbilical cord, forms crucial organs such as the heart, liver, and brain. But even then, the blood of the mother and fetus never mix. The two circulation systems remain separated by the . . . placenta, which acts as a highly selective gatekeeper. While some undesirable compounds do slip past the placental barrier, not every substance from the mother's circulation will make it into the fetal bloodstream.[74]

Thus, the fetal embryo is protected, but not completely isolated. The tragedy of the drug thalidomide, which caused birth defects until it was banned in the 1960s, proved that certain drugs ingested by pregnant women can affect a child's prenatal development.

Nevertheless, researchers have found that "many of the adverse effects attributed to cocaine vanish when scientists factor out the other known risks that can harm the unborn."[75] Dr. Koren surveyed the several dozen published scientific papers on cocaine use during pregnancy. Pooling the data and employing a statistical technique that enabled him to control for factors such as alcohol use, he isolated the effects of cocaine. His study, published in the October 1991 issue of *Teratology*, the top journal in the field, "failed to demonstrate a statistically significant link between cocaine use and premature birth, low birth weight, and certain birth defects."[76] Koren did find some problems due to cocaine use, but they were not as severe as formerly believed.

Other studies have shown that women who use cocaine also usually drink and smoke heavily, and alcohol and tobacco are believed to have negative health effects on babies. Mothers addicted to cocaine are usually negligent in child rearing; thus, their behaviorally disturbed offspring may be that way because of a lack of nurturing rather than the effects of prenatal cocaine use. Some researchers have concluded: "The mothers who give birth to infants labeled 'crack babies' tend to have four things in common— they engage in all kinds of drug use; they neglect their nutrition; they live in an impoverished environment; and they did not receive prenatal care."[77]

While virtually every physician advises strongly against using cocaine, the evidence that "crack babies" have formed a "lost generation" is extremely weak. The hysteria itself, however, may convince many mothers that their children are indeed hopeless. If you're told by authorities that you'll give birth to a zombie, why bother with prenatal care? Under such circumstances, abortion must seem an almost attractive option.

The legal system has overstepped its bounds in its treatment of "crack moms." Hundreds of women have been prosecuted for having taken drugs during pregnancy. Some crack-using mothers have been thrown in jail to isolate them from drugs in the name of helping their babies. In 1989 a Florida woman was convicted not of cocaine possession but of "delivering cocaine to her unborn children."[78] It's not hard to figure where this disturbing trend will lead. Cigarettes and alcohol are also believed to be harmful to an unborn child; we may very well see the jailing of moms who smoke like chimneys and tipple before the millennium is out.

So much of what passes for "education" in the War on Drugs might be more accurately described as "misinformation." The private sector, particularly a compliant media, has played its part. Who can ever forget the ineffable Peter Jennings telling us on the nightly news: "Using it even once can make a person crave cocaine for as long as they [sic] live."[79] There's also the illogic of it all. As Princeton University political scientist Ethan Nadelmann writes, the government has arbitrarily chosen to permit some kinds of drugs while prohibiting others—some of which may be less harmful. Cocaine and heroin are prohibited, although a case can be made that they are "safer" than alcohol and tobacco. In 1985 fewer than 3,500 deaths were caused by the first two substances; the latter *may* have been responsible for a half million deaths that year.[80]

To justify this foolish inconsistency, says Nadelmann, the government has to hoodwink the public with propaganda:

> Many Americans make the fallacious assumption that the government would not criminalize certain [drugs] if they were not in fact dangerous. . . . Then they jump to the conclusion that any of those substances is a form of abuse. The government, in its efforts to discourage people from using illicit drugs, has encouraged and perpetuated these misconceptions not just in its rhetoric but also in its purportedly educational materials.[81]

This, of course, is not to suggest that alcohol and tobacco should be prohibited; Prohibition was tried once and the results—violence, an increase in organized crime, corruption, lack of success in stemming alcohol consumption—were nearly identical to the failures of our current War on Drugs.

Lies, Damned Lies, and Statistics

The humorist Will Rogers once observed that "the income tax has made more liars out of the American people than golf has." If Rogers were alive today, he would be astounded at what drug prohibition has done to our collective veracity.

Since providing information about one's personal (illicit) drug use may lead to prosecution and possible imprisonment, reliable information about such habits is virtually impossible to obtain. Nevertheless, the federal government claims to have precise statistics on drug consumption on a year-by-year basis and, not surprisingly, these cooked-up numbers show that the War on Drugs is a resounding success. The White House's National Drug Control Strategy, presented to Congress in February 1991, claimed the following successes:

Original Goal	*Actual*
Reduce adolescent drug use 10%.	Goal met. Drug use declined 13% from 1988–90.
Reduce occasional cocaine use.	Goal met. Use declined 29% from 1988–90.
Reduce adolescent cocaine use by 20% from 1988–90.	Goal met. Use down by 49%.
Reduce drug-related medical emergencies by 10%.	Goal met. Emergencies down 18%.[82]

The government can claim "victory" if it wants, but these statistics are about as reliable as Zsa Zsa Gabor's answer to the question, "How old are you?" Millions of Americans refuse to tell census snoops how many bathrooms they have; does anyone believe that people will be honest with the government about their *illegal* activities?

At first, it might appear that drug-related emergencies would be accurately reported by hospital emergency rooms. The problem is that such statistics reveal only the *reported* drug emergencies. There is no way of knowing whether the actual number of emergencies is twice, or ten times, or a thousand times higher than the reported number.

For decades, economists have tried to devise methods of measuring the "underground economy": the portion of economic activity that is illegal, including drug dealing, prostitution, gambling, tax evasion, et cetera. Different researchers have come up with estimates that differ by hundreds of billions of dollars annually. There is simply no way to arrive at reliable estimates of such activity; it just can't be done. Consequently, the government's confident and oh-so-precise measures of the extent of illegal drug use should be taken with a huge grain of salt. Besides, they are, after all, a self-evaluation. What government agency ever admitted that it did *not* meet its goals?

There are many indications that the War on Drugs is no more successful than the futile war on alcohol of the 1920s. More intense law enforcement always has the effect of inducing people to turn to more potent drugs. If a drug dealer can smuggle only one suitcase full of drugs into the country, he is likely to fill it with crack cocaine or heroin rather than marijuana. The same thing happened during Prohibition, when beer consumption fell while hard liquor gained ground.[83]

Since needles are illegal in the United States, their shared use has contributed greatly to the spread of AIDS. (Contrast this with the situation in Hong Kong, where the sale and possession of needles are legal and where AIDS as a result of drug injection is extremely rare.) Still, the drug warriors press on, crushing civil liberties underfoot. Drug-enforcement authorities can now seize private property even before an indictment, let alone a fair hearing. The presumption of innocence has been thrown out the window, along with the rest of the Bill of Rights. Former Customs Service Commissioner William von Raab proposed in 1988 that if customs agents couldn't determine what an airplane was up to, they should shoot it down and ask questions later. Incredibly, a majority of the Senate agreed with this nasty police-state idea. William Bennett, a virtual steroid dealer when it comes to ways to put more muscle in the state, proposes sending U.S. troops into Latin America to attack suspected drug laboratories and distribution points. The War on Drugs is no longer metaphorical; real blood is being shed, from the streets of Philadelphia to the beaches of the Florida Keys. And the military, which for a long time was reluctant to enlist in this war, is growing more enthusiastic as calls for defense cuts grow louder. Admiral William Crowe, former chairman of the Joint Chiefs of Staff, candidly admitted in 1990, "Certainly, I think we'll put more emphasis on the drug war. And if there are resources tied to it, why, you'll see the services compete for those, and probably vigorously. We take pride in being accomplished bureaucrats, as well as military men. And I think it's legitimate for military men to try and perpetuate their institution."[84] Spoken like a true bureaucrat, Admiral.

Drug-related crime is still running rampant through American cities, despite beefed-up law enforcement. It is not unusual for upwards of 90 percent of the inmates in some jails to be incarcerated for some drug-related crime, particularly armed robbery or burglary. In spite of all this, the 1991 White House National Drug Control Strategy was "pleased to be able to report that . . . we are embarked on the right path."[85] The path to what the White House does not say.

The Wages of Fighting Sin

As we've said before, governments love crises. They are useful vehicles for engineering tax increases, the revenues from which can be used to bloat the budgets of the relevant bureaucracies. In the absence of a genuine crisis, government suffers from what might be called a "crisis crisis."

The exaggerations and lies tossed about so shamelessly in the War on Drugs fit this description. Just as dozens of federal agencies, from the CIA to the State Department, have jumped on the eco-catastrophe bandwagon, dozens more are clambering aboard the drug train, scrambling for the federal monies hidden in each compartment. An appendix to the White House's National Drug Control Budget discloses that in 1992, $11.7 billion was requested for the U.S. Departments of Justice, Treasury, Transportation, State, Agriculture, Interior, Health and Human Services, Defense, Housing and Urban Development, Education, Labor, and Veterans Affairs; and the Agency for International Development, U.S. Information Agency, CIA, ACTION, U.S. Courts, and, last but not least, something called "Emergencies in the Diplomatic and Consular Service" within the State Department.[86] Even the Fish and Wildlife Service requested $1 million, apparently in response to the cocaine epidemic sweeping the world of rainbow trout. With so many agencies holding a financial stake in the War on Drugs, we can expect the fish stories told by the drug warriors to grow bigger and bigger.

As with all government propaganda, truth is the real loser. "Sixty percent of Americans believe marijuana is physically addictive," writes

Richard J. Dennis, chairman of the Drug Policy Foundation. "Fifty-seven percent believe it is at least as addictive as alcohol and cigarettes; and 76 percent believe its use leads to use of stronger drugs. Fifty-two percent of Americans believe heroin makes people crazy, violent, and psychotic. All those beliefs are unsupported."[87]

Sensible reform of drug policy seems farther away than ever before. There was a window of opportunity in 1977, when President Carter proposed decriminalizing the possession of up to one ounce of marijuana. You'd think that Carter's modest proposal would've succeeded in a nation in which sixty million people have tried marijuana at least once. It didn't. Half a century of preposterous scare stories and lies has taken its toll. Carter's idea went nowhere.

It's time to end the lies. Tell the American people the truth. In the matter of dope and booze and smokes, we could do worse than to recall the words of Abraham Lincoln:

> Prohibition will work great injury to the cause of temperance. It is a species of intemperance within itself, for it goes beyond the bounds of reason in that it attempts to control a man's appetite by legislation and makes a crime out of things that are not crimes. A prohibition law strikes at the very principle upon which our Government was founded.[88]

AIDS and the Great Sex Scare

Uncle Sam has extensive experience in hurling polemics (and interdictions) at alcohol and narcotics; with tobacco, he's making up for lost time. And as the 1980s rolled to a close, he added a new item to this lethal list: sex.

A flood of hysterical prophecies and publications issued from government mouthpieces and printing offices, all bearing the same message: the HIV virus that leads to Acquired Immune Deficiency Syndrome (AIDS) was running rampant through the heterosexual community. *Everyone* was at risk; "anyone can get it," as a doctor at the Walter Reed Army Hospital in Washington, D.C., warned.[89] The high-octane D.C. lobbying firm of Ogilvy & Mather received $4.6 million from the federal government to raise our collective awareness.

They were ably assisted by the middlebrow media, which did its best to fan the panic: *Time*, *Newsweek*, and *U.S. News & World Report* ran sensational stories full of grossly exaggerated figures to prove that AIDS is a disease that "doesn't discriminate," as Group Think had it. Or as *U.S. News & World Report* editorialized ominously: "The disease of *them* suddenly is the disease of *us*. The slow death presumed just a few years ago to be confined to homosexuals, Haitians, and hemophiliacs is now a plague of the mainstream, finding fertile growth among heterosexuals."[90]

(When the predicted breakout of the virus into the heterosexual population never occurred, the nimble spin artists at *U.S. News & World Report* pulled off an impressive jujitsu move: "Heterosexuals, once victims of scare propaganda, now find themselves being pacified with reassurances no more founded in reality."[91] And just who churned out this "scare propaganda," guys?)

Whoever wrote this, and dozens of scare stories like it, was either an ignoramus or a liar. No matter: Americans, by and large, bought it. By November 1987, Gallup revealed that 40 percent of Americans feared falling prey to this remorseless killer.[92] In March 1986 a whopping 65 percent of the respondents to a *Glamour* magazine survey said they were "afraid of contracting AIDS."[93] *Time*, which did so much to mislead Americans about the disease, solemnly intoned in August 1985, "It was the shocking news two weeks ago of actor Rock Hudson's illness that finally catapulted AIDS out of the closet, transforming it overnight from someone else's problem, a 'gay plague,' to a cause of international alarm."[94] (How the unfortunate death of Mr. Hudson, a gay man of legendary promiscuity, achieved this effect is mind-boggling.)

But *Time* was right: AIDS fear gripped the nation. In Iowa and Georgia and Ohio, teenage kids in the backseat of dad's Chevy were refraining from congress, for fear that it would strike them dead within the fortnight.

It was all a lie. There may be plenty of good reasons for Bobby and Suzy not to copulate in that Chevy, but AIDS isn't one of them.

The HIV virus is passed on in five ways: through sexual intercourse, especially involving the anus, with an infected person; by intravenous drug injection using a tainted needle; via transfusion of adulterated blood; through hemophilia-clotting factor; or from an infected mother to a child in the womb. By one estimate of the Centers for Disease Control, 61 percent of people with AIDS are homosexual or bisexual men infected by sexual contacts; 21 percent are IV drug users who shared a needle with an infected person; 7 percent are both homosexual males and IV drug users; 1 percent are hemophiliacs; 2 percent received transfusions of infected blood; 3 percent are of undetermined causes; and 4.5 percent *claim* to have been infected via heterosexual intercourse.[95]

(Some of the material in this section is drawn from the work of Michael Fumento, a courageous journalist whose book *The Myth of Heterosexual AIDS* has been attacked and reviled but not refuted. Malcolm Forbes denounced him in the pages of *Forbes* for spreading his "asinine" heresies;[96] time, however, has proved Fumento right and Forbes wrong. Dead wrong. To its credit, the *New York Times* came to Fumento's rescue with an editorial titled "Why Make AIDS Worse Than It Is?" An excellent question—which Fumento answers.)

From Epidemic to Pandemic

In the early 1980s, news of the "gay cancer" spread throughout the largest cities, particularly San Francisco and New York. Cries began for the federal government to do something. In the spring of 1983, at one of the first AIDS conferences, Congressman Ted Weiss (D-N.Y.) declared, "The AIDS crisis warrants more than a business-as-usual response from both the government and the medical-scientific establishment."[97]

Of course we've gotten business-as-usual, to the nth degree. Federal spending on AIDS-related matters ballooned to $4.274 billion by fiscal year 1992; a powerful coalition of medical researchers and homosexual activists lobbies tenaciously for more, more, more. So potent is this lobby that federal spending on AIDS exceeds that spent on heart disease, which kills 750,000 Americans each year. By contrast, AIDS kills about 25,000 Americans every year and a *total* of a little more than 100,000 Americans during the decade 1981–1991.

Dennis Altman, a gay writer, offered this sharp analysis:

> Once a disease becomes "fashionable," it generates its own estab-
> lishment and vested interests. Aided by politicians, lobbyists and
> the media, the money and attention focused on AIDS in the United
> States since mid-1983 have ensured the development of an AIDS
> industry, involving researchers, doctors, therapists, social workers
> and administrators, who have taken control of the definition and
> management of the disease.[98]

In its early years, this nascent lobby complained bitterly of underfunding by the Reagan administration. The Reaganites were motivated by "homophobia," they charged; if middle-class heterosexuals were dying in tens of thousands, government would mobilize as if for war. Influential Congressman Henry Waxman (D-Calif.) said, "There is no doubt in my mind that if the same disease had appeared among Americans of Norwegian descent, or among tennis players, rather than among gay males, the response of both the government and the medical community would have been different."[99] He had a point.

By 1986, the party line had changed. Talk of the "gay cancer" was stifled. AIDS, we were told, was no longer a disease of promiscuous homosexuals, drug addicts, and the occasional unlucky hemophiliac or recipient of tainted blood. It could happen to anyone. As "Cheers" star Ted Danson lectured the folks out in TV-land in one of numerous government-sponsored commercials, "Anyone. Any type can get it."[100] Such taxpayer-financed television and radio commercials were furnished free of charge to thousands of stations. In one, a blond young man says, "If I, the son of a Baptist minister, living in a rural area, can get AIDS, anybody can."[101] Well, yes, if that son of a Baptist minister shared a needle with an infected person, or got a transfusion of infected blood, or engaged in receptive anal intercourse with an infected person. But the commercial implied that AIDS was rather like lightning: it is as likely to strike a ninety-two-year-old virgin maiden as it is a twenty-four-year-old promiscuous homosexual junkie.

The City of New York plastered the subways with ads reading, "Don't Go Out Without Your Rubbers"[102]—without making a distinction between vaginal intercourse between virgins and anal intercourse in a gay bathhouse. These absurdities were given credence by a mass media barrage typified by *Time*'s assertion that "AIDS is a growing threat to the heterosexual population"[103] and *U.S. News & World Report*'s dubbing of AIDS as "a plague of the mainstream."[104]

Dr. James Curran, Director of AIDS Activity at the Center for Infectious Diseases, told *U.S. News & World Report*: "The infection is spreading among heterosexuals."[105] Douglas A. Feldman, acting executive director of the Queens AIDS Center, wrote in the *New York Times* in 1987: "I fear it is just a matter of time before the pattern of heterosexually transmitted AIDS in the singles bars along First Avenue . . . will begin to look like the pandemic in Africa today."[106]

He was echoed by the two highest-ranking health officials of the U.S.

government. Surgeon General C. Everett Koop, who superintended the mailing of AIDS information to every household in the United States, warned in 1987: "If the heterosexual explosion follows the homosexual explosion, then we are in for unbelievable trouble."[107] Secretary of Health and Human Services Otis R. Bowen added, "I can't emphasize too strongly the necessity of changing lifestyles."[108] The message was clear: single men and women, stop sleeping around—or else.

Reaganite conservatives with an authoritarian bent had a field day with heterosexual AIDS. William Bennett, the Secretary of Education who later became Drug Czar, used the disease as a cudgel with which to beat libidinous impulses out of randy youth. In his pamphlet "AIDS and the Education of Our Children," two million copies of which were distributed at taxpayer expense, Bennett fails to mention anal sex a single time. Indeed, he seems to equate heterosexual and homosexual acts as equally risky.[109] The chilling message of the AIDS alarmists—"safe sex is no sex,"[110] as a University of Miami AIDS bureaucrat put it—dovetailed nicely with the puritan tendencies of some Reaganauts.

Bennett fit right into an administration that made a hash out of federalism by forcing states to adopt mandatory seat-belt laws and the twenty-one-year-old drinking age. He and the head of the White House policy staff, Gary Bauer, hectored states to mandate HIV testing for those applying for marriage licenses—a policy that two states, Illinois and Louisiana, adopted with disastrously wasteful results. Two stalwarts of the right, Senator Jesse Helms (R-N.C.) and Congressman William Dannemeyer (R-Calif.), littered Congress with amendments and bills that would force states to test the blood of the affianced or even quarantine homosexuals. To some on the right, AIDS appeared to be nature's revenge against what they regarded as a sinful practice. Like other "crises," real and manufactured, it offered zealots a perfect excuse to propose draconian measures to curtail practices of which they disapprove.

(While the AIDS hysteria was at its peak, the Reagan-appointed Meese Commission on Pornography was giving Uncle Sam's stamp of approval to another of nanny's dubious claims: that movies and magazines depicting adults engaging in consensual sexual activity encourage crimes of violence such as rape. Among the commissioners was Father Bruce Ritter, the New York City priest who later lost his position as director of Covenant House, a home for runaways, after several of the runaway boys alleged that Ritter had engaged in sex with them.[111])

At this writing, the war against sex continues on both sides, unabated.

And unenlightened. After basketball star Magic Johnson was diagnosed as having the HIV virus in late 1991, newspapers across the country blared in banner headlines: "It Can Happen to Anyone." Johnson and his handlers launched an all-out media blitz: he contracted to write *two* autobiographies, he appeared on Arsenio Hall's popular television talk show, and he collaborated with a professional writer on a lengthy cover story for *Sports Illustrated*. In each and every venue, Johnson has claimed that he became infected through a sex act with a woman—an assertion that many of those who know of Johnson's private life find highly doubtful. When Fumento asked the *Los Angeles Times* sports editor why he didn't pursue the widespread rumors that Johnson is bisexual, he replied, "I don't know what difference it makes. He has it and that's all there is to it. What does it matter?"[112]

It matters because Johnson is being used as the long-awaited proof that heterosexuals, too, are "at risk," to use a favorite locution of social workers, for AIDS. Not a single prominent heterosexual non-drug user has yet fallen prey to the disease; Magic Johnson was, in a macabre way, a godsend to the AIDS lobby. President Bush has appointed him to his Commission on AIDS, where he acts as a highly visible and beloved spokesman for increased government spending. He is also an extraordinarily effective propaganda tool: evidence, at last, that the "explosion" of heterosexual AIDS that Surgeon General Koop warned of is finally here. If Magic Johnson became infected through receptive anal intercourse and is lying to protect his family from embarrassment, that's understandable. Every person deserves dignity and privacy. But if he is lying—and if his lies are furthering the agenda of a power-hungry government and a money-hungry lobby—that's shameful.

The AIDS tragedy is a classic case of government and its handmaidens in the media exaggerating the scope of a problem in order to enlarge the state's powers. When the Surgeon General of the United States, Ted Danson, William Bennett, ACT-UP, Jesse Helms, and Magic Johnson are all shouting the same lie from the rooftops—"AIDS can strike any one of us"—the truth is likely to be drowned in the din.

Michael Fumento has concluded, "The goal of the AIDS industry in general is sheer self-perpetuation."[113] Finding a cure, it seems, takes a backseat. For anyone with a heart, that's a tragedy.

10

The Never Ending Story

The men the American people admire most extravagantly are the most daring liars; the men they detest most violently are those who are trying to tell them the truth.

—H. L. MENCKEN
A Mencken Chrestomathy

IN OUR UNCLE'S HOUSE of propaganda there are many mansions. From soil conservation to smart bombs, nary a program exists that isn't being plugged by bureaucratic flacks. But there are also agencies whose admitted purpose is the dissemination of information. They avoid the P-word, but a rose by any other name . . .

In War

The Founding Fathers of U.S. propaganda were President Woodrow Wilson and George Creel, a crusading newspaperman. On April 13, 1917, Wilson created, by executive order, the Committee on Public Information. He appointed Creel to head it and thus began the most frenzied propaganda campaign in American history.

"The channels of communication were literally choked with official, approved news and opinion,"[1] write historians James R. Mock and Cedric

Larson. The CPI covered every base, and then some. Its components included:

- the Division of News, which issued a mind-boggling 6,000 press releases in two years;
- the Official Bulletin, a daily newspaper of the U.S. government;
- a Foreign Language Newspaper Division;
- Civic and Education Cooperation, which distributed pro-war tracts to schoolchildren;
- a Picture Division and Film Division, which made propaganda films and assisted Hollywood in the production of anti-German silents;
- a Bureau of War Expositions, which organized parades and exhibited captured war weapons; and
- a Bureau of State Fair Exhibits and many other tentacles, including Industrial Relations, Labor Publications Divisions, Service Bureau, Pictorial Publicity, Bureau of Cartoons, Advertising, Four-Minute Men (75,000 men deputized to disrupt public gatherings and deliver four-minute harangues against the Hun), Speaking Division, Syndicate Features, Women's War Work, and Work with the Foreign Born.[2]

For the most part, the CPI avoided crude, Soviet-style hammer-to-the-head propaganda. George Creel called his work "the world's greatest adventure in advertising."[3] Movie stars were recruited to sell bonds and pose for publicity pictures. Hollywood pitched in with feverish classics such as *To Hell with the Kaiser*, *The Kaiser: The Beast of Berlin*, and *Mutt and Jeff at the Front*. (Gore Vidal's novel *Hollywood* gives us a memorable picture of the era. His heroine stars in *Huns from Hell*.)

Reasonable people can disagree on the need for official morale-boosting during time of war. But the CPI went too far by almost any standard. And it succeeded: Mock and Larson write, "The Committee on Public Information had done its work so well that there was a burning eagerness to believe, to conform, to feel the exaltation of joining in a great and selfless enterprise."[4] The repressive measures of the Wilson administration, directed by Attorney General A. Mitchell Palmer, were the logical extensions of the CPI's work.

Opponents of the war, such as socialist leader Eugene V. Debs, were jailed; dissent was not permitted to travel through the mails. The list of censored publications is long: the liberal journal *The Nation*, Georgia populist Tom Watson's various magazines, and the popular Kansas-based socialist newspaper *The Appeal to Reason* were among the banned.

Creel, Palmer, and Wilson gave propaganda a black eye that lasted through the 1920s and '30s. But when war came again, the shiner cleared. An Office of Facts and Figures was set up under poet Archibald MacLeish, who piously intoned, "A democratic government is more concerned with the provision of information to the people than it is with the communication of dreams and aspirations. The duty of government is to provide a basis for judgment; and when it goes beyond that, it goes beyond the prime scope of its duty."[5]

Not all publicists were so high-minded. Max Lerner, for instance, called for "a bold and affirmative attempt to use democratic persuasion . . . as a form of political warfare."[6] Even more brazen was Sherman H. Dryer, who in his 1942 guidebook *Radio in Wartime* wrote: "The strategy of truth is a handicap. . . . Truth . . . will enhance the integrity of our officialdom, but it is a moot question whether it will enhance either the efficiency or the effectiveness of our efforts to elicit concerned action from the public."[7]

Seldom do propagandists speak with Mr. Dryer's admirable candor.

The Office of Facts and Figures was replaced by the more powerful Office of War Information, created by President Roosevelt by executive order on June 13, 1942. A radio broadcaster named Elmer Davis was placed at the helm; George Creel's offer to help was discreetly rejected.

The OWI ranged far afield from mere war propaganda. Its domestic publications advocated the withholding tax and greater government spending on jobs programs—not exactly daggers aimed at the Axis heart. Even a sympathetic historian, John Morton Blum, conceded, "OWI support of other of the President's policies . . . became in some instances indistinguishable from partisan pleading."[8]

MacLeish's strictures fell on deaf ears. One 1943 OWI publication distributed overseas profiled "Roosevelt of America—President, Champion of Liberty, United States Leader in the War to Win Lasting and Worldwide Peace."[9] These glowing tributes, more fitting for a dictator than the elected leader of a democracy, enraged many Americans. Congressman John Taber, ranking Republican on the House Appropriations Committee, called the OWI's output "partly drivel, partly insidious propaganda against Congress and for a fourth term."[10] His Appropriations Committee colleague from Pennsylvania, Representative John Ditter, railed against the "thousands of starry-eyed zealots out to sell their particular pot of gold to a bewildered people . . . [OWI should] go out of the field of producing radio programs, movies, and magazines, and leave that to those who know how."[11]

A majority of Congress agreed. Appalled by the ways that the Roosevelt administration used OWI for its own partisan ends, Congress virtually defunded the agency. Elmer Davis sadly admitted, "We shall be . . . passing back a good deal of the work that we have been doing to . . . the motion picture industry, radio, and others."[12]

Hollywood, especially, shouldered the burden manfully. Since the late '30s, many films had taken an openly interventionist stance. Englishmen, formerly portrayed as snooty ninnies or effete fops, were now valiant gentlemen. Once Hitler broke his word to Stalin, the Russians, too, came in for mild treatment. An egregious piece of Hollywood propaganda was based on *Mission to Moscow*, a pro-Stalin fairy tale written by Joseph Davies, the unspeakably naive returned ambassador to Moscow. The film version of *Mission to Moscow* was released in 1941; as Robert Nisbet writes, "An American movie audience could have logically concluded that the Soviet leaders were all Abraham Lincolns."[13]

Mission to Moscow was a product of Hollywood. While based on the memoir of a U.S. government employee, it was, for the most part, a film made by the private sector. Far more common were movies financed by and made under the supervision of the Signal Corps or other departments of the Armed Services. The greatest of all Hollywood directors, Frank Capra, made a series of seven fifty-minute training films called *Why We Fight* for the U.S. Army. In his autobiography *The Name Above the Title*, Capra recalls the words of General George C. Marshall:

> Young Americans . . . will prove not only equal, but superior to totalitarian soldiers, *if*—and this is a large if, indeed—they are given answers as to *why* they are in uniform, and IF the answers they get are *worth* fighting and dying for. And that, Capra, is our job—and your job. To win this war we must win the battle for men's minds. . . . I think films are the answer. . . . Capra, I want to nail down with you a plan to make a series of documented, factual-information films—the first in our history—that will explain to our boys in the Army *why* we are fighting, and the *principles* for which we are fighting.[14]

Thus were born the finest propaganda movies ever made for the U.S. government—movies that were made, the director admits, as a "counter-attack against *Triumph of the Will*,"[15] the classic Nazi film made by Leni Riefenstahl at the bidding of Adolf Hitler.

Few Americans would quarrel with the production of the *Why We Fight* movies. But the "good" propaganda of World War II bequeathed us a dangerous mindset. As historian Allan M. Winkler noted, in the aftermath of the war "the public fear of the insidious lure of propaganda was now laid to rest."[16] Government had made movies and controlled information as part of a nationwide war effort. We won the war; propaganda helped build support for the president and his strategy. Ergo, propaganda wasn't such a bad thing. By such leaps of logic are chains and shackles forged.

In Peace

In the brave new world after the war, the United States Information Agency, given status as an independent agency in 1953, carried on the overseas propaganda war. The USIA employs more than a thousand press and cultural affairs officers in our foreign embassies; also under its wing are about four thousand foreign nationals and four thousand propagandists in its Washington headquarters. The USIA has enjoyed bipartisan support: the Reagan administration doubled its budget and appointed Heritage Foundation president Edwin J. Feulner, Jr., as chairman of its oversight U.S. Advisory Commission on Public Diplomacy. Like so many other Reagan conservatives who spoke of dismantling the federal government in the heady days of 1980, Mr. Feulner came to enjoy power: he pleaded with Congress not to make "hasty or ill-advised cutbacks"[17] in USIA's budget.

The jewel in the USIA's crown has always been the Voice of America, formerly a project of the Office of War Information. The VOA has won praise from some residents of the crumbled Soviet bloc for providing an alternative to their state-run radio stations; it has also been criticized for "editorials which are consistently hard-line . . . and polemical."[18] Whether twisted and tendentious or the model of evenhandedness, the VOA's editorials and operations are paid for by American taxpayers. Now that communism sits atop the scrapheap of history, is there *any* reason at all why a worker in Houston, Texas, should have taxes taken from his paycheck and shipped across the globe to pay for radio entertainment for Moscow residents?

As with the OWI, the USIA and VOA have softened the average American's aversion to propaganda. Walter R. Roberts, who began writing at the

OWI in 1942 and retired from the USIA in 1986, told the *New York Times*: "The word 'propaganda' has a bad connotation because of the Nazis. But propaganda is not necessarily something that is bad. Basically we Americans cannot understand that a governmental radio station is free from the perception that it should consistently broadcast on behalf of the Government."[19]

If you believe that, we've got some prime Florida swampland we'd like to sell you. Roberts made his statement shortly after the USIA, under pressure from congressional investigators, conceded that it had blacklisted, for ideological reasons, at least ninety-five Americans from speaking under USIA auspices. War is peace. Slavery is freedom. And to one who has toiled long enough in the vineyards of bureaucracy, propaganda is truth.

Taking the USIA's mission one step—or two giant leaps—forward is the National Endowment for Democracy, created at the behest of President Reagan in 1983 to "foster the infrastructure of democracy—the system of a free press, unions, political parties, universities—which allows a people to choose their own way, to develop their own culture, to reconcile their own differences through peaceful means."[20]

This sounds wholesome as mother's milk; it's not. The NED funnels money to four "bipartisan" beneficiaries: the Democratic and Republican parties, the AFL-CIO's Free Trade Union Institute, and the U.S. Chamber of Commerce. These donees use the funds to interfere in the domestic affairs of other nations—or, as President Reagan's speechwriters put it, to "foster the infrastructure of democracy." Sometimes this work is innocuous, or even salutary: inspecting elections in Third World nations for "fairness," for instance. Other projects are positively nocuous. In 1985 the Free Trade Union Institute secretly channeled NED monies to a French student group that served as the student arm of "a security force for right-wing politicians."[21] It also showered the French labor union Force Ouvrière, an anti-Mitterrand organization, with $830,000. There may be—there are—many good reasons for Frenchmen to oppose the presidency of François Mitterrand, but is it really the business of the U.S. government to subsidize the political activities of his opponents? France, after all, is not exactly a fragile new democracy. The "infrastructure" that the NED's defenders talk about is pretty well in place.

More recently, the NED raised eyebrows by sending $400,000 to two Czech parties, Civic Forum and the Public Against Violence, during the 1990 free elections. Representatives of the other twenty-one parties competing in the election were outraged. A Green Party spokesman denounced the grants as "an injustice"—and then demanded, "All the parties should receive an equal share."[22] Is this unmitigated gall or what? Since when has the mission of the U.S. government been to bankroll every non-communist political party in every country in the world? After throwing money at anti-Soviet parties for six years, the NED and its middlemen are now busy handing out American taxpayers' dollars to Russians. Come one, come all: Christian Democrats, Socialists, Liberals—just sign this form and wait in the outer office and we'll process your application ASAP.

The two members of Congress who've led the fight against the NED are Senator Hank Brown (R-Colo.) and Representative John Conyers (D-Mich.). Brown declares: "To institute an international political action committee that interferes with existing democracies makes a sham out of our efforts to advance self-government. For those who have forgotten, America's holding high the torch of freedom means something far different than NED's efforts to manipulate foreign democracies or waste taxpayer dollars."[23]

This last point applies to so many of the propaganda programs we've discussed in this book. Even when the message is benign, taxpayers' money is still being wasted. Michael Kinsley, the *New Republic*'s cheeky TRB columnist, writes of the NED: "What we have here is a pork barrel for intellectuals. Money for study grants, for travel, for conferences, and especially for layers of administration, as the government gives money to the Endowment, which gives it to a Foundation to give it to an Institute to fund a fellowship program. Money for the boys, as Mayor Daley used to say."[24]

The only difference is that Mayor Daley seldom cloaked his pork in the garb of righteousness.

On Stage

No propaganda agency defends itself with greater sanctimony (or pours more venom on its critics) than the National Endowment for the Arts. The NEA was signed into law by that noted lover of the arts, President Lyndon B. Johnson. He inherited it from President Kennedy, who had courted artists and intellectuals with diligence and wit. As Kennedy friend Gore Vidal noted, "He knows the propaganda value of artists and he has . . . tried to win them over."[25]

President Johnson learned the same lesson, and well. Shortly before signing legislation that created a National Council on the Arts, a forerunner to the NEA, Johnson received a memo from ex-Kennedy adviser Arthur Schlesinger, Jr., that was blunt and on the money. Federal spending on the arts, wrote Schlesinger to LBJ, "can strengthen the connections between the Administration and the intellectual and artistic community, something not to be dismissed when victory or defeat next fall [1964] will probably depend on who carries New York, Pennsylvania, California, Illinois and Michigan."[26] In other words, buy off the artists and the wealthy patrons of the arts; subsidize them, and they'll vote for you and perhaps even present you in a favorable light in their works.

The NEA's origin as a cynical attempt to co-opt artists is part of a long and not very honorable tradition. The first large-scale subsidy of artists occurred under President Franklin D. Roosevelt's Works Progress Administration. By 1936, more than forty-five thousand artists, writers, actors, and musicians were cashing WPA checks. As WPA Federal Arts Project Administrator Audrey McMahon explained: "Artists, men of talent and of highly sensitive natures, men who form part of a large group which might easily, under adverse and difficult conditions, become a distinct social problem, have not only been kept from final distress, but their gifts have been directed into the channel of public benefit."[27]

In other words, pay artists *not* to make trouble. The WPA's art projects were eventually scrapped after anti-New Dealers complained that they were mere propaganda and artists complained of the restrictions placed upon them. Orson Welles and John Houseman, for instance, produced Marc Blitzstein's "labor opera" *The Cradle Will Rock* for the Federal Theater Project. As Ronald Brownstein writes, Welles and Houseman persevered "despite attempts from the nervous WPA (already under assault from conservatives for coddling subversives in its arts projects) to stop the show. That experience predictably soured Welles on government theater."[28]

Orson Welles discovered that independence is far nobler than going on the artsy dole. Contemporary artists are learning the same hard lesson. The NEA has been under attack since 1989 for subsidizing artists who defecate and masturbate on stage, recite nonsense verse full of profanities and half-witticisms, and immerse a crucifix in urine. Perhaps, in some eyes, this is art; perhaps it's schlock. But millions of Americans are sick of seeing their tax dollars spent to benefit well-off artists in faraway cities.

But is it propaganda or just pork barrel? Listen to acclaimed novelist George Garrett, who has sat on the NEA's Advisory Literature Panel:

"Once (and whenever) the government is involved in the arts, then it is bound to be a political and social business, a battle between competing factions. The NEA, by definition, supports the arts establishment."[29]

In the performance arts field, for instance, the winners of grants *always* play variations of feminist, socialist, and militantly homosexual themes. An artist whose work suggested, say, that women ought to marry and stay home with the children would *never* receive a grant from the performance arts panel. Never. We're neither endorsing nor condemning feminism or a more traditional concept of womanhood; government should not pay for the propagation of either.

And on Screen

An agency of similar vintage that has committed similar sins is the Corporation for Public Broadcasting. The CPB was also created by President Johnson's stroke of the pen, after a lengthy study by the private Carnegie Commission on Educational Television recommended to Congress that the government create a network of television stations that would be supported by tax dollars and private donations and lead us out of the "vast wasteland" that former Federal Communications Commission Chairman Newton Minnow had deplored. Congress added provisions for public radio to the Carnegie Commission report and sired the CPB, which in turn gave birth to the "fourth network"—the Public Broadcasting Service.

From a modest initial appropriation of $5 million, federal support for public television and radio has grown to almost $400 million in 1991. Despite the claims—made most often during those interminable telethons that interrupt its best programming—that PBS is supported "by viewers like you," well over half of the funding for both public television and radio comes from federal, state, or local governments. In a very real sense, PBS and National Public Radio are state entities.

Many of the shows that PBS broadcasts are unobjectionable: nature documentaries, prestige British dramatizations, "Sesame Street." Others are not. Conservatives have complained for twenty years that National Public Radio is "characterized by an unrelenting left-winger slant with a distinctly nutty twist,"[30] as the right-wing Accuracy in Media charged. Big-budget television programs such as *The Africans* had an undeniable anti-Western bias; PBS's marquee star, Bill Moyers, regularly hosts programs that reflect his liberal humanism. On the other hand, the Nancy

Reagan–hosted *The Chemical People* was a two-parter that promoted the prohibition line on the drug problem. Milton Friedman's series *Free to Choose* proselytized on behalf of the Nobel laureate's libertarian beliefs. There's nothing wrong with television programs that take strong stands or tackle public issues from right, left, or center: what *is* wrong is requiring taxpayers to foot the bill.

Yet after a halfhearted effort to cut the CPB's funds in 1981, the Reagan and Bush administrations have made peace with public broadcasting. Many conservatives have sliced into the PBS pie; when funding was threatened in early 1982, neoconservative Ben Wattenberg went before Congress to plead against any cuts. Wattenberg, by the way, had hosted—and was planning to host another documentary on the network.[31]

No one talks of abolition anymore. The maverick PBS executive Robert J. Chitester, president of WQLN in Erie, Pennsylvania, found few sympathetic Republican ears when he declared during the Reagan years, "Government largesse is a very wasteful way of funding public television," which he said was deteriorating to "some elitist little sideshow."[32] Cable networks such as Arts & Entertainment and The Discovery Channel have made PBS superfluous. Documentarians working for these networks are free to lard their works with opinion—but they are not stamped with the U.S. seal of approval.

Who Wins?

When James Buchanan was awarded the 1986 Nobel Prize in Economics for his work in public-choice theory, critics carped that Buchanan's work, which emphasizes that political decision makers operate out of rational self-interest, merely dressed up common sense in academic garb. Of course politicians, bureaucrats, voters, and special-interest groups act to further their separate self-interests. What else is new? Most of these critics—for example Pulitzer Prize-winning historian Arthur Schlesinger, Jr., and the *New Republic*'s Kinsley, disagreed with Buchanan's generally free-market policy prescriptions. But they accepted the public-choice theory's characterization of government. To adapt President Nixon's famous remark about Keynes, we are all public-choice theorists now.

Public-choice theory predicts—and reality confirms—that government is made up of individuals who, like all others, act in their own self-interest. Self-seeking is as prevalent in government as it is in the private sector:

human nature is such that people tend to do things that enhance their own well-being. These needn't be selfish acts; charity, for instance, may be in the giver's self-interest, and so is the formation of collective groups, clubs, and other organizations.

Given this basic fact of political and economic life, the notion that virtually everything government does serves the interests of those in government is highly credible. Sometimes what is best for politicians and bureaucrats is also in the best interest of the majority of the population. Other times—perhaps most of the time—it is not.

Politicians and bureaucrats are vigorous lobbyists for their pet policies or causes. As we have shown, enormous resources are devoted to advertising and other forms of propaganda that promote the causes of the most powerful special interest of all—government itself.

Government reports, studies, press releases, and press conferences must be treated as skeptically as those of any other special-interest group. An EPA document warning of impending environmental doom, for example, should be treated at least as suspiciously as, say, a report by defense contractors calling for a massive military buildup.

This is not to suggest that environmental problems or threats to national security do not exist. They do. The point is that the environmental regulatory bureaucracy has as much of a vested interest in conjuring up chimerical threats as do the lieutenants of the military-industrial complex. Threats spur Congress and the president to "action"—which always, but always, costs a bundle. The idea that government acts solely in the "public interest" lacks credibility—it is, literally, incredible.

Who Loses?

We have not attempted to quantify the economic effects of government propaganda. We know that it leads to ever-greater expenditures, but given the multifarious forms of propaganda and the uncertainties about just how they affect political decision making, pinning a price tag on the whole shebang would be impossible. We have documented the pervasiveness of federal government propaganda, but we have not peered under every rock in Uncle Sam's mountain; such an undertaking would require a work of encyclopedic heft. Nor have we paid much attention to defense propaganda, except in historical context: many fine books have already been written on the subject.

Government thrives on crisis. Its propaganda, by exaggerating the true extent of social and economic problems, fertilizes the soil of public opinion. In time, it reaps a harvest of broad new powers. Frightened, confused citizens are susceptible to governmental requests to give up their rights and incomes in exchange for the state's promise to "do something" about the crisis. As economic historian Robert Higgs writes:

> Each genuine crisis has been the occasion for another ratchet toward Bigger Government. . . . The ideological imperative that government must "do something," must take responsibility for resolving any perceived crisis, insures new actions. The actions have unavoidable costs, which governments have an incentive to conceal by substituting coercive command-and-control devices for pecuniary fiscal-and-market means of carrying out their chosen policies.[33]

Put simply, the purpose of government propaganda is to expand the public sector while shrinking the private sector and reducing individual freedoms.

Just as relentless propaganda was used to justify communism for decades, propaganda in democratic countries is employed to justify the expansion of failed welfare-state programs. The more we spend on welfare, the worse poverty becomes. The more that is spent on public schools, the more student achievement deteriorates. Public housing is a disgrace in most cities. The welfare state has failed, but government and its allied special-interest groups continue to preach that what is needed is not genuine reform—an American *perestroika*—but more of the same. According to Milton Friedman, the reigning syllogism goes something like this: Major premise: Socialism and the welfare state have been counterproductive, causing most social and economic problems to get worse, not better. Minor premise: Everyone knows this. Conclusion: Therefore, the solution is more socialism and a bigger welfare state.

New proposals for national economic planning are sprouting like toadstools after a rainstorm. We hear calls for a "national energy policy" and a "global environmental policy." The alleged solution to the blight of inner-city housing projects is to build more of the monstrosities. Have student scores on standardized tests plummeted as spending on education has skyrocketed? No problem, just boast, as President Bush has, that your administration is spending more on education than any of its predecessors. Has the welfare system destroyed families and condemned millions of children to squalor and dependence? Then advocate its expansion and damn sincere efforts at reform as "unconscionable," as New York Governor Mario Cuomo has done.

President Bush is a master of this rhetorical misdirection. When his opponent in the 1992 Republican primaries, conservative journalist Patrick J. Buchanan, called for further protectionist measures, Bush sang the praises of free trade and denounced Buchanan's "dangerous isolationism." Yet the Bush administration was the most protectionist in decades.

In the second half of 1991 alone, the Bush administration imposed new textile-import quotas on Nigeria, Egypt, the Philippines, Burma, Costa Rica, Panama, and Pakistan.[34] Hong Kong and Korea were cajoled into drastically reducing their textile exports to the United States as their "contribution" to the Persian Gulf War effort, thereby driving up the price of clothing to the returning soldiers and their families (and everyone else). President Bush, the self-advertised free-trader, also extended restrictions on semiconductor imports, causing the price of this important computer commodity to rise by 15 percent. Import quotas have been extended on machine tools, steel, and even peanuts. Tariffs have been slapped on Japanese minivans, even though the domestic automakers still have almost 90 percent of that market.

Whatever his lips say, George Bush has been "the most protectionist president since Herbert Hoover," charges journalist James Bovard, who adds that Bush's free-trade promises are "worth about as much as his promise not to raise taxes."[35]

Government propaganda is typically anti-market and pro-government intervention; it tends to downplay, ignore, or misrepresent the efficacy of markets while giving a rosy picture—taken straight from the typical high-school textbook—of government's ability to solve social and economic problems. Government propaganda is a manifestation of political entrepreneurship, whereby politicians, bureaucrats, and interest groups attempt to expand their power and incomes by manipulating public perceptions. Government advertisers have much greater latitude to engage in false or misleading advertising than their private counterparts. Where government monopoly exists, the vaunted marketplace of ideas is absent.

The simple solution to all this is to abolish government propaganda.

Short of that, we encourage scholars and citizens to challenge "official" views; welcome dissent, dispute, debate. What Harold Lasswell called propaganda—"the making of deliberately one-sided statements to a mass audience"—is by now deeply embedded in our national government. If the first casualty of propaganda is truth, the second is—or soon will be—our republic.

Appendix 1

Agency	FY 1981	FY 1983	FY 1985
Department of Agriculture	$ 43,665	$ 35,222	$ 35,206
Department of Commerce	6,162	5,486	6,057
Department of Defense	31,748	35,819	46,475*
Department of Education	2,154	2,014	1,700
Department of Energy	43,537	37,304	47,331
Department of Health and Human Services	56,330	47,225	56,083
Department of Housing and Urban Development	2,065	1,931	2,415
Department of the Interior	9,813	9,139	9,516
Department of Justice	7,515	10,218	10,534
Department of Labor	5,090	4,743	4,685
Department of State	16,132	18,653	22,194
Department of Transportation	12,636	12,238	11,610
Department of the Treasury	19,330	22,197	24,775
Agency for International Development	1,872	2,603	2,726
Consumer Product Safety Commission	3,184	2,336	2,385
Environmental Protection Agency	5,203	4,533	6,276
Equal Employment Opportunity Commission	603	933	813
Federal Communications Commission	801	699	492
Federal Deposit Insurance Corporation	294	468	416
Federal Reserve Board	518	608	640
Federal Trade Commission	1,258	1,408	1,205
General Services Administration	561	412	450
Interstate Commerce Commission	2,053	2,039	1,424

Agency	FY 1981	FY 1983	FY 1985
National Aeronautics and Space Administration	11,534	12,721	13,019
National Labor Relations Board	354	355	401
Office of Personnel Management	834	878	746
Securities and Exchange Commission	3,394	3,755	4,308
Small Business Administration	2,115	1,714	1,683
U.S. Information Agency	630	987	988
U.S. Postal Service	9,988	9,431	17,297
Veterans Administration	2,228	2,505	3,086
TOTAL	$ 303,601	$ 290,574	$ 336,756

*Military retirement pay accrual included for first time.

SOURCE: U.S. General Accounting Office, "Public Affairs and Congressional Affairs Activities of Federal Agencies," GAO/GGD-86-24 (Washington, D.C.: GAO, February 1986), pp. 10-11.

Appendix 2

CONGRESSIONAL AFFAIRS OBLIGATIONS BY DEPARTMENT AND AGENCY, FISCAL YEARS 1981, 1983, AND 1985 ($THOUSANDS)

AGENCY	FY 1981	FY 1983	FY 1985
Department of Agriculture	$ 2,867	$ 3,080	$ 3,463
Department of Commerce	2,464	2,253	2,589
Department of Defense	7,912	8,954	13,074*
Department of Education	849	864	1,120
Department of Energy	10,893	11,379	12,698
Department of Health and Human Services	6,955	6,532	6,751
Department of Housing and Urban Development	1,393	1,125	1,502
Department of the Interior	2,860	2,752	2,860
Department of Justice	4,572	5,126	5,365
Department of Labor	4,051	3,425	3,465
Department of State	5,041	5,875	7,338
Department of Transportation	2,914	2,774	3,974
Department of the Treasury	5,348	5,684	6,036
Agency for International Development	11,265	13,486	16,642
Consumer Product Safety Commission	214	174	202
Environmental Protection Agency	1,731	1,807	2,129
Equal Employment Opportunity Commission	253	297	246
Federal Communications Commission	294	315	230
Federal Deposit Insurance Corporation	187	162	240
Federal Reserve Board	254	299	312
Federal Trade Commission	300	288	203
General Services Administration	294	420	399
Interstate Commerce Commission	530	628	609

AGENCY	FY 1981	FY 1983	FY 1985
National Aeronautics and Space Administration	643	825	931
National Labor Relations Board	0	0	0
Office of Personnel Management	368	408	432
Securities and Exchange Commission	181	226	191
Small Business Administration	551	527	558
U.S. Information Agency	-†	313	204
U.S. Postal Service	3,274	4,140	4,384
Veterans Administration	1,244	1,431	1,714
TOTAL	$ 79,702	$ 85,569	$ 99,861

*Military retirement pay accrual included for first time.
†Included in Public Affairs Budget.

SOURCE: U.S. General Accounting Office, "Public Affairs and Congressional Affairs Activities of Federal Agencies," GAO/GGD-86-24 (Washington, D.C.: GAO February 1986), pp. 16–17.

Appendix 3

NUMBER OF FULL-TIME EQUIVALENT PERSONNEL ASSIGNED TO PUBLIC AFFAIRS
AND CONGRESSIONAL AFFAIRS DUTIES BY DEPARTMENT AND AGENCY, FISCAL
YEARS 1981, 1983, AND 1985

	PUBLIC AFFAIRS			CONGRESSIONAL AFFAIRS		
AGENCY	*FY 1981*	*FY 1983*	*FY 1985*	*FY 1981*	*FY 1983*	*FY 1985*
Department of Agriculture	822	718	629	94	100	83
Department of Commerce	141	117	123	61	56	60
Department of Defense	1,179	1,090	1,062	225	228	226
Department of Education	56	43	36	27	37	34
Department of Energy	373	296	286	242	215	210
Department of Health and Human Services	808	725	718	211	195	190
Department of Housing and Urban Development	39	36	33	42	30	33
Department of the Interior	266	213	200	96	85	71
Department of Justice	178	194	184	114	110	114
Department of Labor	153	125	109	98	85	76
Department of State	538	539	581	167	170	192
Department of Transportation	191	260	263	67	72	72
Department of the Treasury	446	412	433	128	125	123
Agency for International Development	35	47	46	233	235	235

AGENCY	PUBLIC AFFAIRS			CONGRESSIONAL AFFAIRS		
	FY 1981	*FY 1983*	*FY 1985*	*FY 1981*	*FY 1983*	*FY 1985*
Consumer Product Safety Commission	58	37	32	7	4	4
Environmental Protection Agency	145	118	153	59	51	54
Equal Employment Opportunity Commission	15	23	18	6	7	6
Federal Communications Commission	32	20	21	9	9	7
Federal Deposit Insurance Corporation	11	11	11	5	5	6
Federal Reserve Board	12	13	13	6	6	6
Federal Trade Commission	46	43	30	9	9	7
General Services Administration	15	10	11	8	10	10
Interstate Commerce Commission	59	51	33	17	14	13
National Aeronautics and Space Administration	173	176	175	23	25	21
National Labor Relations Board	11	10	10	0	0	0
Office of Personnel Management	22	19	19	13	12	12
Securities and Exchange Commission	93	85	85	4	5	4
Small Business Administration	30	28	31	14	14	13
U.S. Information Agency	17	25	27	4	9	6
U.S. Postal Service	139	154	157	63	54	51
Veterans Administration	72	67	70	37	39	43
TOTAL	6,175	5,705	5,599	2,089	2,016	1,982

SOURCE: U.S. General Accounting Office, "Public Affairs and Congressional Affairs Activities of Federal Agencies," GAO/GGD-86-24 (Washington, D.C.: GAO, February 1986), p. 18.

Notes

1. *Welcome to the Jungle*

1. George Orwell, *A Collection of Essays* (Garden City, N.Y.: Doubleday, 1954), pp. 172–73.
2. Michael Choukas, *Propaganda Comes of Age* (Washington, D.C.: Public Affairs Press, 1965), p. 78.
3. Harold Lasswell, "Propaganda," in *The Encyclopedia of the Social Sciences*, vol. XII, ed. E. R. A. Seligman (New York: Macmillan, 1933), p. 521.
4. Choukas, *Propaganda Comes of Age*, p. 15.
5. Eugene McCarthy, *The Crescent Dictionary of American Politics* (New York: Macmillan, 1962), p. 129.
6. Joseph Schumpeter, *Capitalism, Socialism, and Democracy* (New York: Harper & Row, 1950), p. 261.
7. James T. Bennett and Thomas J. DiLorenzo, *Destroying Democracy: How Government Funds Partisan Politics* (Washington, D.C.: Cato Institute, 1985).
8. James M. Beck, *Our Wonderland of Bureaucracy: A Study of the Growth of Bureaucracy in the Federal Government and Its Destructive Effect Upon the Constitution* (New York: Macmillan, 1933), p. 87. "Bureaucracy and Propaganda" is the title of chapter 7.
9. Ibid., p. 91.
10. James Grant, " 'Travelers,' Come Home," *Barron's*, July 1, 1975.
11. John S. Lang, "The Great American Bureaucratic Propaganda Machine," *U.S. News & World Report*, August 27, 1979.
12. As quoted in Tom G. Palmer, "Uncle Sam's Ever-Expanding P.R. Machine," *Wall Street Journal*, January 10, 1985. See also Louis Ludlow, *America Go Bust: An Exposé of the Federal Bureaucracy and Its Wasteful and Evil Tendencies* (Boston: Stratford Company, 1933).
13. Peter Woll, *American Bureaucracy*, 2d ed. (New York: W. W. Norton, 1977), p. 194.
14. U.S. General Accounting Office, "Public Affairs and Congressional Affairs Activities of Federal Agencies," GAO/GGD-86–24 (Washington, D.C.: GAO, February 1986), pp. 9–10.
15. Ibid., p. 2.

16. J. W. Fulbright, *The Pentagon Propaganda Machine* (New York: Liveright, 1970), p. 25n.
17. Lang, "The Great American Bureaucratic Propaganda Machine."
18. Ibid.
19. "100 Leading National Advertisers," *Advertising Age* 62 (September 25, 1991), p. 1.
20. Allan M. Winkler, *The Politics of Propaganda* (New Haven: Yale University Press, 1978), p. 12.
21. Danford L. Sawyer, Head of the U.S. Government Printing Office, *Hearings before the House Appropriations Committee on Legislative Branch Appropriations, FY83*, 97th Cong., 2d Sess., May 10, 14, 1982, p. 14.
22. Copies may be obtained from Superintendent of Documents, Government Printing Office, Washington, D.C. 20402.
23. *U.S. Government Books* (Washington, D.C.: Government Printing Office, January 1991), inside front cover.
24. Karen DeWitt, "U.S. Agency Distributes Pamphlets by Millions," *New York Times*, March 21, 1981. See also Brooks Jackson, "Federal Ink Still Flowing for Pamphlets," *Wall Street Journal*, May 1, 1981.
25. Erwin Leiser, *Nazi Cinema* (New York: Collier Books, 1974), p. 10.
26. William Gildea, "Have You Caught Up with 'Hacksaws, Part III' or 'Swab Your Choppers'?" *TV Guide* January 14, 1978, pp. 26–27.
27. Donald L. Lambro, *The Federal Rathole* (New Rochelle, N.Y.: Arlington House, 1975), pp. 29–30.
28. Quoted in Lambro, *The Federal Rathole*, p. 34.
29. "50,000 Films for Sale," *Newsweek*, March 6, 1967, pp. 90–91.
30. National Audiovisual Center, *Media Resource Catalog* (Capitol Heights, Md.: NAC, various years). A film about male genitals also is offered by NAC. The Department of Defense apparently is convinced that few Americans know how to properly brush their teeth, for it has made or commissioned dozens of films on this topic. See Haynes Johnson and Jack Fuller, "Federal Film-Making Hit," *Washington Post*, August 10, 1972.
31. Gildea, "Have You Caught Up with 'Hacksaws, Part III' or 'Swab Your Choppers'?"
32. Stanley Milgram, *Obedience to Authority* (New York: Harper & Row, 1974), p. 5.
33. Aldous Huxley, *Brave New World Revisited* (New York: Harper, 1958), p. 55.

2. *The Political Economy of Propaganda, or Joe Isuzu Meets Nelson Rockefeller*

1. Joseph Schumpeter, *Capitalism, Socialism, and Democracy* (New York: Harper & Row, 1950), p. 263.
2. Lee Benham, "The Effect of Advertising on the Price of Eyeglasses," *Journal of Law and Economics* 15 (October 1972), pp. 337–52.
3. Amahai Glazer, "Advertising, Information, and Prices: A Case Study," *Economic Inquiry* 19 (October 1981), pp. 661–71.
4. John Cady, *Restricted Advertising and Competition* (Washington, D.C.: American Enterprise Institute, 1976). See also Robert L. Steiner, "Does Advertising Lower Consumer Prices?" *Journal of Marketing* 37 (October 1973), pp. 19–26; Philip Nelson, "Advertising as Information," *Journal of Political Economy* 82 (July/August

1974), pp. 729–54; and Lester G. Telser, "Advertising and Competition," *Journal of Political Economy* 72 (December 1964), pp. 537–62.

5. Senator S. I. Hayakawa, Statement on "Government Competition With Small Business," Subcommittee on Advocacy (Washington, D.C.: Government Printing Office, June 24, 1981), p. 1.

6. James T. Bennett and Thomas J. DiLorenzo, *Underground Government: The Off-Budget Public Sector* (Washington, D.C.: Cato Institute, 1983), pp. 9–11.

7. Richard E. Wagner, "Advertising and the Public Economy," *The Political Economy of Advertising*, ed. David G. Tuerck (Washington, D.C.: American Enterprise Institute, 1976), p. 94.

8. Ibid., p. 97.

9. John Kenneth Galbraith, *The Affluent Society* (Boston: Houghton-Mifflin, 1958), pp. 150–53.

10. Friedrich Hayek, "The Non-Sequitur of the Dependence Effect," *Southern Economic Journal* 27 (April 1961), pp. 346–48.

11. Ibid., p. 346.

12. Ibid.

13. Michael Darby and Edi Karni, "Free Competition and the Optimal Amount of Fraud," *Journal of Law and Economics* 16 (April 1973), pp. 67–88.

14. Richard E. Wagner, "Boom and Bust: The Political Economy of Disorder," *The Theory of Public Choice–II*, ed. James M. Buchanan and Robert D. Tollison (Ann Arbor: University of Michigan Press, 1984), p. 241. See also James Buchanan and Richard Wagner, *Democracy in Deficit* (New York: Academic Press, 1977).

15. Bennett and DiLorenzo, *Underground Government*; Dennis S. Ippolito, *Hidden Spending* (Chapel Hill: University of North Carolina Press, 1984).

16. Bennett and DiLorenzo, *Underground Government*, p. 62.

17. Schumpeter, *Capitalism, Socialism, and Democracy*, p. 262.

18. Ibid., p. 261.

19. Ibid.

20. Ibid.

21. Ibid., p. 263.

22. James L. Payne, "The Congressional Brainwashing Machine," *Public Interest* 100 (Summer 1990), p. 10.

23. Ibid., p. 9.

24. Peter Woll, *American Bureaucracy*, 2d ed. (New York: W. W. Norton, 1977), p. 194.

25. Gordon Tullock, *Welfare for the Well-to-Do* (Dallas, Tex.: The Fisher Institute, 1983), p. 71.

26. Payne, "The Congressional Brainwashing Machine," p. 6.

27. Ibid.

28. Ibid., p. 7.

3. *How Propaganda Builds a Permanent Congress*

1. Fred Barbash, *The Founding* (New York: Simon and Schuster, 1987), p. 132.

2. Ibid.

3. David S. Broder, "Three Keys to 'Incumbent Lock'," *Washington Post*, December 7, 1988.

4. Alexis de Tocqueville, *Democracy in America*, Pt. I, chap. 12, ed. Richard D. Heffner (New York: Mentor Books, 1956), p. 112. Emphasis in original.

5. Hanna Pitkin, *The Concept of Representation* (Berkeley: University of California Press, 1967), p. 201.

6. Robert Weissberg, *Public Opinion and Popular Government* (Englewood Cliffs, N.J.: Prentice-Hall, 1976), p. 170.

7. Neil MacNeil, *Forge of Democracy: The House of Representatives* (New York: David McKay, 1963), p. 451.

8. Roger Davidson and Walter Oleszek, *Congress and Its Members* (Washington, D.C.: Congressional Quarterly Press, 1981), p. 386.

9. Robert A. Burnstein, *Elections, Representation, and Congressional Voting Behavior: The Myth of Constituency Control* (Englewood Cliffs, N.J.: Prentice-Hall, 1989), p. xiv.

10. Ibid., p. 36.

11. Ibid., pp. 104–5.

12. Guy Vander Jagt, "The Permanent Congress Is No Myth," *Washington Post*, June 26, 1989.

13. Ibid.

14. "Addicted to Government," *Wall Street Journal*, January 9, 1990.

15. Ibid.

16. Brooks Jackson, "Constant Congress: Incumbent Lawmakers Use the Perks of Office to Clobber Opponents," *Wall Street Journal*, March 22, 1988.

17. Paul Taylor, "Restive Voters Pick Change at State Level, Stability on Hill," *Washington Post*, November 8, 1990.

18. David E. Rosenbaum, "Democrats Appear to Have a Lock on Congress," *New York Times*, November 7, 1988.

19. "House Incumbents Have 'Wall of Money,' " *Washington Post*, October 5, 1990. See also "Propositions," *Washington Post*, November 8, 1990; "Legislators Would Rather Fight Voters Than Quit," *Washington Post*, November 13, 1990.

20. Gloria Borger, "Congress's $113 Million Junk Mail Habit," *U.S. News & World Report*, August 7, 1989.

21. Walter Pincus, "Senate Panel Cuts Funds for Mailings," *Washington Post*, August 1, 1989.

22. John Pontius, "U.S. Congress Official Mail Costs, Fiscal Year 1972 to Present" (Washington, D.C.: Congressional Research Service of the Library of Congress, June 13, 1989). Some preliminary statistics were also presented for FY 1989. Data are not available from the Postal Service prior to FY 1972.

23. See David Mayhew, "The Case of the Vanishing Marginals," *Polity* 6 (1974), pp. 295–317. See also Everett Carl Ladd, "Public Opinion and the 'Congress Problem,' " *Public Interest* 100 (Summer 1990), pp. 57–67.

24. "Frank Babies," *Wall Street Journal*, September 27, 1989.

25. Ibid.

26. Walter Pincus, "Idaho Mailings No Small Potatoes," *Washington Post*, September 27, 1989.

27. Ibid.
28. "Franks A Lot: Senators Spend $53 Million in Franked Mass Mailings in 1987–88," *Common Cause News*, June 16, 1989.
29. Charles R. Babcock, "Frankly, an Election-Year Avalanche," *Washington Post*, September 19, 1988.
30. Ibid.
31. Walter Pincus, "Freshmen and Franked Mail," *Washington Post*, July 18, 1990.
32. Howard Schneider, "Dyson Leads Md. Delegation to Mailbox as Franking Privileges End," *Washington Post*, July 12, 1990.
33. Babcock, "Frankly, an Election-Year Avalanche."
34. "The Better Congress Bureau," *Wall Street Journal*, March 7, 1988.
35. Walter Pincus, "Mountain of Mailings Grows Ever Taller: as Election Year Franked Mail Hits Record Proportions, Senate Pressures for House Limits," *Washington Post*, July 21, 1989.
36. Walter Pincus, "House's Quasi-Private Entrepreneurs," *Washington Post*, July 26, 1988.
37. U.S. Congress, House Commission on Congressional Mailing Standards, *Regulations on the Use of the Congressional Frank by Members of the House of Representatives* (Washington, D.C.: Government Printing Office, 1989), p. vii.
38. Ibid., p. 8.
39. Ibid., p. 7.
40. Ibid., p. 9.
41. Ibid., p. 15.
42. Ibid., p. 21, emphasis added.
43. Ibid., p. 24.
44. Tom Kenworthy, "House Members Turn Mailings into Powerful Political Weapon," *Washington Post*, June 19, 1990.
45. Borger, "Congress's $113 Million Junk Mail Habit." It is illegal for a frank to be used to send mail *to* a member of Congress and information on party affiliation cannot be requested on franked mail.
46. Ibid.
47. U.S. Congress, House Commission on Congressional Mailing Standards, *Regulations*, p. 22.
48. Pincus, "Mountain of Mailings."
49. William Safire, "Prince of Perks," *New York Times*, October 16, 1989. See also Walter Pincus, "Enmity Sharpens Frank-Mail Clash," *Washington Post*, October 2, 1989.
50. Kenworthy, "House Members Turn Mailings into Powerful Political Weapon."
51. Ibid.
52. Babcock, "Frankly, an Election-Year Avalanche."
53. Jack Anderson and Dale Van Atta, "Congress's Self-Congratulatory Mail," *Washington Post*, February 28, 1990.
54. "Phony Reform for Congressional Mail," *New York Times*, October 7, 1989.
55. Pincus, "Senate Panel Cuts Funds for Mailings." See also Safire, "Prince of Perks."
56. "Frank Babies."
57. "Politics as Usual," *Los Angeles Times*, September 28, 1989.

58. Safire, "Prince of Perks." See also Walter Pincus, "For House Staffs, Funds for Pay Raise," *Washington Post*, July 25, 1990; Walter Pincus, "House Members Escalate Costly First-Class Mailings: Spending Triples in Three Months as Lawmakers Find Way to Circumvent Limits on Newsletters," *Washington Post*, August 1, 1990.

59. Schneider, "Dyson Leads Md. Delegation to Mailbox."

60. Walter Pincus, "3 Who Would Curb 'Frank' Use It Fully," *Washington Post*, July 24, 1990. See also Jack Anderson and Dale van Atta, "Congressional Junk Mail," *Washington Post*, July 31, 1990.

61. Walter Pincus, "3 Who Would Curb 'Frank' Use It Fully."

62. As the restrictions were being considered, Senator Alfonse M. D'Amato (R-N.Y.), tainted by the savings-and-loan scandal, spent $2.65 million of taxpayers' money to send 16.7 million pieces of mail to his constituents in the six months ending September 30, 1989. See Walter Pincus, "D'Amato Flooded Mails as Limits Were Debated," *Washington Post*, January 3, 1990.

63. Walter Pincus, "Senate Panel to Consider Big Increases in Taxpayer-Financed Free Mailings," *Washington Post*, June 13, 1990.

64. Walter Pincus, "House Votes to Limit Franked Mail," *Washington Post*, October 22, 1990.

65. Walter Pincus, "Disclosure Rules May Cut House Mailings," *Washington Post*, November 8, 1990.

66. Babcock, "Frankly, an Election-Year Avalanche."

67. Tom Kenworthy, "House Incumbents Ride the Airwaves," *Washington Post*, October 17, 1990.

68. Walter Pincus, "Senate Seeks High-Tech Ways to Get Out the Word," *Washington Post*, July 29, 1989.

69. Ibid.

70. David R. Mayhew, *Congress: The Electoral Connection* (New Haven: Yale University Press, 1974), p. 49.

71. Andres Rosenthal, "On the Air: $97 Million Spent in '86," *New York Times*, July 14, 1987. See also Mayhew, *Congress: The Electoral Connection*, p. 50; and for more information on the taxpayer-financed advantages of incumbents, see Don Lambro, *Washington: City of Scandals* (Boston: Little, Brown, 1984), especially chapters 3 and 4.

72. John Dutton, "Overlooking the Perk Advantage," *Washington Times*, May 25, 1990.

73. U.S. Bureau of the Census, *Historical Statistics of the United States, Colonial Times to 1957* (Washington, D.C.: Government Printing Office, 1960), Series Y 249, p. 710.

74. Ibid.

75. Jackson, "Constant Congress." See also "The Unelected," *Wall Street Journal*, July 5, 1988.

76. Bruce Cain, John Ferejohn, and Morris Fiorina, *The Personal Vote: Constituency Service and Electoral Independence* (Cambridge: Harvard University Press, 1987), p. 61.

77. Mark Liedl, "100 Days of the 101st Congress," *Indianapolis Star*, May 29, 1989.

78. Pincus, "For House Staffs, Funds for Pay Raise."

79. Milton Gwirtzman, "Far Too Many People on Capitol Hill," *New York Times*, May 14, 1988.

80. Mark Bisnow, "Memo to Congress: Fire Half Your Staff," *Washington Post*, January 17, 1988.
81. Randall B. Ripley and Grace Franklin, *Congress, the Bureaucracy, and Public Policy*, 4th ed. (Chicago: Dorsey Press, 1987), p. 43.
82. Morris P. Fiorina, *Congress: Keystone of the Washington Establishment*, 2d ed. (New Haven: Yale University Press, 1989), p. 58.
83. Ripley and Franklin, *Congress, the Bureaucracy, and Public Policy*, pp. 47–48.
84. Bisnow, "Memo to Congress."
85. Fiorina, *Congress: Keystone of the Washington Establishment*, pp. 54–55.
86. To reach the maximum number of constituents, some members use vans equipped as offices that travel throughout their districts or states to bring services to constituents.
87. Congressional Management Foundation, *Frontline Management: A Guide for Congressional District/State Offices* (Washington, D.C.: CMF, 1989), pp. 5–6. The book was sponsored by AT&T.
88. Michael Kiernan, "Your Guy in Washington," *U.S. News & World Report*, August 7, 1989.
89. Congressional Management Foundation, *Frontline Management*, foreword.
90. "Constituent Service Tops Survey as Key to Political Success," *Washington Post*, December 18, 1989.
91. Pincus, "Freshmen and Franked Mail."
92. Ibid.
93. Charles Clapp, *The Congressman: His Job as He Sees It* (Washington, D.C.: Brookings Institution, 1963), p. 84.
94. Kenneth Olson, "The Service Function of the United States Congress," *Congress: The First Branch of Government* (Washington, D.C.: American Enterprise Institute for Public Policy Research, 1966), p. 344.
95. Fiorina, *Congress: Keystone of the Washington Establishment*, p. 90.
96. Dutton, "Overlooking the Perk Advantage."
97. John Dillin, "PAC Power Draws Calls for Reform," *Christian Science Monitor*, February 22, 1989. For a definition of PACs, see Larry J. Sabato, *PAC Power: Inside the World of Political Action Committees* (New York: W. W. Norton, 1984), p. 3.
98. Ibid.
99. U.S. Federal Election Commission, *Campaign Expenditures in the United States, 1977–1986: Reports on Financial Activity Data*, computer files, (Washington, D.C.: USFEC, 1988).
100. Charles R. Babcock, "78 Senators Reach PACs' Million Mark," *Washington Post*, August 1, 1990.
101. Ibid. See also Dillin, "PAC Power Draws Calls for Reform."
102. "PAC Support Scorecard: The House," *Washington Post*, May 11, 1989.
103. Sabato, *PAC Power*, table 3–2, p. 75.
104. Ross K. Baker, *The New Fat Cats: Members of Congress as Political Benefactors* (New York: Priority Press, 1989), table 1, p. 75. For additional insights into the role of PACs in supporting incumbents far more generously than challengers, see Larry Margasak, "PACs Give Candidates $93.7 Million," *Washington Post*, August 31, 1990; Helen Dewar, "Cash Showing High Interest in Incumbents," *Washington Post*, October 31, 1990; "House Incumbents Maintaining Huge Fund-Raising Advantage," *Washington*

Post, October 31, 1990; George Thayer, *Who Shakes the Money Tree? American Campaign Financing Practices from 1789 to the Present* (New York: Simon and Schuster, 1973); Douglas Caddy, *How They Rig Our Elections* (New Rochelle, N.Y.: Arlington House, 1975); Ann B. Matasar, *Corporate PACs and Federal Campaign Financing Laws: Use or Abuse of Power?* (New York: Quorum Books, 1986).

105. Amatai Etzioni, *Capital Corruption: The New Attack on American Democracy* (New York: Harcourt Brace Jovanovich, 1984), p. 42.

106. W. P. Welch, "Campaign Contributions and Legislative Voting: Milk Money and Dairy Price Supports," *Western Political Quarterly* 35 (December 1982), pp. 478–95.

107. John P. Frendreis and Richard W. Waterman, "PAC Contributions and Legislative Behavior: Senate Voting on Trucking Deregulation," *Social Science Quarterly* 66 (June 1985), pp. 401–12.

108. Henry W. Chappell, "Campaign Contributions and Voting on the Cargo Preference Bill," *Public Choice* 36 (1981), pp. 301–12; Cletus G. Coughlin, "Domestic Content Legislation: House Voting and the Economic Theory of Regulation," *Economic Inquiry* 23 (October 1985), pp. 437–48.

109. Jonathan I. Silberman and Garey C. Durden, "Determining Legislative Preferences on the Minimum Wage: An Economic Approach," *Journal of Political Economy* 84 (April 1976), pp. 317–29; Sam Peltzman, "Constituent Interest and Congressional Voting," *Journal of Law and Economics* 27 (April 1984), pp. 181–210; Marick F. Masters and Asghar Zardkoohi, "The Determinants of Labor PAC Allocations to Legislators," *Industrial Relations* 25 (Fall 1986), pp. 328–38; Marick F. Masters and Asghar Zardkoohi, "Congressional Support for Unions' Positions Across Diverse Legislation," *Journal of Labor Research* 9 (Spring 1988), pp. 149–65; James B. Kau and Paul H. Rubin, "The Impact of Labor Unions on the Passage of Economic Legislation," *Journal of Labor Research* 2 (Fall 1981), pp. 133–45; and James B. Kau and Paul H. Rubin, *Congressmen, Constituents, and Contributors* (Boston: Martinus Nijhoff, 1982).

110. Henry W. Chappell, "Campaign Contributions and Congressional Voting: A Simultaneous Probit-Tobit Model," *Review of Economics and Statistics* 64 (February 1982), pp. 77–83; Diana Evans, "Oil PACs and Aggressive Contribution Strategies," *Journal of Politics* 50 (November 1988), pp. 1047–56; Janet M. Grenzke, "PACs and the Congressional Supermarket: The Currency Is Complex," *American Journal of Political Science* 28 (May 1984), pp. 259–81; John R. Wright, "PACs, Contributions, and Roll Calls: An Organizational Perspective," *American Political Science Review* 79 (June 1985), pp. 400–14; and John R. Wright, "PAC Contributions, Lobbying, and Representation," *Journal of Politics* 51 (August 1989), pp. 713–29. For a discussion of how PAC money guarantees "access" to legislators, see Laura I. Langbein, "Money and Access: Some Empirical Evidence," *Journal of Politics* 48 (November 1986), pp. 1052–62; Arthur Denzau and Robert Mackay, "Gatekeeping and Monopoly Power of Committees: An Analysis of Sincere and Sophisticated Behavior," *American Journal of Political Science* 27 (November 1983), pp. 740–61; and Woodrow Wilson, *Congressional Government: A Study in American Politics* (Boston: Houghton-Mifflin, 1885). Committee membership is crucial for obtaining PAC contributions, as shown by a large and growing literature. For example, see Richard F.

Fenno, *Congressmen in Committees* (Boston: Little, Brown, 1973); George Goodwin, Jr., *The Little Legislatures* (Amherst: University of Massachusetts Press, 1970); Kenneth A. Shepsle, *The Giant Jigsaw Puzzle: Democratic Committee Assignments in the Modern House* (Chicago, Ill.: University of Chicago Press, 1978); Michael Munger, "Allocation of Desirable Committee Assignments: Extended Queues Versus Committee Expansion," *American Journal of Political Science* 32 (May 1988), pp. 317–44; and Barry R. Weingast and William J. Marshall, "The Industrial Organization of Congress; or, Why Legislatures, Like Firms, Are Not Organized as Markets," *Journal of Political Economy* 96 (February 1988), pp. 132–63. Other characteristics of members of Congress, such as seniority, ideology, "home district," and electoral margin, have also been found to influence the allocation of PAC money. See Michael Munger, "A Simple Test of the Thesis That Committee Jurisdictions Shape Corporate PAC Contributions," *Public Choice* 62 (1989), pp. 181–86; James W. Endersby and Michael Munger, "The Impact of Legislator Attributes on Union PAC Campaign Contributions," *Journal of Labor Research* 13 (Winter 1992), pp. 79–97; and Jill Abramson and Brooks Jackson, "Debate Over PAC Money Hits Close to Home as Lawmakers Tackle Campaign-Finance Bill," *Wall Street Journal*, March 7, 1990.

111. Richard Morin and Charles R. Babcock, "Out-of-State Donations to Candidates Are on the Rise," *Washington Post*, July 31, 1990.

112. Ibid. Under federal law, contributions of less than $200 do not have to be reported. Another case of out-of-state contributions concentrated in a particular industry is given by Senator Tim Wirth (D-Colo.) and the cable television industry. See Charles R. Babcock, "The Senator and the Special Interest," *Washington Post*, November 6, 1990.

113. "Foreign-Financed PACs Under Fire," *Insight*, November 5, 1990.

114. Etzioni, *Capital Corruption*, p. 4.

115. Baker, *The New Fat Cats*, pp. 2–3.

116. The Coelho saga is interesting and provides important insights into the power of political action committees. Readers interested in an in-depth treatment of Coelho's political maneuvers and the corruption created by the PAC system of campaign finance should consult Brooks Jackson, *Honest Graft: Big Money and the American Political Process*, rev. ed. (Washington, D.C.: Farragut Publishing, 1990). Coelho permitted Jackson, a journalist, to have complete access to his fund-raising activities. This book is a highly detailed account of how money is raised from PACs and how it is used to influence policy. See also Abramson and Jackson, "Debate Over PAC Money Hits Close to Home."

117. "Congress: Money to Burn," *Newsweek*, April 30, 1990.

118. Ibid. For examples of the personal use of campaign funds, see James T. Bennett and Thomas J. DiLorenzo, *Destroying Democracy: How Government Funds Partisan Politics* (Washington, D.C.: Cato Institute, 1984), p. 394; and Baker, *The New Fat Cats*, p. 65.

119. Brooks Jackson, "Representatives' Use of Funds Draws Criticism," *Wall Street Journal*, January 18, 1989.

120. Charles R. Babcock, "Hill Fund-Raising: Better Safe Than Sorry? Despite Overflowing War Chests, Congressional Incumbents Keep Up Pressure for Donations," *Washington Post*, September 26, 1990. See also, for example, R. Kenneth Godwin, *One*

Billion Dollars of Influence: The Direct Marketing of Politics (Chatham, N.J.: Chatham House, 1988); Philip M. Stern, *The Best Congress Money Can Buy* (New York: Pantheon Books, 1988).

121. George Hackett, "Rule by Permanent Congress: Bulging War Chests Give Incumbents a Big Edge," *Newsweek*, June 6, 1988.

122. Mark Liedl, "100 Days of the 101st Congress."

123. Carol Hardy, "House and Senate Standing Committees and Subcommittees with Jurisdiction over National Drug Abuse Policy," Report #88–634 GOV (Washington, D.C.: Congressional Research Service of the Library of Congress, September 27, 1988).

124. Mark E. Liedl, "What Is Congress Trying to Hide?" *Wall Street Journal*, August 15, 1989.

125. Ibid.

126. Mark Liedl, "Too Many Chefs in Congress," *Washington Post*, August 21, 1989.

127. Ralph K. Huitt, "Congress, the Durable Partner," *Lawmakers in a Changing World*, ed. E. Frank (Englewood Cliffs, N.J.: Prentice-Hall, 1966), p. 20. A survey of the literature on oversight is given in B. A. Rockman, "Legislative-Executive Relations and Legislative Oversight," *Legislative Studies Quarterly* 9 (August 1984), pp. 387–440.

128. Federal government scandals are beyond the scope of this analysis, but there is a vast (and growing) literature on scandals in Congress and in the executive branch. See, for example, Don Lambro, *Washington—City of Scandals: Investigating Congress and Other Big Spenders* (Boston: Little, Brown, 1984); Diana B. Henriques, *The Machinery of Greed* (Lexington, Mass.: Lexington Books, 1986); John A. Gardiner, *The Politics of Corruption* (New York: Russell Sage Foundation, 1970); Blair Bolles, *How to Get Rich in Washington: Rich Man's Division of the Welfare State* (New York: W. W. Norton, 1952); Charles Peters, *Blowing the Whistle: Dissent in the Public Interest* (New York: Praeger Publishers, 1972); George C. S. Benson, *Political Corruption in America* (Lexington, Mass.: Lexington Books, 1978); Elizabeth Drew, *Politics and Money: The New Road to Corruption* (New York: Macmillan, 1983); and William J. Chambliss, *On the Take: From Petty Crooks to Presidents*, 2d ed. (Bloomington: Indiana University Press, 1988).

129. J. W. Davis, *The National Executive Branch* (New York: Free Press, 1970), pp. 133–34. See also M. S. Ogul, *Congress Oversees the Bureaucracy* (Pittsburgh, Penn.: University of Pittsburgh Press, 1976).

130. Ripley and Franklin, *Congress, the Bureaucracy, and Public Policy*, p. 220.

131. A discussion of pork-barrel spending is beyond the scope of this analysis, but the practice is legion throughout the federal government. For examples of pork-barrel boondoggles, see John A. Ferejohn, *Pork Barrel Politics: Rivers and Harbors Legislation, 1947–1968* (Stanford, Calif.: Stanford University Press, 1974); Doug Bandow, *The Politics of Plunder: Misgovernment in Washington* (New Brunswick, N.J.: Transaction Publishers, 1990); and Don Lambro, *Fat City: How Washington Wastes Your Taxes* (South Bend, Ind.: Regnery/Gateway, 1980). With regard to the savings-and-loan scandal, see Charles R. Babcock, "Fund-Raising Memos Detail Cranston's Courting of Donor Keating," *Washington Post*, October 7, 1990.

132. Liedl, "What Is Congress Trying to Hide?"

133. National Institutes of Health, *1988 NIH Almanac* (Bethesda, Md.: NIH, 1988), pp. 18–19.

134. Mackubin Thomas Owens, "Micromanaging the Defense Budget," *Public Interest* 100 (Summer 1990), p. 136.

135. Ibid., p. 140.

136. Liedl, "What Is Congress Trying to Hide?"

137. For example, see Jeremy Rabkin, "Micromanaging the Administrative Agencies," *Public Interest* 100 (Summer 1990), pp. 116–30.

138. L. Gordon Crovitz, "Micromanaging Foreign Policy," *Public Interest* 100 (Summer 1990), p. 106.

139. "Congress on the Line," *Wall Street Journal*, May 11, 1990.

140. Mark Liedl, "Congress's Busywork: 'Constituent Service' Has Replaced Governing," *Washington Post*, January 28, 1990. Emphasis in original.

141. Paulette Thomas, "S&L Bailout Makes Lawmakers a Bit Thriftier About Doling Out Help to Their Constituents," *Wall Street Journal*, November 6, 1989.

142. Liedl, "What Is Congress Trying to Hide?"

143. Dutton, "Congress by Computer?" *Washington Post*, May 6, 1990.

144. U.S. Congress, House Committee on Science, Space, and Technology, *Africa and Hunger: Prospects for Sustainable Development in Sub-Saharan Africa, Hearings before the Subcommittee on Water and Power Resources*, 99th Cong., 1st sess., September 19, 1985, p. 327. Asner actually testified twice on this issue; see also U.S. Congress, House Committee on Interior and Insular Affairs, *Irrigation in Drought and Famine–Affected Countries, Hearings before the Subcommittee on Water and Power Resources*, 99th Cong., 1st sess., July 23, 1985, pp. 5–9.

145. Dutton, "Congress by Computer?" See also Milton Gwirtzman, "Far Too Many People on Capitol Hill," *New York Times*, May 14, 1988.

146. Henry Precht, "The Invisible Government in Washington," *Christian Science Monitor*, July 14, 1989.

147. "The Unelected," *Wall Street Journal*, July 5, 1988.

148. "Power Reading," *Wall Street Journal*, May 22, 1989.

149. Ibid. Staff members are also legally permitted to enjoy the largess of lobbyists and special-interest groups. See "Lobbyists Pay for Trips as Clean Air Bill Looms," *Washington Post*, March 6, 1989.

150. Jeffrey H. Birnbaum, "Many Ex-Aides to Congressional Tax Writers Now Lobby for Companies to Undo '86 Reforms," *Wall Street Journal*, August 15, 1989.

151. "Top Capitol Aide's Trips Are Paid For by Industries," *New York Times*, March 6, 1989.

152. Michael J. Malbin, *Unelected Representatives: Congressional Staff and the Future of Representative Government* (New York: Basic Books, 1980).

153. See Gordon S. Jones and John A. Marini, ed., *The Imperial Congress* (New York: Pharos Books, 1989) and James T. Bennett and Manuel Johnson, *The Political Economy of Federal Government Growth* (College Station, Tex.: Center for Research and Education in Free Enterprise, Texas A&M University, 1980), p. 140.

154. Dutton, "Congress by Computer?"

155. One wonders how much political anguish and fallout would accompany federal

legislation regarding broccoli, given President Bush's publicly stated aversion to it? Would such a law be vetoed?

156. "The Year Congress Stopped," *New York Times*, December 22, 1987.

157. Thomas P. Slaughter, *The Whiskey Rebellion: Frontier Epilogue to the American Revolution* (New York: Oxford University Press, 1986), pp. 196ff. The negotiations were not successful, and Washington used troops to suppress the rebellion.

158. George J. Stigler, *The Intellectual and the Marketplace* (Cambridge: Harvard University Press, 1984), p. 23.

159. U.S. Minimum Wage Study Commission, *Report* (Washington, D.C.: Government Printing Office, 1981), vol. 1, p. xiii.

160. Simon Rottenberg, "National Commissions: Preaching in the Garb of Analysis," *Policy Review* 23 (Winter 1983), p. 139.

161. Patrick J. Sloyan, "Another Blue-Ribbon Blunder; The Pay-Raise Fiasco: Governing by Old-Boy Commission," *Washington Post*, February 12, 1989.

162. Charles Krauthammer, "Congressional Cowardice," *Washington Post*, January 6, 1989.

163. Mark Liedl, "Congress's Best Vote in '89 Was to Adjourn," *Orange County Register*, January 8, 1990.

164. U.S. General Services Administration, *Eighteenth Annual Report of the President on Federal Advisory Committees: Fiscal Year 1989* (Washington, D.C.: GSA, January 9, 1990), pp. 1–11, passim.

165. On this point, see Susan F. Rasky, "Congress Says: 'A Commission Made Us Do It'," *New York Times*, January 29, 1989.

166. John H. Fund, "Term Limitation: An Idea Whose Time Has Come," *Policy Analysis* no. 141 (Washington, D.C.: Cato Institute, October 30, 1990), p. 17.

167. Ibid.

4. *Gimme Shelter, Gimme Food, Gimme . . .*

1. For a detailed discussion of how the poverty threshold was developed, see Mollie Orshansky, "Counting the Poor: Another Look at the Poverty Profile," *Social Security Bulletin* 51 (October 1988), pp. 25–51. This article is a reprint of the original, which was published in the January 1965 issue of *Social Security Bulletin*.

2. "The 1990 Federal Poverty Income Guidelines," *Social Security Bulletin* 53 (March 1990), p. 15. The threshold varies with family size: for the contiguous forty-eight states and the District of Columbia, it ranges from $6,280 for one person to $21,260 for a family of eight. Separate (and higher) thresholds are computed for Alaska and Hawaii, where the cost of living is higher. Within the forty-eight contiguous states and the District of Columbia, costs of living are not taken into account in calculating the threshold. It is assumed that the same poverty threshold appropriate for a family living in a high-cost city, such as Manhattan, is also appropriate for a family living in a rural area where the cost of living is much lower.

3. "Relief Is No Solution," *New York Times*, February 2, 1962.

4. William E. Simon, *A Time for Action* (New York: Reader's Digest Press, 1980), p. 91.

5. For example, an article in *Business Week*, March 26, 1984, entitled "Why There's No

Welfare Fat Left to Trim," concluded that "current programs are very close to the minimum level of support that a wealthy society has decided to provide to its poorest citizens. . . . Congress readily agreed to Reagan's proposals for deep slashes in a broad array of welfare programs. . . . As a result of this clean sweep, politicians and welfare experts generally agree that there is little room left for additional cuts." The article also noted, however, that after adjusting for inflation, spending on welfare programs was about the same in 1984 as it was in 1980. A similar story in the March 26, 1984, *U.S. News & World Report*, "The Desperate World of America's Underclass," concluded that "by many accounts, life for the urban underclass became bleaker in recent years. Since 1980, a harsh economy and cuts in federal social-welfare programs have combined to reduce by 9.4 percent the average income for the poorest one-fifth of American households. . . ."

6. Vee Burke, "Cash and Non-Cash Benefits for Persons with Limited Income: Eligibility Rules, Recipient and Expenditure Data FY 86–88" (Washington, D.C.: Congressional Research Service of the Library of Congress, October 24, 1989), p. 6. Also see U.S. Congress, House Committee on Ways and Means, *Background Material and Data on Programs Within the Jurisdiction of the Committee on Ways and Means: 1989 Edition* (Washington, D.C.: Government Printing Office, 1989), p. 152.

7. U.S. Bureau of the Census, *Money Income and Poverty Status in the United States: 1988*, P–60, Number 166, p. 109.

8. U.S. Congressional Budget Office, *The Food Stamp Program: Income or Food Supplementation?* (Washington, D.C.: CBO, 1966), p. xiv. It is possible that food stamps do not increase food consumption at all. Recipients may spend so much less of their own income on food that total food expenditures may not increase or increase only slightly. As evidence of this effect, James Bovard cited a Department of Agriculture study showing that "each additional dollar of food stamp payments increased food consumption by only 14 cents." See James Bovard, "How Federal Food Programs Grew and Grew," *Policy Review* 26 (Fall 1983), p. 47.

9. Isabel V. Sawhill, "Poverty in the U.S.: Why Is It So Persistent?" *Journal of Economic Literature* 26 (September 1988), p. 1079.

10. Robert Rector, Kate Walsh O'Beirne, and Michael McLaughlin, "How 'Poor' Are America's Poor?" *Backgrounder* no. 791 (Washington, D.C.: The Heritage Foundation, September 21, 1990), p. 4. Much of the discussion and data in this chapter are taken from this source and other publications of The Heritage Foundation. We gratefully acknowledge the permission granted by The Heritage Foundation to use these materials.

11. "Welfare and Poverty" (Dallas, Tex.: National Center for Policy Analysis, 1983), p. 7.

12. John L. Weicher, "Mismeasuring Poverty and Progress," *Cato Journal* 6 (Winter 1987), pp. 715–30.

13. James T. Bennett and Thomas J. DiLorenzo, *Destroying Democracy: How Government Funds Partisan Politics* (Washington, D.C.: Cato Institute, 1985), especially chapters 8 and 9.

14. Jonathan R. Hobbs, "Welfare Needs and Welfare Spending," *Backgrounder* no. 219 (Washington, D.C.: The Heritage Foundation, October 13, 1982), p. 4.

15. U.S., Bureau of the Census, *Measuring the Effects of Benefits and Taxes on Income and Poverty: 1986*, P–60, No. 164–RD–1, pp. 158, 163, 170, 183.

16. This definition was taken from the *Random House College Dictionary*; similar definitions can be found in any dictionary.
17. United Nations, *Compendium of Housing Statistics* (New York: United Nations, 1983), pp. 251–61.
18. Organization for Economic Cooperation and Development, *Living Conditions in OECD Countries* (Paris: OECD, 1986), p. 133.
19. U.S. Department of Commerce, Bureau of the Census, and U.S. Department of Housing and Urban Development, Office of Policy Development and Research, *American Housing Survey for the United States in 1987*, Current Housing Reports H–150–87, (Washington, D.C.: Government Printing Office, 1987), pp. 34, 36, 40, 44, 84, 114, 304. It should also be noted that 58 percent of "poor" homeowners are not elderly.
20. U.S. Department of Energy, Energy Information Administration, *Housing Characteristics 1987* (Washington, D.C.: Government Printing Office, 1989), p. 87.
21. Doug Bandow, "Reagan Yields to the Kiwi Lobby?" *New York Times*, July 3, 1984.
22. U.S. Department of Labor, Bureau of Labor Statistics, "Consumer Expenditures in 1988," *USDL Press Release*, February 26, 1990, No. 90–96.
23. U.S. Department of Agriculture, Human Nutrition Information Service, *Low-Income Women 19–50 Years and Their Children 1–5 Years, 4 days: 1985*, CSF II Report 85–5 (Washington, D.C.: USDA, 1988), p. 50. U.S. Department of Agriculture, Human Nutrition Information Service, *Women 19–50 Years and Their Children 1–5 Years, 4 Days: 1985*, CSF II Report 85–4 (Washington, D.C.: USDA, 1987), p. 42.
24. Human Nutrition Information Service, *Women 19–50 and Their Children*, p. 42.
25. Human Nutrition Information Service, *Low-Income Women 19–50*, pp. 72, 73; Human Nutrition Information Service, *Women 19–50 and Their Children*, p. 65.
26. U.S. Congress, Congressional Budget Office, *Feeding Children: Federal Child Nutrition Policies in the 1980s* (Washington, D.C.: CBO, 1980), p. 58. Emphasis added.
27. For a discussion of this episode and additional references, see Bovard, "How Federal Food Programs Grew and Grew," pp. 43–44.
28. A far less expensive way to prevent malnutrition is to simply fortify foods with vitamins. The Congressional Budget Office indicated as early as May 1980 that "vitamin fortification could provide for 100 percent of a child's recommended dietary allowance for less than $3.00 a year in ingredient costs." Even after adjusting for inflation, the costs of nutritional supplements would be only a tiny fraction of the total spent on supplemental food programs. Even the health-conscious eater must be confused about what constitutes good nutrition. The federal government, which has an alphabet soup of 42 agencies that deal with nutrition and more than 125 relevant federal programs, puts out conflicting signals. According to the GAO, information "is given piecemeal and sometimes is duplicative, conflicting, and confusing." Consider the recommendations made in federal government reports on polyunsaturated fat. Five reports indicated that good nutrition requires an increase in polyunsaturated fats; five others indicated that polyunsaturated fats should not be increased. Further clouding the issue, one government report specified that polyunsaturated fat should be increased "for high risk groups." Is it any wonder that the average consumer is confused?
29. Morton Paglin, *Poverty and Transfers In-Kind* (Stanford, Calif.: Hoover Institution Press, 1980), p. 64.
30. Ibid., table 8, p. 61.

31. Edgar K. Browning, *Redistribution and the Welfare System* (Washington, D.C.: American Enterprise Institute for Public Policy Research, 1975), p. 2. Roger A. Freeman, *The Growth of American Government: A Morphology of the Welfare State* (Stanford, Calif.: Hoover Institution Press, 1975), p. 144, n. 47. Edward C. Banfield, *The Unheavenly City Revisited* (Boston: Little, Brown, 1974), p. 134. Timothy Smeeding, "The Anti-Poverty Effects of In-Kind Transfers," *Journal of Human Resources* 12 (Summer 1977), pp. 360–78. Martin Anderson, *Welfare* (Stanford, Calif.: Hoover Institution Press, 1987).

32. Leonard Beeghley, "Illusion and Reality in the Measurement of Poverty," *Social Problems* 31 (February 1984), pp. 322. See also Leonard Beeghley, *Living Poorly in America* (New York: Praeger, 1983).

33. Beeghley, "Illusion and Reality," p. 327.

34. Ibid., p. 328.

35. Ibid., p. 331.

36. U.S. Congress, Joint Economic Committee, Staff Study of the Subcommittee on Fiscal Policy, *Welfare in the 70's: A National Study of Benefits Available in 100 Local Areas*, Studies in Public Welfare, Paper No. 15, 93d Cong., 2d sess., July 22, 1974, pp. 6–8.

37. Charles Murray, *Losing Ground: American Social Policy, 1950–1980* (New York: Basic Books, 1984). Charles Murray, *In Pursuit: Of Happiness and Good Government* (New York: Simon and Schuster, 1988). These effects have also been verified by others. See, for example, Sheldon Danziger, Robert Haveman, and Robert Plotnick, "How Income Transfer Programs Affect Work, Savings, and the Income Distribution: A Critical Review," *Journal of Economic Literature* 19 (September 1981), pp. 975–1028. Additional sources are provided in their extensive bibliography.

38. Marvin Olasky, "Beyond the Stingy Welfare State: What We Can Learn from the Compassion of the 19th Century," *Policy Review* 54 (Fall 1990), pp. 2–14. See also Marvin Olasky, *The Tragedy of American Compassion* (Washington, D.C.: Regnery Gateway, 1992).

39. U.S. Bureau of the Census, *Income Distribution in the United States*, prepared by Herman P. Miller (Washington, D.C.: Government Printing Office, 1966), p. 1.

40. Pamela Roby, "The Poverty Establishment," *The Poverty Establishment*, ed. Pamela Roby (Englewood Cliffs, N.J.: Prentice-Hall, 1974), p. 5.

41. Edgar K. Browning, "Inequality and Poverty," *Southern Economic Journal* 55 (April 1989), p. 819. The survey to which Browning refers is found in J. R. Kearl, Clayne L. Pope, Gordon C. Whiting, and Larry T. Wimmer, "A Confusion of Economists?" *American Economic Review* 69 (May 1979), pp. 28–37. See also, U.S. Congress, Joint Economic Committee, *The American Distribution of Income: A Structural Problem*, prepared by Lester C. Thurow, 92d Cong., 2d sess., March 17, 1972, p. 1; and Victor R. Fuchs, "Redefining Poverty and Redistributing Income," *Public Interest* 8 (Winter 1967), p. 89.

42. See Karl Brunner, "Economic Inequality and the Quest for Social Justice," *Cato Journal* 6 (Spring/Summer 1986), p. 153. National Conference of Catholic Bishops, *Economic Justice for All* (Washington, D.C.: United States Catholic Conference, 1986), p. 91.

43. Browning, "Inequality and Poverty," p. 820.

44. Robert Rector and Kate Walsh O'Beirne, "Dispelling the Myth of Income Inequality," *Backgrounder* no. 710 (Washington, D.C.: The Heritage Foundation, June 6, 1989), p. 13. Other researchers have also shown that the inequality of income is markedly reduced by making adjustments similar to those made by Rector and O'Beirne. See, for example, Frank Levy, *Dollars and Dreams* (New York: Russell Sage Foundation, 1987); Greg Duncan, *Years of Poverty, Years of Plenty* (Ann Arbor: University of Michigan Press, 1984); and James Davies, France St-Hilaire, and John Whalley, "Some Calculation of Lifetime Tax Incidence," *American Economic Review* 74 (September 1984), pp. 633–49.

45. Browning, "Inequality and Poverty," p. 20.

46. Andrei Kuteinkov, "Soviet Society—Much More Unequal Than U.S.," *Wall Street Journal*, January 26, 1990. For a more detailed discussion, see Paul Craig Roberts, *Alienation and the Soviet Economy: The Collapse of the Socialist Era*, rev. ed. (Oakland, Calif.: Independent Institute, 1990).

47. Kuteinkov, "Soviet Society."

48. Ibid.

49. Cassandra Chrones Moore, "Housing Policy in New York: Myth and Reality," *Policy Analysis* no. 132 (Washington, D.C.: Cato Institute, 1990), p. 1.

50. See Charles Baird, *Rent Control: The Perennial Folly* (Washington, D.C.: Cato Institute, 1977) and William Tucker, *The Excluded Americans: Homelessness and Housing Policies* (Washington, D.C.: Regnery Gateway, 1990).

51. Assar Lindbeck, *The Political Economy of the New Left: An Outsider's View*, 2d ed. (New York: Harper & Row, 1977), p. 39.

52. William Tucker, "The Source of America's Housing Problem: Look in Your Own Back Yard," *Policy Analysis* no. 127 (Washington, D.C.: Cato Institute, 1990), p. 17. Tucker also discusses the effects of zoning on the housing market.

53. Carl F. Horowitz, "Washington's Continuing Fiction: A National Housing Shortage," *Backgrounder* no. 783 (Washington, D.C.: The Heritage Foundation, August 22, 1990), p. 2.

54. Ibid.

55. Ibid., p. 8.

56. U.S. Bureau of the Census, *Construction Reports*, Series C-25, "New One-Family Houses Sold and for Sale," 1970, 1988.

57. Horowitz, "Washington's Continuing Fiction," p. 9.

58. *Who's Buying Houses in America: Chicago Title's 14th Annual Survey of Recent Home Buyers* (Chicago, Ill.: Chicago Title and Trust Company, 1990). See also the 1980 edition.

59. Horowitz, "Washington's Continuing Fiction," p. 9.

5. *Getting Down on the Farm*

1. P. J. O'Rourke, *Rolling Stone*, July 12, 1990, p. 10.

2. James MacGregor Burns, *Roosevelt: The Lion and the Fox, 1882–1940* (New York: Harcourt Brace Jovanovich, 1956), p. 194.

3. Bruce L. Gardner, *The Governing of Agriculture* (Lawrence, Kans.: The Regents Press of Kansas, 1981).

4. Elmer Learn, Philip Martin, and Alex McCally, "American Farm Subsidies: A Bumper Crop," *Public Interest* 84 (Summer 1986), pp. 66–78.

5. James Bovard, *The Farm Fiasco* (San Francisco: Institute for Contemporary Studies, 1989), p. 62.

6. Ibid., p. 63.

7. Cited in *Journal of Commerce*, May 17, 1988, p. 1.

8. Clifton B. Luttrell, *The High Cost of Farm Welfare* (Washington, D.C.: Cato Institute, 1989), p. 105.

9. Bovard, *The Farm Fiasco*, p. 64.

10. U.S. Department of Agriculture, *Sugar and Sweetener: Outlook and Situation Report* (Washington, D.C.: Government Printing Office, September 1986).

11. Bovard, *The Farm Fiasco*, p. 62.

12. U.S. Government Accounting Office, *Congressional Decision Needed on Necessity of Federal Wool Program* (Washington, D.C.: GAO, 1982), p. 17.

13. Bovard, *The Farm Fiasco*, p. 68.

14. U.S. General Accounting Office, *Federal Wool Program*, p. 24.

15. National Wool Growers Association, "Analysis of the National Wool Act" (Washington, D.C.: NWGA, 1985), p. 12.

16. Bovard, *The Farm Fiasco*, p. 80.

17. U.S. General Accounting Office, *Federal Price Support for Honey Should Be Phased Out* (Washington, D.C.: GAO, 1985), p. 20, cited in Bovard, *The Farm Fiasco*, p. 78.

18. Julius Duscha, *Taxpayers' Hayride* (Boston: Little, Brown, 1964), p. 44.

19. Burns, *Roosevelt*, p. 195

20. Arthur Schlesinger, Jr., *The Coming of the New Deal* (Boston: Houghton-Mifflin, 1959), p. 61.

21. Ibid., p. 40.

22. Ibid.

23. Duscha, *Taxpayers' Hayride*, p. 43.

24. Don Doig, "The Farming of Washington," *Policy Analysis* no. 27 (Washington, D.C.: Cato Institute, August 24, 1983), p. 9.

25. Cited in Bovard, *The Farm Fiasco*, p. 91.

26. Ibid., p. 92.

27. Luttrell, *The High Cost of Farm Welfare*, p. 41.

28. Ibid., p. 47.

29. See Peter Bauer, *Dissent on Development* (Cambridge: Harvard University Press, 1972); and Peter Bauer, *Reality and Rhetoric: Studies in the Economics of Development* (Cambridge: Harvard University Press, 1984).

30. Bovard, *The Farm Fiasco*, p. 127.

31. Luttrell, *The High Cost of Farm Welfare*, p. 84.

32. Henry Hazlitt, *Economics in One Lesson* (New York: Arlington House, 1979). Governmental issuers of credit, such as the FmHA, are exempt from taxes and from many of the rules, regulations, and red tape that burden private-sector lenders, especially banks. Also, the FmHA and other federal lending agencies have direct access to the federal Treasury, that is, the taxpayers' pockets.

33. Bovard, *The Farm Fiasco*, pp. 128–35.

34. U.S. General Accounting Office, *Farmers Home Administration's Losses Have Increased Significantly* (Washington, D.C.: GAO, December 1988).
35. U.S. General Accounting Office, *Farmers Home Administration, Problems and Issues Facing the Emergency Loan Program* (Washington, D.C.: GAO, November 1987), p. 42.
36. Doig, "The Farming of Washington," p. 12.
37. Chester C. Davis, "The Problem of Agricultural Adjustment," *Journal of Farm Economics* 16 (February 1934), p. 89.
38. USDA statistics cited in Brad Knickerbocker, "Corporate Giant on the Land Poses Some Big Questions," *Christian Science Monitor*, July 28, 1980.
39. Ibid.
40. William Robbins, "Some Farmers Thriving as Others Go Under," *New York Times*, February 19, 1983.
41. Cited in David Kline, "The Embattled Independent Farmers," *New York Times*, November 29, 1981.
42. E. W. Kieckhefer, "Farm Policy Expected to Draw Further Debate," *Memphis Commercial Appeal*, February 16, 1987.
43. Luttrell, *The High Cost of Farm Welfare*, p. 96.
44. Ibid.
45. Ibid.
46. Lloyd D. Teigen, *Agricultural Parity* (Washington, D.C.: U. S. Department of Agriculture, 1987).
47. U.S. Bureau of the Census, *Household Wealth and Asset Ownership* (Washington, D.C.: Government Printing Office, 1980).
48. Bovard, *The Farm Fiasco*, p. 50.
49. Ibid., p. 44.
50. Ibid.
51. Ibid., p. 47.
52. Ibid.
53. Ralph Robey, *Roosevelt vs. Recovery* (New York: Harper & Row, 1934), p. 117, cited in Bovard, *The Farm Fiasco*, p. 56.
54. *Congressional Record*, House, September 28, 1985, p. 7860.
55. Luttrell, *The High Cost of Farm Welfare*, p. 61.
56. Ibid., p. 62.
57. Ibid.
58. *World Food Nutrition Study: Enhancement of Food Production for the United States*, Report of the Board of Agriculture and Renewable Resources (Washington, D.C.: National Academy of Sciences, 1975), p. 61.
59. *Feeding Children: Federal Child Nutrition Policies in the 1980s* (Washington, D.C.: U.S. Congressional Budget Office, 1980), p. 61.
60. J. Patrick Madden and Marion D. Yoder, *Program Evaluation: Food Stamps and Commodity Distribution in Rural Areas of Central Pennsylvania*, Agricultural Experiment Station Bulletin no. 78 (University Park: Pennsylvania State University Press, 1972).
61. Statement of Senator Hubert H. Humphrey, *Food Stamp Hearings*, Subcommittee on Agriculture and General Legislation of the Committee on Agriculture and Forestry,

U.S. Senate, *Food Stamp Reform*, Part 1 (Washington, D.C.: Government Printing Office, 1975), p. 107.

62. H. L. Mencken, "The Husbandman," in *A Mencken Chrestomathy* (New York: Alfred A. Knopf, 1949), p. 360.

6. *Fuel for the Propaganda Machine*

1. Thomas Sowell, *Knowledge and Decisions* (New York: Basic Books, 1980), p. 219.
2. American Forest Council, *Managing the Future of America's Forests* (Washington, D.C.: AFC, 1989), pp. 1–2.
3. Martin Morse Wooster, "Selling Shortages Short," *Public Opinion* 11 (November/December 1988), p. 48.
4. Ibid., p. 49.
5. Robert H. Nelson, "Mythology Instead of Analysis: The Story of Public Forest Management," *Forestlands*, ed. Robert T. Deacon and M. Bruce Johnson (San Francisco: Pacific Institute for Public Policy Research, 1985), p. 26.
6. Randall O'Toole, *Reforming the Forest Service* (Washington, D.C.: Island Press, 1988), p. 20.
7. U.S. Department of Agriculture, Forest Service, *Timber Depletion, Lumber Prices, Lumber Exports, and Concentration of Timber Ownership* (Washington, D.C.: Government Printing Office, 1920), p. 3.
8. Ibid.
9. Ibid., pp. 70–71.
10. Ibid., p. 71.
11. Ibid.
12. Ibid.
13. Ibid., p. 72.
14. Karen L. Waddell, Daniel D. Oswald, and Douglas S. Powell, *Forest Statistics of the United States, 1987*, Resource Bulletin PNW-RB-168 (Portland, Ore.: U.S. Department of Agriculture, Forest Service, Pacific Northwest Research Station, 1989), table 2, p. 21.
15. U.S. Department of Agriculture, Forest Service, *FY 1989 U.S. Forest Planting Report* (Washington, D.C.: USDA, 1990), p. 4.
16. Ibid., p. 5.; American Forest Council, *Managing the Future of America's Forests*, pp. 2ff.
17. American Forest Council, *Managing the Future of America's Forests*, p. 2.
18. Marion Clawson, "Forests in the Long Sweep of History," *Science* 205 (June 15, 1979), pp. 1171–72.
19. Robert Nelson, "Mythology Instead of Analysis," p. 52.
20. Ibid., p. 71. Nelson reproduces some of the Forest Service forecasts of future timber growth, inventory, and consumption to show that the agency has repeatedly underestimated growth and overestimated consumption.
21. U.S. Department of Interior, U.S. Geological Survey, *Papers on the Conservation of Mineral Resources* (Washington, D.C.: Government Printing Office, 1909), pp. 45–46.
22. U.S. Geological Survey, "The Oil Supply of the United States," *Bulletin of the American Association of Petroleum Geologists* 6 (January-February 1922), p. 45.

23. Herman Kahn, William Brown, and Leon Martel, *The Next Two Hundred Years: A Scenario for America and the World* (New York: William Morrow, 1974), p. 93.
24. Milton R. Copulos, "Natural Gas Deregulation: Time to Finish the Job," *Backgrounder* no. 535 (Washington, D.C.: The Heritage Foundation, September 26, 1986), p. 2.
25. Milton R. Copulos, "Time to Decontrol Natural Gas Prices," *Executive Memorandum* no. 38 (Washington, D.C.: The Heritage Foundation, October 10, 1983), p. 1; Copulos, "H.R. 4227: How to Keep Natural Gas Supplies Short and Prices High," *Issue Bulletin* no. 108 (Washington, D.C.: The Heritage Foundation, June 12, 1984), p. 1.
26. Copulos, "Natural Gas Deregulation," p. 3.
27. David I. Meiselman, in the foreword, *Forty Centuries of Wage and Price Controls*, by Robert Schuettinger and Eamonn Butler (Thornwood, N.Y.: Caroline House, 1979), pp. 3–4.
28. When shortages of natural gas arose in the bitter winter of 1976–77, natural gas supplies to some large commercial users were interrupted so that service could be maintained to homes and hospitals. Congress responded by passing the Fuel Use Act as part of the 1978 National Energy Act. The Fuel Use Act prohibited the use of natural gas in large industrial and utility boilers and required large consumers to pay above-market prices for the natural gas they use. (This is also called the Incremental Pricing Program.) Thus, the distortions introduced by price controls engendered additional regulations and market restraints.
29. Copulos, "Natural Gas Deregulation," p. 4.
30. Dominick T. Armentano, *Antitrust and Monopoly: Anatomy of a Policy Failure* (New York: Wiley-Interscience, 1983), p. 73.
31. For a more detailed discussion of the "capture" of regulatory agencies, see Sam Peltzman, "Toward a More General Theory of Regulation," *Journal of Law and Economics* 19 (August 1976), pp. 211–40.
32. William E. Simon, *A Time for Truth* (New York: McGraw-Hill, 1978), p. 53.
33. Milton R. Copulos, "Salvaging the Synthetic Fuels Corporation," *Backgrounder* no. 423 (Washington, D.C.: The Heritage Foundation, April 12, 1985), p. 3.
34. Milton R. Copulos, "America's Looming Energy Crisis: The Causes," *Backgrounder* no. 578 (Washington, D.C.: The Heritage Foundation, April 29, 1987), p. 5.
35. William E. Simon, "Tilting at Windfall Profits," *Policy Review* 11 (Winter 1980), p. 21.
36. Burt Schorr, "Our Blurred Energy Blueprint," *Wall Street Journal*, November 8, 1974.
37. James P. Gannon, "All Roads Are Steep in U.S. Drive to Achieve Energy Independence," *Wall Street Journal*, March 7, 1974. See also "Project Independence," *Wall Street Journal*, March 12, 1974.
38. William Tucker, "Time to Turn Off the Synfuels Tap," *Reader's Digest* (August 1985), p. 17.
39. "Shattered Hope for Synfuels," *Time*, August 19, 1985.
40. Milton R. Copulos, "Reagan's Fading Energy Agenda," *Backgrounder* no. 204 (Washington, D.C.: The Heritage Foundation, August 17, 1982), p. 9.
41. Walter S. Mossberg, "When U.S. Set Up That Oil Reserve, It Left One Thing Out," *Wall Street Journal*, March 15, 1979.
42. Ibid.

43. "CIA Energy Study Issues Grim Forecast: Demand Will Far Exceed Supply by 1985," *Wall Street Journal*, April 19, 1977.

44. "Thermostat Follies," *Wall Street Journal*, August 17, 1979. See also Judy Bachrach, "William Simon: The Energetic Czar," *Washington Post*, January 13, 1975; and "Do, DOE, DONE," *Wall Street Journal*, August 7, 1978.

45. "Jimmy Carter on the Run," *Wall Street Journal*, June 14, 1977.

46. Herbert A. Merklein and William P. Murchison, *Those Gasoline Lines and How They Got There* (Dallas, Tex.: Fisher Institute, 1981), p. 81.

7. The Sky Is Falling!

Source of the epigram is David M. Graber, "Mother Nature as a Hothouse Flower," *Los Angeles Times Book Review*, October 27, 1989.

1. Cited in Jonathan Schell, "Our Fragile Earth," *Discover*, October 1987, p. 87.

2. Cited in Dixy Lee Ray, *Trashing the Planet* (Washington, D.C.: Regnery Gateway, 1990), p. 170.

3. Ibid.

4. Thomas J. DiLorenzo, "Does Capitalism Cause Pollution?" Center for the Study of American Business *Issue Paper* (St. Louis, Mo.: CSAB at Washington University in St. Louis, August 1991).

5. Donella Meadows, Dennis Meadows, Jorgen Randers, and William Behrens, *The Limits to Growth* (New York: Potomac Associates Books, 1974), p. 9.

6. Ibid., p. 29.

7. Ibid., p. 190.

8. Ibid., pp. 192–93.

9. Ibid., p. 194.

10. James T. Bennett and Thomas J. DiLorenzo, *Destroying Democracy: How Government Funds Partisan Politics* (Washington, D.C.: Cato Institute, 1985), p. 143.

11. Lord Zuckerman, "Science, Technology, and Environmental Management," *Who Speaks for the Earth*, ed. Maurice Strong (New York: W. W. Norton, 1973), p. 70.

12. See Bennett and DiLorenzo, *Destroying Democracy*, p. 144.

13. Ibid.

14. Ibid.

15. U.S. Council on Environmental Quality and Department of State, *Global 2000 Report to the President* (Washington, D.C.: CEQ, 1980).

16. Ibid., vol. 2, p. 712.

17. Herman Kahn and Ernest Schneider, "Globaloney 2000," *Policy Review* 16 (Spring 1981), p. 131.

18. Julian Simon, "Global Confusion, 1980: A Hard Look at the *Global 2000* Report," *Public Interest* 62 (Winter 1981), pp. 4, 8.

19. Ibid., p. 6.

20. Ibid., p. 20.

21. Ibid.

22. Ibid.

23. Ibid.

24. See Julian Simon, *The Ultimate Resource* (Princeton, N.J.: Princeton University

Press, 1981); idem, *Population Matters* (New Brunswick, N.J.: Transaction Books, 1990).

25. Warren Brookes, "The Global Warming Panic," *Forbes*, December 25, 1989.
26. Ibid.
27. Interview with Warren Brookes, April 5, 1990.
28. Brookes, "The Global Warming Panic."
29. S. Fred Singer, "Global Warming: Do We Know Enough to Act?" Center for the Study of American Business *Formal Publication* no. 104 (St. Louis, Mo.: CSAB at Washington University in St. Louis, March 1991).
30. Ray, *Trashing the Planet*, p. 33.
31. Ibid.
32. Singer, "Global Warming," p. 4.
33. Brookes, "The Global Warming Panic."
34. Ibid.
35. James Hansen, "The Greenhouse Effect: Effect on Global Temperatures and Regional Heat Waves," testimony before the U.S. Senate Committee on Energy and Natural Resources, June 1988.
36. Cited in Brookes, "Global Warming Panic."
37. Ibid.
38. T. R. Karl et al., *Historical Climatology*, Series 4–5 (Asheville, N.C.: National Oceanic and Atmospheric Administration, National Climate Data Center, 1988).
39. The law of large numbers states that as a sample size of a probability distribution increases, the likelihood that the sample mean diverges significantly from the population mean approaches zero.
40. Brookes, "The Global Warming Panic."
41. Karl et al., *Historical Climatology*.
42. Patrick J. Michaels, *Sound and Fury: The Science and Politics of Global Warming* (Washington, D.C.: Cato Institute, 1992).
43. William Gray, "Strong Association Between West African Rainfall and U.S. Landfall of Intense Hurricanes," *Science*, September 14, 1990, pp. 1251–56; S. B. Idso, R. C. Balling, Jr., and R. S. Cervany, "Carbon Dioxide and Hurricanes, Implications of Northern Hemisphere Warming for Atlantic/Caribbean Storms," *Meteorology and Atmospheric Physics* 42 (December 1990), pp. 259–63.
44. "Climate Impact Response Functions," Report of a Workshop at Coolfont, West Virginia, September 11–14, 1989, by the Intergovernmental Panel on Climate Change, National Climate Office, United Nations. "Noise" refers to distortions introduced into data series by such means as measurement errors and changes in the definitions of variables. Noise may be random ("white noise") or systematic ("coherent noise"). The interested reader may consult Ulf Grenander and Murry Rosenblatt, *Statistical Analysis of Stationary Time Series* (New York: John Wiley, 1957), pp. 37, 41–42, 46, 158–59.
45. Brookes, "The Global Warming Panic."
46. "Warming Up to the Facts," *Wall Street Journal*, January 11, 1991.
47. Ibid.
48. David Brookes, "Journalists and Others for Saving the Planet," *Wall Street Journal*, October 5, 1989.

49. S. Fred Singer and Candice Crandall, "Misled by Lukewarm Data?" *Washington Times*, May 30, 1991.
50. Ray, *Trashing the Planet*, p. 46.
51. Ibid.
52. Hugh W. Ellsaesser, "The Holes in the Ozone Hole II," *Cato Journal* 12 (1992), in press.
53. Ray, *Trashing the Planet*, p. 46.
54. Report to the U. S. National Bureau of Standards, April 1989, cited in ibid., p. 47.
55. Ray, *Trashing the Planet*, p. 66. Ironically, the process of removing sulfur dioxide by smokestack scrubbing creates an almost equivalent amount of carbon dioxide. In addition, about three tons of limestone sludge are created for every one ton of sulfur dioxide that is eliminated by limestone scrubbers. The 1990 Clean Air Act Amendments will create an additional thirty million tons of limestone sludge a year and no one knows what to do with it. By requiring heavy investments in smokestack technology, the law will also delay the building of new, more technologically advanced, and significantly cleaner power plants. Far from being a global panacea, the 1990 Clean Air Act Amendments will likely create more, not less, pollution while imposing billions of dollars of economic and environmental costs on the economy.
56. Brookes, "The Global Warming Panic."
57. Edward C. Krug, "Fish Story: The Great Acid Rain Flimflam," *Policy Review* 52 (Spring 1990), pp. 44–48.
58. Ibid., pp. 44, 45.
59. Ibid., p. 46.
60. Ibid.
61. Ibid., p. 55.
62. Ibid., p. 46.
63. Ibid.
64. Ibid.
65. Ibid.
66. Cited in Ray, *Trashing the Planet*, p. 61.
67. Quoted in Terry Eastland, "The Deep Six," *American Spectator*, February 1992, p. 46.
68. Statement on CBS's "60 Minutes," December 30, 1990.
69. Eastland, "The Deep Six."
70. Krug, "Fish Story," p. 48.
71. Elizabeth Whelan, *Toxic Terror* (Ottawa, Ill.: Jameson Books, 1985), p. xiii.
72. Ibid., p. 2.
73. Ibid., p. 11.
74. Ibid., p. 2.
75. See Whelan, *Toxic Terror*; Edith Efron, *The Apocalyptics* (New York: Simon and Schuster, 1984).
76. Cited in Ray, *Trashing the Planet*, p. 83.
77. Ibid.
78. Gary Slutsker, "Paratoxicology," *Forbes*, January 8, 1990.
79. Ray, *Trashing the Planet*, p. 84.
80. Cited in Slutsker, "Paratoxicology."

81. Ray, *Trashing the Planet*, p. 85.
82. Ibid., p. 86.
83. Ibid.
84. Slutsker, "Paratoxicology."
85. Ibid.
86. Ray, *Trashing the Planet*, p. 86.
87. Ibid.
88. Ibid.
89. Cited in Robert James Bidinotto, "The Great Apple Scare," *Reader's Digest*, October 1990, pp. 53, 57.
90. Ibid., pp. 53–54.
91. Cited in Warren Brookes, "How the EPA Launched the Hysteria About Alar," *Detroit News*, February 25, 1990.
92. Bidinotto, "The Great Apple Scare."
93. Ibid.
94. Ibid. Emphasis added.
95. Brookes, "How the EPA Launched the Hysteria About Alar."
96. Whelan, *Toxic Terror*, p. 109.
97. Ray, *Trashing the Planet*, p. 86.
98. Virginia I. Postrel, "The Green Road to Serfdom," *Reason*, April 1990, p. 28.

8. *Compelling Belief*

1. Statement by Steven Higgerson, quoted in Murray Rothbard, "Historical Origins," *The Twelve-Year Sentence*, ed. William F. Rickenbacker (New York: Open Court, 1974), p. 15.
2. Ibid.
3. S. Alexander Rippa, *Education in a Free Society* (New York: David McKay, 1967), p. 110.
4. Ibid.
5. As quoted in Colin Greer, *The Great School Legend* (New York: Basic Books, 1972), p. 62.
6. William Bennett, *Our Children and Our Country* (New York: Simon and Schuster, 1988), p. 212.
7. E. G. West, *Education and the State* (London: Institute for Economic Affairs, 1970), p. 72.
8. Ibid.
9. Rickenbacker, *The Twelve-Year Sentence*, back cover.
10. Steve Lowrey, "Young Blacks Born after His Death Spur New Interest in Malcolm X," *Rochester Democrat & Chronicle*, December 30, 1991.
11. Stephen Arons and Charles Lawrence III, "The Manipulation of Consciousness: A First Amendment Critique of Schooling," *The Public Monopoly*, ed. Robert B. Everhart (San Francisco: Pacific Institute for Public Policy Research, 1982).
12. Phyllis Schlafly, "NEA Teaches Disrespect," *Chattanooga News–Free Press*, August 3, 1991.

13. Joel H. Spring, "Sociological and Political Ruminations," in Rickenbacker, *The Twelve-Year Sentence*, p. 142.
14. Ibid.
15. *Eclectic Review*, January 1843, p. 580, cited in George Smith, "Nineteenth-Century Opponents of State Education," in Everhart, *The Public School Monopoly*.
16. Ibid.
17. Ibid.
18. Ibid., p. 125.
19. Ibid., p. 126.
20. John Stuart Mill, *On Liberty* (New York: W. W. Norton, 1975), pp. 98–99.
21. Joel Spring, *Conflict of Interests: The Politics of American Education* (New York: Longman, 1988), p. 125.
22. Ibid., p. 127.
23. Mary Turner, Kenneth Switzer, and Charlotte Redden, *American Government* (Columbus, Ohio: Merrill, 1987), p. 482.
24. Ibid.
25. "The Reregulation President," *Wall Street Journal*, June 17, 1991.
26. Ibid.
27. "Senator Amnesia," *Wall Street Journal*, July 2, 1991.
28. Allen Kownslar and Terry Smart, *Civics: Citizens and Society* (New York: McGraw-Hill, 1983), p. 188.
29. Robert Crandall, "Review of Clean Coal/Dirty Air" by Bruce Ackerman and W. Hassler, *Bell Journal of Economics* 12 (Autumn 1981), p. 678.
30. Ibid., p. 679.
31. Kownslar and Smart, *Civics*, p. 188.
32. Ibid.
33. Ibid.
34. Robert Crandall and S. M. Beser, "The Deregulation of Cable Television," *Law and Contemporary Problems* 44 (Winter 1981), pp. 81–107.
35. Kownslar and Smart, *Civics*, p. 189.
36. Ibid.
37. Dominick Armentano, *Antitrust and Monopoly* (New York: Wiley, 1982).
38. William Baumol and Janus Ordover, "Use of Antitrust to Subvert Competition," *Journal of Law and Economics* 28 (May 1985), pp. 247–66.
39. Ronald Coase, "Economists and Public Policy," *Large Corporations in a Changing Society*, ed. J. F. Weston (New York: New York University Press, 1975), pp. 182–84.
40. Mary Turner, Cathryn Long, John Bower, and Elizabeth Lott, *Civics: Citizens in Action* (Columbus, Ohio: Merrill, 1986), p. 364.
41. Turner, Switzer, and Redden, *American Government*, p. 567.
42. Ibid., p. 570.
43. Ibid.
44. Ibid., p. 579.
45. Ibid.
46. Ibid.
47. Ibid.
48. James T. Bennett and Thomas J. DiLorenzo, *Unfair Competition: The Profits*

of Nonprofits (Lanham, Md.: Madison Books, 1988), especially chapters 2 and 7.

49. See, for example, Doug Bandow, *The Politics of Plunder: Misgovernment in Washington* (New Brunswick, N.J.: Transaction Publishers, 1990), p. 192.
50. Turner, Switzer, and Redden, *American Government*, p. 489.
51. William Hartley and William Vincent, *American Civics* (New York: Harcourt Brace Jovanovich, 1979), p. 115.
52. Alexander Hamilton, James Madison, and John Jay, *The Federalist Papers* (New York: New American Library, 1961), p. 77.
53. Ibid., p. 78.
54. Ibid., p. 77.
55. Ibid., p. 79.
56. Ibid., p. 80.
57. Ibid.
58. Charles Sykes, *The Hollow Men: Politics and Corruption in Higher Education* (Washington, D.C.: Regnery Gateway, 1990), p. 70. See also Allan Bloom, *The Closing of the American Mind* (New York: Simon and Schuster, 1987).
59. Nat Hentoff, "No Free Lunch for Artists," *Washington Post*, March 24, 1990.
60. James S. Coleman, "A Quiet Threat to Academic Freedom," *National Review*, March 18, 1991, p. 28.
61. Ibid., p. 30.
62. Ibid., p. 31.
63. Ibid.
64. Ibid., p. 32.
65. Ibid., p. 34.
66. Ibid.
67. E. C. Pasour, "Financial Support and Freedom of Inquiry in Agricultural Economics," *Minerva*, Spring 1988, p. 51.
68. Ibid., p. 37.
69. M. R. Benedict, *Farm Policies of the United States 1790–1950* (New York: Twentieth Century Fund, 1953), p. 514.
70. Pasour, "Financial Support," p. 38.
71. Ibid., p. 37.
72. Milton Friedman, "Liberalism's Crackup," *Forbes*, November 1989, p. 33.
73. Ibid.
74. " '60s Protesters, '80s Professors," *U.S. News & World Report*, January 16, 1989, p. 54.
75. Sykes, *The Hollow Men*, p. 22.
76. Ibid., p. 33.
77. Ken Emerson, "Only Correct," *New Republic*, February 18, 1991, p. 18.
78. Sykes, *The Hollow Men*, p. 54.
79. Paul Hollander, "From Iconoclasm to Conventional Wisdom: The Sixties in the Eighties," *Academic Questions*, Fall 1989, p. 11.
80. Sykes, *The Hollow Men*, p. 54.

81. Ibid.

82. Dozens of examples of this phenomenon are provided in Dinesh D'Souza, *Illiberal Education* (New York: Free Press, 1991).

83. Dinesh D'Souza, "Multiculturalism 101," *Policy Review* 56 (Spring 1991), p. 22.

84. Ibid.

85. Ibid.

86. Ibid.

87. Ibid., p. 23.

88. Ibid., p. 24.

89. Ibid.

90. Ibid.

91. Ibid.

9. *Dope, Booze, Smokes, and Sex*

1. Ludwig von Mises, *Human Action: A Treatise on Economics*, 3d. rev. ed. (Chicago: Henry Regnery, 1966), pp. 733–34.

2. Deanna Hodgin, "Neo-Prohibition Puts Squeeze on Napa Valley Wine Industry," *Insight*, April 29, 1991. See also James T. Bennett, *Health Research Charities: Image and Reality* (Washington, D.C.: Capital Research Center, 1990).

3. John Kobler, *Ardent Spirits: The Rise and Fall of Prohibition* (New York: G. P. Putnam's Sons, 1973), p. 87.

4. J. C. Furnas, *The Late Demon Rum* (New York: G. P. Putnam's Sons, 1965), p. 45.

5. Ibid., pp. 44–45.

6. Kobler, *Ardent Spirits*, p. 143.

7. James H. Timberlake, *Prohibition and the Progressive Movement* (Cambridge: Harvard University Press, 1963), p. 50.

8. Ibid., p. 53.

9. Ibid., p. 27.

10. Ibid., p. 80.

11. Furnas, *The Late Demon Rum*, p. 101.

12. Timberlake, *Prohibition and the Progressive Movement*, p. 121.

13. Bennett, *Health Research Charities: Image and Reality*, pp. 45–56, 59–100, especially pp. 52–53.

14. "Blueprint for Success: Countdown 2000—Ten Years to a Tobacco-Free America" (Washington, D.C.: Tobacco-Free America, 1990), pp. iii–v.

15. Ibid., pp. iii, v, 7, 19.

16. Alex Kozinski, "Who's Afraid of Commercial Speech?" (Washington, D.C.: Washington Legal Foundation, September 21, 1990), p. 3.

17. Kobler, *Ardent Spirits*, p. 147.

18. U.S. Congress, Senate, *A Bill to Amend the Public Health Service Act*, 101st Cong., 2d sess., June 26, 1990, S. 2795.

19. *A Bill to Amend the Public Health Service Act*, pp. 2–5.

20. Kobler, *Ardent Spirits*, p. 200.

21. Hans J. Eysenck, "Smoking and Health," *Smoking and Society*, ed. Robert D. Tollison (Lexington, Mass.: D. C. Heath, 1986), p. 70.

22. R. Jeffrey Smith, "Low-Level Radiation Causes More Deaths Than Assumed, Study Finds," *Washington Post*, December 20, 1989.

23. Gary Kamiya, "The Cancer Personality," *Hippocrates* (November/December 1989), pp. 92–93.

24. Richard L. Stroup and John C. Goodman, "Making the World Less Safe: The Unhealthy Trend in Health, Safety and Environmental Regulation," *Journal of Regulation and Social Costs* 1 (January 1991), p. 21.

25. See Jacob Sullum, "Smoke and Mirrors," *Reason*, February 1991. For a more rigorous discussion of the errors made in assessing the social costs of smoking, see Dwight R. Lee, "Environmental Economics and the Social Cost of Smoking," *Contemporary Policy Issues* 9 (January 1991), pp. 83–92.

26. C. Everett Koop, quoted in "Interview of Surgeon General C. Everett Koop," *New York Times*, December 13, 1985.

27. U.S. Congress, House Committee on Energy and Commerce, *Cigarettes: Advertising, Testing, and Liability, Hearings before the Subcommittee on Transportation, Tourism, and Hazardous Materials*, on H.R. 4543, 100th Cong., 2d sess., May 4, June 8 and 29, 1988, pp. 441–42.

28. Ibid., p. 442.

29. Douglas J. Den Uyl, "Smoking, Human Rights, and Civil Liberties," *Smoking and Society*, ed. Robert D. Tollison (Lexington, Mass.: D. C. Heath, 1986) p. 211.

30. R. Emmett Tyrell, "Environmental Tobacco Smoke and the Press," *Clearing the Air: Perspectives on Environmental Tobacco Smoke*, ed. Robert D. Tollison (Lexington, Mass.: D. C. Heath, 1988), p. 75.

31. Sullum, "Smoke and Mirrors," p. 33.

32. Gray Robertson, "Building-Related Illnesses: Tobacco Smoke in Context," in *Clearing the Air: Perspectives on Environmental Tobacco Smoke*, ed. Robert D. Tollison (Lexington, Mass.: D. C. Heath, 1988), p. 37.

33. Discrimination against obese people is already being practiced. Sharon L. Russell of St. Petersburg, Florida, was dismissed from Salve Regina College, a nursing school in Newport, Rhode Island, in 1985 because of her weight. Russell sued the college for discrimination and won an award of $44,000 in federal court. The U.S. Supreme Court overturned the award. See "Court Overturns Award to Overweight Nurse," *Washington Times*, March 21, 1991.

34. Gabrielle Glaser, "Minority Billboards," Associated Press, November 2, 1989.

35. Anthony Ramirex, "Cigarette Marketing to Blacks Draws Fire," *Orange County Register*, January 14, 1990.

36. "Tobacco Gifts Blocked, Says Ex-Colonel," *Charlotte Observer*, October 14, 1990.

37. Rene Sanchez, "Huffing and Puffing Over Tobacco Grant," *Washington Post*, June 7, 1990.

38. Shaun Assael, "Why Big Tobacco Woos Minorities," *Adweek*, January 29, 1990.

39. Ibid.

40. As quoted in Walter S. Ross, *Crusade: The Official History of the American Cancer Society* (New York: Arbor House, 1987), p. 197.

41. Jesse Steinfeld, William Griffiths, Keith Ball, and Robert M. Taylor, ed., *Proceedings*

of the Third World Conference on Smoking and Health, vol. II: *Health Consequences, Education, Cessation Activities, and Governmental Action*, NIH 77–1413 (Bethesda, Md.: National Institutes of Health, 1975), p. 829. Emphasis added.

42. Ibid., p. 854.
43. "Tobacco Unit Tells Youth Not to Smoke," *Boston Globe*, December 12, 1990.
44. Jerome L. Himmelstein, *The Strange Career of Marihuana* (Westport, Conn.: Greenwood Press, 1983), p. 62.
45. Ibid., p. 60.
46. Ibid., p. 54.
47. Ibid., p. 26.
48. Arnold S. Trebach, *The Heroin Solution* (New Haven: Yale University Press, 1982), p. 51.
49. Ibid.
50. Ibid.
51. Richard Lawrence Miller, *The Case for Legalizing Drugs* (New York: Praeger, 1991), p. 90.
52. Ibid., p. 9.
53. Ibid., pp. 57–58.
54. Ibid., p. 58.
55. Ibid., p. 19.
56. The White House, *National Drug Control Strategy* (Washington, D.C.: Government Printing Office, 1991).
57. U.S. Office of National Drug Control Policy, *State Drug Control Status Report* (Washington, D.C.: Government Printing Office, 1990), p. 1.
58. Ibid.
59. Ibid., p. 13.
60. David Boaz, "The Consequences of Prohibition," *The Crisis in Drug Prohibition*, ed. David Boaz (Washington, D.C.: Cato Institute, 1990), p. 5.
61. Ibid.
62. Miller, *The Case for Legalizing Drugs*, p. 92.
63. U.S. Office of Drug Control Policy, *State Drug Control Status Report*, p. 20.
64. "Propaganda," *City Paper*, Washington, D.C., December 6, 1991.
65. Ibid.
66. Ibid.
67. Ibid.
68. Ibid.
69. Ibid.
70. Ibid.
71. Ibid.
72. Kathy Fackelmann, "The Crack–Baby Myth," *City Paper*, Washington, D.C., December 13, 1991.
73. Ibid.
74. Ibid.
75. Ibid.
76. Ibid.
77. Ibid.

78. Ibid.
79. Ibid.
80. Lewis H. Lapham, "A Political Opiate," *The Crisis in Drug Prohibition*, ed. David Boaz (Washington, D.C.: Cato Institute, 1990), p. 141.
81. Ethan Nadelmann, "U.S. Drug Policy: A Bad Export," *Foreign Policy* 70 (Spring 1988), pp. 83–108.
82. The White House, *National Drug Control Strategy*.
83. Boaz, "The Consequences of Prohibition," p. 3.
84. Center for Defense Information, "The Pentagon's War on Drugs: The Ultimate Bad Trip," (Washington, D.C.: CDI, 1992), vol. XXI, no. 1, p. 5.
85. The White House, *National Drug Control Strategy*, p. 1.
86. Ibid., pp. 140–41.
87. Richard J. Dennis, "Toward a Moral Drug Policy," *The Crisis in Drug Prohibition*, ed. David Boaz (Washington, D.C.: Cato Institute, 1990), p. 92.
88. Kobler, *Ardent Spirits*, pp. 63–64.
89. Michael Fumento, *The Myth of Heterosexual AIDS* (New York: Basic Books, 1990), p. 16.
90. Ibid., p. 3.
91. "AIDS and 'Straights': Unsettling Questions," *U.S. News & World Report*, August 17, 1987.
92. Fumento, *The Myth of Heterosexual AIDS*, p. 10.
93. "This Is What You Thought," *Glamour*, March 1986.
94. "AIDS: A Growing Threat," *Time*, August 12, 1985.
95. Fumento, *The Myth of Heterosexual AIDS*, p. 16.
96. Malcolm Forbes, "Why Did *Forbes* Run Fumento's Fulminations on AIDS?" *Forbes*, July 10, 1989.
97. Kevin M. Cahill, ed., *The AIDS Epidemic* (New York: St. Martins, 1983), p. 158.
98. Fumento, *The Myth of Heterosexual AIDS*, p. 322.
99. Ibid. p. 200.
100. Ibid., p. 215.
101. "Media and the Message," *Commonweal*, November 6, 1987, p. 612.
102. Fumento, *The Myth of Heterosexual AIDS*, p. 160.
103. "The Big Chill: Fear of AIDS," *Time*, February 16, 1987.
104. Fumento, *The Myth of Heterosexual AIDS*, p. 3.
105. "Interview with Dr. James Curran," *U.S. News & World Report*, August 5, 1985.
106. Cited in Paula A. Treichler, "AIDS, Gender, and Biomedical Discourse," *AIDS: The Burdens of History*, ed. Elizabeth Fee and Daniel M. Fox (Berkeley: University of California Press, 1988), p. 212.
107. Fumento, *The Myth of Heterosexual AIDS*, p. 72.
108. Ibid., p. 227.
109. Ibid., p. 192.
110. "Call to Battle," *Time*, November 10, 1986.
111. Martin Morse Wooster, "Reagan's Smutstompers," *Reason*, April 1986, pp. 26–33.
112. Michael Fumento, "Do You Believe in Magic?" *American Spectator*, February 1992.

113. Fumento, *The Myth of Heterosexual AIDS*, p. 350.

10. *The Never Ending Story*

1. James R. Mock and Cedric Larson, *Words That Won the War* (New York: Russell & Russell, 1968), p. 11.
2. Ibid., pp. 68–74.
3. Allan M. Winkler, *The Politics of Propaganda* (New Haven: Yale University Press, 1978), p. 3.
4. Mock and Larson, *Words That Won the War*, p. 6.
5. John Morton Blum, *V Was for Victory* (New York: Harcourt Brace Jovanovich, 1976), p. 22.
6. Ibid., p. 26.
7. Ibid., p. 27.
8. Ibid., p. 45.
9. Winkler, *The Politics of Propaganda*, p. 66.
10. Blum, *V Was for Victory*, p. 40.
11. Ibid.
12. Ibid., p. 41.
13. Robert Nisbet, *Roosevelt and Stalin: The Failed Courtship* (Washington, D.C.: Regnery Gateway, 1988), p. 16.
14. Frank Capra, *Frank Capra: The Name Above the Title* (New York: Macmillan, 1971), p. 327.
15. Ibid., p. 329.
16. Winkler, *The Politics of Propaganda*, p. 149.
17. Edwin J. Feulner, Jr., "A Message from the Chairman," *United States Advisory Commission on Public Diplomacy 1986 Report* (Washington, D.C.: United States Information Agency, 1986), p. 3.
18. Christopher Madison, "Under Wick, the USIA Has a Bigger Budget, New Digs and an Image Problem," *National Journal*, June 9, 1984, p. 1136.
19. "Department of Great Communicators," *New York Times*, March 22, 1986.
20. David Boaz, "Money for the Boys," *Libertarian Outlook*, August 1985, p. 12.
21. Mark Schapiro and Annette Levy, "NED to the Rescue," *New Republic*, December 23, 1985.
22. Stephen Engelberg, "U.S. Grant to Two Czech Parties Is Called Unfair Interference," *New York Times*, June 10, 1990.
23. *Congressional Record*, House, December 18, 1985, p. 12562.
24. TRB, "Intellectual Pork Barrel," *New Republic*, July 2, 1984.
25. Bill Kauffman, "Subsidies to the Arts: Cultivating Mediocrity," *Policy Analysis* no. 137 (Washington, D.C.: Cato Institute, August 8, 1990), p. 5.
26. Ibid.
27. Ibid., p. 2.
28. Ronald Brownstein, *The Power and the Glitter* (New York: Pantheon, 1990), p. 94.
29. Kauffman, "Subsidies to the Arts," p. 12.

30. *AIM Report* (Washington, D.C.: Accuracy in Media, July 2, 1983), p. 1.

31. Congressional Arts Caucus *Update*, March 12, 1982.

32. Neil Hickey, "Public TV: Why Reports of Its Death Seem Premature," *TV Guide*, December 11, 1982.

33. Robert Higgs, *Crisis and Leviathan: Critical Episodes in the Growth of American Government* (New York: Oxford University Press, 1987), p. 261.

34. James Bovard, "George Bush: Protectionist," *Free Market*, March 1992, p. 1.

35. Ibid.

Index

About the Authors

James T. Bennett is an Eminent Scholar at George Mason University and holds the William P. Snavely Chair of Political Economy and Public Policy in the Department of Economics. He received his Ph.D. from Case Western Reserve University in 1970 and has specialized in research related to public policy issues, the economics of government and bureaucracy, labor unions, and health charities. He is founder and editor of the *Journal of Labor Research* and has published more than 60 articles in professional journals such as the *American Economic Review, Review of Economics and Statistics, Policy Review, Public Choice,* and *Cato Journal.* His books include *The Political Economy of Federal Government Growth* (1980), *Better Government at Half the Price* (1981), *Deregulating Labor Relations* (1981), *Underground Government: The Off-Budget Public Sector* (1983), *Destroying Democracy: How Government Funds Partisan Politics* (1986), *Unfair Competition: The Profits of Nonprofits* (1988), *Health Research Charities: Image and Reality* (1990), *Health Research Charities II: The Politics of Fear* (1991). He is an adjunct scholar of the Heritage Foundation and a member of the Mont Pelerin Society and the Philadelphia Society.

Thomas J. DiLorenzo is Professor of Economics in the Sellinger School of Business and Management at Loyola College in Maryland. He holds a Ph.D. in Economics from Virginia Polytechnic Institute and State University and is the author of over 50 articles in academic journals such as the *American Economic Review, Economic Inquiry, Southern Economic Journal, Public Finance Quarterly,* and *Public Choice.* He is the coauthor of four other books, including *Underground Government: The Off-Budget Public Sector; Destroying Democracy: How Government Funds Partisan Politics; Unfair Competition: The Profits of Nonprofits;* and *Patterns of Corporate Philanthropy: The Suicidal Impulse.*

319

Dr. DiLorenzo has also published in popular journals such as *Policy Review, Reason,* and *Society,* and has contributed articles to numerous newspapers including the *Wall Street Journal, Christian Science Monitor, Newsday,* and many others. He is a member of the Mont Pelerin Society, an adjunct scholar of the Cato Institute, and an adjunct fellow of the Center for the Study of American Business at Washington University in St. Louis.